SharePoint® 2010 Administration
Instant Reference

SharePoint® 2010 Administration
Instant Reference

Randy Williams

Milan Gross

Wiley Publishing, Inc.

Acquisitions Editor: Agatha Kim
Development Editor: Stef Jones
Technical Editor: Randy Muller
Production Editor: Eric Charbonneau
Copy Editor: Liz Welch
Editorial Manager: Pete Gaughan
Production Manager: Tim Tate
Vice President and Executive Group Publisher: Richard Swadley
Vice President and Publisher: Neil Edde
Book Designer: Maureen Forys, Happenstance Type-O-Rama
Proofreader: Scott Klemp, Word One
Indexer: Ted Laux
Project Coordinator, Cover: Katherine Crocker
Cover Designer: Ryan Sneed
Cover Image: © kycstudio/iStockPhoto

Copyright © 2011 by Wiley Publishing, Inc., Indianapolis, Indiana

Published simultaneously in Canada

ISBN: 978-1-118-02234-4 (pbk)
ISBN: 978-1-118-11851-1 (ebk)
ISBN: 978-1-118-11853-5 (ebk)
ISBN: 978-1-118-11852-8 (ebk)

No part of this publication may be reproduced, stored in a retrieval system or transmitted in any form or by any means, electronic, mechanical, photocopying, recording, scanning or otherwise, except as permitted under Sections 107 or 108 of the 1976 United States Copyright Act, without either the prior written permission of the Publisher, or authorization through payment of the appropriate per-copy fee to the Copyright Clearance Center, 222 Rosewood Drive, Danvers, MA 01923, (978) 750-8400, fax (978) 646-8600. Requests to the Publisher for permission should be addressed to the Permissions Department, John Wiley & Sons, Inc., 111 River Street, Hoboken, NJ 07030, (201) 748-6011, fax (201) 748-6008, or online at http://www.wiley.com/go/permissions.

Limit of Liability/Disclaimer of Warranty: The publisher and the author make no representations or warranties with respect to the accuracy or completeness of the contents of this work and specifically disclaim all warranties, including without limitation warranties of fitness for a particular purpose. No warranty may be created or extended by sales or promotional materials. The advice and strategies contained herein may not be suitable for every situation. This work is sold with the understanding that the publisher is not engaged in rendering legal, accounting, or other professional services. If professional assistance is required, the services of a competent professional person should be sought. Neither the publisher nor the author shall be liable for damages arising herefrom. The fact that an organization or Web site is referred to in this work as a citation and/or a potential source of further information does not mean that the author or the publisher endorses the information the organization or Web site may provide or recommendations it may make. Further, readers should be aware that Internet Web sites listed in this work may have changed or disappeared between when this work was written and when it is read.

For general information on our other products and services or to obtain technical support, please contact our Customer Care Department within the U.S. at (877) 762-2974, outside the U.S. at (317) 572-3993 or fax (317) 572-4002.

Wiley also publishes its books in a variety of electronic formats and by print-on-demand. Not all content that is available in standard print versions of this book may appear or be packaged in all book formats. If you have purchased a version of this book that did not include media that is referenced by or accompanies a standard print version, you may request this media by visiting http://booksupport.wiley.com. For more information about Wiley products, visit us at www.wiley.com.

Library of Congress Cataloging-in-Publication Data is available from the publisher.

TRADEMARKS: Wiley, the Wiley logo, and the Sybex logo are trademarks or registered trademarks of John Wiley & Sons, Inc. and/or its affiliates, in the United States and other countries, and may not be used without written permission. SharePoint is a registered trademark of Microsoft Corporation. All other trademarks are the property of their respective owners. Wiley Publishing, Inc., is not associated with any product or vendor mentioned in this book.

10 9 8 7 6 5 4 3 2 1

Dear Reader,

Thank you for choosing *SharePoint 2010 Administration Instant Reference*. This book is part of a family of premium-quality Sybex books, all of which are written by outstanding authors who combine practical experience with a gift for teaching.

Sybex was founded in 1976. More than 30 years later, we're still committed to producing consistently exceptional books. With each of our titles, we're working hard to set a new standard for the industry. From the paper we print on, to the authors we work with, our goal is to bring you the best books available.

I hope you see all that reflected in these pages. I'd be very interested to hear your comments and get your feedback on how we're doing. Feel free to let me know what you think about this or any other Sybex book by sending me an email at `nedde@wiley.com`. If you think you've found a technical error in this book, please visit `http://sybex.custhelp.com`. Customer feedback is critical to our efforts at Sybex.

Best regards,

Neil Edde
Vice President and Publisher
Sybex, an Imprint of Wiley

Acknowledgments

While my name may be on the cover, publishing a book is definitely a team effort. The Sybex team has been incredibly patient, supportive, and immensely valuable during each phase. Deep thanks go to Agatha Kim, our acquisitions editor, for her polite but effective steps to keep the project on track; Randy Muller for his technical editing and helpful suggestions; Pete Gaughan, editorial manager, for his quick answers; and Eric Charbonneau, production editor, and Liz Welch, copy editor, both of whom ensure the book is polished to a high sheen. In particular, however, I'd like to acknowledge Stef Jones, our development editor. I worked hard to ensure my first drafts were clear and concise—I felt pretty good about them. When the first chapter reviews came back all "marked up," I felt a bit like a high school freshman. But, after reading the detailed changes and suggestions, the improvements were obvious, and I knew we had someone special on our team. Thanks to her, what you are holding is not just a good book but a great one.

Of course, let me also thank Milan Gross, the book's coauthor. I wasn't ready to make the commitment to be the sole author, and I really enjoyed teaming up with you on this.

I'd like to also acknowledge Wen He and Chyan Yee Goh. Both were involved in content review, and it is genuinely appreciated. If you have any concerns with clarity, technical accuracy, or value, only Milan and I are to blame.

The SharePoint community is simply fantastic and unlike any other technical community out there. Many toil writing books or blogs, tweeting, speaking, running user groups, or providing answers on forums—not for money, but in the spirit of "sharing the point." I learn so much from you and thank you for your contributions. You are my second family and some of my closest friends. 'Til the next SharePint!

Lastly, and most importantly, let me thank my lovely wife Gigi for her support and understanding. Her sacrifices helped make this book a reality, and her love has made all my dreams come true.

—Randy Williams

When Randy invited me to join him in writing this book, I welcomed the offer with both excitement and trepidation. Having written for previous books, I knew how much effort goes into putting together a publication like this. Fortunately, the team at Sybex is the best I've ever worked with and was instrumental to the success of the book. I would like to thank Agatha Kim for her flexibility with deadlines as I worked to fit authoring into an otherwise packed schedule. I am also grateful to Stef Jones for her uncanny ability to edit a topic that is still unfamiliar to the world at large and suggest clarifications on even the most technical points. I also thank Liz Welch and Eric Charbonneau for their amazing job of bringing the text into better focus through their own editorial gifts; Randy Muller, for his technical insights; and the rest of the Sybex team without whom this book would not have happened.

I also need to thank my senior managers at Synergy, Chris Bayot and Ben Creamer, for their tireless dedication and efforts to keep all but the most critical matters from landing on my desk. I definitely would not have found the time for this book without them.

Finally, I would like to thank my friend and colleague, Randy Williams, for the opportunity to share in the writing of this book and for the countless thoughtful conversations we've shared over the years. I have never known a finer professional, or a better person.

—Milan Gross

About the Authors

Randy Williams is a senior architect and trainer for Synergy. He has over 20 years of eclectic IT experience and for the past 15 years has been architecting and developing Microsoft-based solutions. He has a master's degree in information systems along with a number of certifications. From 2009 to 2011, he was awarded the Microsoft Most Valuable Professional (MVP) in SharePoint. Randy writes for *Windows IT Pro* and *SharePoint Pro* magazines and speaks at conferences worldwide. Randy is now based in San Diego, having just relocated back to the U.S. after running Synergy's Southeast Asia operations from Singapore. In his leisure, Randy enjoys spending time with his wife, Gigi. Together, they hike, travel, go to the beach, and like to watch scary movies together. And, sometimes, he enjoys reading a good, nontechnical book.

Milan Gross is a principal for Synergy. Beginning with the early days of Windows, Milan has worked with virtually every piece of Microsoft technology that has led to the evolution of what is today SharePoint. Milan has spent over 15 years delivering training and consulting on Microsoft technologies in the U.S., Australia, Singapore, India, and China. He has been an invited speaker at TechEd in Australia, China, and Malaysia and has spoken at numerous other SharePoint events around the world. He holds the MCSD, MCSE, MCDBA, and MCT certifications from Microsoft as well as a master's degree from the University of Pennsylvania. Milan currently lives in Singapore where he heads the Asia Pacific region of Synergy and is deeply involved in the Microsoft community. In his spare time, Milan enjoys running, scuba diving, and spicy Asian cooking.

Contents

Introduction	xix

Part I: Deploying SharePoint 2010 — 1

Chapter 1: Installing SharePoint 2010 — 3

Prepare for Installation	4
Understanding the SharePoint Installation	4
Understanding the Creation of Service Accounts	8
Install SharePoint 2010	9
Installing Prerequisites	10
Installing SharePoint Binaries	12
Creating or Joining a Server Farm	15
Perform Postinstall Operations	23
Adjusting Diagnostic Logging	24
Resolving the HTTP 401.1 Unauthorized Error	25
Creating a Web Application and Site Collection	25
Installing Office Web Apps	25
Installing Language Packs	27
Installing a Fix for WCF Data Services	28
Apply Updates	28
Understanding Update Types	28
Understanding the Update Process	29
Installing Updates to a Farm	30
Automate the Installation	33
Configuring AutoSPInstaller	34
Installing Prerequisites Without Internet Access	36

Chapter 2: Creating and Managing Web Applications — 39

Understand Web Applications	40
Working with SharePoint Web Application Components	40
How SharePoint Web Applications Work	42
Create a Web Application Using Central Administration	44
Choose an Authentication Type	44
Configure IIS Website Settings	45
Configure Security	46
Configure the Public URL	52
Configure the Application Pool	52
Configure the Content Database	53
Configure Service Application Connections	54

Create a Web Application Using PowerShell 55
Configure IIS Settings 56
    Configuring the IIS Logging Path 57
    Configuring the SSL Certificate 58
Configure Additional Settings 60
    Configuring General Settings 61
    Configuring Resource Throttling 63
    Disabling SharePoint Designer 64
    Configuring Blocked File Types 65
Extend or Delete a Web Application 65
    Benefits of Extending a Web Application 65
    Extending a Web Application 66
    Managing Alternate Access Mappings 68
    Unextending and Re-extending a Web Application 70
    Deleting a Web Application 71

Chapter 3: Creating and Managing Site Collections 73
Create Site Collections 74
    Defining Managed Paths 74
    Creating a Site Collection Using Central Administration 77
    Creating a Site Collection Using PowerShell 79
    Configuring Quota Templates Using Central Administration 80
    Specifying the Content Database 82
    Enabling Self-Service Site Creation 84
Manage Site Collections 85
    Managing Site Collections Using Central Administration 85
    Managing Site Collections Using PowerShell 88
Manage Site Settings 90
    Managing the Site Collection Gallery 91
    Managing the Look and Feel of Web Pages 96
    Managing Site Administration 101
    Managing Site Collection Administration 104

Chapter 4: Creating Service Applications 109
Understand Service Applications 110
    Understanding the Service Application Framework 110
    Understanding Service Instances 112
Create and Delete Service Applications 112
    Creating a Service Application 113
    Deleting a Service Application 115
    Managing Service Application Administrators 116
Configure the Built-in Service Applications 117
    Configuring the Access Services Application 118
    Configuring the Business Data Connectivity Service Application 119
    Configuring the Excel Services Application 122
    Configuring the PerformancePoint Services Application 130

Configuring the Secure Store Service Application	132
Configuring the State Service Application	135
Configuring the Visio Graphics Service Application	135
Configuring the Web Analytics Service Application	137
Configuring the Word Automation Service Application	137
Configuring the PowerPoint Service Application	139
Configuring the Word Viewing Service Application	139
Associate Service Applications to Web Applications	140

Chapter 5: Scaling and High Availability   143

Understand Farm Topologies	144
Understanding the Single-Server Farm	145
Understanding the Two-Server Farm	145
Understanding the Three-Server Farm	146
Understanding the Medium-Server Farm	147
Understanding the Large Farm	148
Configure Servers and Services	150
Adding and Removing Servers from a Farm	150
Managing SharePoint Services	153
Scale Out Web Servers	156
Configuring Windows-Based NLB	157
Using a Hardware-Based Load Balancer	165
Running Central Administration on Multiple Servers	166
Scale Out Application Servers	168
Understanding Cross-Farm Services	169
Configuring Cross-Farm Services	170
Scaling the Search Service	175
Scale Out Database Servers	182
Adding New SQL Servers	183
Scaling Using Database Mirroring	184
Scaling Using Clustered SQL Servers	185

Part II: Configuring SharePoint 2010   187

Chapter 6: Configuring System Settings   189

Manage Content Databases	190
Adding a Content Database	190
Removing a Content Database	193
Configuring a Content Database	194
Moving a Content Database	196
Manage Email and Text Messages (SMS)	197
Configuring Incoming Email	197
Configuring Outgoing Email	203
Configuring SMS Messaging	204
Manage Solutions	206
Managing Farm Solutions	206

xiv   Contents

Managing User Solutions	211
Manage Features	215
Activating and Deactivating Features	216
Using PowerShell to Manage Features	218

Chapter 7: Configuring the User Profiles and My Sites Services   221

Configure the User Profile Service Application	223
Configuring Accounts and Permissions	224
Preparing the Farm for Supporting My Sites	225
Creating the User Profile Service Application	228
Starting the User Profile Services	232
Configure User Profile Properties	233
Configuring a Property for Import	233
Configuring a Property for Export	235
Creating a Custom Property Mapping	236
Configure User Profile Synchronization	238
Creating a Synchronization Connection	238
Performing Synchronization	241
Configuring Synchronization Settings	242
Editing Connection Filters	243
Manage User Profiles	244
Viewing Profiles and Editing a Profile	244
Creating a New Profile	245
Deleting a Profile	245
Configure Audiences	246
Creating an Audience	246
Editing an Audience	248
Deleting an Audience	248
Scheduling Audience Compilation	249
Configure My Sites and Social Networking	249
Setting Up My Sites	250
Configuring Trusted Host Locations	252
Configuring Personalization Site Links	253
Publishing Links to Office Client Applications	254

Chapter 8: Configuring the Search Service   255

Configure the Search Service Application	257
Configuring the Search Service Accounts	257
Configuring the SharePoint Foundation Search Service	258
Creating the SharePoint Search Service	260
Configure Crawler Impact Rules	262
Configure Farm Search Administration	263
Configuring Farm-Level Search Settings	265
Configuring Search Topology	265
Create a New Content Source	267

Creating a New Content Source	267
Types of Content Sources	269
Manage Crawls	271
Managing Crawl Schedules	271
Managing Crawl Rules	273
Viewing the Crawl Log	275
Define Server Name Mappings	276
Configure Databases and Host Distribution Rules	277
Creating Additional Crawl Databases	277
Creating a Host Distribution Rule	277
Configure IFilters and File Types	278
Understanding IFilters and File Formats	278
Installing IFilters	279
Editing File Types	279
Configuring File Icons	280
Reset the Index	280
Understand FAST for SharePoint 2010	281

Chapter 9: Configuring Search Scopes and Search Results   283

Manage Search Scopes	284
Creating Shared Search Scopes	285
Creating a Site Collection Search Scope	288
Assigning a Search Scope	289
Configuring Search Center Tabs for Search Scopes	291
Create Metadata Property Mappings	294
Viewing Crawled Properties	295
Creating a New Managed Property	296
Configure Authoritative Pages	297
Define Keywords and Best Bets	299
Creating a Keyword	299
Adding a Best Bet	300
Remove Items from Search Results	302
Configure Federated Search	302
Creating a Federated Location	303
Importing a Federated Location	307
Editing, Copying, Deleting, or Exporting a Federated Location	308
Configuring a Federated Search Web Part	308
View Search Reports	309

Chapter 10: Configuring Document Management   311

Configure Versioning and Approval	312
Enabling Document Versioning	312
Restoring a Document Version	314
Requiring Explicit Checkout	315

  Taking Ownership of Checked-Out Files   317
  Configuring Draft Item Security   318
  Enabling and Configuring Content Approval   319
 Create Views   321
 Create Content Types   324
 Create Document Sets   327
 Configure Document IDs   328
 Configure the Content Organizer   330
  Configuring Content Organizer Settings   330
  Creating Content Organizer Rules   331

Chapter 11: Configuring the Managed Metadata Service   333

 Configure Content Type Syndication   334
  Creating the Content Type Syndication Hub   335
  Configuring the Content Type Hub   338
 Configure Term Sets   342
  Using the Term Store Tool   343
  Creating a Term Set Group   345
  Creating a Term Set   347
  Importing and Exporting a Term Set   349
  Creating and Configuring a Term   349
 Use Term Sets   350
  Creating a Managed Metadata Column   351
  Using a Managed Metadata Column   353
  Configuring Metadata Navigation   354
 Manage Enterprise Keywords   356
  Enabling Keyword Tagging   357
  Viewing Keywords   358
  Modifying, Deleting, and Moving Keywords   358
  Blocking Keywords   359

Chapter 12: Configuring Records Management   361

 Understand Records Management in SharePoint   362
 Configure In-Place Records Management   363
  Activating the In-Place Records Management Feature   364
  Configuring Record Declaration Settings   364
  Configuring Lists and Libraries for Records Management   365
  Declaring and Undeclaring Records Manually   367
  Declaring Records Through Workflow   369
  Declaring Records Through a Retention Policy   371
 Configure a Records Center   372
  Creating a Records Center Site   373
  Creating Libraries in a Records Center   374
  Configuring Organizer Rules for Submitted Records   375
  Creating Custom Send To Connections   377

Submitting Records	379
Configure Information Management Policies	381
Creating an Information Management Policy	382
Creating a Site Collection Policy	387
Configure eDiscovery and Holds	388
Creating a Hold Definition	389
Searching for Items to Hold	389
Holding and Releasing Individual Items	390

Chapter 13: Configuring Web Content Management and Publishing   391

Configure Publishing Features	392
Activating the Site Collection Publishing Infrastructure Feature	393
Activating the SharePoint Server Publishing Feature	394
Creating a Publishing Page	394
Selecting a Page Layout	397
Understanding Page Properties	399
Creating Reusable Content	401
Configure SharePoint 2010 Caching	403
Configuring Publishing Cache Profiles	403
Configuring the Output Cache	407
Configuring the Object Cache	409
Configuring the BLOB Cache	411
Configure Content Deployment	413
Configuring Content Deployment Paths	415
Configuring Content Deployment Jobs	418

Part III: Managing SharePoint 2010   421

Chapter 14: Managing Security   423

Configure Farm-Level Security	424
Configuring Farm Administrators	424
Configuring Managed Accounts	426
Configuring Service Accounts	430
Configure Web Application Security	430
Configuring Web Application Policies	431
Configuring Permission Policy Levels	433
Managing Anonymous Access	434
Configuring Antivirus Settings	435
Configure Site Collection Security	436
Adding or Removing Site Collection Administrators	437
Creating Permission Levels	438
Managing SharePoint Groups	440
Managing Permission Inheritance	442
Managing Permissions	444

Contents

Chapter 15: Managing Auditing, Monitoring, and Analytics — 449

Manage Auditing and Audit Reports — 450
   Configuring Site Collection Auditing — 451
   Managing Audit Log Growth and Size — 453
   Viewing Audit Reports — 454
Configure Web Analytics Reporting — 457
   Configuring Web Analytics — 457
   Viewing Analytics Reports — 459
Use the Health Analyzer — 463
   Reviewing Problems and Solutions — 464
   Reviewing Rule Definitions — 466
Configure Diagnostic Logging — 466
   Working with the Event Log — 467
   Working with the Trace Log — 468
   Configuring Diagnostic Logging Settings — 469
Manage Timer Jobs — 470
   Viewing Timer Jobs — 471
   Running a Timer Job — 472
   Managing Timer Job Schedules — 472

Chapter 16: Managing Backup and Restore — 473

Back Up the Farm — 474
   Performing a Complete Farm Backup — 474
   Understanding Farm Backup Sets — 480
   Using PowerShell to Automate Farm Backups — 481
Restore the Farm — 484
   Understanding Farm Restore — 485
   Using Central Administration to Restore the Farm — 486
Back Up and Restore a Site Collection — 488
   Using Central Administration to Back Up
     a Site Collection — 489
   Using PowerShell to Back Up a Site Collection — 489
   Using PowerShell to Restore a Site Collection — 490
Export and Import a Website, List, or Library — 491
   Using Central Administration to Export — 492
   Using PowerShell to Export — 493
   Using PowerShell to Import — 494
Recover Data from an Unattached
  Content Database — 495
   Restoring a Content Database — 496
   Using Central Administration to Recover Data from
     an Unattached Content Database — 497
   Restoring or Importing Content — 498

Index — 499

Introduction

There are a lot of SharePoint books out there, and you might be wondering, why another? We know that different people buy books for different reasons. In this book, we cater to the busiest of professionals. We respect your time and understand that many of you don't have time to read an 800-page tome. You need quick answers to real questions such as "How do I apply a cumulative update?" or "What steps are needed to configure network load balancing?" The answers we give are concise and come with easy-to-follow, step-by-step instructions. In some cases, we also answer the *why* questions that are common with complex products like SharePoint. As you read, you'll find many notes, tips, and warnings, helping you avoid the common and not-so-common pitfalls.

One of our goals was to focus on topics needed most by today's administrators. We include content that is not found elsewhere or is scattered among too many places to easily put together. In the book, you will learn how to:

- Build and scale your SharePoint environment to meet user demand
- Preserve and protect SharePoint content
- Deliver an effective search platform
- Keep your SharePoint servers healthy
- Manage SharePoint using Central Administration and PowerShell

While this book can be read from cover to cover, each chapter is fairly discrete, so in many cases, you can flip right to the section you need. Where relevant, we refer you to other sections, chapters, or external links for more information. This is a hands-on guide, and our ultimate goal is for this to be the one book that you carry around in your backpack. Bring it into the server room or war room. Annotate it, flag its pages—use it like any good multitool.

What You Need

Other than an open and eager mind, there is nothing specific that you will need before delving in. Of course, as you start to build and deploy SharePoint environments, you'll need physical or virtual hardware and software that SharePoint requires. This is spelled out for you in Chapter 1.

In most chapters, you will find PowerShell cmdlets (pronounced "command-lets") that can be used to perform administrative tasks. For these, you must use a specially configured PowerShell interface called SharePoint 2010 Management Shell. This is the same PowerShell engine that is part of Windows Server 2008, but it auto-registers all of the SharePoint cmdlets that can be used. You can find the shortcut here: Start ➤ All Programs ➤ Microsoft SharePoint 2010 Products ➤ SharePoint 2010 Management Shell. Since you'll use SharePoint 2010 Management Shell regularly, you might want to pin the shortcut to the Start menu or link to it from your taskbar.

Who Should Read This Book

Whether you are a seasoned SharePoint administrator or just now starting out in SharePoint, you'll find useful content in here. As much as possible, we avoid making assumptions about any SharePoint background you may or may not have.

Those with a SharePoint background will probably use the book more as a reference guide. Those of you who are starting out are encouraged to read the first four chapters to get your footing with terminology and essential concepts. From there, you can move into any other chapter with relative ease.

If you are a SharePoint designer or developer, we cover many relevant concepts, but most of the material is focused on the needs of IT professionals.

Since SharePoint is built on top of many other systems, there are other products and technologies you should understand to get the most out of this book. You will benefit from the following:

- Rudimentary knowledge of Active Directory and Domain Name System (DNS)
- Experience working with Windows Server 2008 or Windows Server 2008 R2

- Overall familiarity with IIS and SQL Server
- Basic understanding of Windows networking

How to Contact the Authors

We welcome feedback from you about this book or other books you'd like to see from us in the future.

To reach Randy or get more information about his work, visit his website at www.synergyonline.com/randy. You can also follow him on Twitter (@tweetraw).

Milan can be reached via his blog at www.synergyonline.com/milan or on LinkedIn at www.linkedin.com/in/milangross.

Sybex strives to keep you supplied with the latest tools and information you need for your work. Please check their website at www.sybex.com, where we'll post additional content and updates that supplement this book if the need arises. Enter **SharePoint Instant Reference** in the Search box (or type the book's ISBN—**9781118022344**), and click Search to get to the book's update page.

PART I
Deploying SharePoint 2010

IN THIS PART

CHAPTER 1: Installing SharePoint 2010. 3

CHAPTER 2: Creating and Managing Web Applications. 39

CHAPTER 3: Creating and Managing Site Collections 73

CHAPTER 4: Creating Service Applications. 109

CHAPTER 5: Scaling and High Availability. 143

1

Installing SharePoint 2010

IN THIS CHAPTER, YOU WILL LEARN TO:

▶ **PREPARE FOR INSTALLATION** (Pages 4 – 9)
- Understanding the SharePoint Installation (Page 4)
- Understanding the Creation of Service Accounts (Page 8)

▶ **INSTALL SHAREPOINT 2010** (Pages 9 – 23)
- Installing Prerequisites (Page 10)
- Installing SharePoint Binaries (Page 12)
- Creating or Joining a Server Farm (Page 15)

▶ **PERFORM POSTINSTALL OPERATIONS** (Pages 23 – 28)
- Adjusting Diagnostic Logging (Page 24)
- Resolving the HTTP 401.1 Unauthorized Error (Page 25)
- Creating a Web Application and Site Collection (Page 25)
- Installing Office Web Apps (Page 25)
- Installing Language Packs (Page 27)
- Installing a Fix for WCF Data Services (Page 28)

▶ **APPLY UPDATES** (Pages 28 – 33)
- Understanding Update Types (Page 28)
- Understanding the Update Process (Page 29)
- Installing Updates to a Farm (Page 30)

▶ **AUTOMATE THE INSTALLATION** (Page 33 – 37)
- Configuring AutoSPInstaller (Page 34)
- Installing Prerequisites Without Internet Access (Page 36)

The first step in using SharePoint in an organization is deploying the product. With SharePoint, deployment is much more involved than running a simple wizard and clicking Next, Next, Finish. This chapter breaks down the installation into major stages and provides you with the step-by-step procedures, pointing out the pitfalls that you must avoid along the way.

Prepare for Installation

Before jumping into the actual installation, there are two important preparation items that we need to cover. Understanding and completing the preparation steps will ensure that your installation goes smoothly, preventing you from having to reformat your servers and start all over again. These two preparation items are:

- Understanding the SharePoint installation process, including the farm, server roles, and requirements
- Creating the necessary service accounts

Understanding the SharePoint Installation

SharePoint 2010 is different from other Microsoft server systems, and the installation steps reflect its uniqueness. The installation and configuration process is broken up into many steps. Knowing these steps, being prepared with the necessary input, and understanding the output are the keys to success. SharePoint also has its own set of terms and definitions. The broad terms that apply to SharePoint as a whole are introduced here. This section covers these areas:

- The farm
- The three server roles found in a SharePoint farm
- SharePoint's hardware and software requirements

Understanding the Farm

SharePoint 2010 has been designed to scale from just a few users to tens of thousands. In terms of server counts, this can be just one or dozens. In SharePoint, a farm consists of all servers that share a configuration database, and they collectively provide the content and services needed.

Although it is easy to add and remove servers from the farm and adjust a server's services, the servers and their farm are very tightly connected, like a close-knit family. The configuration database is the brain and heart of the farm. In many ways it seems alive, and there are synchronization jobs that run that are analogous to a heartbeat.

SharePoint's farm is so close, literally, that you normally cannot separate the servers across a wide area network (WAN). For example, the network latency between a web server and a database server should be no more than 1 millisecond, something that's nearly impossible to do as you add network distance and the usual switches and routers into the mix. In other words, all the farm servers should be co-located in the same datacenter.

You may be wondering, "How do I scale SharePoint to support global or multi-national companies?" A short answer for now is that this process usually involves setting up multiple farms, one in each major region. This topic is more thoroughly covered in Chapter 5, "Scaling and High Availability."

Understanding Server Roles

Within the farm, there are three primary roles that a server can have. In very small farms (e.g., one or two servers), these roles will be shared on the same machine. As the farm expands, they often become more dedicated. Before installing SharePoint and creating the farm, we recommend that you define the servers and their roles. Although the roles are somewhat adaptable, it's best to know up-front in order to avoid rework.

The three roles are web front end (WFE) server, application server, and database server. The basic communication between these roles and the browser client is depicted in Figure 1.1.

Figure 1.1: Communication between browser and server roles

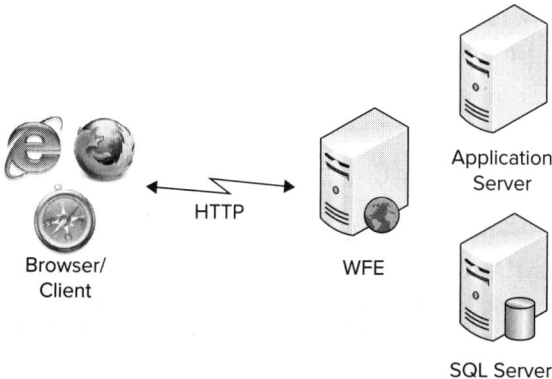

Web Front End The web front end (WFE) is a web server, based on Internet Information Services (IIS), that receives direct HTTP (or HTTPS) requests from end user or client applications. A request could be from the browser for a web page or it could be a web service request from a client like Microsoft Word. Multiple WFE servers can be used with load balancing as covered in Chapter 5.

Application Server An application server also runs IIS, but it is configured differently than WFE servers. Specifically, it runs designated service applications (these are introduced in Chapter 4, "Creating Service Applications"). An application server may run services such as index (part of search) or Office Web Apps. Application servers receive their requests from the WFE servers, not directly from client machines. Multiple application servers can be used and automatically provide fault tolerance and load-balancing capabilities.

Database Server Database servers run Microsoft SQL Server and form the data tier for SharePoint. These servers receive requests from both WFE and application servers. SharePoint 2010 uses many types of databases, including a configuration database and multiple content and service application databases. SharePoint supports clustered SQL servers, database mirroring, and multiple SQL servers to provide scalability and fault tolerance. Details are covered in Chapter 5.

> **NOTE** While it's easy to classify servers in these three roles, they sometimes overlap in functionality. In particular, it is common to run certain service applications on WFE servers for performance reasons. Other than this exception, these roles are distinct.

Understand SharePoint Requirements

Since SharePoint scales out to multiple servers across each server role, you do not need super-powerful, scaled-up servers. Selecting the right number of CPU cores and amount of memory depends on many factors and is still as much of an art as it is a science. This concept is expanded on in more detail in Chapter 5. Table 1.1 lists the recommended minimum requirements that you must meet for each server role, assuming it will be for production use.

Table 1.1: Hardware requirements

Role	CPU Cores (64-bit)	Memory	Disk
WFE	4	8 GB	80 GB free
Application	4	8 GB	80 GB or more free; see later in this section.
Database	4	8 GB	Varies; see later in this section

NOTE A development or evaluation environment can function with less CPU and memory. At an absolute minimum, you should have two cores and 4 GB of RAM.

Estimating the amount of disk space needed can be much harder and is based directly on how much content is stored. For a WFE, the amount of space needed is relatively fixed and 80 GB is a comfortable amount. An application server, in particular a server running a query component (used with search), may have additional local space requirements. Estimating disk space needed for a query server is covered in Chapter 5. Estimating disk space needed for a database server depends on the amount of content stored in SharePoint. To calculate the space needed, see the article "Storage and SQL Server Capacity Planning and Configuration" at http://technet.microsoft.com/en-us/library/cc298801.aspx.

Table 1.2 describes SharePoint's software requirements. The most notable point to keep in mind is that SharePoint requires 64-bit operating systems (OSs) and SQL servers.

Table 1.2: Software requirements

Component	Minimum Version Required
Operating system	64-bit Windows Server 2008 with SP2 64-bit Windows Server 2008 R2
SQL Server	64-bit SQL Server 2005 SP3 and CU3 64-bit SQL Server 2008 with SP1 and CU2 (or CU5+) 64-bit SQL Server 2008 R2
Active Directory	Functional level should be Windows Server 2003

In addition to these requirements, SharePoint will install a number of prerequisites during the installation process, as explained in the "Installing Prerequisites" section later in this chapter. To learn more about the hardware and software requirements, see

http://technet.microsoft.com/en-us/library/cc262485.aspx

> **NOTE** While not supported for production use, SharePoint 2010 can be installed on top of Windows Vista or Windows 7. This is commonly done for a development environment. To learn more on how to build a development environment on these operating systems, see http://msdn.microsoft.com/en-us/library/ee554869.aspx and http://blogs.msdn.com/b/cjohnson/archive/2010/10/28/announcing-sharepoint-easy-setup-for-developers.aspx.

Understanding the Creation of Service Accounts

This section covers the service accounts that must be created prior to starting the SharePoint installation. Just as with other server applications, service accounts are the Active Directory (AD) domain accounts that each service uses. Since SharePoint provides a multitude of services, a number of service accounts are needed. Which ones you need depend on which services you use. This section covers the minimum necessary accounts for a basic installation. As you learn more about service applications in Chapters 4, 7, 8 and 9, others are introduced.

Table 1.3 introduces the three accounts that are needed for installation.

Table 1.3: Service accounts needed for installation

Account Type	Purpose	Details and Permissions
Install account	Account used to install SharePoint and create or join a farm	Domain account Local administrator on each WFE and application server Has a login to database server with dbcreator and securityadmin server role permissions
SQL Server service account	Account used to run MSSQLSERVER engine service	Domain account (recommended) Permissions to UNC Path where farm backup is stored
Farm account (aka database access account)	Creates databases and runs key farm services	Domain account
Application Pool account(s)	Executes requests received by a web application	Domain account Used when creating web applications; see Chapter 2

The permissions listed in Table 1.3 are the minimum permissions that must be manually granted. SharePoint or the OS will automatically grant additional permissions. When creating your service accounts, here are the security best practices you should follow:

- When creating these accounts in AD, it is best to store them along with other service accounts in a separate organizational unit (OU).
- Consistently follow a naming convention for your accounts. For example, name each account starting with "SP."
- SharePoint can detect accounts whose passwords are about to expire and automatically change the passwords for you. (This is covered in more detail in Chapter 14, "Managing Security.") If your security policy requires password expiration, it is best to follow that and you can rest knowing that SharePoint makes this process easy to manage.
- Configure these service accounts following the "principle of least privilege," meaning that you do not grant additional permissions other than the minimum that are needed.

Install SharePoint 2010

Now that you understand the farm and have created your service accounts, you are ready to install. As you will learn in this section, there are three main steps to installing SharePoint 2010:

1. Installing prerequisites
2. Installing SharePoint binaries
3. Creating or joining the farm

This section assumes the OS and SQL Server have already been installed and configured as per the requirements listed previously. This installation section applies to all farm sizes, from a single server to a multiserver farm.

NOTE Before starting the installation, be sure to log into the server with the install account that you created.

This section won't go into detail on how to configure the OS or SQL Server, but here are a few quick tips:

- For your WFE and application servers, create two partitions, C: and D:. Make C: a minimum of 40 GB with the balance of space on D:.
- For your WFE and application servers, there is no need to add any roles or features. This will be done automatically for you.
- For your SQL server, format the partitions that will be used for data and log with a 64KB allocation unit size.
- For your SQL server, set the database default location to appropriate drive partitions with ample space.

Other than these, there are no special SharePoint configuration requirements to keep in mind when installing the OS or SQL Server.

Each of these installation steps covered below applies to all WFE and application servers that will make up your farm. The steps do *not* apply to any dedicated SQL servers that you will use.

SharePoint allows you to add servers to and remove servers from the farm with relative ease. Thus, when installing SharePoint, you do not have to have all the servers prepared and ready. To start, you will just need SQL Server and the first WFE that will be part of the farm ready to go.

> **TIP** Assuming you are creating a multiserver farm, we recommend that your database server(s) be dedicated to the database role. In other words, do not run WFE or application server roles on your SQL server. This is why you do not install SharePoint on your database servers. Furthermore, if possible, it's best to have your SQL server dedicated to your SharePoint farm and not be shared with other non-SharePoint applications.

Installing Prerequisites

Installing prerequisites is the first step in the installation process. In addition to the basic OS requirements covered already, SharePoint requires a number of additional items prior to starting the basic installation. Fortunately, there is an automated process that handles all of these for you. This process is called the Prerequisites Installer, and it can be started from the SharePoint Server installation splash screen.

Figure 1.2 shows SharePoint Server's installation splash screen. You can start the installation program by running setup.cmd or by using AutoPlay from the DVD. If you are installing SharePoint Foundation (SPF), you should run SharePointFoundation.exe.

Figure 1.2: SharePoint Server installation splash screen

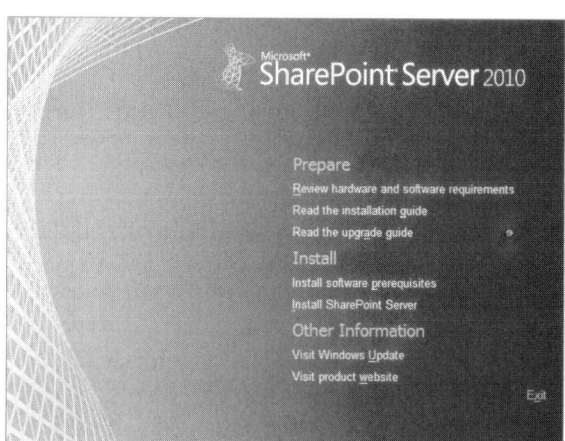

When you start the Prerequisites Installer, a separate program will start and greet you with the wizard shown in Figure 1.3.

Figure 1.3: SharePoint Preparation Tool wizard

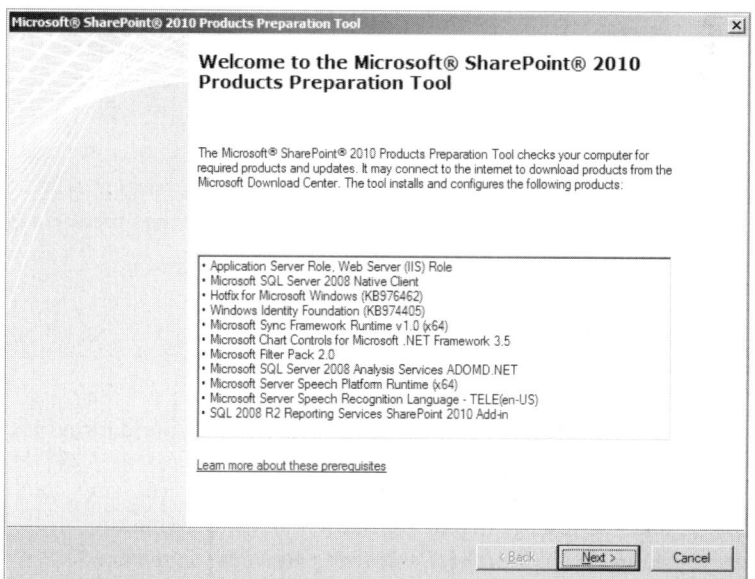

For most of the components, the installer will try to download the appropriate version from the Internet. Components that are already installed in a matching version are skipped. During the installation of these components, the server may need to be rebooted. If it does, after you log back in, the installer will resume from where it left off.

> **NOTE** If the server does not have an active Internet connection, the download will fail and the installer will stop. The workaround for this is to predownload these components from another machine. We explain how to do this in the "Automate the Installation" section, later in this chapter.

The installer keeps a detailed log of each activity, which can be used to troubleshoot any problems. This log file is stored in the folder specified by the TEMP environment variable. To easily find this folder, click Start and type in **%temp%**. Inside this folder, look for a file named PrerequisiteInstaller.<DateTimeStamp>.log. You can open and view this file in Notepad.

Installing SharePoint Binaries

Once the prerequisites are successfully installed, you are ready for the second step. This step will install all of the SharePoint binaries into the file system and otherwise prepare the server to be part of a farm.

This part of the installation can also be launched from the splash screen in the Install section (see Figure 1.3, earlier in this chapter) or manually via the setup.exe program found in the folder for the DVD.

When you install SharePoint binaries, you have the option of automatically applying a service pack or cumulative updates. This process is called *slipstreaming*. For more information on how to do this, see www.toddklindt.com/blog/Lists/Posts/Post.aspx?ID=230.

Installing SharePoint Foundation

If you are installing SPF, here are the steps you follow:

1. From the splash screen, choose Install SharePoint Foundation.
2. Accept the Software License Terms.
3. Assuming you are not installing SharePoint onto a domain controller, you are prompted whether you want to create a stand-alone or a server farm. In almost all cases, you'll want to create a server farm. See Figure 1.4.

Figure 1.4: Choose Standalone or Server Farm

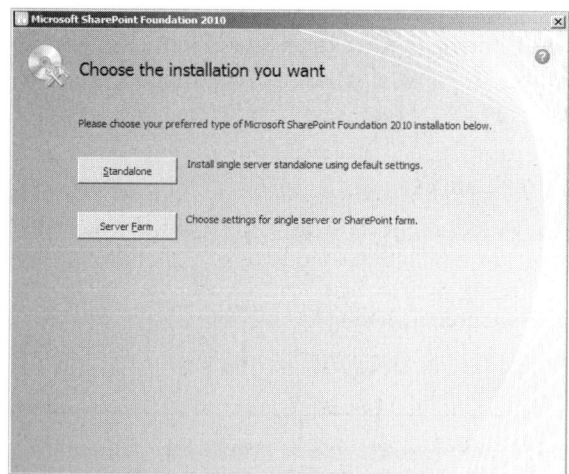

4. On the Server Type tab, select Complete. Be careful as the default is Stand-alone even though you avoided it in the previous step. See Figure 1.5.

Figure 1.5: Choose Complete or Stand-alone

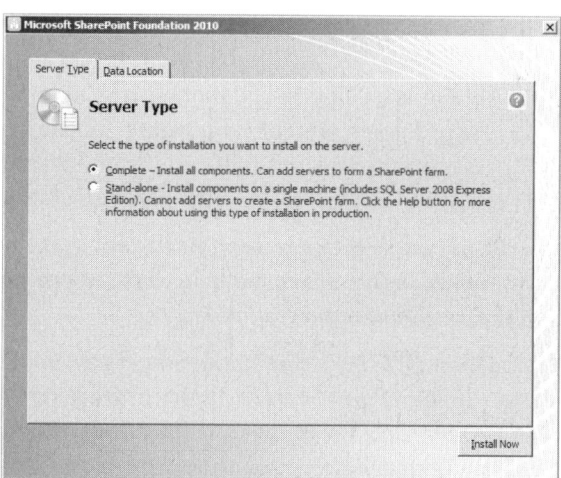

WARNING Creating a stand-alone farm is seldom recommended. It is a special farm that always contains a single server and it can never scale out to multiple servers. Installing a stand-alone farm also installs SQL Server Express locally and cannot use a separate SQL installation you may already have.

5. On the File Location tab, enter a data location. This is the folder to where SPF's search index files are stored. By default, these are stored on the C: drive. If you expect SharePoint to index a lot of content, it is best to move this storage location to a separate partition (e.g., D:).

Installing SharePoint Server

Installing SharePoint Server (SPS) is similar to installing SPF. Here are the steps you follow:

1. From the splash screen, choose Install SharePoint Server.
2. Enter your standard or enterprise license key.

> **WARNING** No matter which type of license key you enter, SPS's installation program installs the same set of files. SharePoint simply enables or disables features according to the license type. If you enter in a standard key, you can upgrade to enterprise at a later date to unlock the additional features. However, you cannot downgrade from enterprise to standard without rebuilding the farm.

3. Accept the Software License Terms.
4. Assuming you are not installing SharePoint onto a domain controller, you are prompted whether you want to create a stand-alone or server farm. In almost all cases, you'll want to create a server farm. See Figure 1.4 in the previous section.
5. On the Server Type tab, select Complete. Be careful as the default is stand-alone even though you avoided it in the previous step. See Figure 1.5 in the previous section.
6. On the File Location tab, choose a file location. These are folders where a portion of SharePoint Server's binary files are stored. By default, these are stored on the C: drive. If your C: drive is smaller than the 40 GB recommendation, you should move this storage location to another drive letter.

After you provide all this input, the SharePoint binaries are installed. During installation, a detailed log of each activity is made, which can be used to troubleshoot any problems. These log files are stored in the same folder as the prerequisite installer log files, based on the TEMP environment variable. Inside this folder, look for a file named `SharePoint Server Setup (<long_number>).log` or `Microsoft SharePoint Foundation 2010 Setup (<long_number>).log`. These files can be opened and viewed in Notepad.

> **TIP** SharePoint 2010 has the ability to track or block installations, which helps you prevent unauthorized deployments. For more information, see "Track or Block SharePoint Server 2010 Installations" located at http://technet.microsoft.com/en-us/library/ff730261.aspx.

Creating or Joining a Server Farm

With prerequisites and the SharePoint binaries installed, you are ready for the final and most important part of the installation: creating a new or joining an existing server farm. Both of these can be done from either a wizard or the command line.

The wizard is called the SharePoint 2010 Products Configuration Wizard. You can automatically launch this wizard at the end of the previous installer stage. The wizard is the easiest way to create or join a farm.

Creating a Server Farm

You must create a farm if this is the first server in the farm. Creating a farm creates a new configuration database in SQL Server. SharePoint also creates the Central Administration web application, which is used to administer the farm. Finally, this step installs services, registers SharePoint's features, and secures the server and the farm.

Creating a Farm Using the Configuration Wizard

When using the SharePoint 2010 Products Configuration Wizard to create a farm, here are the steps you go through:

1. Start the Configuration Wizard. This wizard can be run from the end of the previous installer phase or by choosing Start ➢ All Programs ➢ Microsoft SharePoint 2010 Products ➢ SharePoint 2010 Products Configuration Wizard.

   You are greeted with the initial screen shown in Figure 1.6.

Figure 1.6: Starting the Configuration Wizard

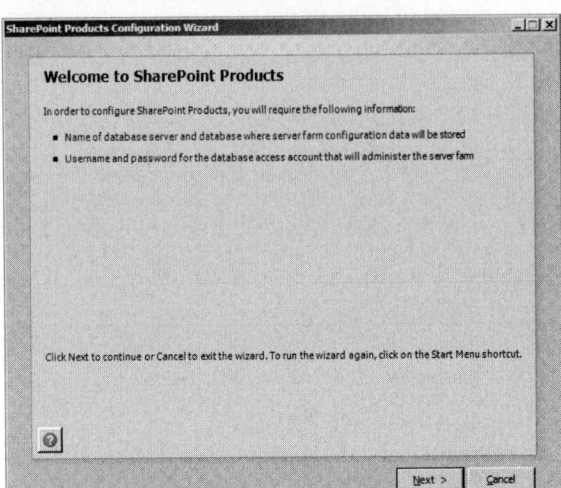

2. Acknowledge the warning that services may be restarted.
3. Specify whether you wish to create a new server farm by selecting Create A New Server Farm, as shown in Figure 1.7.

Figure 1.7: Create or connect to an existing farm

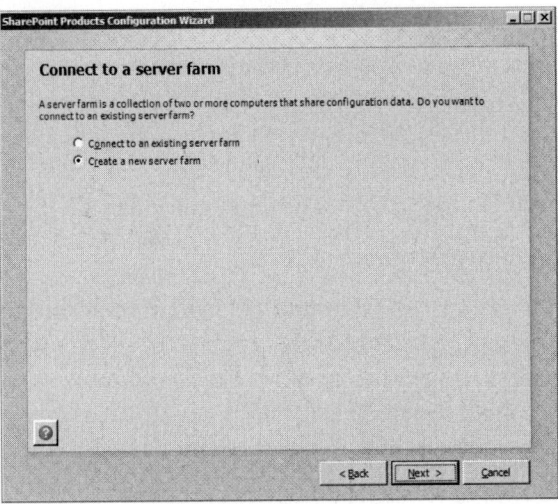

4. Specify the name of your database server and a name for the configuration database, as shown in Figure 1.8. When specifying the

Install SharePoint 2010

database server name, it's best to create a SQL Alias, which allows you to use an alternate name instead of the actual SQL server name. This can ease maintenance especially if you need to move databases to a different server. To learn how create a SQL Alias, see the article titled "How to Setup and Use a SQL Server Alias" available at http://www.mssqltips.com/tip.asp?tip=1620

Figure 1.8: Specify configuration database settings

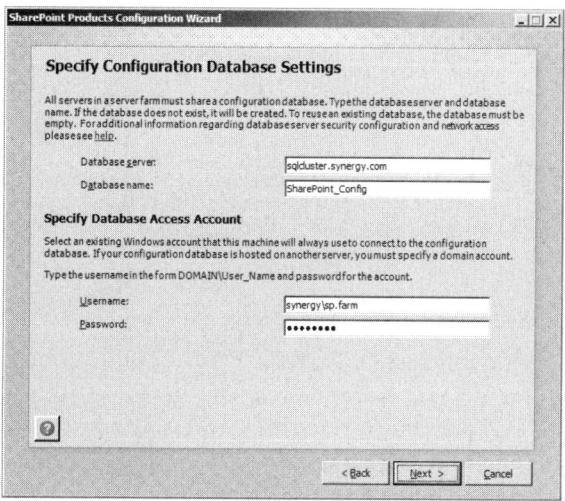

5. In the second half of the Specify Configuration Database Settings screen, specify the farm account (also known as the database access account) and password. This is one of the service accounts mentioned in the "Understanding the Creation of Service Accounts" section. Among other things, this account is used to create new databases on the SQL server.

6. Create a farm passphrase, as shown in Figure 1.9. The passphrase is an extra level of security. Whenever a new server is added to this farm, the passphrase must be entered. The passphrase must be in the form of a complex password.

A complex password has a minimum of eight characters and includes at least three of the following:

- English uppercase letters (A–Z)
- English lowercase letters (a–z)

- Numerals (0–9)
- Non-alphanumeric characters (such as !, $, #, %)

Figure 1.9: Create a farm passphrase

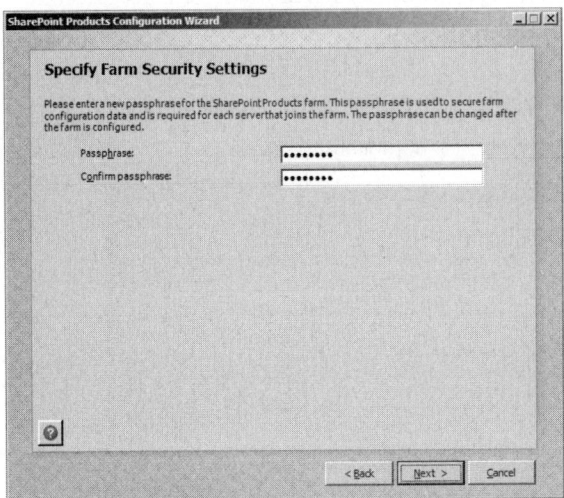

7. Provide the TCP port number for the Central Administration Web Application. By default, a random port is shown; you can either keep this or change it. See Figure 1.10.

Figure 1.10: Configure the Central Administration Web Application

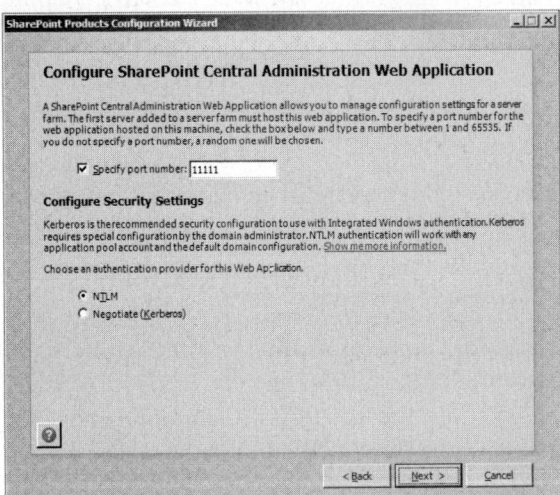

Install SharePoint 2010   **19**

8. On the same screen, choose the security settings (authentication type) for your web application. Your two options are NTLM (Windows NT LAN Manager) and Kerberos. Kerberos is a better choice security-wise and also more efficient, but it requires additional configuration in your domain to be in place.

9. Review your settings to begin creating the farm, as shown in Figure 1.11. Click Next to start the creation.

Figure 1.11: Review configuration settings

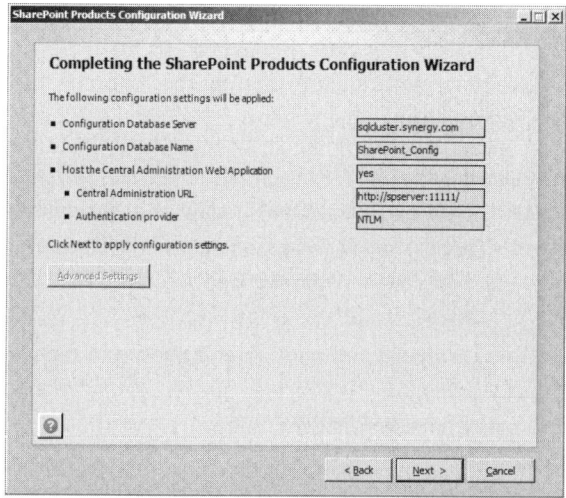

10. Wait a few minutes and click Finish when the process completes.

The farm is now created and Central Administration will start.

Creating a Farm Using *PSCONFIG.EXE*

The command-line program used to create or join a farm is `PSConfig.exe`. There are two key advantages to using this command instead of the graphical wizard:

- You can automate this step through script.
- You can specify the name for the Central Administration Web Application content database.

In contrast, when you use the wizard, it will autogenerate a not-so-friendly name like `SharePoint_AdminContent_48cedae2-4d1f-42f8-8293-f19b621dc0fa`.

To create a farm using `PSConfig.exe`, follow these steps:

1. Change into the directory `Program Files\Common Files\Microsoft Shared\Web Server Extensions\14\BIN`.

> **TIP** A SharePoint administrator frequently runs commands from this BIN folder. This folder is located in what is called the SharePoint Root, or 14 Hive. By adding a new entry to your PATH environment variable, you can run these commands from any command prompt (including PowerShell) without having to manually enter this long folder path.

2. Run the following command, substituting the correct values for those shown in angle brackets:

   ```
   psconfig -cmd configdb -create -server <SqlServerName>
   -database <ConfigDatabaseName> -user <FarmAccount>
   -password <FarmPassword> -passphrase <Passphrase>
   -admincontentdatabase <AdminContentDatabaseName>
   ```

A sample of this command and its output is shown in Figure 1.12.

Figure 1.12: Creating farm using `PSConfig.exe`

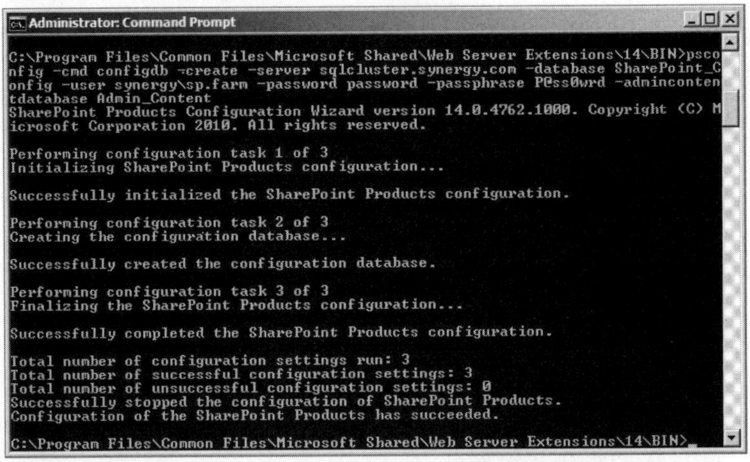

> **NOTE** If you get a permissions error running this command, be sure that you are running the command as an administrator. To do so, right-click the Command Prompt shortcut and select Run As Administrator.

3. Run the Configuration Wizard to finish creating the farm (Start ➤ All Programs ➤ Microsoft SharePoint 2010 Products ➤ SharePoint 2010 Products Configuration Wizard). This part can also be scripted with `PSConfig.exe`, but the resulting configuration is the same.
4. When prompted, choose Do Not Disconnect From This Server Farm.
5. Provide the TCP port number for the Central Administration Web Application.
6. Choose the authentication type for your web application: NTLM or Kerberos.
7. Review your settings and click Next.
8. Wait a few minutes and click Finish when the process completes.

The farm is now created and Central Administration will start. By default, log files for the Configuration Wizard and `PSConfig.exe` are stored in the `Program Files\Common Files\Microsoft Shared\Web Server Extensions\14\LOGS` folder. You can consult these logs to troubleshoot any problems you have. The filename format is `PSCDiagnostics_<Date-Time>_<Random Number>.log`.

Joining an Existing Server Farm

Any new server that will become a WFE or application server must be added to the farm. Here's what you will need in order to join a new server to an existing farm:

- Server OS installed and joined to the domain
- SharePoint prerequisites installed
- SharePoint binaries installed
- Name of your SQL Server where the farm configuration database is stored
- Name of your configuration database
- Farm passphrase (this can be reset if unknown)
- Must be logged in with the domain installer account, which is a local administrator

Here are the steps to join a server into an existing farm:

1. Start the Configuration Wizard by choosing Start ➤ All Programs ➤ Microsoft SharePoint 2010 Products ➤ SharePoint 2010 Products Configuration Wizard.

You are greeted with the initial screen in the wizard, as shown in Figure 1.6 earlier in this chapter.

2. Acknowledge the warning that services may be restarted.
3. Select the Connect An Existing Server Farm radio button, as shown in Figure 1.7.
4. Enter the name of the database server where the configuration database is stored and click the Retrieve Database Names button. Confirm that the right configuration database is selected. See Figure 1.13.

Figure 1.13: Specifying configuration database settings

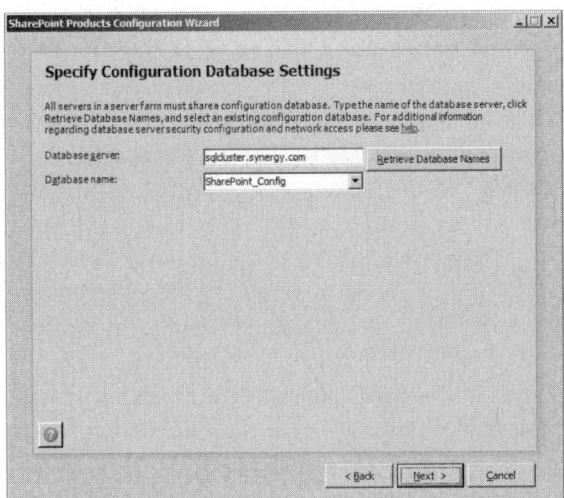

If you cannot connect to the database server, check the following areas:

- Be sure you are logged in with the installer account.
- Check the incoming firewall settings on the SQL server.
- Ensure Named Pipes and/or TCP/IP Protocols are enabled for the SQL Server Network Configuration. (This is specified in SQL Server Configuration Manager on the SQL server.)

5. Enter the passphrase for the farm (the one you defined when you created the farm). See Figure 1.14.

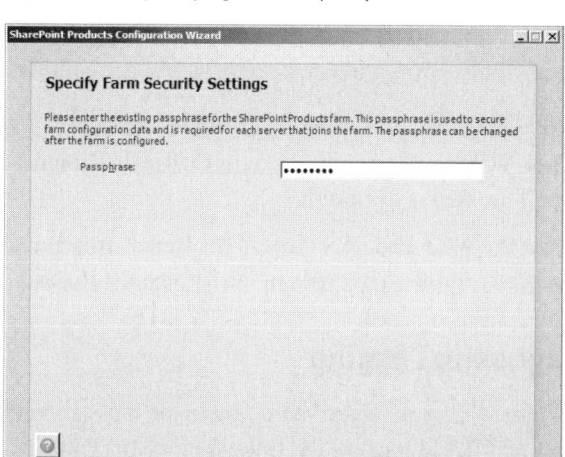

Figure 1.14: Specifying the farm passphrase

NOTE If the passphrase is unknown, you can reset it from any of the other farm servers by using the `Set-SPPassPhrase` PowerShell cmdlet.

6. Review your settings. Clicking the Advanced Settings button allows you to host the Central Administration Web Application on this server. By default, the Central Administration Web Application is hosted only on the first machine that created the farm, but you can move it to another server or run it on multiple servers. How to run the Central Administration Web Application on another server is covered in Chapter 5, "Scaling and High Availability."

When the process completes, you have joined the farm.

Perform Postinstall Operations

Now that your installation is complete, there are a few additional operations that you should do to ensure your farm is properly configured from the start. Some of these are covered in later chapters in more detail. Here is a list of what should be done:

- Adjust diagnostic logging path to ensure your C: drives don't get filled up with SharePoint log entries.

- Resolve the problematic HTTP 401.1 Unauthorized error (aka loopback fix).
- Create a web application and site collection to host content.
- Install language packs. This step is optional.
- Install Office Web Apps to view and edit Office documents from SharePoint. This step is optional.
- Apply the fix for WCF Data Services. This step is optional and provides support for certain types of custom applications.

Adjusting Diagnostic Logging

By default, SharePoint will store its text-based trace log files (also called Unified Logging System [ULS] logs) in the following folder: `Program Files\Common Files\Microsoft Shared\Web Server Extensions\14\LOGS`. The problem is that for busy environments, you can fill up your `C:` drive with these log entries.

The solution is to move these log entries off your `C:` drive and onto a different partition such as `D:`. To do so:

1. On all WFE and application servers, create a new folder to store your trace logs (for example, `D:\Logs\SharePoint`).
2. Start Central Administration (Start ➤ All Programs ➤ Microsoft SharePoint 2010 Products ➤ SharePoint 2010 Central Administration).
3. Click Monitoring and then select Configure Diagnostic Logging.
4. In the Trace Log setting, adjust the path to match the one you defined in step 1, as shown in Figure 1.15.

Figure 1.15: Changing the path for the trace log

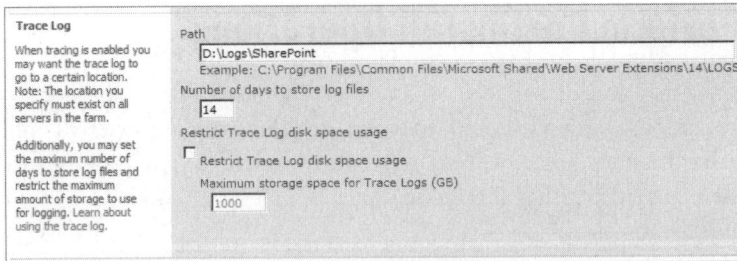

Configuring diagnostic logging is covered in more detail in Chapter 15, "Managing Auditing, Monitoring, and Analytics."

Resolving the HTTP 401.1 Unauthorized Error

Windows Server 2008 and 2008 R2 have a security feature that prevents the WFE itself from browsing to FQDN server names (i.e., `intranet.company.com`) it hosts. This is only an issue from the web server and does not affect external clients.

This feature, while worthwhile from a security posture, wreaks havoc with SharePoint by breaking a number of regular operations. Microsoft has posted two methods to solve the problem: `http://support.microsoft.com/kb/896861`. For a production server, you are advised to go with method 1 and push out this setting with a Group Policy. For a development or test environment, method 2 is acceptable and an easier fix.

Creating a Web Application and Site Collection

Before SharePoint can be used by regular users, you must create a web application and a site collection. The web application defines the URL and how users will authenticate (e.g., Windows, Forms). The site collection holds the content (e.g., websites, documents, list items) users store in SharePoint. Chapter 2, "Creating and Managing Web Applications," explains how to create web applications, and Chapter 3, "Creating and Managing Site Collections," describes site collections.

Installing Office Web Apps

Office Web Apps is an optional add-in that lets you view and edit Word, Excel, PowerPoint, and OneNote files right from the browser. To use Office Web Apps, you must download and install it separately. It's easiest to install Office Web Apps before creating the farm, but you can do it afterward as well.

Installing Office Web Apps Before Creating The Farm

To install Office Web Apps before creating the farm, follow these steps:

1. After installing the SharePoint binaries, install Office Web Apps by running the setup program.
2. Accept the Software License Terms.

3. Enter your license key.
4. Choose a file location.
5. When the installation completes, proceed to create the farm as described in "Creating a Server Farm," earlier in this chapter.
6. When adding new servers to the farm, be sure to install Office Web Apps before joining the server to the farm.

Installing Office Web Apps on an Existing Farm

If you are installing Office Web Apps to an existing farm, follow these steps. Steps 1–6 must be done on each WFE and application server in the farm.

1. Install Office Web Apps by running the setup program.
2. Accept the Software License Terms.
3. Enter your license key.
4. Choose a file location.
5. Close the installation program.
6. Run the SharePoint Configuration Wizard to register the new components.

These final two steps need to be done only once for the farm:

7. From Central Administration, create new service applications for Word Viewing Service, PowerPoint Service Application, and Excel Service Application. Details are covered in Chapter 4.
8. Designate the server(s) in the farm on which you want to run the services provided by Office Web Apps. Details are covered in Chapter 5.

> **NOTE** When you install Office Web Apps, SharePoint will modify its default behavior to start opening Office documents in the browser. This can cause problems if Office Web Apps is installed but not fully configured yet. When installing Office Web Apps into an existing farm with active users, consider scheduling downtime to complete the installation and configuration.
> For more details and other workarounds, see http://technet.microsoft.com/en-us/library/ff431687.aspx#bkmk_addtl_conf.

Installing Language Packs

SharePoint has built-in multilingual capabilities. You can even have individual websites configured to support multiple languages. For example, you can have a team site that some users use in English and others use in German.

> **NOTE** SharePoint doesn't automatically translate content between languages—it only adjusts the menu commands and built-in application pages to display in that language.

For SharePoint to support multiple languages, you must download and install each additional language pack that you intend on using. Unlike the previous version of SharePoint, you do not need to install both the Foundation and Server language packs if you are running SPS.

- Download SPS 2010 language packs from

    www.microsoft.com/downloads/details.aspx?FamilyID=046f16a9-4bce-4149-8679-223755560d54

- Download SPF 2010 language packs from

    www.microsoft.com/downloads/en/details.aspx?FamilyID=646E311A-AAF3-4D30-B03C-2F3C70D19A22

Here are the steps to install a language pack in your farm. These steps must be done on every WFE and application server in your farm. The order of the servers is not important, and you can install language packs on multiple servers at the same time.

1. Install the language pack (ServerLanguagePack.exe).
2. Run the SharePoint Configuration Wizard to register the language pack for the server. There are no inputs that you need to provide.

> **NOTE** For some languages such as Arabic or Chinese, you must download and install additional files for the OS. To install, go to Control Panel, click Region And Language, choose Keyboards And Languages, and then select Install/Uninstall Languages.

To learn more about installing language packs for SharePoint, see

   http://technet.microsoft.com/en-us/library/cc262108.aspx

Installing a Fix for WCF Data Services

SharePoint 2010 has built-in support for Representational State Transfer (REST)-based web services. REST is a type of web service that allows you to easily read and write from SharePoint lists and libraries from client programs. In SharePoint, this ability is provided by software called WCF Data Services (formerly called ADO.NET Data Services). SharePoint does not use this as a built-in capability, but if you will be writing and deploying custom applications for SharePoint, you might need to apply a hotfix to correct a problem. This problem only exists on Windows Server 2008 R2 and Windows 7.

Download the hotfix here:

    www.microsoft.com/downloads/en/details.aspx?familyid=
    3e102d74-37bf-4c1e-9da6-5175644fe22d&displaylang=en

You will need to install the hotfix on each WFE server.

Apply Updates

From time to time you will need to apply a hotfix, cumulative update, or service pack to your farm. How each of these is installed and applied to your farm can vary in SharePoint 2010. Before going through the specific steps to apply an update, it helps to first understand how updates are designed.

Understanding Update Types

In general, Microsoft makes two types of SharePoint updates available: service packs and cumulative updates.

> **Service Packs (SPs)** Just as with most systems, SPs are a collection of fixes and sometimes new features that go through a rigorous testing process prior to release. SPs in SharePoint 2010 are expected to be cumulative. For example, SP2 should include all the fixes that were part of SP1. How often SPs are released can vary widely, but it's reasonable to expect one every 12–18 months or so.
>
> **Cumulative Updates (CUs)** CUs are regular updates, released every two months. A CU addresses issues that have been resolved since the last SP or CU. In some cases, CUs may be a collection of

individual hotfixes rolled up into one download. In other cases, they may be hotfixes that are released at the same time but downloaded and installed separately. Unlike SPs, these updates have not been as thoroughly tested, and you should only consider installing them if you are building a new farm or you need to fix a specific problem that a CU addresses.

In rare cases, perhaps to correct an urgent security issue, Microsoft may release a critical on-demand fix. In most cases, these are applied the same way as a CU.

Here is a common question: "I'm running SPS 2010. Do I need to install both the SPF and the SPS update?" The answer varies on a case-by-case basis, but the safe reply to this question is yes. Take the October 2010 CU, for example. In this case, the SPS update includes the SPF update. However, it does not hurt to apply both, so if you are ever in doubt, apply both. Just make sure that you install the SPF update before the SPS one.

Understanding the Update Process

When you are applying SPs or CUs to SharePoint, there are two primary aspects to the process:

- Install the update's binary files
- Upgrade the database schema

In some cases these steps need to be performed together and in other cases compatibility mode applies, which means the steps can be performed at different times.

Understanding Primary Aspects of the Update

Installing the update's binary files is the easy part. You simply run the update (normally an EXE), and it installs the necessary files. This process usually takes just a few minutes or so per server.

Upgrading the database schema is the more involved operation, in terms of time. This step is usually done with the SharePoint Configuration Wizard and involves upgrading the database to align with the build of the new binary files that were installed. How long this takes depends on several factors, but the two primary factors are the size of your content databases and the speed of your SQL servers (in particular the disk channel).

Understanding Compatibility Mode

In prior versions of SharePoint, administrators were required to perform both of these update operations together. That is, after you installed the update on each server, you had to then immediately run the Configuration Wizard to upgrade the database.

In SharePoint 2010, some updates will fall within a "compatibility mode boundary." In other words, they are backward compatible. This means that you can just install the update to all servers and then defer the database upgrade until a later date, usually as part of scheduled downtime. How long can you defer? There is no firm rule, but you are advised to defer no longer than a few weeks.

In general, it is expected that most hotfixes and CUs will fall within this compatibility mode, assuming you are running the most recent SP. This means that you can apply these types of updates and defer the database upgrade. SPs, since they are much larger and complex, are not expected to be backward compatible. When this happens, a new boundary is established. So, when you apply an SP, you will need to run the database upgrade immediately after installing the update's binaries. How this works is shown in Figure 1.16.

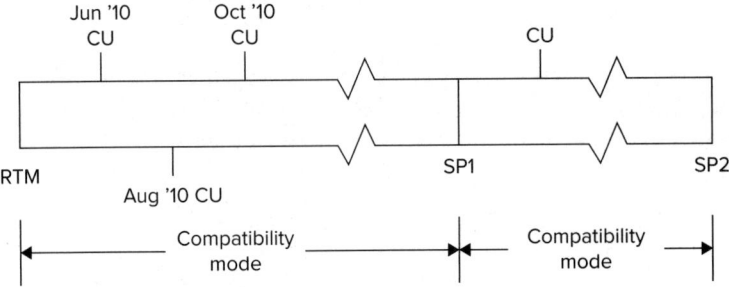

Figure 1.16: Compatibility mode boundaries

Installing Updates to a Farm

Now that you have an understanding of the types of updates, here are the steps you need to go through depending on whether or not the update is backward compatible.

> **WARNING** SharePoint updates that have been applied cannot be rolled back. Thus, before applying any type of update to the farm, you should run a complete farm backup.

Installing a Service Pack

Applying an update that is not backward compatible (e.g., a service pack) must be done during scheduled downtime. Here are the steps:

1. If you are load balancing your WFE servers, pause the load balancer. If not, you can just stop the World Wide Web Publishing Service (W3SVC) on each WFE server.
2. Install the update on the server hosting Central Administration.
3. Install the update on the remaining servers.
4. Run the Configuration Wizard on the server hosting Central Administration to upgrade all databases. Much welcomed in SharePoint 2010, you now have a percentage complete status bar, as shown in Figure 1.17.

Figure 1.17: Percentage complete

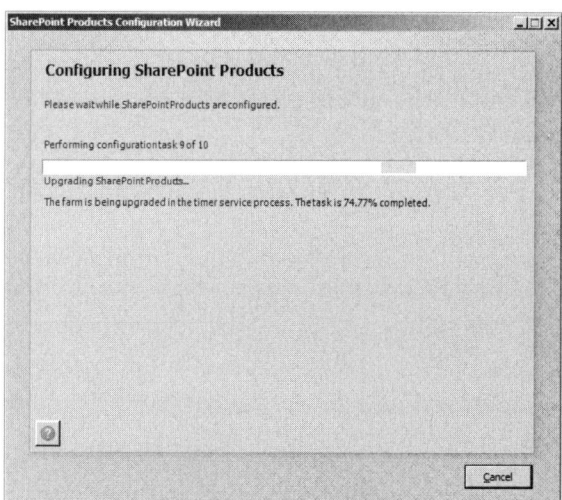

5. Verify the upgrades were successful.
6. Run the Configuration Wizard on the remaining servers. These can all be run in parallel.
7. Resume the load balancer or restart the W3SVC services.
8. Test and validate.

Installing a Backward-Compatible Update

Applying an update that is backward compatible involves two parts. One is to install the binaries, and the second (which can be deferred) is running the upgrade. The first part can be done with minimal downtime if you are load balancing your WFE servers.

If you are load balancing, follow these steps to install the binaries:

1. Remove approximately half of your servers from the load balancer. If you have three servers, you can just remove one.
2. Install the update on the server(s) removed. Do not run the Configuration Wizard.
3. After confirming the update installed successfully, remove the remaining server(s) from the load balancer.
4. Add the server(s) that were removed in step 1 to the load balancer.
5. Install the update on the server(s) removed in step 3. Do not run the Configuration Wizard.
6. Install the update on the remaining servers in the farm. Do not run the Configuration Wizard.
7. Add the server(s) that were removed in step 3 to the load balancer.
8. Test and validate.

If you are not load balancing, follow these steps to install the binaries:

1. Install the update on the server that is your WFE. Do not run the Configuration Wizard.
2. After confirming the update installed successfully, install the update on the remaining servers in the farm. Do not run the Configuration Wizard.
3. Test and validate.

At this point, your binaries have been applied, and your databases will be flagged as needing an upgrade. If at this point in Central Administration you choose Upgrade And Migration and then select Review Database Status, you will see what's shown in Figure 1.18. You are now running in a deferred upgrade state. During your next scheduled maintenance window, you should complete the upgrade.

Figure 1.18: Content databases in compatibility range

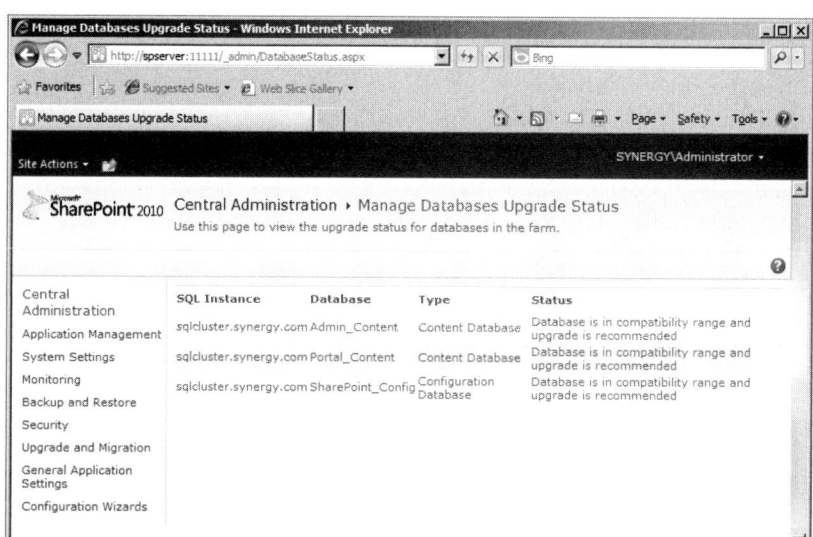

To complete the upgrade and align the database schema with binaries, follow these steps:

1. If you are load balancing your WFE servers, pause the load balancer. If not, you can just stop the W3SVC service on each WFE server.
2. Run the Configuration Wizard on the server hosting Central Administration to upgrade all databases. Check the percentage complete status bar, as shown in Figure 1.17, earlier in this section.
3. Verify the upgrades were successful.
4. Run the Configuration Wizard on the remaining servers. These can all be run in parallel.
5. Resume the load balancer or restart the W3SVC services.
6. Test and validate.

Automate the Installation

As you can see, performing a SharePoint installation manually is quite a lot of work. In addition, as servers and farms are added, there is always the risk of missing or misconfiguring a step. Having automated scripts guarantees consistency in each farm you build. Therefore, if you expect to build farms on a regular basis, it is essential to have a set of automation scripts in your toolkit.

Fortunately, the SharePoint community has come to the rescue by providing an excellent package that automates nearly every detail, including the provisioning of many services. It also supports single- or multiserver farms. The package is called AutoSPInstaller and can be downloaded from CodePlex at http://autospinstaller.codeplex.com.

Configuring AutoSPInstaller

While AutoSPInstaller is easy to use and can be adapted to specific needs, it does help to understand the installation process. This section provides an overview of how to use AutoSPInstaller. More details can be found on the AutoSPInstaller page on CodePlex. This package is regularly updated, so the features may vary from what is covered in this section.

Here are the steps to use AutoSPInstaller to automate the creation of a farm:

1. Create a new installation folder to hold all files used for installation.

2. Copy the contents of the SharePoint ISO or actual disc into this new folder. If you just have an EXE, you can extract it using this syntax:

   SharePoint.exe /extract:E:\SP.Install

3. Download and unzip AutoSPInstaller into your installation folder (e.g., E:\SP.Install).

4. Inside the SP.Install folder, edit the config.xml file and add your SharePoint Server Product Key. This is the line that begins with <PIDKEY>.

5. Inside the SP.Install folder, edit the SetInputs.xml file. This file provides detailed instructions on how the automated installation works. Among other settings, you must provide the name of your SQL server, database names, and the farm account. The farm account's password and farm passphrase are optional—if they are not specified, you will be prompted for them during the installation. In this file, you also have the option of installing many service accounts such as Search or Managed Metadata. See Figure 1.19 for a snapshot of just a few of these settings.

Figure 1.19: AutoSPInstaller configuration settings

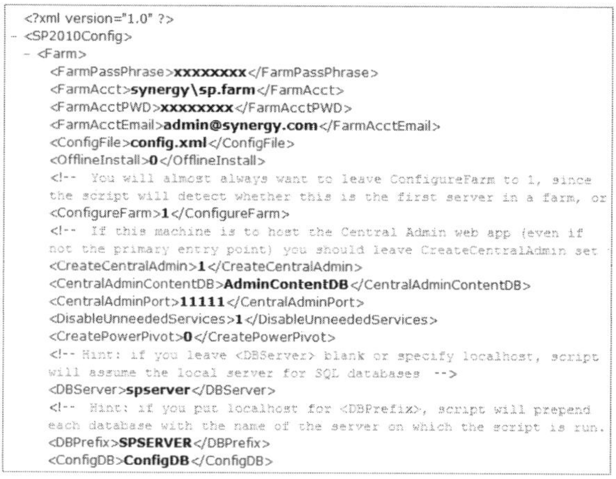

```xml
<?xml version="1.0" ?>
- <SP2010Config>
  - <Farm>
      <FarmPassPhrase>xxxxxxxx</FarmPassPhrase>
      <FarmAcct>synergy\sp.farm</FarmAcct>
      <FarmAcctPWD>xxxxxxxx</FarmAcctPWD>
      <FarmAcctEmail>admin@synergy.com</FarmAcctEmail>
      <ConfigFile>config.xml</ConfigFile>
      <OfflineInstall>0</OfflineInstall>
      <!-- You will almost always want to leave ConfigureFarm to 1, since
      the script will detect whether this is the first server in a farm, or -->
      <ConfigureFarm>1</ConfigureFarm>
      <!-- If this machine is to host the Central Admin web app (even if
      not the primary entry point) you should leave CreateCentralAdmin set -->
      <CreateCentralAdmin>1</CreateCentralAdmin>
      <CentralAdminContentDB>AdminContentDB</CentralAdminContentDB>
      <CentralAdminPort>11111</CentralAdminPort>
      <DisableUnneededServices>1</DisableUnneededServices>
      <CreatePowerPivot>0</CreatePowerPivot>
      <!-- Hint: if you leave <DBServer> blank or specify localhost, script
      will assume the local server for SQL databases --> 
      <DBServer>spserver</DBServer>
      <!-- Hint: if you put localhost for <DBPrefix>, script will prepend
      each database with the name of the server on which the script is run. -->
      <DBPrefix>SPSERVER</DBPrefix>
      <ConfigDB>ConfigDB</ConfigDB>
```

6. Optionally, add any SPs and/or CUs that you want to have automatically applied (slipstreamed) into the Updates folder. When adding, be sure to manually extract the contents of each update.

7. Optionally, add any language packs into the LanguagePacks folder.

8. Log into the server using your SharePoint install account.

9. From the AutoSPInstaller folder, run the Launch.bat file to begin. As it runs, AutoSPInstaller will log all of its activities into RTF-formatted files that it places on the desktop. It also logs output into the console window, as shown in Figure 1.20.

Figure 1.20: Initial console output from AutoSPInstaller

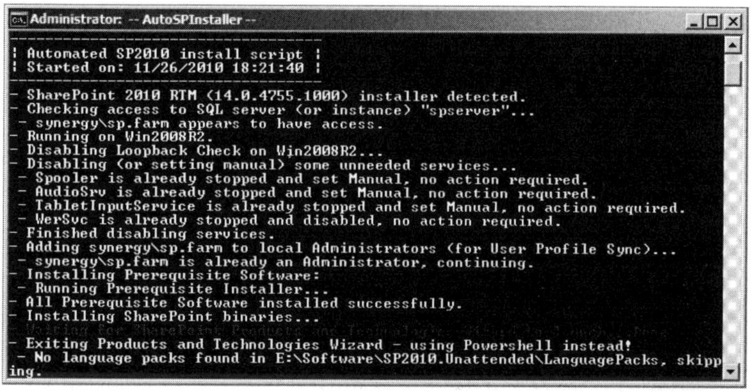

```
Administrator: --AutoSPInstaller--
| Automated SP2010 install script |
| Started on: 11/26/2010 18:21:40 |

- SharePoint 2010 RTM (14.0.4755.1000) installer detected.
- Checking access to SQL server (or instance) "spserver"...
- synergy\sp.farm appears to have access.
- Running on Win2008R2.
- Disabling Loopback Check on Win2008R2...
- Disabling (or setting manual) some unneeded services...
  - Spooler is already stopped and set Manual, no action required.
  - AudioSrv is already stopped and set Manual, no action required.
  - TabletInputService is already stopped and set Manual, no action required.
  - WerSvc is already stopped and disabled, no action required.
- Finished disabling services.
- Adding synergy\sp.farm to local Administrators (for User Profile Sync)...
  - synergy\sp.farm is already an Administrator, continuing.
- Installing Prerequisite Software:
  - Running Prerequisite Installer...
- All Prerequisite Software installed successfully.
- Installing SharePoint binaries...
- Exiting Products and Technologies Wizard - using Powershell instead!
  - No language packs found in E:\Software\SP2010.Unattended\LanguagePacks, skipp
ing.
```

Here are a few limitations with AutoSPInstaller and other issues that you should be aware of:

- AutoSPInstaller does not currently automate the installation of Office Web Apps.
- All service accounts will use the same application pool identity.
- AutoSPInstaller is designed to work with SharePoint Server. To fully automate the installation of SharePoint Foundation, the script needs to be modified.

Installing Prerequisites Without Internet Access

An automated installation, just like a manual one, attempts to download the prerequisite files from the Internet during installation. If the server does not have Internet access, the install will fail. The workaround for this is to predownload these files and tell the installer to use these predownloaded files instead. Here are the steps:

1. Download all prerequisites using a PowerShell script located at http://autospinstaller.codeplex.com/releases/view/44442.
2. Store these files these in the `PrerequisiteInstallerFiles` folder.
3. In your installer folder (e.g., `E:\SP.Install`), create a text file named `PrerequisiteInstaller.Arguments.txt` with the following values on one long line:

    ```
    /SQLNCli:PrerequisiteInstallerFiles\sqlncli.msi
    /ChartControl:PrerequisiteInstallerFiles\MSChart.exe
    /KB976462:PrerequisiteInstallerFiles\Windows6.1-KB976462-v2-x64.msu
    /IDFXR2:PrerequisiteInstallerFiles\Windows6.1-KB974405-x64.msu
    /Sync:PrerequisiteInstallerFiles\Synchronization.msi
    /FilterPack:PrerequisiteInstallerFiles\FilterPack\FilterPack.msi
    /ADOMD:PrerequisiteInstallerFiles\SQLSERVER2008_ASADOMD10.msi
    /Speech:PrerequisiteInstallerFiles\SpeechPlatformRuntime.msi
    ```

/SpeechLPK:PrerequisiteInstallerFiles\
MSSpeech_SR_en-US_TELE.msi
/ReportingServices:PrerequisiteInstallerFiles\
rsSharePoint.msi

NOTE This arguments file will vary slightly depending on whether you are using Windows Server 2008 or 2008 R2. This example assumes you are using 2008 R2. It also assumes you are using US English for the base language. For details on how to adjust these values, see http://technet.microsoft.com/en-us/library/ff686793.aspx.

2
Creating and Managing Web Applications

IN THIS CHAPTER, YOU WILL LEARN TO:

▸ **UNDERSTAND WEB APPLICATIONS** (Pages 40 – 44)

▸ **CREATE A WEB APPLICATION USING CENTRAL ADMINISTRATION** (Pages 44 – 54)
  - Choose an Authentication Type (Page 44)
  - Configure IIS Website Settings (Page 45)
  - Configure Security (Page 46)
  - Configure the Public URL (Page 52)
  - Configure the Application Pool (Page 52)
  - Configure the Content Database (Page 53)

▸ **CONFIGURE SERVICE APPLICATION CONNECTIONS** (Pages 54 – 55)

▸ **CREATE A WEB APPLICATION USING POWERSHELL** (Pages 55 – 56)

▸ **CONFIGURE IIS SETTINGS** (Pages 56 – 60)

▸ **CONFIGURE ADDITIONAL SETTINGS** (Pages 60 – 65)

▸ **EXTEND OR DELETE A WEB APPLICATION** (Pages 65 – 72)

Once SharePoint has been installed and a farm has been created, the next logical step is to create one or more SharePoint web applications. SharePoint web applications are specially configured ASP.NET web applications that are hosted inside Internet Information Services (IIS). These web applications expose the content found within SharePoint websites, so they are an integral part of building a SharePoint environment.

Understand Web Applications

Creating a SharePoint web application requires many configuration settings, and some are difficult to change once the application has been created. Thus, it's important to highlight some of the key architectural components that make up a SharePoint web application prior to creation. Understanding these components will ensure you have the knowledge to effectively create and manage your SharePoint web applications. This section covers the major components found within a SharePoint web application and briefly discusses how they work within IIS.

Working with SharePoint Web Application Components

Logically, a SharePoint web application holds multiple site collections. In fact, that's the purpose of a SharePoint web application: to provide a URL where site collections can be mounted. Before we go too much further, it helps to have a basic grasp of site collections and how they are stored on disk. More details on site collections are covered in Chapter 3, "Creating and Managing Site Collections."

Exploring Site Collection Basics

A site collection is a collection of SharePoint websites organized in a hierarchy, just like folders. Many SharePoint artifacts and configuration settings are shared throughout a site collection. Some of these artifacts include master pages, content types, web parts, templates, and, perhaps most importantly, security. Each site collection has a single top-level or root website, which is where these shared artifacts are stored. Websites also contain lists and libraries where user content such as tasks, calendar entries, and documents are found. While SharePoint can support thousands of site collections per web application, most use a much smaller number.

Working with Content Databases

Content databases are stored in SQL Server and hold all the content and metadata associated with site collections. When you create a new web application, a new content database is also created. A site collection is created within a web application. When a site collection is created, it is stored within one of the web application's content databases. Here are some key rules to remember when working with content databases:

- A site collection cannot be spread across multiple content databases.
- A content database is associated with just one web application.
- A web application can have multiple content databases.
- A content database cannot be spread across separate web applications.
- Content databases should be kept as small as possible—in general, do not exceed 200 GB for each one.

Figure 2.1 depicts the relationship between SharePoint web applications, content databases, and site collections.

Figure 2.1: Relationship between web applications, content databases, and site collections

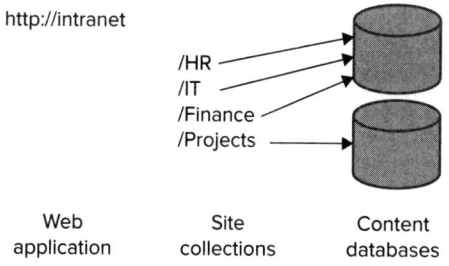

> **NOTE** SharePoint 2010 also allows you to store content outside of the content database, in the file system. This is done by configuring Remote BLOB Storage (RBS) for a particular content database. RBS is commonly used when you have very large content databases (more than 500 GB) and need to use a cheaper form of storage. With RBS, only the files stored in lists and libraries (the files are the BLOBs, or Binary Large Objects) within SharePoint websites are stored in the file system. All other content and metadata is still stored in the content database and the rules associated with content databases and site collections (including quotas) still apply. To learn more about RBS and how to install and configure it, see the article "Install and Configure Remote BLOB Storage (RBS) with the FILESTREAM Provider (SharePoint Foundation 2010)" at http://technet.microsoft.com/en-us/library/ee663474.aspx.

How SharePoint Web Applications Work

Internally, SharePoint web applications are complex ASP.NET web applications. Fortunately, knowing all the details about the inner workings is not important. This section focuses on just the essentials.

Understanding SharePoint's Relationship with IIS

At a basic level, a SharePoint web application is an IIS-configured web site. It consists of IIS properties such as authentication type, application pool, and binding details such as host header (i.e., the URL), IP address, and TCP port. As you will learn shortly, most of these settings are configured from SharePoint—SharePoint administrators do not regularly go into IIS to adjust these settings.

When a SharePoint web application is created, a new IIS website is created on each web front end (WFE) server along with a few files and subfolders located at `C:\inetpub\wwwroot\wss\VirtualDirectories\<host header & port>`. In this folder, a very important file named `web.config` exists. This is an ASP.NET configuration file that configures the IIS website to be a SharePoint web application. There are occasions where you need to manually modify this file (covered elsewhere in this book).

> **NOTE** Understanding terminology in SharePoint is tricky. In particular, the word *site* is a troublesome as it means different things in different contexts. For example, you have IIS websites, SharePoint site collections, and SharePoint websites. An IIS website is completely different from a SharePoint website. What you need to remember is that an IIS website is associated with a SharePoint web application.

Using Application Pools

An application pool is used by IIS to process and execute requests that are received by the WFE server. It is associated with the IIS website and SharePoint web application.

You must specify which application pool to use when creating a new SharePoint web application. You have the option of creating a new application pool or sharing (reusing) an existing one. From a security standpoint, it's best to have separate application pools for each web application. However, this approach does consume more RAM on the WFE servers, which affects performance, especially if you have limited memory.

An application pool gobbles up memory quickly because it can be very active. It also does a great deal of caching. For production environments, this amount can vary widely but usually falls between 200 MB and 8 GB. Due to the large amount of RAM used by the cache, it is essential to ensure your WFE servers have sufficient RAM to avoid excessive paging (using disk when RAM is unavailable). Microsoft recommends having no more than 10 application pools per farm, but this is not a hard limit.

> **NOTE** Technically, an application pool is a Windows process named w3wp.exe and is often called the worker process. As with any Windows process, it requires an associated user account. The account associated with w3wp.exe is called the application pool identity.

Create a Web Application Using Central Administration

Web applications can be created from the Central Administration GUI or PowerShell. To create a web application using Central Administration, follow these steps:

1. Open Central Administration (Start ➤ All Programs ➤ Microsoft SharePoint 2010 Products ➤ SharePoint 2010 Central Administration).
2. Click Application Management, then choose Manage Web Applications
3. In the ribbon, click New. The Create New Web Application dialog box appears.
4. Specify each of the settings and click OK. You need to configure the following settings:
    - Authentication Type
    - IIS Web Site Settings
    - Security
    - Public URL
    - Application Pool
    - Content Database
    - Service Application Connections

We'll explain how to configure each setting in the next few sections. It may take a minute or longer for the web application to be created. While it is running, SharePoint is creating and configuring a new IIS website on each WFE server. It is also creating a new content database on the SQL server specified.

Choose an Authentication Type

The first setting in the Create New Web Application dialog box asks you to choose the authentication method to be used. (See Figure 2.2.)
You have two choices here: Claims-Based Authentication or Classic Mode Authentication.

Figure 2.2: Choose an authentication type

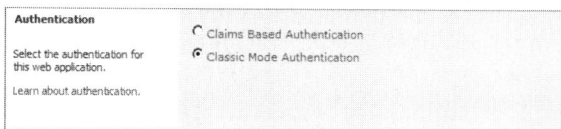

Claims-Based Authentication (CBA)   Also called Claims, Claims-Based Authentication is new to SharePoint 2010 and is based on Windows Identity Foundation. If you will be using Forms-Based Authentication (FBA) or a trusted identity provider such as Windows Live (e.g., Hotmail), you must use Claims. It can be used with Active Directory or Lightweight Directory Access Protocol (LDAP) authentication as well and even allows you to have multiple authentication types based on the same URL. Claims works by exchanging Security Assertion Markup Language (SAML)-based tokens between identity providers.

Classic-Mode Authentication   This is the mechanism that was supported in previous versions of SharePoint. It is the easiest to configure but you should choose it only if you will be using Windows Authentication alone. If you plan on using SharePoint only as an intranet and will be integrating with Active Directory, Classic mode works just fine.

Configure IIS Website Settings

As shown in Figure 2.3, the IIS Web Site section of the Create New Web Application dialog box allows you to configure the IIS website's bindings. In most cases, you will be creating a new IIS website, but SharePoint also lets you convert an existing IIS website into a SharePoint web application. This option is helpful if you have removed SharePoint from an IIS website and need to re-extend it. How and why you might want to do this is covered in the section "Extend or Delete a Web Application," later in this chapter.

Figure 2.3: Configuring IIS website settings

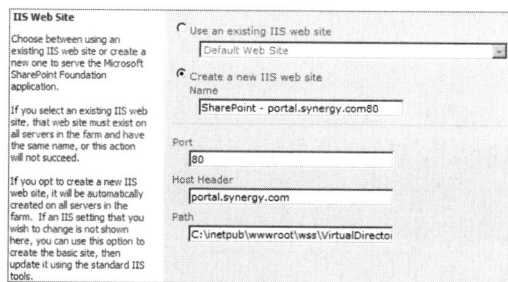

IIS uniquely identifies each website it manages by using three different settings: IP Address, Host Header, and TCP Port. Each IIS website (and SharePoint web application) must have at least one unique value out of these settings. When creating a SharePoint web application, however, you cannot specify the IP address. Initially, SharePoint will bind the IIS website to all unassigned addresses. If you need to bind it to a specific IP address, then you must modify the bindings in IIS after the web application has been created. Be sure to make this modification on all WFE servers.

The host header becomes the friendly name or fully qualified domain name (FQDN) that you will use for the web application. Within Domain Name System (DNS), you will need to be sure that this name resolves to the address of your WFE server or, if you are using network load balancing (NLB), the cluster IP address for your WFE cluster. Configuring an NLB cluster is covered in Chapter 5, "Scaling and High Availability."

Optionally, you can change the website path. By default, this points to a folder path on the C: drive. It only takes a small amount of space, however, so there is no reason to change it.

Configure Security

The security options available depend on whether you chose Claims or Classic authentication. Both types of authentication support anonymous users and Secure Sockets Layer (SSL). You turn these settings on and off in the Security Configuration section of the Create New Web Application dialog box (see Figure 2.4).

Figure 2.4: Security Configuration settings

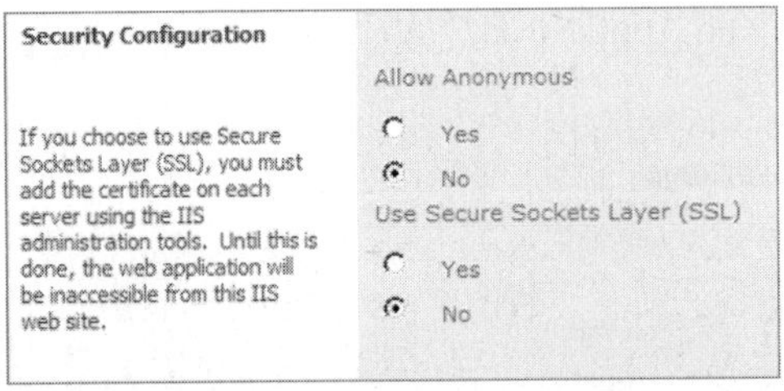

Anonymous users are guest users who do not log in. It is common for public-facing Internet websites to allow anonymous users. For more detail, see Chapter 14, "Managing Security."

SSL is used to encrypt traffic from the client across the Internet to your web servers. If you choose to use SSL, you must load and bind an SSL certificate to the website in IIS after you create the web application. You cannot do this through SharePoint, however; you must use IIS Manager. These steps are covered in the "Configure IIS Settings" section later in this chapter.

Configuring Claims-Based Authentication

Claims is the most flexible form of authentication. With it, you can configure multiple authentication types associated to a single URL on a web application. For example, employees can authenticate using Active Directory, and contractors can authenticate using FBA.

The options available when you choose Claims-Based Authentication are shown in Figure 2.5.

Figure 2.5: Claims Authentication Types security settings

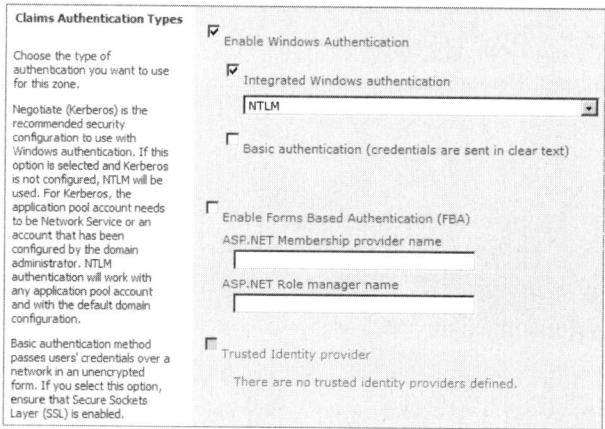

With Claims, you have the option of selecting from one to three primary forms of authentication: Windows, FBA, and Trusted Identity provider. While Claims-Based Authentication is much more powerful than Classic authentication, configuring Claims is a bit more complex.

There are minor differences between Claims and Classic from the user's perspective. For example, the People Picker (the screen where users and groups are granted permissions) is slightly different. If Claims-Based Authentication is configured, users can see and choose users and groups from multiple security realms. For example, both users who exist in Active Directory and users who exist in an external LDAP provider might show up in the People Picker.

Figure 2.6 shows the People Picker when using Classic authentication (top) and when using Claims (bottom) with both Windows Authentication and FBA.

Figure 2.6: People Picker when using Classic (top) and Claims (bottom) authentication

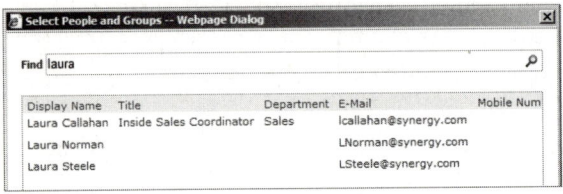

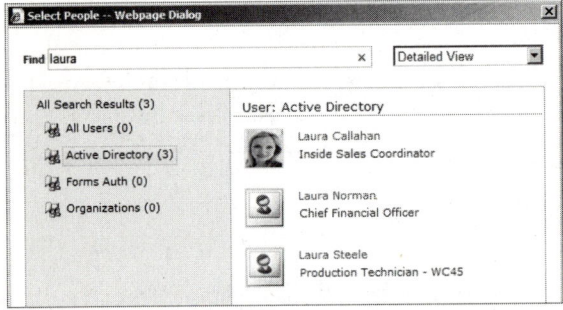

Configuring Windows Authentication

When you enable Windows Authentication, you need to choose whether to use NTLM (Windows NT LAN Manager) or Kerberos. NTLM works with Active Directory and doesn't require any additional configuration. While it's easier to configure, it has three main drawbacks in comparison with Kerberos:

- It is less secure.
- It requires more network packets when authenticating.
- It doesn't support delegation.

Kerberos is an industry-standard form of authentication and also works with Active Directory. It overcomes the limitations associated with NTLM but requires additional configuration. It can be hard to troubleshoot and confirm Kerberos is working unless you have a solid grasp of how it works.

If you choose Kerberos, you need to configure service principal names (SPNs) for SQL Server and each SharePoint web application. For more information on configuring Kerberos with SharePoint, see the article "Configure Kerberos Authentication (SharePoint Server 2010)" here:

http://technet.microsoft.com/en-us/library/ee806870.aspx

NOTE You might be curious why the dialog box says Negotiate (Kerberos). Negotiate means that IIS tells the client that both Kerberos and NTLM are supported, and the client determines which method to use.

If you choose Windows Authentication, you also have the option of enabling Basic Authentication. This is a simple authentication scheme where the user's credentials are sent unencrypted. It is normally used with older browsers. If you select this option, be sure that SSL is in place to ensure that passwords cannot be obtained by devices listening on the network.

Configuring Forms-Based Authentication

FBA is only available when using Claims-Based Authentication. FBA presents users with a web page where they enter their username and password. A default web page is available (see Figure 2.7), or you can design a custom web page.

Figure 2.7: FBA login web page

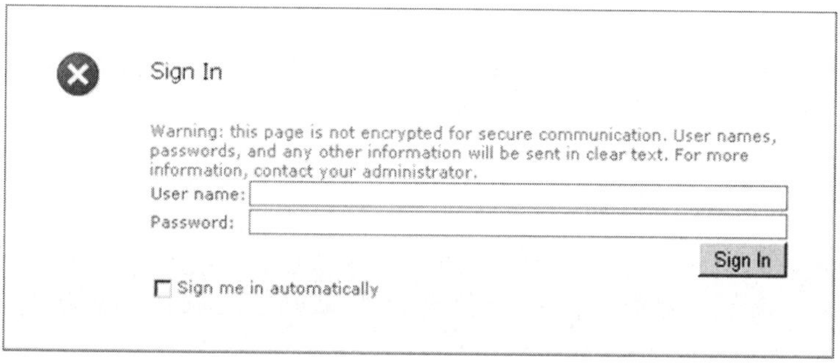

If you enable FBA, you must define which providers will be used for authenticating membership (i.e., users) and managing roles (i.e., groups). For these, you can use Active Directory, LDAP, SQL Membership Provider, or any custom provider that can plug into ASP.NET membership services. FBA works by taking the username and password received from the web page and passing it off to the provider for validation.

To use FBA, you must edit various web.config files with the settings to be used for the membership and role provider. Here is a brief overview of the steps that you must complete on each WFE server:

1. Edit the web.config file for the Central Administration Web Application and add the settings for the membership and role manager that will be used.

2. Edit the web.config file for the Security Token Service Application (located in Program Files\Common Files\Microsoft Shared\Web Server Extensions\14\WebServices\SecurityToken). The changes you make here are exactly the same as with step 1.

3. Create your new SharePoint web application. For the FBA section, as shown in Figure 2.5 earlier in this chapter, enter the ASP.NET membership provider name and the role manager name. These names were specified in steps 1 and 2.

4. Edit the web.config file for the newly created web application and add the same membership and role manager settings used in steps 1 and 2.

When modifying these web.config files, you should make backups first and be very careful—the syntax is complex and varies depending on the provider that is used. For two different examples on how to configure FBA, see the following articles:

- "Configure Forms-Based Authentication for a Claims-Based Web Application (SharePoint Server 2010)":

    http://technet.microsoft.com/en-us/library/ee806890.aspx

- "Configuring Forms Based Authentication for SharePoint 2010 Using IIS7" on Donal Conlon's blog:

    http://donalconlon.wordpress.com/2010/02/23/configuring-forms-base-authentication-for-sharepoint-2010-using-iis7

> **TIP** You can download a configuration utility that can help you configure and push out these web.config changes to all your WFE servers. To read more and download the utility, see the article "SharePoint 2010 Forms Based Authentication Configuration Manager" at http://blogs.technet.com/b/speschka/archive/2010/07/28/sharepoint-2010-forms-based-authentication-configuration-manager.aspx.

Configuring a Trusted Identity Provider

A trusted identity provider allows SharePoint to use a custom or third-party claims provider. For example, you can use Windows Live ID accounts to authenticate users to SharePoint. Before you can select an identity provider, you must first configure one using PowerShell. This process is somewhat complex and the details are beyond the scope of this book. For more information, see the article "Configure Claims-Based Authentication Using Windows Live ID (SharePoint Foundation 2010)." This article contains steps to configure SharePoint to use Live ID as a claims provider. It is available here:

http://technet.microsoft.com/en-us/library/ff973114.aspx

Configuring Classic Authentication

Compared to Claims, configuring Classic authentication is much easier. You must specify whether NTLM or Kerberos will be used. Configuring Kerberos with Classic authentication is the same as with Claims and is discussed in the "Configuring Windows Authentication" section earlier in this chapter. The other setting defines whether SSL is to be used. Figure 2.8 shows the settings for creating a web application with Classic authentication selected.

Figure 2.8: Security Configuration settings for Classic authentication

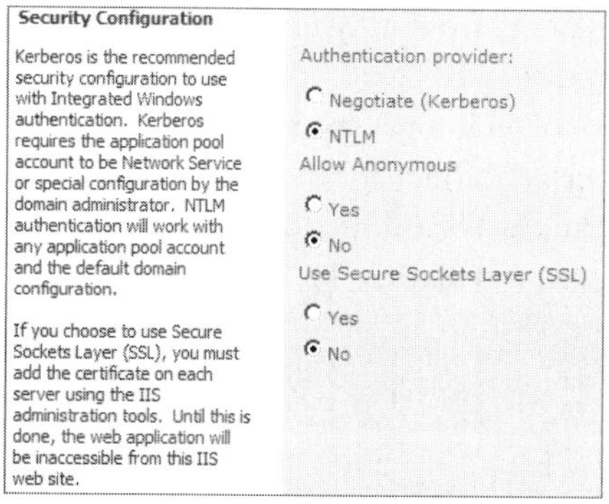

Configure the Public URL

The public URL is the web application URL that SharePoint recognizes and uses when generating links on web pages. The public URL can also be changed after creating the web application. More details on how and when to adjust this setting are found later in this chapter in the "Managing Alternate Access Mappings" section.

Configure the Application Pool

As described earlier, the application pool is the worker process and account that executes client requests on the WFE server. When creating a web application, you can either create a new application pool or reuse an existing one. The interface for configuring the application pool is shown in Figure 2.9.

Figure 2.9: Configuring application pool settings

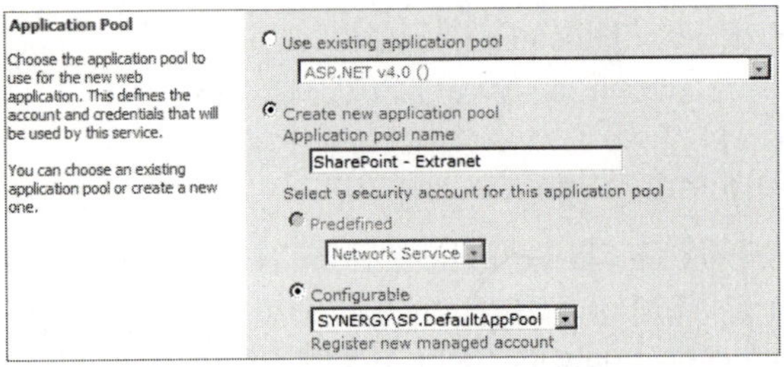

Application Pool	
Choose the application pool to use for the new web application. This defines the account and credentials that will be used by this service. You can choose an existing application pool or create a new one.	○ Use existing application pool [ASP.NET v4.0 ()] ● Create new application pool Application pool name [SharePoint - Extranet] Select a security account for this application pool ○ Predefined [Network Service] ● Configurable [SYNERGY\SP.DefaultAppPool] Register new managed account

Reusing an application pool is more efficient in terms of memory usage but introduces a small security risk, because a single application pool account has access to multiple web applications. Another small risk with sharing application pools is that if the application pool is recycled (restarted), it momentarily affects requests from all web applications sharing it.

When creating a new application pool, you must specify the name of the Windows account to be used as a security account for the application pool. An application pool account is almost always a domain user account, like other service accounts, as discussed in Chapter 1, "Installing

SharePoint 2010." The account to be used for the application pool must first be configured as a managed account (this means that SharePoint can manage the account's password). Managed accounts are covered in more detail in Chapter 14.

Configure the Content Database

As described in the "Understand Web Applications" section, content databases hold site collections that are associated with the web application. When creating a web application, you must create a new content database. The interface for configuring the content database is shown in Figure 2.10.

Figure 2.10: Configuring the content database

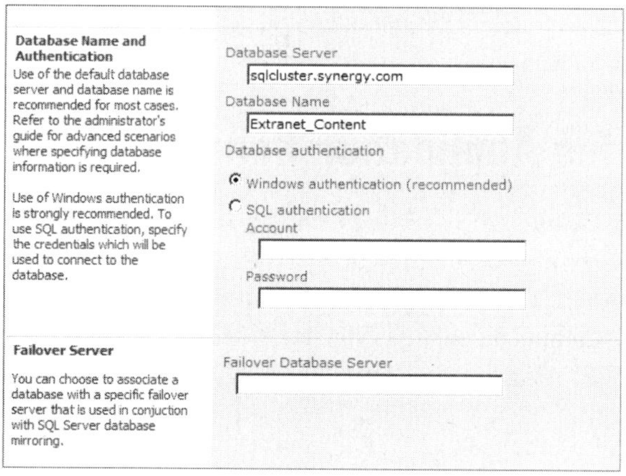

TIP Using a consistent database naming convention is important when creating new content databases. The main reason is for disaster recovery purposes if you ever need to restore a content database. Consistent names are also much easier and cleaner to follow when viewing the list of databases from SQL Server. The default database name of WSS_Content is too generic and not indicative of what or whose content is stored there. Better examples are HR_Content, Projects_Content_DB_1, or MySites_Content_1. The use of _1 is just a numbering convention, allowing you to track multiple content databases associated to the web application.

In the Database Server field shown in Figure 2.10, you can specify the SQL server to be used for this database. Choosing a different SQL server allows you to scale your database tier to multiple servers if needed. Just make sure your SharePoint farm account (defined when the farm was created, as covered in Chapter 1) has securityadmin and dbcreator permissions on the SQL server.

In the Failover Server section, you can specify the server name of a mirrored SQL server. To use this setting, you must have database mirroring configured. Scaling out multiple database servers and database mirroring is introduced in Chapter 5.

The Database Authentication settings shown in Figure 2.10 specify how the application pool account connects to the SQL server. Windows Authentication is recommended because no password information is sent over the wire. If you use SQL authentication, you must make sure that the SQL server is configured to allow SQL authentication and a login account has already been created.

Configure Service Application Connections

The Service Application Connections settings, shown in Figure 2.11, allow you to associate your new web application to existing service applications. In other words, this web application can call into and consume these services, such as Search. Service applications are covered in Chapter 4, "Creating Service Applications."

Figure 2.11: Configuring Service Application Connections settings

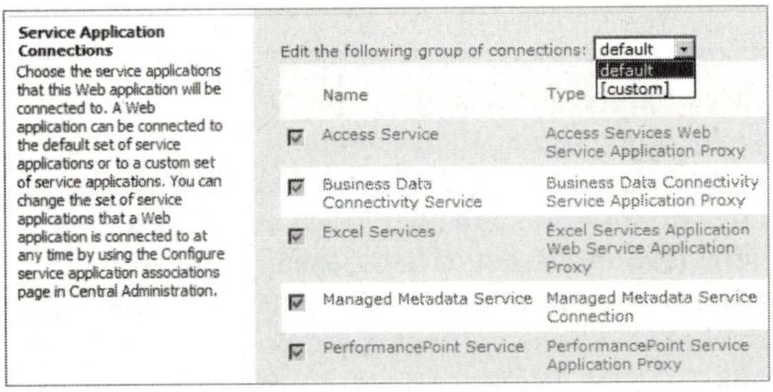

To set up service application connections, follow these steps:

1. In the list labeled "Edit the following group of connections," select a preconfigured group or Custom.

2. If you choose Custom, select each of the service applications you want to associate. You can change these associations at any time by going to Central Administration, click Application Management and then choose Configure Service Application Associations.

Create a Web Application Using PowerShell

Now that you know how to create a web application using the Central Administration GUI, it's time to learn how to do it from script. Using a script is helpful if you need to create many web applications or regularly re-create them and need to ensure it is done consistently each time.

The PowerShell cmdlet is `New-SPWebApplication`. The full syntax covers most of the settings presented in Central Administration.

```
New-SPWebApplication -ApplicationPool <String> -Name
<String> [-AdditionalClaimProvider
<SPClaimProviderPipeBind[]>] [-AllowAnonymousAccess
<SwitchParameter>] [-ApplicationPoolAccount
<SPProcessAccountPipeBind>] [-AssignmentCollection
<SPAssignmentCollection>] [-AuthenticationMethod
<String>] [-AuthenticationProvider
<SPAuthenticationProviderPipeBind[]>] [-Confirm
[<SwitchParameter>]] [-DatabaseCredentials
<PSCredential>] [-DatabaseName <String>]
[-DatabaseServer <String>] [-HostHeader <String>]
[-Path <String>] [-Port<UInt32>] [-SecureSocketsLayer
<SwitchParameter>] [-ServiceApplicationProxyGroup
<SPServiceApplicationProxyGroupPipeBind>]
[-SignInRedirectProvider
<SPTrustedIdentityTokenIssuerPipeBind>]
[-SignInRedirectURL <String>] [-Url <String>] [-WhatIf
[<SwitchParameter>]][<CommonParameters>]
```

To learn more about the various parameter values, use the following PowerShell cmdlet:

```
Get-Help New-SPWebApplication -detailed
```

> **NOTE** When running this or any SharePoint-based PowerShell cmdlet, be sure to use the SharePoint 2010 Management Shell. It can be found at Start ➤ All Programs ➤ Microsoft SharePoint 2010 Products.

The following is a script that you can use to create your next web application using PowerShell. Simply adjust the values for the variables. The web application will use Classic authentication. You will also need to ensure that the account defined by $appPoolAccount is already configured as a managed account.

```
$name = "Extranet"
$hostHeader = "extranet.synergy.com"
$url = "https://" + $hostHeader
$port = 443
$appPoolName = "Extranet_AppPool"
$appPoolAccount = "SYNERGY\SP.DefaultAppPool"
$dbServer = "sqlcluster.synergy.com"
$dbName = "Extranet_Content"

New-SPWebApplication -Name $name -hostHeader ↵
$hostHeader -Port $port -URL $url -SecureSocketsLayer ↵
-ApplicationPool $appPoolName -ApplicationPoolAccount ↵
(Get-SPManagedAccount $appPoolAccount) -DatabaseServer ↵
$dbServer -DatabaseName $dbName
```

Configure IIS Settings

While SharePoint manages most of the settings used for the IIS website, a few settings must be changed using IIS Manager. The most common ones that you need to adjust are covered in this section.

> **WARNING** The web application settings that SharePoint allows you to configure (TCP Port, Application Pool, and others) should not be changed directly in IIS. Why? SharePoint keeps track of these settings in the configuration database. If the settings are changed directly in IIS, SharePoint and IIS become out of sync and problems will result.

Configuring the IIS Logging Path

IIS logs all requests made by clients and writes them in a series of text-based log files. It captures each web page request, such as `default.aspx`, and all of the resources found on the page—including images, scripts, and CSS files. A single page request can result in 20 or more lines in the log file. Multiply this by hundreds of requests by thousands of users and the result is millions of lines for just a single day!

By default, IIS stores the logs on the `C:` drive of your WFE server. If SharePoint receives a lot of requests, a major disk space problem for your system partition can quickly develop. You should change this log path in any environment, such as production, which is expected to have a large number of requests. This change needs to be done only once for each WFE server. Here are the steps:

1. Go into IIS Manager for each WFE server.
2. In the Connections panel on the left, select the server name.
3. In the Features view shown in the middle panel, select Logging.
4. For the log file, change the directory to a more suitable drive and folder. For example, in Figure 2.12 we've changed the path for the log files to `D:\Logs\IIS`.

Figure 2.12: Configuring the IIS logging path

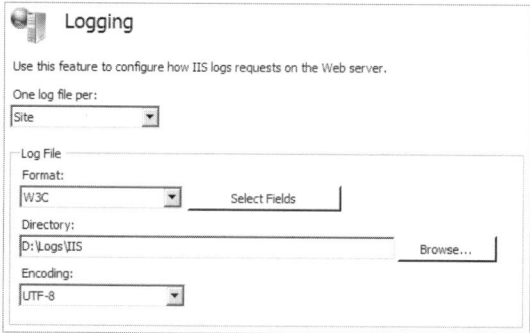

5. Click Apply in the Actions panel on the right to save. This change will be applied to all current IIS websites and any new ones created in the future.

NOTE IIS does not have a built-in way to archive old log files. You can either manually delete old IIS log files periodically, or you can use a script to automate deletion. You will find many scripts available online, such as "Simple PowerShell script to clean up IIS log files" at http://codeasis.com/ShowArticle.aspx?ID=152.

Configuring the SSL Certificate

If SSL was enabled when you created the web application, you will need to load and bind a certificate to the IIS website. There are three parts to this process: creating the certificate request, loading the certificate into IIS, and binding it to the IIS website.

NOTE Incidentally, this process is the same with any IIS website, so it's not specific to SharePoint.

To create a certificate request, follow these steps:

1. Start IIS Manager on any one of the WFE servers.
2. In the Connections panel on the left, select the server name.
3. In the Features view (the middle part of the screen), double-click Server Certificates.
4. In the Actions panel on the right, select Create Certificate Request.
5. Fill out the Request Certificate form as shown in Figure 2.13. Ensure that the entry in the Common Name field matches the host header you specified when you created the web application. When you are finished, click Next.

Figure 2.13: Creating an SSL certificate request

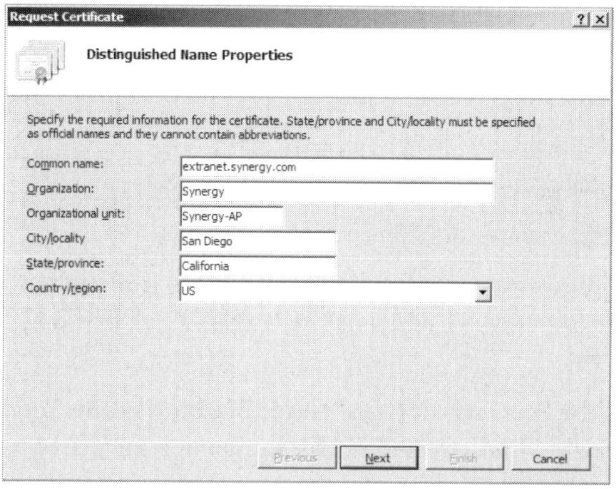

6. Select the appropriate cryptographic setting and bit length. Which settings you use depends on which third-party provider (such as VeriSign or Thawte) or other service (e.g., Microsoft Certificate Services) you are requesting the certificate from. Click Next.

7. Enter a filename and click Finish to save the certificate request as a file. This request is a Base64 encoded text file and must be submitted to the certificate provider. In most cases, you can paste the text file's contents into the web page where you order/request the certificate.

The certificate you receive back from the provider is a single file, usually with a .cer extension. The next task is to load this certificate on each of the WFE servers. Once the certificate is obtained, go into IIS Manager for each WFE server and follow these steps:

1. In the Connections panel on the left, select the server name.
2. In the Features view, double-click Server Certificates.
3. In the Actions panel on the right, select Complete Certificate Request.
4. In the dialog box, browse to the CER file and provide a friendly name for the certificate (that is, a name that will help you recognize the certificate later).

Now that the certificate is loaded, the final procedure is to bind it to the IIS website. These steps must also be done on each WFE server within IIS Manager.

1. In the Connections panel on the left, expand the current server name.
2. Expand Sites and select the correct IIS website.
3. In the Features view, double-click SSL Settings.
4. If you are requiring an SSL connection (that is, you are not allowing unencrypted HTTP sessions), select the check box and click Apply.
5. Return to the Features view and select Bindings in the Actions panel. The Site Bindings dialog box shown in Figure 2.14 appears.

Figure 2.14: Configuring IIS Website Bindings

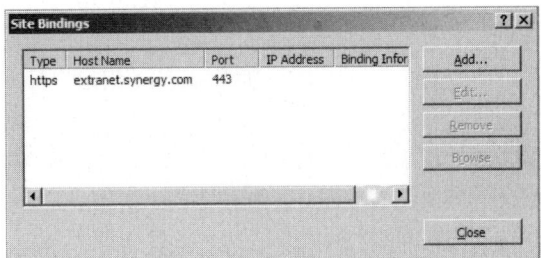

6. Select the binding entry and click the Edit button.
7. In the SSL Certificate drop-down, select the certificate and click OK.

Configure Additional Settings

Once you've created the web application and made the IIS adjustments, there are a few additional settings that you might want to change in order to fine-tune how your web application will function. This section covers the most commonly used settings found within Central Administration on the Web Applications Management page (click Application Management, then select Manage Web Applications).

Configuring General Settings

The General Settings section includes a wide range of settings, from maximum file size, to alerts thresholds, to how recycle bins are used. You can find these configuration options by clicking General Settings in the ribbon (see Figure 2.15).

Figure 2.15: Configuring General Settings

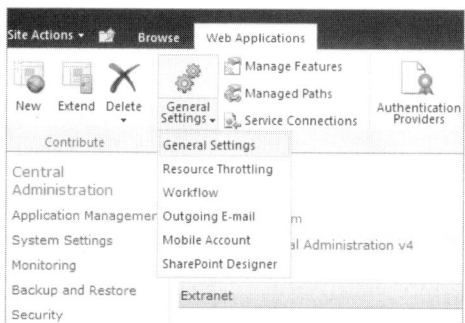

Some of the settings are described here:

Default Time Zone Each web application has a default time zone setting that determines what time zone the root website of each site collection created will use. If you do not specify one, the time zone of the WFE server is used. While you can change the time zone for websites by modifying Regional Settings, it's easier to set the most common time zone to be the default here.

Default Quota Template A quota template is used to restrict the amount of space used in a site collection. A newly-created web application does not have a default quota template assigned. Unless you set a default quota template here, a newly created site collection is not assigned a quota, and the site collection can grow uncontrolled, causing space problems within its content database. We recommend setting a default quota template to ensure a quota is automatically applied to new site collections. Quota templates are covered in more detail in Chapter 3.

Browser File Handling The Browser File Handling setting tells SharePoint to add a special value in the HTTP header when downloading certain file types. The default setting is Strict, which prevents the browser from automatically opening these files. This setting is designed to eliminate a security risk that is posed if a file is corrupted or written to exploit a known security hole.

> **NOTE** As of this writing, the Browser File Handling setting works only with Internet Explorer 8 and 9. Other browsers ignore this setting.

The Strict setting prevents PDF files from automatically opening up in the browser using the Adobe Reader plug-in. Instead, it forces users to save the file and open it on the computer. If security is the top priority in your environment, the best practice is to keep the setting as Strict. Otherwise, you might consider changing the value to Permissive.

Maximum Upload Size By default, SharePoint limits any single file (or group of files if using the multiple file upload) to 50 MB. This limit is controlled at the web application level. You can change the setting to allow files as large as 2 GB.

> **TIP** Even if you increase the maximum upload size, you may still have issues uploading large files. The most common reason is because of a timeout. To resolve the problems, follow the steps in the article "Error Message When You Try to Upload a Large File to a Document Library on a Windows SharePoint Services 3.0 Site" at http://support.microsoft.com/kb/925083. This Knowledgebase article was written for SharePoint 2007, but it still applies to 2010 if you adjust the path from 12\TEMPLATE\LAYOUTS to 14\TEMPLATE\LAYOUTS.

> **TIP** If you are running SharePoint on Windows Server 2008 (not 2008 R2), the maximum upload size is also restricted by the operating system and IIS 7.0. You will need to increase the maximum upload size in the web.config file. See the article "You Cannot Upload Files That Are Larger than 28 MB on a Windows Server 2008-Based Computer That Is Running Windows SharePoint Services 3.0" at http://support.microsoft.com/kb/944981 for more information on how to make this change.

Configuring Resource Throttling

One of the new features in SharePoint 2010 is a restriction on the number of list or library items that can be returned in a single request. This is called large list throttling and it helps prevent expensive queries from causing major performance problems. By default, SharePoint limits any request to 5,000 items, as shown in Figure 2.16. Requests that exceed this limit are not executed and an error message is returned.

Figure 2.16: Configuring Resource Throttling settings

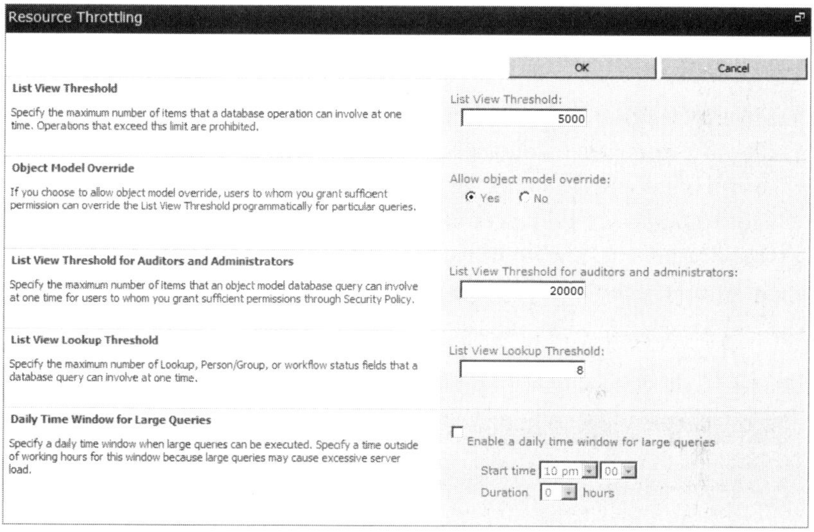

Users who are administrators or auditors (as defined by the web application policy) can request up to 20,000 items, assuming Object Model Override is enabled and custom code is used.

Custom processing jobs that run during night hours or other slow periods may run special queries that exceed the resource throttling thresholds. Fortunately, there is a setting shown at the bottom of Figure 2.16, Daily Time Window For Large Queries, that addresses this need. By enabling the daily time window, you can turn off throttling for one or more hours.

> **TIP** As a general rule, it is a best practice to ensure that lists and libraries do not grow so large that this throttling is applied. You can do so by ensuring that list and library views have an item limit set to display only a small subset of items per page (by default, the item limit is set to 30 and can be adjusted when you are configuring the view). Folders can also be used to help manage size limits since most queries only return items from a single folder. For more details, please refer to the white paper titled "Designing Large Lists Maximizing Lists Performance" downloadable from www.microsoft.com/downloads/en/details .aspx?FamilyID=fd1eac86-ad47-4865-9378-80040d08ac55.

Disabling SharePoint Designer

SharePoint Designer is a powerful application that provides useful features to administrators, site owners, and designers. However, this power comes at the risk of potentially breaking websites. As a farm administrator, you have the option of disabling certain aspects of SharePoint Designer for web applications. As shown in Figure 2.17, there are four ways of controlling how SharePoint Designer can be used within a web application.

Figure 2.17: Disable SharePoint Designer

SharePoint Designer Settings	
Allow SharePoint Designer to be used in this Web Application Specify whether to allow users to edit sites in this Web Application using SharePoint Designer.	☑ Enable SharePoint Designer
Allow Site Collection Administrators to Detach Pages from the Site Template Specify whether to allow site administrators to detach pages from the original site definition using SharePoint Designer.	☑ Enable Detaching Pages from the Site Definition
Allow Site Collection Administrators to Customize Master Pages and Layout Pages Specify whether to allow site administrators to customize Master Pages and Layout Pages using SharePoint Designer.	☑ Enable Customizing Master Pages and Layout Pages
Allow Site Collection Administrators to see the URL Structure of their Web Site Specify whether to allow site administrators to manage the URL structure of their Web site using SharePoint Designer.	☑ Enable Managing of the Web Site URL Structure
	OK Cancel

These four settings can also be controlled by site collection administrators at the site collection level; however, any setting turned off for the web application takes precedent over the site collection setting. For more information on each of these settings, see the article

"Managing SharePoint Designer 2010" at http://office.microsoft.com/en-us/sharepoint-designer-help/managing-sharepoint-designer-2010-HA101838275.aspx.

Configuring Blocked File Types

The Blocked File Types setting defines what file extensions are allowed to be uploaded as list attachments or library items. By default, file extensions that introduce a security risk are prohibited. As part of a governance strategy, you may need to add or remove entries. For example, if MP3 files should be disallowed, simply add the .mp3 extension to the list of entries.

Extend or Delete a Web Application

The ability to extend or delete a web application is very useful in a number of situations. This section covers:

- Extending web applications
- Defining alternate access mappings and zones
- Solving various administrative challenges involving your web applications

Benefits of Extending a Web Application

Extending a web application is one of the true versatilities of SharePoint. Extending a web application allows you to expose the same set of content to a different set of users, typically with a different URL and form of authentication.

For example, say that Acme Corp. has been using SharePoint as their intranet for the past year. Their internal URL is http://acme-intranet and it uses Windows Authentication. Management then decides that external suppliers must be able to collaborate with Acme on some of the same content. In other words, they want to create an extranet.

A solution to this requirement is to extend the current web application to a new URL—perhaps https://extranet.acme.com—and use FBA. Acme site administrators can then grant access to external users so that both internal and external users can collaborate on the same content. Of course, there are DNS, firewall, and a number of security issues that need to be addressed, but SharePoint supports the core requirement.

When you extend a web application, another IIS website is created with new binding information, but the content databases (and site collections contained therein) and application pool are shared. You also specify which form of authentication will be used for the extended instance.

> **NOTE** When extending a web application, the extended instance will always use the same authentication type (i.e., Claims or Classic). This presents problems if you want to use FBA for external users but your intranet is currently configured using Classic authentication. You can migrate from Classic to Claims using a PowerShell script, but there are some known issues. Note that once the web application is set to Claims, it cannot be migrated back to Classic. See the article "Migrate from Classic-Mode to Claims-Based Authentication (SharePoint Server 2010)" at http://technet.microsoft.com/en-us/library/gg251985.aspx for more information.

Extending a Web Application

From SharePoint's perspective, extending a web application is surprisingly easy. In the following steps, the scenario is based on the one used earlier, extending Acme Corp's intranet to an extranet. Here are the steps using Central Administration:

1. Choose Application Management, then select Manage Web Applications.

2. Select the web application you want to extend and click the Extend button in the ribbon, as shown in Figure 2.18.

Figure 2.18: Extending a web application

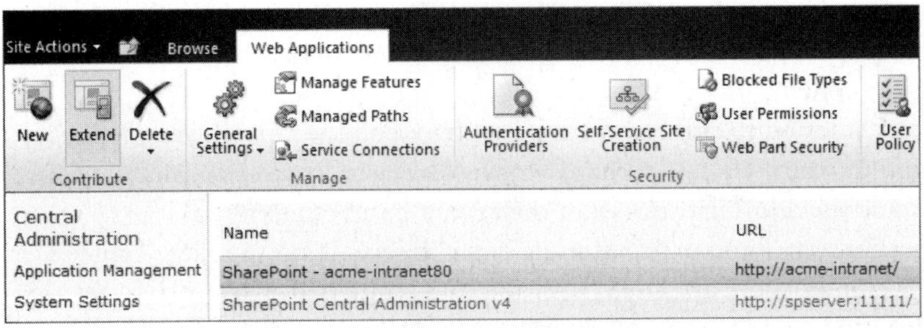

3. The dialog box that appears is similar to the one you see when creating a new application but with fewer options. Fill out the options for the new IIS website. The top half is shown in Figure 2.19.

Figure 2.19: Configuring the extended IIS website

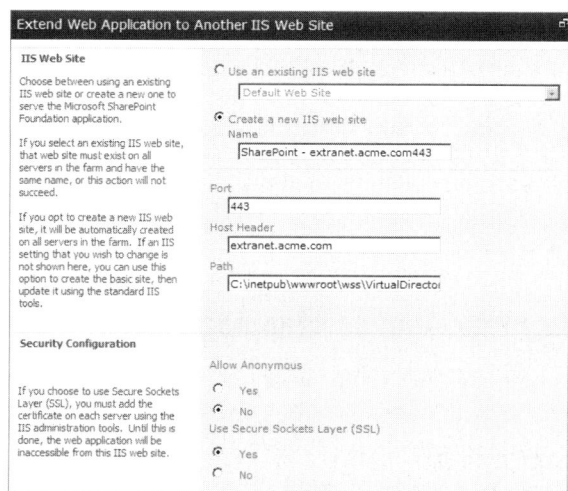

4. For authentication types, configure as appropriate. The options presented here depend on whether the original web application was created with Claims or Classic. For Acme's requirement, only FBA has been enabled.

   SharePoint will generate a public URL that can be changed if needed. The public URL is covered in the "Managing Alternate Access Mappings" section later in this chapter.

5. Specify the zone for this extended instance. Zones are also covered in the "Managing Alternate Access Mappings" section. For this scenario, Extranet has been selected, as shown in Figure 2.20.

Figure 2.20: Configuring the public URL and zone

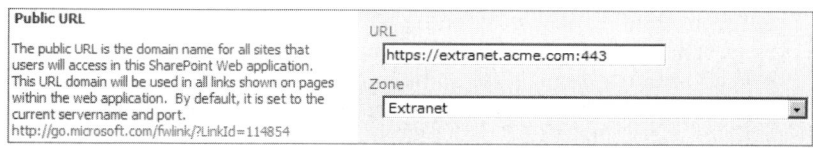

This process creates a new IIS website and a new `web.config` file. Entries in the SharePoint configuration database point this website to the same content database(s) that are used by the original web application. From SharePoint's perspective, it is still one web application with an alternate form of access.

> **NOTE** When extending the web application, SharePoint does not copy the `web.config` file from the original IIS website. Instead, it creates a new one, adding settings that it is aware of, such as custom SharePoint Solution Packages (WSP files) that have been deployed. If you have manually made any changes to the `web.config` file, you will have to apply them manually to the newly created `web.config` file as well.

Managing Alternate Access Mappings

Alternate access mappings (AAMs) provide additional URLs that can be used as part of a web application. When you extend a web application, SharePoint automatically creates a new AAM. In the previous scenario, both `http://acme-intranet` and `https://extranet.acme.com` are access mappings for the same web application. Assuming that `http://acme-intranet/ProjectA/Documents` is a valid URL, then so is `https://extranet.acme.com/ProjectA/Documents`.

Understanding Alternate Access Mappings

Each web application supports up to five different access mappings. This means that each web application can only be extended a maximum of four times. When creating an access mapping, you use a label to categorize what type of mapping you are using. This label is called a zone. The five zones are Default, Intranet, Internet, Extranet, and Custom. The zone is just a label and has no noticeable impact on functionality. The Extranet zone was chosen as shown in Figure 2.20 since it is the most reasonable category, but another zone could have been chosen.

> **NOTE** When you create a new web application, the URL provided becomes the first access mapping and is labeled as the default zone. While the zone name is just a label, the default zone is a bit special because it's used for some internal functions. Therefore, you must always have a default zone for each web application.

Understanding Public and Internal URLs

In addition to allowing multiple URLs to point to a single content database, an AAM also ensures that links on SharePoint's web pages are correct for the type of user. This is the purpose of the public URL. In other words, the public URL is used to set the base URL for links on the web pages that are returned. For example, when viewing the list of documents in a library from the default zone (i.e., http://acme-intranet), the URL for a file is http://acme-intranet/ProjectA/Documents/RocketLauncher.docx. This same document for an extranet user becomes https://extranet.acme.com/ProjectA/Documents/RocketLauncher.docx. Each zone has its own, unique public URL.

Each AAM zone also has an internal URL. The internal URL is the address that is used when making an HTTP request. For example, in the browser's address bar when requesting a page, you see http://acme-intranet. In this case, the internal URL is http://acme-intranet. At this point you're probably wondering *why do we need another URL?* That is, wouldn't the internal URL and public URL be the same? In most cases, yes, but there are some useful exceptions.

The most common situation where these URLs are different is when you are using a firewall as a reverse proxy, as depicted in Figure 2.21. In this case, the user connects to https://extranet.acme.com. This request is received by the reverse proxy device and repackaged as a new internal request using http://acme-intranet. When the SharePoint WFE replies with the response, it structures the links in the correct URL for the user. The reverse proxy receives the response from SharePoint and repackages again back as the response for the user.

Figure 2.21: Public and internal URLs

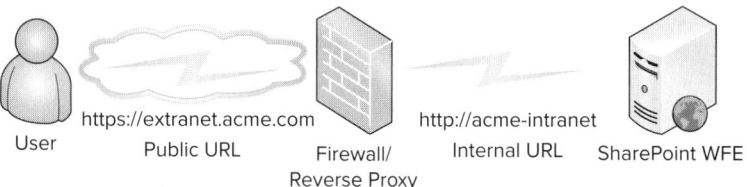

User   https://extranet.acme.com/   Firewall/   http://acme-intranet   SharePoint WFE
          Public URL   Reverse Proxy   Internal URL

Editing Alternate Access Mappings

Central Administration provides a special page for viewing and editing the AAMs for each web application. This page is mostly used to add or edit internal URLs or edit public URLs for your web application zones. You access this screen by going to System Settings, then selecting Configure Alternate Access Mappings. Initially, this screen will show you the mappings for all web applications, but the mappings can be filtered by selecting a single web application (called a mapping collection in this screen). Figure 2.22 shows the filtered view of the mappings for the Acme intranet and extranet.

Figure 2.22: AAM entries for Acme

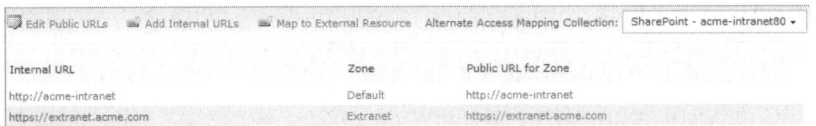

You can perform the following tasks on the AAM page:

- To edit a public mapping, click the Edit Public URLs link and change as needed.
- To change the internal URL for a zone, click the internal URL link.
- To add additional internal URLs, click the link as shown in Figure 2.22.

> **NOTE** The excellent article "Plan Alternate Access Mappings (Windows SharePoint Services)" at http://technet.microsoft.com/en-us/library/cc288609(office.12).aspx describes AAM and how to configure SharePoint for a reverse proxy scenario. While it's written for SharePoint 2007, it still applies to 2010.

Unextending and Re-extending a Web Application

You might want to unextend and re-extend a web application. The most common need is to change the bindings (e.g., TCP port or host header) for a web application's zone. SharePoint doesn't provide a simple way to do this, so it involves removing (or unextending) SharePoint from an IIS website and then re-extending it with the new settings.

Here are the steps to unextend and re-extend a web application's zone:

1. Start Central Administration.
2. Go to Application Management and click Manage Web Applications.

3. Select the web application you want to unextend.
4. Click the down arrow under the Delete button in the ribbon.
5. Select Remove SharePoint From IIS Web Site, as shown in Figure 2.23.

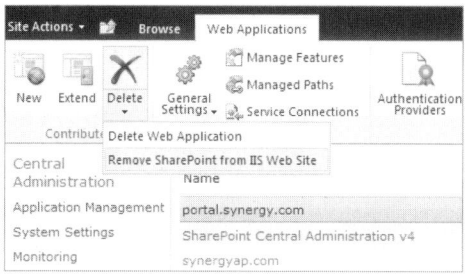

Figure 2.23: Unextending a SharePoint web application

6. Select the zone you wish to unextend and click OK.

If you unextend the default zone, SharePoint still recognizes this URL and keeps track of it in the configuration database, but the zone becomes inactive. If you unextend any other zone, the zone is removed from SharePoint.

Now that the zone has been unextended, the steps to re-extend are the same as extending any web application:

1. From the same Manage Web Applications screen, select the web application that you wish to re-extend.
2. Select the Extend button in the ribbon.
3. For the IIS website section, you can either reuse the previous website (assuming you didn't delete it), or re-create it with the new and correct bindings. Either way, the result is the same.

Deleting a Web Application

Deleting a web application removes all references to the web application, its zones, and its configuration settings. When deleting a web application, you have the option of also deleting all the content databases and IIS websites.

To delete a web application, follow these steps:

1. Start Central Administration.
2. Go to Application Management, and then select Manage Web Applications.

3. Select the web application you want to delete.
4. Select the Delete button from the ribbon.
5. Choose whether to keep the content databases and IIS websites, as shown in Figure 2.24.

Figure 2.24: Deleting a SharePoint web application

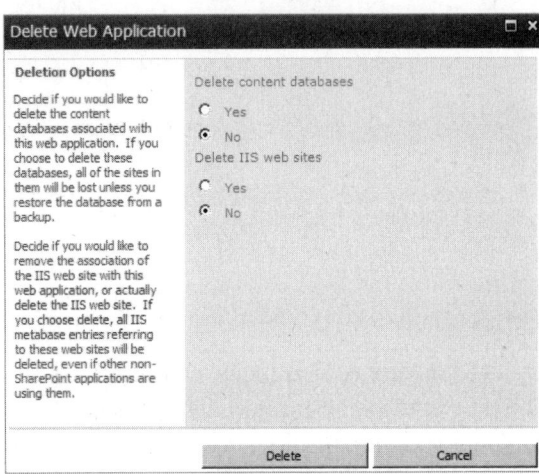

WARNING Deleting a web application, its content databases, and its IIS websites is an irreversible action when using these steps. To re-create the configuration you must restore from backup.

You can also use the Remove-SPWebApplication PowerShell cmdlet to delete a web application.

TIP One not-so-obvious advantage of deleting a web application and preserving the IIS websites and content databases is if you want to change the application pool associated with a web application. While SharePoint lets you change the application pool identity easily (select Security, then choose Configure Service Accounts), you are unable to change the application pool itself. Thus, the only way to do this is to delete the web application, re-create it, and reapply the settings, including re-associating all of the content databases.

3
Creating and Managing Site Collections

IN THIS CHAPTER, YOU WILL LEARN TO:

▶ **CREATE SITE COLLECTIONS (Pages 74 – 85)**
- Defining Managed Paths (Page 74)
- Creating a Site Collection Using Central Administration (Page 77)
- Creating a Site Collection Using PowerShell (Page 79)
- Configuring Quota Templates Using Central Administration (Page 80)
- Specifying the Content Database (Page 82)
- Enabling Self-Service Site Creation (Page 84)

▶ **MANAGE SITE COLLECTIONS (Pages 85 – 90)**
- Managing Site Collections Using Central Administration (Page 85)
- Managing Site Collections Using PowerShell (Page 88)

▶ **MANAGE SITE SETTINGS (Pages 90 – 108)**
- Managing the Site Collection Gallery (Page 91)
- Managing the Look and Feel of Web Pages (Page 96)
- Managing Site Administration (Page 101)
- Managing Site Collection Administration (Page 104)

A *site collection* is an organized hierarchy of SharePoint websites that share security, navigation, look and feel, and many other properties. A site collection is stored in a content database and is associated with a web application. Creating site collections is typically reserved for a SharePoint farm administrator, but day-to-day management of site collections is often delegated to site collection administrators. Site collection administrators are specially trained power users who are often not IT specialists.

This chapter's focus is on the tasks that are commonly handled by the farm administrator. However, it does touch on complex site collection administrator duties as well to ensure you have a well-rounded understanding of site collections.

Create Site Collections

Site collections can be created in a number of ways. This section covers creation of site collections using either Central Administration or PowerShell.

> **TIP** Planning site collections is an important step and should be part of an overall governance strategy. Planning is beyond the scope of this chapter. For more information on planning, see the article "Plan Sites and Site Collections (SharePoint Server 2010)" at http://msdn.microsoft.com/en-us/library/cc263267.aspx.

Defining Managed Paths

A managed path is the site collection portion of the URL that is appended to the web application URL. Each site collection must have a unique managed path. An example of where the managed path fits in with a complete URL is shown in Figure 3.1.

Figure 3.1: Breakdown of a SharePoint URL

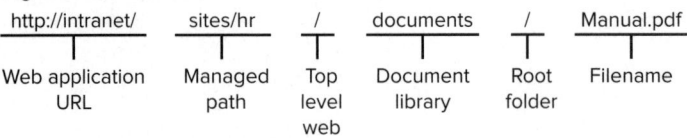

The managed path to be used for a new site collection must exist prior to creating the site collection. SharePoint supports two different types of managed paths: explicit and wildcard.

Explicit Managed Path   This type of path contains a fixed value that can be used once for a single site collection—for example, HR.

Wildcard Managed Path   This type of path allows you to define a portion of the URL that applies to multiple site collections in this web application. A precreated wildcard path with the name sites already exists for each web application, and it functions like sites/*, where * is specified when the site collection is created, as shown in Figure 3.3. For example, you could create a site collection with the complete managed path of sites/projects. In this case the projects portion is the wildcard. The complete managed path must be unique in the web application.

> **NOTE**   Despite the existence of a managed path named (root), all site collections exist at the same level and there is no hierarchy among the site collections. So, http://intranet/ (the root site collection) and http://intranet/HR are all peer site collections associated with the http://intranet web application.

Creating and Deleting Managed Paths Using Central Administration

You can create managed paths easily by using Central Administration. Here are the steps:

1. Click Application Management, then select Manage Web Applications.
2. Select the desired web application and click Managed Paths in the ribbon. You are taken to the dialog box shown in Figure 3.2.

Figure 3.2: Creating a managed path

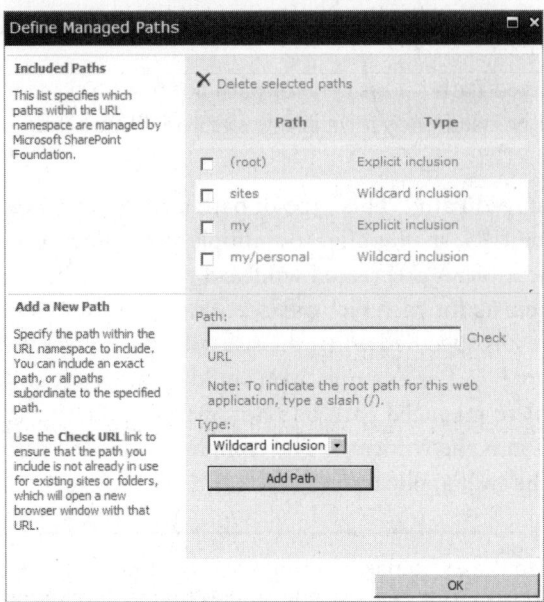

3. In the Add A New Path section, enter the path to be used. You can use forward slashes if desired.
4. Specify the type: wildcard or explicit.
5. Click the Add Path button to add the path.
6. Optionally, repeat steps 3–5 to add more managed paths.
7. Click OK when you've finished.

The Define Managed Paths dialog box can also be used to delete managed paths:

1. In the Included Paths section, select the managed paths you want to delete.
2. Click the Delete Selected Paths link at the top of the dialog box.

WARNING Be careful to avoid deleting managed paths that are in use. SharePoint will let you do this, and doing so will immediately cause all sites in that site collection to display 404 errors. If this happens, just re-create the managed path exactly how it existed previously.

Creating Managed Paths Using PowerShell

To create a managed path using PowerShell, use the `New-SPManagedPath` cmdlet. Here is the basic syntax:

```
New-SPManagedPath <relative path> -WebApplication 
<URL> [-Explicit]
```

The following example creates a new explicit managed path that is mounted at http://intranet/projects:

```
New-SPManagedPath projects -WebApplication 
http://intranet -Explicit
```

Creating a Site Collection Using Central Administration

Creating a site collection using Central Administration is quite easy. Here are the steps:

1. Start Central Administration. (Start ➤ All Programs ➤ Microsoft SharePoint 2010 Products ➤ SharePoint 2010 Central Administration.)

2. In the Application Management section, click Create Site Collections. You are taken to the screen to create a new site collection; the upper half of this screen is shown in Figure 3.3.

Figure 3.3: Creating a site collection

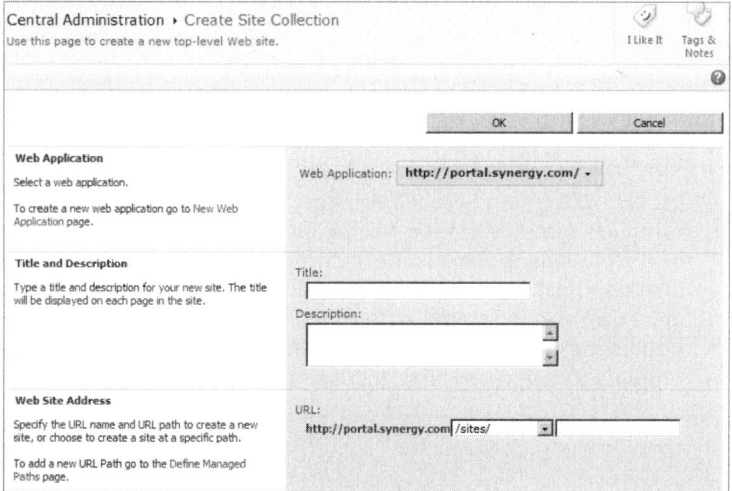

3. Before filling out anything else, be sure that the correct web application is selected.

4. Provide the title and description. When you create a site collection using Central Administration, a top-level website is created automatically, and these settings become the title and description for that website. The title and description can also be changed after the site collection has been created.

5. Enter the website address. You can specify either an explicit managed path or a wildcard managed path. (See the section "Defining Managed Paths" for more information.)

6. Select the website template to be used for the top-level website. (See Figure 3.4.) As with creating any website in SharePoint, the template cannot be changed after creation, so choose carefully. The templates available are based on the site definitions that have been installed. If you are not sure which template, you can choose Select Template Later from the Custom tab.

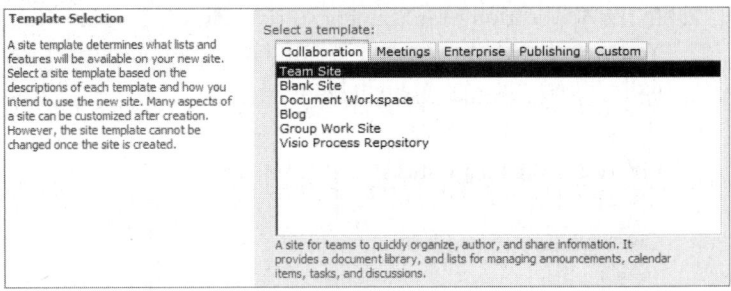

Figure 3.4: Selecting the top-level website template

NOTE Choosing Select Template Later is handy when the farm administrator doesn't know which template to use for the top-level website. This issue is common in situations when the farm administrator is creating the site collection for another site collection administrator. After the site collection is created, one of the designated site collection administrators must specify the template to use when first accessing the site collection.

7. Specify the primary site collection administrator and, optionally, a secondary site collection administrator. (See Figure 3.5.) It is a best practice in most situations to have a secondary site collection administrator. SharePoint allows you to have more than two site collection administrators, but you can specify a maximum of two when you create the site collection. The site collection administrator must be an individual and cannot be a security group or role. Once the site collection has been created, you can add additional administrators by choosing Site Collection Administrators from the Site Settings menu.

Figure 3.5: Specifying site collection administrators

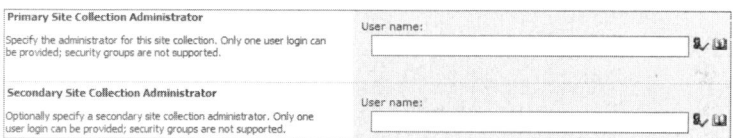

8. Specify whether you want to use a quota template. (See Figure 3.6.) A quota controls two facets of site collection usage: how much space can be used and how many resources are available for sandboxed solutions. The quota can be changed after the site collection has been created. Quotas are covered in more detail later in the "Configuring Quota Templates Using Central Administration" section.

Figure 3.6: Specifying a quota template

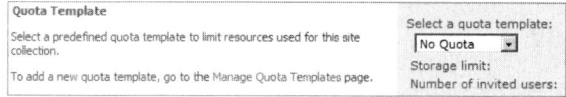

9. Click OK to create the site collection.

Creating a Site Collection Using PowerShell

The main cmdlet to create a new site collection is `New-SPSite`. It is a powerful command and you can use it in many ways. Here is the syntax with the most common switches:

```
New-SPSite <absolute URL> -OwnerAlias <String> 
-OwnerEmail <String> [-ContentDatabase 
```

```
<String>] [-Description <String>] ⏎
[-Name <String>] [-QuotaTemplate ⏎
<SPQuotaTemplatePipeBind>] [-Template <String>]
```

> **TIP** To learn more about the various parameter values that you can include, use the following PowerShell cmdlet: `Get-Help New-SPSite -detailed`.

Here are some examples showing how the command can be used:

- Create a site collection that uses the team site template (STS#0) for the top-level website:

    ```
    New-SPSite http://intranet/HR -OwnerAlias ⏎
    domain\user -OwnerEmail user@domain.com ⏎
    -Name "HR Portal" -Template STS#0
    ```

- This example creates a site collection and stores it in a specific content database (the content database must already exist):

    ```
    New-SPSite http://intranet/ITS -OwnerAlias ⏎
    domain\user -OwnerEmail user@domain.com ⏎
    -Name "ITS Projects" -ContentDatabase ⏎
    ITS_Content
    ```

To identify the list of web templates, use the `Get-SPWebTemplate` cmdlet.

Configuring Quota Templates Using Central Administration

A quota template is a reusable definition for limiting space and resource usage in a site collection. Assigning a quota template ensures that consistent limits are applied to site collections and also allows you to easily adjust these limits. Without using a quota, site collections and content databases can balloon to unmanageable sizes. Thus, we highly recommend that you use quotas for site collections.

> **TIP** Having a default quota template is recommended to ensure that newly created site collections have a quota applied. To specify a default quota template when creating site collections, go to the General Settings for a web application, as covered in Chapter 2, "Creating and Managing Web Applications."

A quota template can be assigned during site collection creation or at any point after. Here are the steps to create a quota template using Central Administration:

1. Select Application Management, and then choose Specify Quota Templates. You are taken to the screen shown in Figure 3.7.

Figure 3.7: Managing quota templates

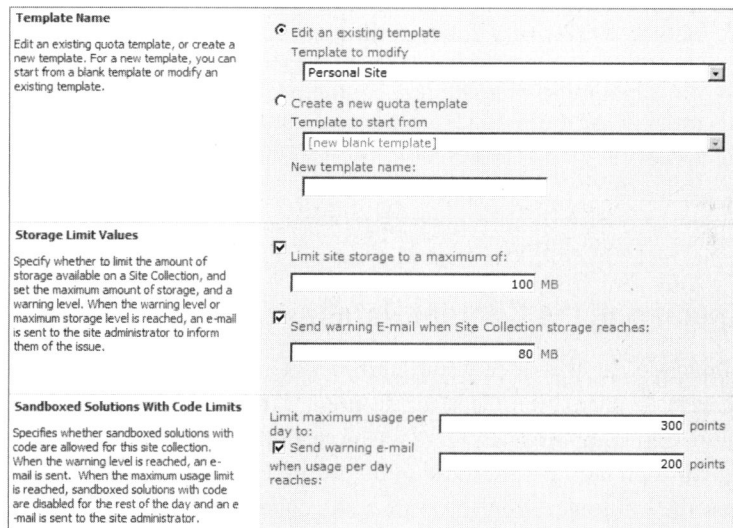

2. Click the Create A New Quota Template radio button.
3. Optionally, in the Template To Start From menu, select an existing template to copy the settings.
4. Type a new name for the template. Template names must be unique in the farm.
5. Optionally, in the Storage Limit Values section, enable and enter the maximum amount of space in MB to be used in the quota template. When this limit is reached, no new items can be added and most changes to websites throw an error.
6. Optionally, enable and enter a warning limit. When space exceeds this value, emails are sent to the primary and secondary site collection administrators advising them that the limit has been exceeded.

7. In the section Sandboxed Solutions With Code Limits, enter the number of resource points that are allowed in the site collection. More details on sandboxed solutions are covered in the "Managing the Solutions Gallery" section later in this chapter.

8. Click OK to save the new quota template.

NOTE Space used by items in the end-user recycle bin (associated with each website) counts as part of the site collection quota. When users see the storage quota limit error, many decide to delete files (i.e., move them to the end-user recycle bin), assuming that will resolve the problem. However, items must also be deleted from the end-user recycle bin to resolve the problem. For more information, see "Managing Recycle Bins" later in this chapter.

Specifying the Content Database

Managing the size of content databases is an important task for a SharePoint farm administrator. Content databases were introduced and defined in Chapter 2, and one of the recommendations is to keep the size of each content database under 200 GB. Unfortunately, when using Central Administration to create a site collection, you cannot directly specify in which content database the site collection will be created. This means SharePoint automatically selects the content database when creating a new site collection. As you will learn, this isn't always the best option.

To help explain, look at an example web application's four content databases, as shown in Figure 3.8.

Figure 3.8: Content databases

Database Name	Database Status	Database Read-Only	Current Number of Site Collections	Site Collection Level Warning	Maximum Number of Site Collections
Blue_Content	Started	No	3	5	10
Green_Content	Started	No	2	5	10
Red_Content	Started	No	1	5	10
Yellow_Content	Stopped	No	0	5	10

Let's suppose that Red_Content's single site collection is very large, totaling 100 GB. Blue_Content and Green_Content have several small site collections, each totaling less than 1 GB. Yellow_Content has no site collections, and it has been taken offline, as shown by the label Stopped in the Database Status column.

> **NOTE** In SharePoint, when a database is labeled "Offline" or "Stopped," it only means that SharePoint does not select this content database when creating (or restoring) a site collection. Any existing site collections currently stored in a content database marked Stopped are not affected in any way.

When SharePoint selects the content database, it selects the one that is "most available," determined by the number of new site collections that can be stored in the content database. This is calculated by subtracting the current number from the warning level. If the warning level has been reached, it is calculated from the maximum level.

In this example, Red_Content is considered the most available since, of the databases that are not stopped, it has the fewest site collections.

> **TIP** To summarize, SharePoint doesn't look at the *size* of the content database but the *number of site collections* stored to determine which database is most available.

A better way to manage space is to set the content database yourself, especially if you expect this new site collection to grow large. Although you cannot do this directly using Central Administration, here are some workaround steps that achieve the same goal:

1. Decide which content database to use.
2. Using Central Administration, select all the other content databases and set them as Offline (or Stopped). This prevents SharePoint from creating new site collections in those databases.
3. Create the site collection.

The content database can be selected directly when creating the site collection using PowerShell. This is a better option if you have many content databases, and it becomes too tedious to manually set them as Offline. We covered this topic in the "Creating a Site Collection Using PowerShell" section earlier in this chapter.

Enabling Self-Service Site Creation

Self-service site creation is a way of granting regular users the ability to create their own site collections. It's a very special capability and we do not usually recommend that you use it. Although there are some advantages, such as the convenience factor, here are some of the notable drawbacks:

- No approval process
- Difficulty in controlling site collection sprawl
- Difficulty in setting the content database for new site collections
- Difficulty in limiting who has permissions to create new site collections

Here are the steps to enable this ability for a web application in Central Administration:

1. Click Application Management, then select Manage Web Applications.
2. Select the desired web application and click Self-Service Site Creation in the ribbon.
3. In the dialog box, click the On radio button and then click OK.

For users to create a site collection, they must access the _layouts/scsignup.aspx page from within a web application—for example, http://intranet/_layouts/scsignup.aspx.

When Self-Service Site Creation is enabled, any user who has at least Read permissions in any site collection can create another site collection in the web application. This is because the Read permission level automatically includes the Self-Service Site Creation permission.

> **TIP** A more viable option would be to develop custom code and use that as an alternative. How to accomplish this is beyond the scope of this book.

> **WARNING** If you opt to use Self-Service Site Creation, we strongly advise you to set a default quota template for your web application. Doing so ensures that space is restricted for the new site collection.

Manage Site Collections

After a site collection is created, and certainly during its lifetime, there are additional configuration settings that need to be adjusted. This section covers the settings commonly managed using Central Administration and PowerShell.

Managing Site Collections Using Central Administration

This section explores common administrative tasks using Central Administration and covers managing quotas, using locks, and deleting site collections.

Managing Quotas and Locks

Once you create a quota template, you can assign it to one or more site collections in the farm. Here are the steps to assign a quota template using Central Administration:

1. Select Application Management, then choose Configure Quotas and Locks. You are taken to the screen shown in Figure 3.9.

   Figure 3.9: Assigning a quota template

   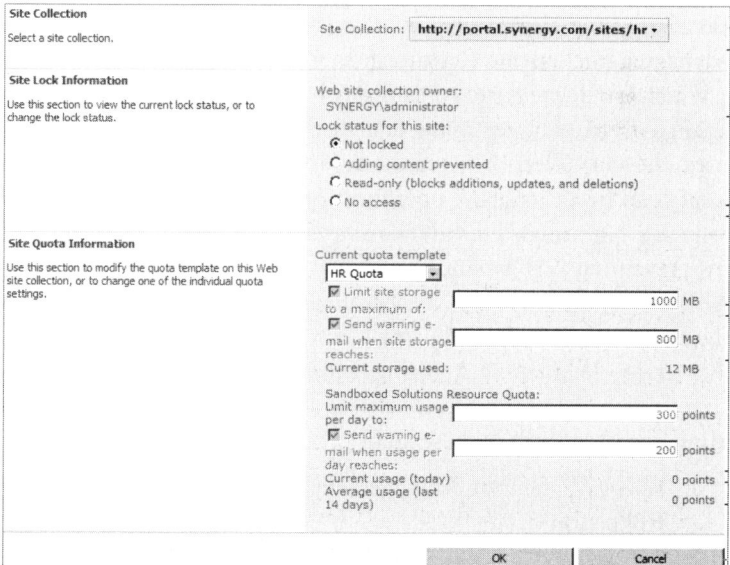

2. Select the site collection.

3. Under Site Quota Information, select a quota template from the Current Quota Template drop-down list.

4. Click OK to save.

You can also create a one-time quota for a single site collection. This allows you to set a limit without first having to create a quota template. To do this, select the Individual Quota template and fill in the quota values as needed.

From the same screen in Figure 3.9, you can also place a lock on one of the site collections. A lock is used to temporarily suspend certain types of activities and is usually done in special cases such as troubleshooting corruption or performing a migration. In some cases, SharePoint also places a read-only site collection lock when doing a site collection backup.

SharePoint is smart enough to detect when a content database has been marked read-only. When this happens, SharePoint treats all site collections in that content database as read-only until the read-only option for the database is set back to False.

Deleting a Site Collection Using Central Administration

Site collections can be deleted when they are no longer needed. Site collection administrators can delete the site collections they own, and farm administrators can delete any site collection. Site collections that are deleted can only be recovered by doing a restore, as covered in Chapter 16, "Managing Backup and Restore."

When you delete a site collection, SharePoint initially flags the site collection as deleted by removing it from the site map. For all practical purposes, the site collection is removed. However, since the complete removal of data can be an intensive operation, SharePoint creates a timer job that is run at a later time. This allows SharePoint to remove the data gradually, preventing performance problems. The timer job is called Gradual Site Delete and, by default, is scheduled to run daily. This and other timer jobs can be run on demand using Central Administration as covered in Chapter 15, "Managing Auditing, Monitoring, and Analytics."

For a farm administrator to delete a site collection from Central Administration, follow these steps:

1. Select Application Management, then choose Delete A Site Collection.

2. Select the web application and site collection.

3. Double-check that you have selected the correct one and then click the Delete button.

For a site collection administrator to delete a site collection, follow these steps:

1. Log into the site collection and connect to the top-level site.
2. Click Site Actions ➢ Site Settings.
3. Under Site Actions category, select Delete This Site.
4. Confirm the URL is correct and click Delete.

You can also delete a site collection using PowerShell. See "Deleting a Site Collection Using PowerShell" later in this chapter.

Automatically Deleting Unused Site Collections

SharePoint is able to detect when site collections go unused and then email site collection administrators asking if the site should be kept or deleted. Emails are sent to the primary and secondary site collection administrators. The email contains links to confirm the site is in use or to approve its deletion.

SharePoint can also automatically delete unused site collections if these email notices go unanswered. These settings are managed at the web application level and, by default, are turned off.

Follow these steps to turn on and configure this setting from Central Administration:

1. Click Application Management, then choose Confirm Site Use And Deletion. You are taken to the screen in Figure 3.10.

Figure 3.10: Configuring site use confirmation and deletion

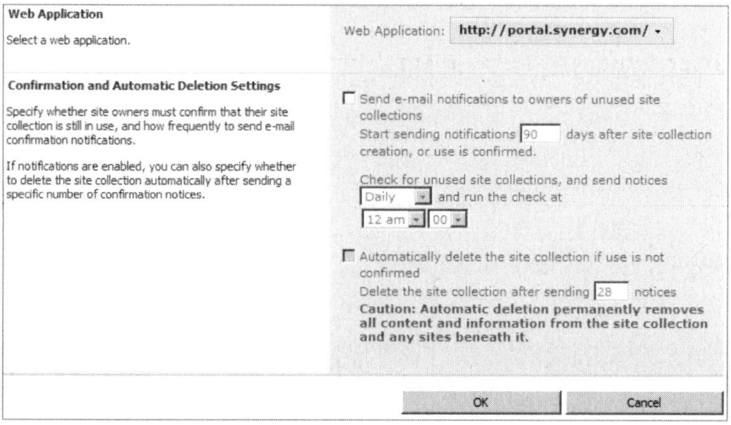

2. Select the web application.

3. To enable SharePoint to send email when site collections are not being used, select the check box labeled "Send e-mail notifications to owners of unused site collections."

4. Configure the number of days that the site collection should be unused prior to sending out notifications. By default, this is 90 days, as shown in Figure 3.10.

5. Adjust the frequency and time of day that site collections are checked for use. This can be daily, weekly, or monthly.

6. Optionally, enable automatic deletion by selecting the check box labeled "Automatically delete the site collection if use is not confirmed." If this is enabled, configure the number of notices that will be sent prior to automatic deletion.

For more details and other recommendations on how to handle unused site collections, see the article "Manage Unused Web Sites (SharePoint Server 2010)" at http://technet.microsoft.com/en-us/library/cc262420.aspx.

Managing Site Collections Using PowerShell

PowerShell provides a near endless amount of administrative control. The following PowerShell commands are supported when directly working with site collections:

```
Backup-SPSite, Get-SPSite, Get-SPSiteAdministration,
Move-SPSite, New-SPSite, Remove-SPSite, Restore-SPSite,
Set-SPSite, Set-SPSiteAdministration
```

This section covers common administrative tasks. For more examples of using PowerShell to administer SharePoint 2010, see SharePoint MVP Gary Lapointe's blog, SharePoint Automation, at http://blog.falchionconsulting.com.

Enumerating Site Collections

The cmdlets that list site collections are Get-SPSite and Get-SPSiteAdministration. These commands are very similar, but farm administrators should use Get-SPSiteAdministration to ensure all site collections properties can be returned, even those you may not have direct access to.

Here are some of the primary parameters:

```
Get-SPSiteAdministration [-AssignmentCollection
<SPAssignmentCollection>] [-Filter <ScriptBlock>]
[-Limit <String>] [-ContentDatabase <String>]
```

Here are some useful examples:

- List all site collections URLs associated with a certain web application:

    ```
    Get-SPSiteAdministration http://intranet/*
    -Limit all
    ```

- List all properties for all site collections in a particular content database:

    ```
    Get-SPSiteAdministration -ContentDatabase
    SP_Portal_Content -Limit all | Select *
    ```

- Show the space used for all site collections in the current farm:

    ```
    Get-SPSiteAdministration -Limit all |
    select Url, @{Name="Space";expression=
    {$_.Usage.Storage/1MB}}
    ```

- Show the first 10 site collections owned by a particular user:

    ```
    Get-SPSiteAdministration -Limit 10
    -Filter {$_.Owner -eq "domain\user"}
    ```

Moving a Site Collection to a Different Content Database

Moving a site collection from one content database to another is a snap with the Move-SPSite PowerShell cmdlet. Here are a couple examples on how it can be used:

- Move one site collection to a different content database (provided both databases are on the same SQL Server):

    ```
    Move-SPSite http://intranet/HR
    -DestinationDatabase HR_Content_DB
    ```

- Use the pipe command combined with `Get-SPSiteAdministration` to move multiple site collections from one content database to another:

  ```
  Get-SPSiteAdministration -ContentDatabase ↵
  Old_Content_DB | Move-SPSite ↵
  -DestinationDatabase New_Content_DB
  ```

Deleting a Site Collection Using PowerShell

To delete a site collection using PowerShell, here is the basic syntax:

```
Remove-SPSite <URL> [-Confirm]
```

Unlike Central Administration, PowerShell will not automatically create a timer job and delete the site collection gradually. Instead, it begins the deletion immediately. To issue a timer job and match how the Central Administration executes a deletion, include the `-GradualDelete` switch. This switch is recommended if you are deleting a large site collection during peak hours. Here is an example of deleting a site collection gradually and suppressing confirmation:

```
Remove-SPSite http://intranet/sites/projects -GradualDelete
-Confirm:$false
```

Manage Site Settings

The instructions in this and the following sections of this chapter pertain to tasks performed by site collection administrators. Certainly, in many smaller organizations the site collection administrator may in fact be the same person as the farm administrator, but the larger the company and more formal the delegation is, this role may become more decentralized.

That said, a whole book could be written on what tasks a site collection administrator has. It's a powerful and important role! In this chapter, the objective is to focus on the more technical and less intuitive aspects of site collection administration. So, whether you are just providing technical support to site collection administrators or handling these tasks yourself, you will find value in this section.

NOTE The options you have for managing the site collection will vary depending on whether you're running SharePoint Foundation (SPF) or SharePoint Server (SPS). Where there are differences, we'll point them out. When running SPS, options also vary depending on whether the SharePoint Server Publishing Infrastructure site collection feature is enabled. When this feature is enabled, many additional options, such as setting master pages, working with page layouts, and configuring navigation, are made available.

Managing the Site Collection Gallery

A *gallery* is a collection of SharePoint artifacts that can be shared across multiple websites in a site collection. In many cases, such as the Web Part gallery, the galleries act as special document libraries where files are stored. For the top-level website in a site collection, there are seven visible galleries that can be managed from the Site Settings page. The first three galleries are also visible in websites underneath the top level:

- Site Columns
- Site Content Types
- Master Pages And Page Layouts
- Web Parts
- List Templates
- Themes
- Solutions

Managing Master Pages And Page Layouts

The Master Pages And Page Layouts gallery is available when working with a publishing website that is part of SPS 2010. For SPF or any non-publishing site, the gallery stores master pages only.

Master Pages Master pages define the core framework of SharePoint's web pages in a website. They exist to ensure a consistent look and feel across web pages and websites in a site collection and separate a page's content from its look and feel. For out-of-the-box master pages, they control top and quick launch navigation, the ribbon, breadcrumbs, the Site Actions menu, and much more. In other words, they provide the base functionality of a web page.

Page Layouts Page layouts reference master pages and are used with publishing pages to manage the layout of content stored on the page. Page layouts are available when you are working with a publishing site collection that is part of SPS 2010. For SPF or any nonpublishing site collection, the gallery stores master pages only.

Organizations looking to implement a custom brand do so by developing a custom master page. Those looking to publish pages that have a consistent layout do so by developing a custom page layout. You can share master pages and page layouts across the site collection by uploading them to the Master Pages And Page Layouts gallery.

> **NOTE** SharePoint Designer can also be used to create master pages and page layouts and is able to publish directly to the gallery. Using SharePoint Designer is outside the scope of this book.

To upload a custom master page (.master extension) or a page layout (.aspx extension) to the gallery, follow these steps:

1. Ensure you are signed in as a site collection administrator or as someone who has Design or Full Control permissions.
2. Navigate to the top-level website in a site collection.
3. Click Site Settings ➢ Site Actions.
4. Within Galleries, select Master Pages And Page Layouts.
5. In the ribbon, click the Documents tab and then click Upload Document, as shown in Figure 3.11.

Figure 3.11: Uploading a new file

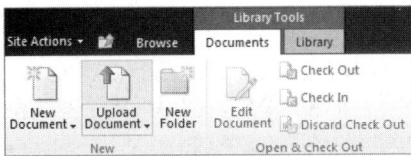

6. Browse to the file and upload it to the gallery.
7. A dialog box pops up asking for the content type which is either page layout or publishing master page. Choose the correct one based on the file uploaded and fill in any metadata. At this point, the file is checked in as a draft (minor) version.

8. To publish the file as a major version, click the down arrow for the file to show the context menu for this file. See Figure 3.12.

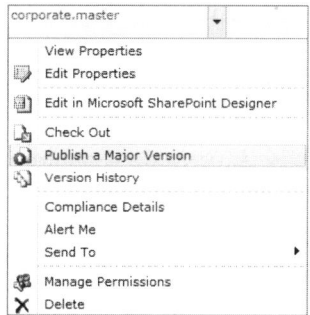

Figure 3.12: Publishing a file as a major version

9. Select Publish a Major Version.
10. Before the page is available to all users, it must be approved. From the same context menu for the file, select Approve/Reject.
11. In the dialog box, select Approved.

At this point, the page is ready to be used by all users. For a custom page layout, this layout page can be selected when creating a new publishing page. For a master page, this master can be selected and applied to websites in this site collection. How to apply a master page is covered later in the "Applying a Master Page" section.

> **NOTE** Master pages and page layouts can also be deployed by creating a custom feature. This is usually done by a developer and instructions are outside the scope of this book. One advantage of a custom feature is that you can easily deploy the master page or page layout to multiple site collections.

Managing Web Parts

The Web Part gallery stores the web parts that can be added to pages within the site collection. Each web part available is referenced by a web part definition file that has either a `.dwp` or a `.webpart` extension. Web parts that can be added to a page are displayed in the Web Part Picker, as shown in Figure 3.13.

Figure 3.13: Web Part Picker

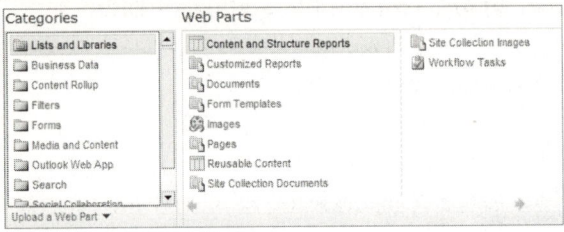

Each site collection's Web Part gallery is initially populated only with out-of-the-box web parts. Custom web parts can be developed and deployed, and many third-party web part packages are available as well.

Although a site collection administrator can manually upload a new web part definition file into the gallery, this is rarely done as there are other deployment steps that are needed prior to using a new web part. Deploying web parts along with other forms of custom code is covered in the "Managing the Solutions Gallery" section and in Chapter 6, "Configuring System Settings."

However, site collection administrators commonly adjust the permissions of web parts. Many organizations want to restrict the web parts that can be added to pages. In other words, they want to remove certain web parts from the picker shown in Figure 3.13. The recommended way to do this is to change the permissions of the definition files in the Web Part gallery. Any user who does not have at least the Read permission to a web part definition file will not see the web part in the gallery. The steps you go through to change permissions are the same as with any item in a list or library. Follow these steps to change permissions for a single web part definition file:

1. From the top-level website, click Site Actions ➢ Site Settings.
2. Under Galleries, select Web Parts.
3. Items in the site collection's Web Part gallery are displayed in pages of 30 items. Click the Edit icon next to the web part you want to change.
4. In the dialog box that appears, click the Manage Permissions button in the ribbon.

5. Click the Stop Inheriting Permissions button and click OK to confirm this action. (By default, the web part definition file inherits its permissions from the gallery.)

6. Adjust permissions as necessary.

Managing the Solutions Gallery

User (aka sandboxed) solutions are packages of custom code that can be easily and safely deployed within a site collection. This type of custom code can include web parts, features, event handlers, and others. No manual deployment is needed for this code, and the code is safe—it cannot destabilize a web application. SharePoint ensures this safety by running the code in a special worker process with restricted access.

Each user solution consists of a single file with the .wsp extension. Internally, this is a Windows cabinet file, which is like a Zip file, where the code and configuration files are stored. To deploy the user solution, you perform two tasks:

1. Upload the WSP file to the Solutions gallery.

2. Activate the solution to make it available for use.

Each user solution is tracked for usage and the total usage for all user solutions is counted against a resource quota on the site collection. Resource usage is measured by looking at many counters, including CPU, RAM, and the number of SharePoint queries issued. This usage is converted into a point total, which is the basis for the resource quota. By default, this is 300 points. You will find more details on how these resource points are calculated in Chapter 6.

The resource quota is a daily quota, and the resource total for all user solutions is reset to zero each day by a timer job. If a quota is in use and the resource point total for that day is reached, user solutions will stop running for that site collection. Figure 3.14 shows how resource points are displayed in the Solutions gallery.

Figure 3.14: User solutions resource quota display

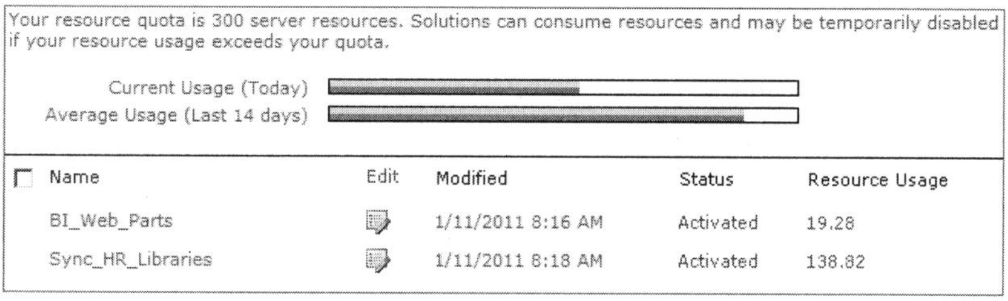

Name	Edit	Modified	Status	Resource Usage
BI_Web_Parts		1/11/2011 8:16 AM	Activated	19.28
Sync_HR_Libraries		1/11/2011 8:18 AM	Activated	138.82

Your resource quota is 300 server resources. Solutions can consume resources and may be temporarily disabled if your resource usage exceeds your quota.

Current Usage (Today)
Average Usage (Last 14 days)

Here is how a site collection administrator can upload and activate a user solution:

1. From the top-level website, click Site Actions ➢ Site Settings.
2. Under Galleries, select Solutions.
3. Above the ribbon, click the Solutions tab.
4. Click the Upload Solutions button in the ribbon.
5. Browse to and upload a user solution.
6. After it uploads, click the Activate button as shown in Figure 3.15. This deploys the solution to the site collection and makes it available for use.

Figure 3.15: Activating a user solution

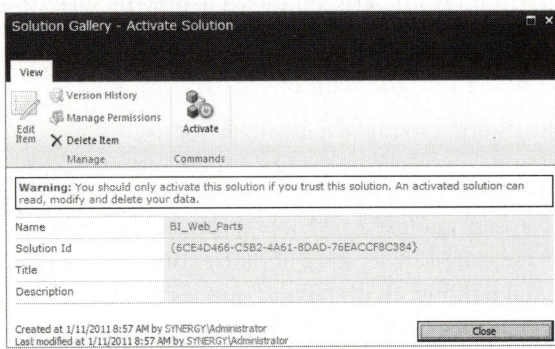

Additional information on managing both user and farm solutions is provided in Chapter 6.

Managing the Look and Feel of Web Pages

This section covers some of the common tasks relating to the cosmetics and functionality of SharePoint web pages. These sections relate to the Look and Feel category found on the Site Settings menu.

Applying a Master Page

In SPS 2010, applying a master page changes the assigned master page for one or more websites in a site collection. When changing the master page, you have the option of cascading the change to all lower-level websites.

In SPS 2010, the master page can be applied in two different ways, depending on whether it applies to a publishing or a nonpublishing page:

As a Site Master Page The Site Master Page setting applies the master page to all publishing pages in the website. A publishing page is a page usually found in the pages library within a publishing site. Publishing pages are based on a page layout.

As a System Master Page The System Master Page setting applies to nonpublishing pages, including the following:

- Form pages. An example of a form page is the New Item dialog (NewForm.aspx) for a tasks list.

- View pages, which apply to built-in or custom views on a list or library; for example, the All Documents (AllItems.aspx) view for a document library.

- Application pages, which are special pages that originate from the _layouts virtual directory. SharePoint has hundreds of built-in application pages such as the Site Settings page (settings.aspx).

To change the master page for a website, follow these steps:

1. Ensure you are signed in as a site collection administrator or as someone who has Design or Full Control permissions.

2. Click Site Actions ➤ Site Settings.

3. Under Look and Feel, select Master Page. You are shown the dialog that is shown in part in Figure 3.16. If you don't see Master Page as an option, read the note on the next page.

Figure 3.16: Changing the master page for a website

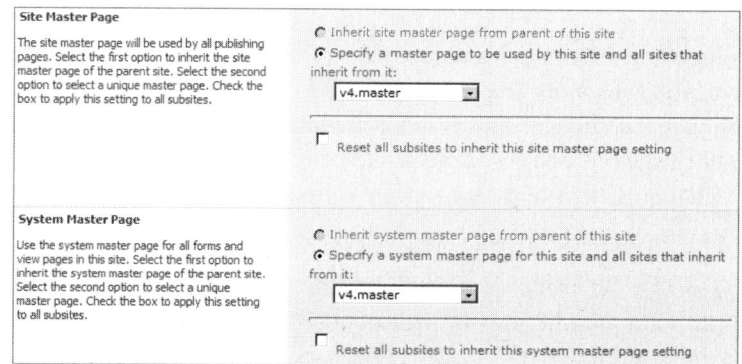

4. Adjust the site master and/or system master page. The pages available come from the master page gallery.

5. Optionally, choose to reset all subsites to match these settings. This will also override the master page setting for all websites beneath this website in the hierarchy.

From this same master page settings screen, you can also apply a custom cascading-style sheet (CSS). CSS adjusts cosmetics such as fonts, borders, certain images, and the positioning of HTML controls.

> **NOTE** Users of SPF do not have this option to change the master page in this way. The SPF master page can only be changed using SharePoint Designer or custom code. If you are using SPS, the site collection must have the "SharePoint Server Publishing Infrastructure" feature activated and the website that you are changing must have the "SharePoint Server Publishing" feature activated.

Changing and Applying a Site Theme

Changing the site theme allows you to adjust certain fonts and colors for your web pages. Unlike changing the master pages or CSS, it does not change the layout or positioning of the content. The site theme gets merged with the master page and CSS to produce the desired cosmetics.

SharePoint has nearly 20 built-in themes, and custom themes can be easily created using a Windows theme-creating program such as PowerPoint 2010. Custom themes have a .thmx extension and must be uploaded into the themes gallery for the site collection.

When applying a theme, you can also make minor changes to the theme such as adjustments to font colors and the body font. The changed theme can automatically be applied to subsites. SharePoint also gives you the ability to preview how the new theme will appear without applying the change. This is helpful when you are trying to find the right theme but don't want to affect other users currently using the site.

Changing the site theme is quite simple. Here are the steps:

1. Ensure you are signed in as a site collection administrator or as someone who has Design or Full Control permissions.

2. Click Site Actions ➢ Site Settings.

3. Under Look And Feel, select Site Theme.
4. Select the theme from the list available.
5. Optionally, adjust the colors and fonts as shown.
6. Optionally, preview the theme to confirm the settings.
7. Choose whether to apply this theme to just this one website or this website and all its subsites.
8. Click Apply to save your changes.

Managing Site Collection Navigation

In SharePoint, two primary forms of navigation exist:

Global or Top-Link Navigation   Refers to the menu available just above the content area where the ribbon is visible. It is normally used for navigation across a wide number of websites in this site collection. This type of navigation is referred to as global since it can be inherited globally across websites in the site collection.

Current Navigation   By default, this is shown in the quick launch area, which is to the left of the content area. It is used to navigate to content commonly used within a single website. For example, you typically see links to lists and libraries here.

Figure 3.17 shows these forms of navigation for a typical team site.

Figure 3.17: Global and current navigation

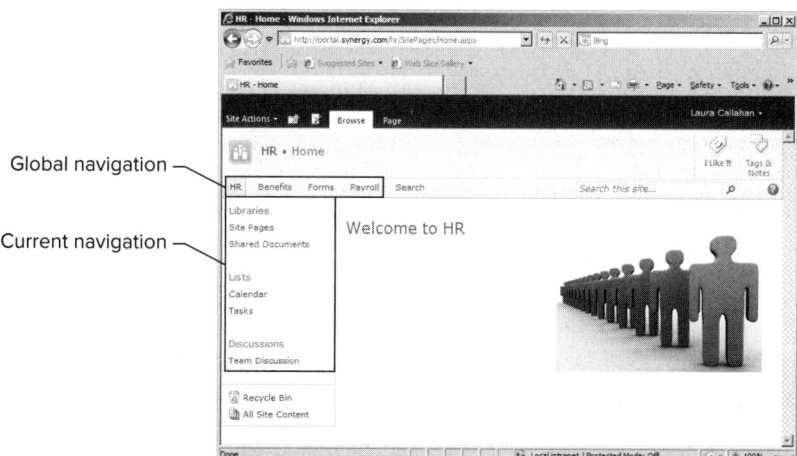

> **NOTE** Other forms of navigation—such as breadcrumb, tree view, and metadata—also exist. Metadata navigation is covered in Chapter 11, "Configuring the Managed Metadata Service," but the other forms are not covered in this book.

The options that you have for configuring global and current navigation vary whether you are using SPF or SPS. For SPF, your options are limited and you can only make very basic changes. The limited options also apply to SPS site collections that are not using the publishing feature. This section assumes you are using SPS with the SharePoint Server Publishing site collection feature activated.

To configure navigation for the site collection, follow these steps:

1. Ensure you are signed in as a site collection administrator or as someone who has Design or Full Control permissions.
2. Click Site Actions ➢ Site Settings.
3. Under Look And Feel, select Navigation.
4. Under Global Navigation, adjust the settings as needed. These settings control whether links are dynamically added when new subsites or pages are created.
5. Under Current Navigation, adjust the settings as needed.
6. Optionally choose how links should be sorted.
7. The greatest flexibility is within the Navigation Editing And Sorting section, as shown in Figure 3.18. Here you can manually order, hide, insert, and even create multilevel links.

Figure 3.18: Configuring navigation links and sorting

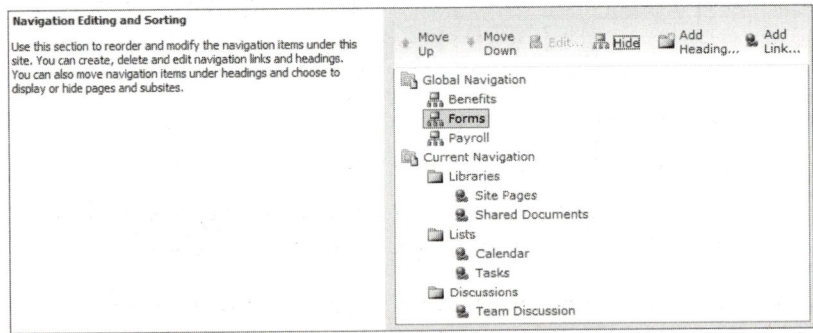

8. Click OK when you finish to save your changes.

> **NOTE** When you are creating a new website, the default setting is not to inherit global navigation settings from the parent. If you want inheritance, it is best to specify this when creating a new website. Do so by clicking the More Options button (using the Silverlight interface) and then selecting Yes to inherit the top link bar.

Managing Site Administration

This section relates to settings in the Site Administration category found on the Site Settings menu. Although many of these settings apply to just a single website, some apply to the whole site collection. The topics emphasized in this section continue to focus on common tasks that apply to the site collection.

Managing Regional Settings

Regional settings determine the time zone and control how numbers, dates, and time are displayed and sorted on web pages. They are very similar to Windows regional settings. Each website can have its own set of regional settings. As users of websites may be spread across the globe, adjusting these settings ensures an understandable and consistent experience for all. For example, if you have a project site mainly for users in Singapore, you can adjust the regional settings for them.

When you create a new site collection, the time zone used for the top-level site matches the default configured for the web application. If no default for the web application was set, the site collection uses the time zone configured for the operating system on the WFE server. When you create new subsites in the site collection, the regional settings will match those of the parent website.

To adjust the regional settings for a website, follow these steps:

1. Click Site Actions ➢ Site Settings.
2. Under Site Administration, select Regional Settings.
3. Adjust the regional settings as needed for this website. If this is a top-level site, you can apply these changes to all subsites.

Users can also override a website's regional settings with their own personal settings. This is useful when users of the website are in different regions. For example, you might have a project in which most of the users are in Singapore but a few are located in Germany.

Personal settings are specific to a site collection. To override a website's settings and define personal settings for all SharePoint websites in this site collection, follow these steps.

1. Click your login name, located in the upper-right corner, by default.
2. Click My Settings.
3. Select My Regional Settings.
4. Clear the Always Follow Web Settings check box at the top.
5. Adjust the regional settings as needed.
6. Click OK to save.

Managing RSS Settings

Really Simple Syndication (RSS) allows SharePoint to expose list and library content as RSS feeds, which can be consumed by client RSS reader applications. RSS must be enabled both at the site collection level and on the individual website.

To enable RSS for the site collection, follow these steps:

1. Go to the top-level website in the site collection.
2. Click Site Actions ➢ Site Settings.
3. Under Site Administration, select RSS.
4. Select the Allow RSS Feeds In This Site Collection check box.
5. Optionally, enable RSS for this single website and adjust any of the advanced settings, such as Copyright.
6. Click OK to save.

> **NOTE** To allow the Windows Explorer search engine built into Windows 7 to connect and integrate with SharePoint, you must ensure site collection RSS feeds are enabled. More details on configuring Search for the client are covered in Chapter 9, "Configuring Search Scopes and Search Results."

Managing Content and Structure

Users of SPS have a powerful website management tool called Site Content and Structure. The following are just some of the useful tasks that can be performed using this gem:

- Get a hierarchical view of all websites in the site collection.
- Copy or move a website to another location.
- Quickly go to the settings or permission page for a website.
- Remove multiple websites, including subsites, lists, and libraries in one operation.

The Site Content and Structure utility is shown in Figure 3.19.

Figure 3.19: SharePoint Site Content and Structure

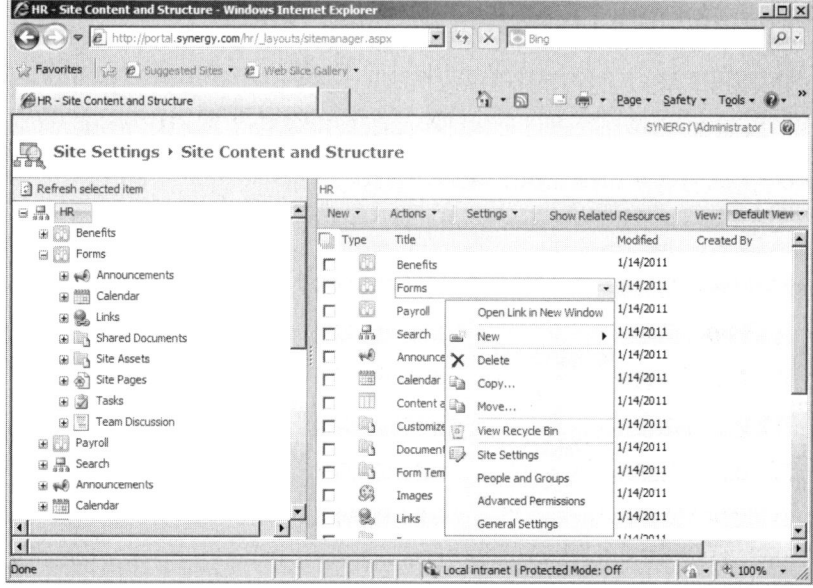

When working with this tool, take note of the following caveats:

- Only content within the site collection can be managed.
- You cannot move or copy websites between site collections.
- Moving or copying websites can change their permissions depending on how security inheritance is configured.

- Copying websites does not preserve all settings when the site is duplicated. For example, currently running workflow and unique permissions are lost.

There are several ways you can access this utility:

- If the SharePoint Server Publishing Infrastructure site collection feature is enabled, you have a link to it called Content And Structure from the Site Administration menu within Site Settings.
- If the SharePoint Server Publishing website feature is enabled, you have a link to it called Manage Content And Structure from the Site Settings menu.
- If no publishing features are enabled, you can navigate directly to it by entering the website URL followed by `_layouts/sitemanager.aspx`—for example, `http://intranet/HR/_layouts/sitemanager.aspx`.

Managing Site Collection Administration

This section applies to settings in the Site Collection Administration category found only at the top-level Site Settings page. Only site collection administrators or those granted Full Control at the web application policy can access these menu items.

The Site Collection Administration category contains many links, and some that are only visible when certain features are activated. This chapter focuses on the common ones that are not covered in other areas of the book.

Managing Recycle Bins

When a user deletes an item, folder, list, or library, the contents are placed in the recycle bin for the website. This is often called the end-user recycle bin or first-stage recycle bin. Items that are removed from this first recycle bin are then moved to a second-stage recycle bin shared at the site collection level.

> **NOTE** Deleting a website is different from deleting an individual item, folder, list, or library. A deleted website is immediately removed from SharePoint and can only be recovered by doing a restore, as covered in Chapter 16.

Regular users with at least Contribute permissions can restore items from the first-stage recycle bin. Only site collection administrators can restore from the second-stage recycle bin.

To restore items from the first-stage recycle bin, follow these steps:

1. Access the website and click the Recycle Bin link found in the quick launch navigation menu.
2. Select the item(s) to recover and click the Restore Selection link.

To restore items from the second-stage recycle bin, follow these steps:

1. Click the Recycle Bin link from the Site Collection Administration menu. (This initially takes you to a virtual view showing all files that are stored in all first-stage recycle bins. A site collection administrator can also restore from the first-stage recycle bin from this view.)
2. Click Deleted From End-User Recycle Bin to see all items deleted from all first-stage recycle bins. This is the second-stage recycle bin.
3. Select the item(s) to recover and click the Restore Selection link.

Restoring from either recycle bin puts the file back in the location it was before it was deleted. In other words, restoring from the second-stage recycle bin does not put the file back into the first-stage recycle bin.

In addition to these site collection options, recycle bins can be administered at the web application level. Settings here apply to all site collections in the web application. Here are the steps to manage this from Central Administration:

1. Click Application Management, then select Manage Web Applications.
2. Select the desired web application and click the General Settings button in the ribbon.
3. In the resulting dialog, scroll down to the Recycle Bin settings, as shown in Figure 3.20.

Figure 3.20: Recycle Bin settings

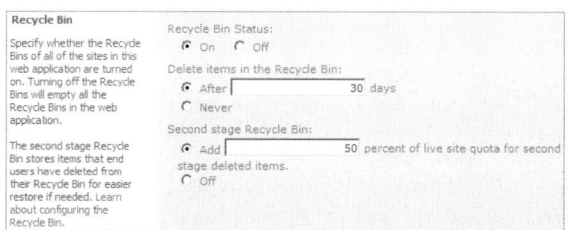

Here are some tips to remember when working with recycle bins:

- Turning off the recycle bin as shown in Figure 3.20 will immediately empty all recycle bins for all site collections in the web application.
- Space used by all first-stage recycle bins counts against your site collection quota.
- The second-stage recycle bin also has a size quota, which is configured as a percentage of the site collection quota (by default, 50 percent, as shown in Figure 3.20).
- Files that are aged from the first-stage recycle bin are automatically deleted and do not go into the second stage.
- The age countdown for an item begins when it is initially deleted. For example, assume that items are only kept for the default of 30 days, as shown in Figure 3.20. If an item is deleted on June 1 and then moved from the first-stage recycle bin to the second-stage recycle bin on June 30, it will only stay in the second-stage recycle bin for one more day.

Managing Portal Site Connection

As covered in the "Managing Site Collection Navigation" section, each site collection independently maintains its own global navigation. This can be a problem if multiple site collections are being used and need to be linked together. For example, say each business unit has its own site collection and they can be accessed from the master portal. When navigating into the HR portal, the HR site collection navigation takes over, and you have lost your link back to the master portal. This can easily cause confusion and frustration among users.

Portal site connection is a feature that provides one simple solution to this problem. From each "subordinate" site collection (e.g., each business unit), you add a portal site connection back to the "top level" site collection. This feature is also used frequently with My Sites to link back to a separate portal since each My Site is a separate site collection.

> **NOTE** The words "subordinate" and "top level" are used with quotes here since, technically, all site collections are peers and no hierarchy among them exists despite what the URL might suggest.

Manage Site Settings

To add a portal site connection to link from one site collection to another, follow these steps:

1. Access the subordinate site collection that needs to link back to another.
2. Navigate to the top-level website.
3. Click Site Actions ➤ Site Settings.
4. In Site Collection Administration category, select Portal Site Connection.
5. Specify the name and the URL for the other site collection and click OK to save. See Figure 3.21.

Figure 3.21: Configuring the portal site connection

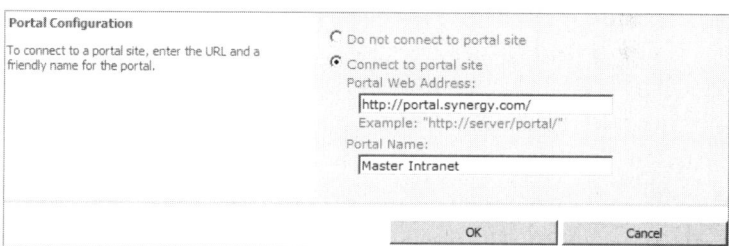

After you add the connection, Figure 3.22 shows how this appears from the up navigation control. Prior to adding the portal site connection, the HR link was the topmost link in the hierarchy.

Figure 3.22: Link to top-level portal

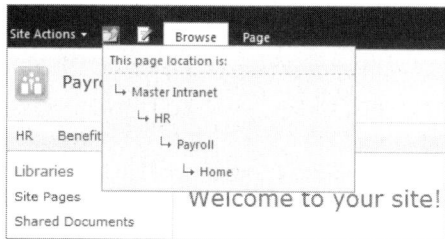

Managing SharePoint Designer

The "Disabling SharePoint Designer" section in Chapter 2 covers how SharePoint Designer can be used across a web application. See Figure 2.17 in Chapter 2 for a screen shot of this.

The same four settings that can be set at the web application level can also be set at the site collection level, giving a lower level of granularity. However, any setting that is disabled at the web application level takes precedence over the site collection setting.

To adjust SharePoint Designer's capabilities within a site collection, follow these steps:

1. Navigate to the top-level website of the site collection.
2. Click Site Actions ➢ Site Settings.
3. In Site Collection Administration category, select SharePoint Designer Settings.
4. Disable as needed.
5. Click OK to save.

4
Creating Service Applications

IN THIS CHAPTER, YOU WILL LEARN TO:

▶ **UNDERSTAND SERVICE APPLICATIONS (Pages 110 – 112)**
- Understanding the Service Application Framework (Page 110)
- Understanding Service Instances (Page 112)

▶ **CREATE AND DELETE SERVICE APPLICATIONS (Pages 112 – 117)**
- Creating a Service Application (Page 113)
- Deleting a Service Application (Page 115)
- Managing Service Application Administrators (Page 116)

▶ **CONFIGURE THE BUILT-IN SERVICE APPLICATIONS (Pages 117–140)**
- Configuring the Access Services Application (Page 118)
- Configuring the Business Data Connectivity Service Application (Page 119)
- Configuring the Excel Services Application (Page 122)
- Configuring the PerformancePoint Services Application (Page 130)
- Configuring the Secure Store Service Application (Page 132)
- Configuring the State Service Application (Page 135)
- Configuring the Visio Graphics Service Application (Page 135)
- Configuring the Web Analytics Service Application (Page 137)
- Configuring the Word Automation Service Application (Page 137)
- Configuring the PowerPoint Service Application (Page 139)
- Configuring the Word Viewing Service Application (Page 139)

▶ **ASSOCIATE SERVICE APPLICATIONS TO WEB APPLICATIONS (Pages 140 – 141)**

Understand Service Applications

Service applications in SharePoint 2010 are a set of independent processes that allow for both flexibility and scalability in farm architecture. Sometimes referred to as *shared services*, each application provides specific functionality—such as data connectivity or centralized metadata—to the SharePoint farm. Administrators can create one instance of a service and share it across the entire farm or create multiple instances to partition information to different web applications in the farm.

Service applications take the place of the Shared Service Provider that was found in the SharePoint 2007 architectural model, extending the concept of supporting services by providing administrators with more granular configuration options.

Understanding the Service Application Framework

Service applications are designed to let administrators choose how and where to host the functionality provided by SharePoint. Later in this chapter we'll go through configuring each of the service applications in detail. For now it is important to understand the relationship among service applications, service proxies, and services running on the server. Table 4.1 lists each of the service applications available in the different versions of SharePoint 2010.

Table 4.1: SharePoint 2010 service applications

Product Version	Service Applications	Purpose
SharePoint Foundation 2010	Application Discovery and Load Balancer	Load balancing of service applications
	Business Data Connectivity Service	Data retrieval and updating service for line-of-business databases and web services
	Security Token Service	Handles requests for Claims-Based Authentication
	Usage and Health Data Collection	Gathers and stores usage and health data in the logging database

Table 4.1: SharePoint 2010 service applications

Product Version	Service Applications	Purpose
SharePoint Server 2010 Standard Edition	Web Analytics Service	Collects and reports on user page requests and search queries
	Managed Metadata Service	Supports syndicated content type hubs and managed term sets
	Search Service	Provides indexing and searching functionality
	Secure Store Service	Provides an encrypted credential store
	State Service	Stores data that needs to be accessed between pages
	User Profile Service	Provides My Sites, User Profiles, and Audiences
SharePoint Server 2010 Enterprise Edition	Access Services	Executes and renders Access database applications as websites
	Excel Services	Executes and renders Excel workbooks as web pages
	PerformancePoint Service	Generates business intelligence dashboards from multidimensional data
	Visio Graphics Service	Executes and renders Visio files as web pages
	Word Automation Service	Server-side programmatic manipulation of Word files
Office Web Applications	PowerPoint Service Application	Online viewing and editing of PowerPoint files
		PowerPoint Broadcast feature, which delivers a PowerPoint presentation in a multicast mode
	Word Viewing Service	Online viewing and editing of Word documents

Service applications can provide their services to one or more web applications (for more information on web applications, see Chapter 2, "Creating and Managing Web Applications") in the farm via a service application proxy, which acts as a communication link between the service application and the web applications that it supports. This allows for great flexibility in the application architecture, with one service application providing services to multiple web applications and one web application consuming services from multiple service applications.

Understanding Service Instances

Service applications are connected to service instances, which run on specific SharePoint servers. A *service instance* is the process that executes on one or more SharePoint servers to deliver the functionality of the service application to the farm. A service application requires at least one instance of the service be running on one of the servers. But in many cases the same service application can run on multiple SharePoint servers, providing both scalability and fault tolerance to the farm. Service applications and service instances operate at different levels in the SharePoint application architecture; service applications are objects defined within the SharePoint configuration database and represent logical sets of configuration settings. Service instances are physical programs that run on servers in the farm and host the service application objects for execution.

Service instances are managed separately from service applications. Whereas service applications are created centrally and apply across servers in the farm, service instances are started and stopped on specific servers in the farm. You can find full details on starting and stopping services in Chapter 5.

Create and Delete Service Applications

Service applications can be created in one of two ways. There are advantages and disadvantages to each method.

>**Running the Farm Configuration Wizard** The wizard automates the creation of service applications. Using the wizard has the advantage of being fast and simple, but the wizard will assign all service applications to one application pool with a single service

account. The wizard will also create all the service databases using an automatic naming convention, which includes a GUID in the name.

Manually Creating Each Application This approach is more time consuming than using the wizard but offers you greater flexibility in configuring and naming the applications.

Creating a Service Application

You can run the Farm Configuration Wizard immediately after the completion of the farm installation process or at any point after that.

Running the Farm Configuration Wizard

To run the Farm Configuration Wizard, follow these steps:

1. From the SharePoint 2010 Central Administration Web Application, under Application Management, click Configuration Wizards.

2. On the Configuration Wizards page, click Launch The Farm Configuration Wizard.

3. Click the Start The Wizard link.

4. On the Configuration page, either select an existing managed account (covered in detail in Chapter 14, "Managing Security") or enter credentials to create a new managed account. This account will act as the service account for the application pool and will be granted ownership rights on all the service databases. The account should be an Active Directory domain account but does not require any explicit permissions assigned to it. Select the services you want to configure and click Next. The process may take several minutes to complete.

Creating a Service Application Manually

Some service applications have unique configuration steps and will be covered in detail individually in later sections of this chapter or in other chapters. These steps can be used to manually create each service application:

1. From the SharePoint 2010 Central Administration Web Application, under Application Management, click Manage Service Applications.

2. From the ribbon, click the New menu and select the type of service application you want to create, as shown in Figure 4.1. For this example, choose Access Services.

Figure 4.1: Choosing a service application to create

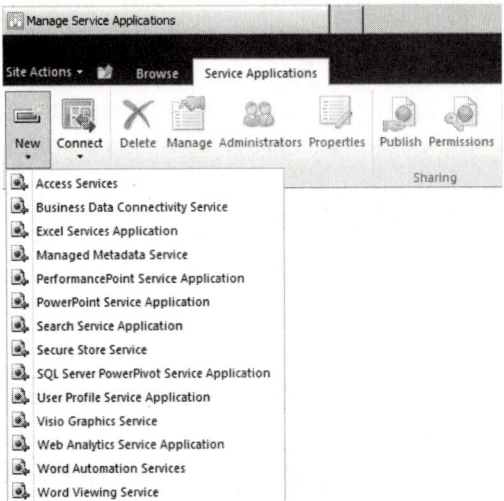

3. In the dialog box shown in Figure 4.2, enter a name for your service.

Figure 4.2: Create New Access Services Application dialog box

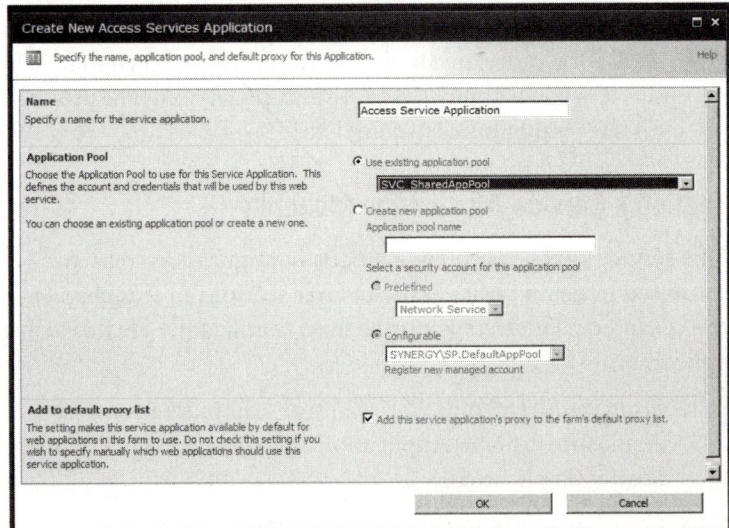

4. All services require an application pool to be created or assigned. (Application pools—the process spaces within which SharePoint code executes—are covered in detail in Chapter 2.) Select an existing application pool to share process resources between web applications or create a new one to isolate the web service application resources. To create a new application pool, enter a name and select a managed account as its service account.

5. Some service applications provide the option Add To Default Proxy List, which is selected by default. Uncheck this option if this application will be used for only one web application.

6. A few service applications create databases during their initial configuration. These are the Business Data Catalog, Managed Metadata Service, Secure Store Service, and User Profile Service Application. For these, include the following information:

    - Enter the server name of the SQL server that will host the database.
    - Enter the name of the database.

TIP It is a good idea to use a consistent naming convention for all databases.

   - Select either Windows Authentication or SQL Authentication (used generally for Internet-facing farms with a firewall in front of the SQL server).
   - For fault-tolerant farms that use mirrored database servers, enter the failover database server that will host the mirror.

Deleting a Service Application

When you no longer need a service application, you can delete it. Deleting the service application will remove it from the proxy group that it is a part of but does not stop the associated server service from running if there is one. Only farm administrators can delete a service application.

Follow these steps to delete a service application:

1. From SharePoint 2010 Central Administration, under Application Management, click Manage Service Applications.
2. Click the row of the service application to be deleted.

3. From the ribbon, click Delete.

4. In the resulting dialog box, you have the option to delete the service database by checking the option Delete Data Associated With The Service Applications. If there is no data associated with the service application or it is no longer going to be used then it makes sense to delete the unused databases. In cases where the service application may be re-created again or the databases are being relocated to a different SQL Server then leave the box unchecked.

5. Click OK.

Managing Service Application Administrators

You can delegate management of a service application to someone who is not a farm administrator. This approach allows you to distribute the maintenance of services to several staff members while restricting their access to specific services. Service application managers can open the Service Applications page (_admin/ServiceApplications.aspx) but will only see those service applications that they have permissions to manage. Only farm administrators can delegate service applications to others.

1. From SharePoint 2010 Central Administration, under Application Management, click Manage Service Applications.

2. Click the row of the service application for which you are changing the administrators.

3. From the ribbon, click Administrators, as shown in Figure 4.3.

Figure 4.3: Click Administrators on the ribbon

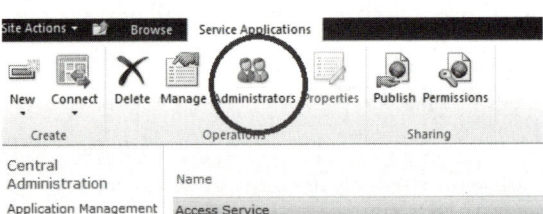

4. In the resulting dialog box, browse for or type the username of the person you want to add; then click Add.

5. To complete the delegation, check the Full Control option for the user, as shown in Figure 4.4.

Figure 4.4: Check the Full Control in this dialog box

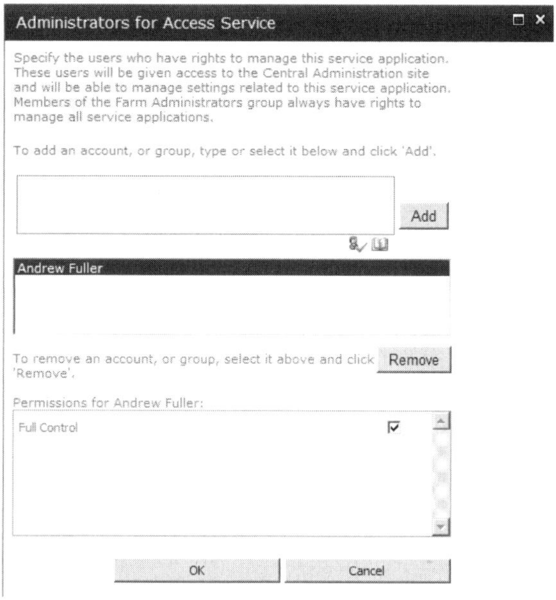

6. Click OK.

Configure the Built-in Service Applications

Once you create a service application, you can begin configuring it. This section describes the configuration steps and settings for the following applications:

- Access Services
- Business Data Connectivity Services
- Excel Services
- PerformancePoint Services
- Secure Store Service
- State Service
- Visio Graphics Service
- Web Analytics Service

- Word Automation Service
- PowerPoint Service
- Word Viewing Service

> **NOTE** Not all service application configuration is covered in this section. The User Profile Service is covered in Chapter 7, "Configuring the User Profiles and My Sites Service." The Search Service will be covered in Chapter 8, "Configuring the Search Service," and the Managed Metadata Service will be covered in Chapter 11, "Configuring the Managed Metadata Service."

Configuring the Access Services Application

Access Services allows Access 2010 databases to be imported into SharePoint and converted to online, web-based applications that retain all the functionality of the offline version. Data tables, forms, and reports become accessible via a SharePoint Access website, which can be shared among multiple users. This service requires that the server service Access Database Service be started on at least one server using the Services On Server screen. Starting and stopping services are covered in Chapter 5, "Scaling and High Availability."

Once the Access Services application has been created and the service started, the service is ready to use. In cases where this service will be used extensively, performance and scalability issues may occur. You can address such issues by modifying the service settings. To do so, use the following steps:

1. From SharePoint 2010 Central Administration, under Application Management, click Manage Service Applications.
2. On the Manage Service Applications page, click the link for the Access Services application.
3. Change the appropriate settings as described next.
4. Click OK to save the settings.

You can configure the following types of elements:

Lists and Queries You can restrict the complexity and size of the data tables and queries executed within the database.

The Types of Objects an Access Services Application Can Contain The Application Objects section controls the Maximum Application Log Size, which defaults to 3,000 records but can be increased to retain additional entries over time by setting it to a larger value. You can make it unlimited in size by setting it to –1.

Behavior of Sessions The Session Management section controls the amount of RAM and open connection resources that can be used. These settings can be lowered to reduce the memory consumption on the server.

Memory Utilization This section controls the total physical memory available to Access Services. The default value of –1 sets the limit to 50 percent of the memory on the server. This value can be reduced to minimize contention with other processes.

Templates The Maximum Template Size setting limits users, by default, to 30 MB Access Template (.accdt) files. This value can be changed to any positive number or set to –1 for unlimited size.

For the full list of configurations available, see the article "Set Up and Configure Access Services (SharePoint Server 2010)" at:

http://technet.microsoft.com/en-us/library/ee748653.aspx

Configuring the Business Data Connectivity Service Application

Business Connectivity Services (BCS) provides a middle tier of data services to SharePoint sites and custom applications. Once configured with external content types, the BCS acts as an object broker for abstracted data objects that encapsulate the query and authentication parameters of connections to external data sources. This service requires that the server service Business Data Connectivity Service be started on at least one server using the Services On Server screen. Connections are defined as external content types, each of which represents a query to a database or web service along with the parameter definitions and authentication details. External content types can then be displayed on site pages as external lists, which give users the ability to display and, in some cases, edit the data exposed by the connection.

Most of the creation and configuration of external content types is done through SharePoint Designer 2010, but the configuration of permissions and management is handled at the service level. You can perform the following configuration tasks through the Manage Service Applications interface:

- Import a BDC (Business Data Connectivity) model
- Set permissions for external content type objects
- Set permissions on the metadata store

To modify these settings, do the following:

1. From SharePoint 2010 Central Administration, under Application Management, click Manage Service Applications.

2. On the Manage Service Applications page, click the link for the Business Data Connectivity Service application. A portion of the View External Content Types page is shown in Figure 4.5.

Figure 4.5: View External Content Types

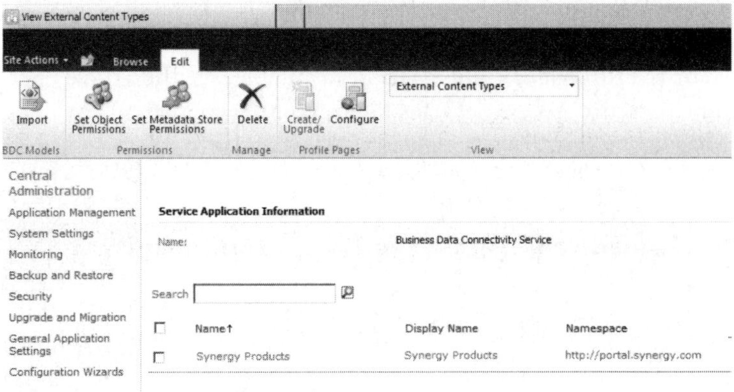

Importing a BDC Model

Business data connections are defined through external content types managed by the BDC. A farm administrator can import a BDC Model XML file created by a developer that contains one or more external content types. Perform the following steps:

1. On the ribbon, click the Import button.
2. Click Browse, navigate to the XML file, and click Open.

3. Click Import.
4. The service will validate the file and import it into the service database.

Setting Object Permissions

Once you've either imported an external content type or created one using SharePoint Designer 2010, you must set permissions to allow users to query data through the object.

While developers and data analysts may create external content types, only BCS administrators can assign permissions. Use these steps to configure external content type permissions:

1. To configure object permissions, check the box next to an External Content Type; then, from the Ribbon, click Set Object Permissions.
2. In the resulting dialog box, do one of the following:
   - Enter the name of a user or group and click Check Names.
   - Browse for a user or group account.
3. Click Add.
4. Check the box next to the permissions you want to assign to this user or group, as shown in Figure 4.6.

Figure 4.6: Set Object Permissions dialog box

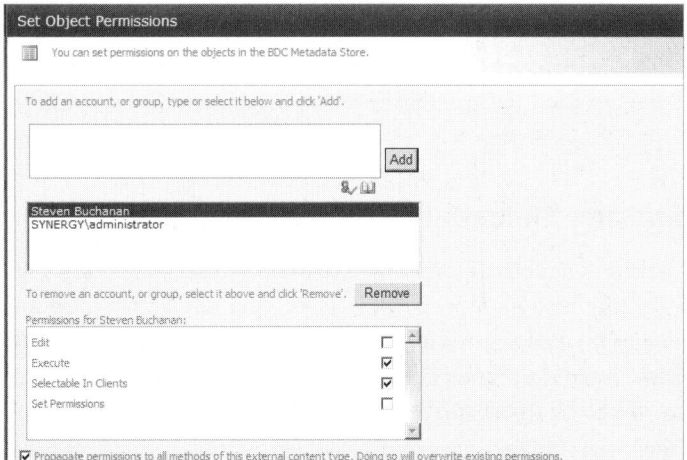

Edit   Create external content types and import models.

Execute   Create, read, update, delete, or query an external content type.

Selectable In Clients   Create and configure an external list from an external content type, allowing it to be displayed on a page.

Set Permissions   Change the permissions of the object. You must grant at least one account the Set Permissions right.

5. Click OK.

Setting Metadata Store Permissions

The Set Metadata Store Permissions are similar to the Set Object Permissions described in the previous section. Using this command, farm or service administrators can set permissions on the entire metadata store:

1. To configure metadata store permissions, from the ribbon select Set Metadata Store Permissions.

2. In the resulting dialog box, do one of the following:

   - Enter the name of a user or group and click Check Names.
   - Browse for a user or group account.

3. Click Add.

4. Check the box next to the appropriate permissions for the object

   The permissions for the metadata store are the same as the permissions for an external content type, as described in the previous section.

Configuring the Excel Services Application

Excel Services enables SharePoint 2010 to load, execute, and recalculate Excel workbooks in a server-side process and render a workbook as a web page. The service lets you view large workbooks without downloading and opening them on the client and allows elements of workbooks to be displayed in Excel Web Access web parts as part of a business intelligence dashboard. This service requires that the server service Excel Calculation Services (ECS) be started on at least one server using the Services On Server screen.

You can configure the following settings for Excel Services:

- Global settings for security, memory, and load balancing
- Trusted file locations
- Trusted data connection libraries
- Trusted user-defined function assemblies

Configuring Global Settings

The Global Settings configuration page is used to modify security, memory, and load balancing settings for Excel Services. Use the following steps to configure these settings:

1. From SharePoint 2010 Central Administration, under Application Management, click Manage Service Applications.

2. On the Manage Service Applications page, click the link for the Excel Services application.

3. On the Manage Excel Services Application page, click Global Settings, as shown in Figure 4.7.

Figure 4.7: Manage Excel Services Application page

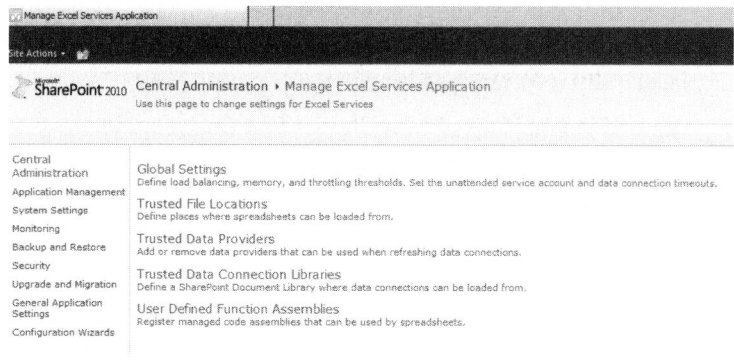

4. In the Security section of the Excel Services Application Settings page, configure the following settings:

   File Access Method Two methods are available. The Impersonation method opens files outside of SharePoint using the account of the user logged onto the site. The Process

Account method uses the service account. In most cases, you should select Process Account. The Impersonation method should only be used when Kerberos authentication has been configured in SharePoint. For more details on Kerberos, see the article "Configure Kerberos Authentication (SharePoint Server 2010)" at http://technet.microsoft.com/en-us/library/ee806870.aspx.

Connection Encryption This setting determines whether Excel Services should require a Secure Sockets Layer (SSL) connection to the SharePoint front end. You should require encryption if it is possible to configure SSL or IP Internet Protocol Security (IPsec) over the connection and you want to prevent usernames and passwords from being exposed on the network.

Allow Cross Domain Access This setting determines whether files from one HTTP domain can be displayed on a page in a different HTTP domain. This setting should be turned on only when necessary in multidomain environments.

5. In the Load Balancing section, choose one of the following options:

   Workbook URL The workbook URL is used to select the ECS process used to open the workbook. This ensures that the same ECS session is used for all requests made to that workbook. This option is selected by default and is the generally recommended setting.

   Round Robin With Health Check A round-robin load-balancing model is used to select the ECS process used to open a workbook. This setting is useful when multiple Excel Services application servers are configured and a small number of workbooks will be accessed by a relatively large number of users.

   Local If an ECS session is available on the local SharePoint server, then it is used; otherwise, a round-robin model is used. Local is a hybrid setting that is appropriate when multiple Excel Services instances are running on SharePoint web front end servers.

6. In the Session Management section, enter the Maximum Sessions Allowed Per User value. The default is 25. When the maximum

number of sessions is exceeded, additional sessions for that user will be blocked until some sessions expire. Enter −1 for unlimited sessions.

7. In the Memory Utilization section, configure the following settings:

    Maximum Private Bytes The maximum amount (in MB) of memory allocated for the ECS process. The largest amount you can enter is equivalent to 50 percent of the physical memory on the machine.

    Memory Cache Threshold The percentage of the Maximum Private Bytes value that is used for objects that are no longer in use. Retaining objects in cache longer may allow them to be reused more often but will consume more space. Enter 0 to disable caching.

    Maximum Unused Object Age The maximum time (in minutes) that an object not in use in a session will remain in memory. Valid values: −1 (no maximum); from 1 through 34560 (24 days).

8. In the Workbook Cache section, configure the following settings:

    Workbook Cache Location The file system location of the workbook file cache on the SharePoint server. If this value is empty, SharePoint creates a subdirectory in the system temporary directory.

    Maximum Size Of Workbook Cache The maximum disk space (in MB) that can be allocated to workbooks that are currently in use by ECS. The default is 40 GB.

    Caching Of Unused Files Select this check box to enable caching of files that are no longer in use by ECS sessions.

9. In the External Data section, configure the following settings:

    Connection Lifetime The maximum time (in seconds) a connection may remain open. When a connection exceeds this time it is closed.

    Unattended Service Account The Unattended Service Account is used for authentication when no authentication is provided in an Office Data Connection (ODC) file. Enter the Application ID defined in the Secure Store Service (SSS) that holds the credentials.

10. Click OK to save the settings.

Configuring Trusted File Locations

Specifying trusted file locations is essential for Excel Services to function. Excel files will not be loaded and processed by Excel Services unless they are in a trusted location. Use the following steps to configure a trusted location:

1. From SharePoint 2010 Central Administration, under Application Management, click Manage Service Applications.

2. On the Manage Service Applications page, click the link for the Excel Services application.

3. On the Manage Excel Services Application page, click Trusted File Locations, as shown in Figure 4.7, earlier in this chapter.

4. Click Add Trusted File Location.

5. In the Location section, configure the following settings:

    Address   Enter the URL or UNC path of the site or directory that holds Excel files that Excel Services is allowed to execute.

    Location Type   Choose the protocol used by Excel Services to connect to the location. The options are Microsoft SharePoint Foundation (which is a SharePoint library), a UNC path pointing to a Windows file share, or an HTTP URL pointing to a web address.

    Trust Children   Specify whether all subsites and subfolders underneath the location are to be trusted as well.

    Description   Add a text description of the location to explain the purpose of trusting it.

6. In the Session Management section, configure the following settings:

    Session Timeout   The length of time (in seconds) that a session will remain in memory after the last request is received. If no further requests are received in this time, the session is shut down. Valid values: from –1 (no timeout) through 2,073,600 (24 days). The value 0 means that the session expires at the end of a single request.

    Short Session Timeout   Similar to Session Timeout, except that the time is measured from the first request and applies only if no further requests are made. Valid values: from –1 (short session timeout is disabled) through 2,073,600 (24 days). The value 0 means that the session expires at the end of a single request.

New Workbook Session Timeout Similar to the Session Timeout, except that it applies only to new workbook sessions. Valid values: from –1 (no timeout) through 2,073,600 (24 days). The value 0 means that the session expires at the end of a single request.

Maximum Request Duration The maximum duration (in seconds) of a single request in a session. Valid values: from –1 (no timeout) through 2,073,600 (24 days).

Maximum Chart Render Duration The maximum time (in seconds) spent rendering any single chart. Valid values: from –1 (no timeout) through 2,073,600 (24 days).

7. In the Workbook Properties section, configure the following settings:

    Maximum Workbook Size The maximum size (in MB) of a workbook that can be opened by ECS. Valid values: from 1 through 2,000.

    Maximum Chart or Image Size The maximum size (in MB) of a chart or image that can be opened by ECS. Valid values: any positive integer.

8. In the Calculation Behavior section, configure the following settings:

    Volatile Function Cache Lifetime The maximum time (in seconds) that a computed value for a volatile function is cached for automatic recalculations. Valid values: –1 (calculated once on load); 0 (always calculated); from 1 through 2,073,600 (24 days).

    Workbook Calculation Mode Determines the calculation mode for the workbook. The modes are as follows: File uses the mode specified in the workbook. Manual recalculates only when a Calculate request is received. Automatic forces recalculation any time a dependent value is changed. Automatic Except Data Tables is like Automatic but ignores values in data tables.

9. In the External Data section, configure the following settings:

    Allow External Data The None setting allows no connections to data outside the workbook. Trusted Data

Connection Libraries Only allows only ODC files stored in Data Connection Libraries that are also trusted by Excel Services. Trusted Data Connection Libraries And Embedded allows both trusted Data Connection Libraries and ODC files embedded inside workbooks.

Warn On Refresh When enabled, this setting displays a warning before refreshing external data for files in this location.

Display Granular External Data Errors When enabled, this setting displays detailed error messages when an external connection to data fails.

Stop When Refresh On Open Fails When this setting is enabled, if a file is set to refresh data connections when it is opened and the file refresh fails and the user does not have Open Item permissions on the workbook, then the Open operation will abort.

External Data Cache Lifetime The maximum time (in seconds) that the system can use external data query results. There are separate settings for Automatic refresh (Periodic/On-Open) and Manual refresh. For both, valid values are −1 (never refresh after first query); from 0 through 2,073,600 (24 days).

Maximum Concurrent Queries Per Session The maximum number of external data queries that can execute concurrently in a single session. Valid values: any positive integer.

Allow External Data Using REST When enabled, requests from the REST API can refresh external data connections. This setting has no effect if Allow External Data is set to None.

10. In the User-Defined Functions section, choose whether external assemblies containing user-defined functions may be called from workbooks in this trusted location.

Configuring Trusted Data Connection Libraries

A data connection library holds Office Data Connection (ODC) or Universal Data Connection (UDC) files. Excel Services can be configured to trust specific libraries that hold connection files that have been approved as safe to use. To add a trusted library, follow these steps:

1. From SharePoint 2010 Central Administration, under Application Management, click Manage Service Applications.
2. On the Manage Service Applications page, click the link for the Excel Services application.
3. On the Manage Excel Services Application page, click Trusted Data Connection Libraries, as shown in Figure 4.7, earlier in this chapter.
4. Click Add Trusted Data Connection Library.
5. On the Add Trusted Data Connection Library page, enter the URL of the library and a description that explains its purpose.
6. Click OK.

Configuring User-Defined Function Assemblies

Excel Services does not support macros or Visual Basic for Applications (VBA) code inside Excel files. For any code to execute, it must be compiled into a .NET assembly that exposes user-defined functions that can be called in a workbook much like normal Excel functions can. The assemblies must be registered in order to be recognized by Excel Services. To register a user-defined assembly, follow these steps:

1. From SharePoint 2010 Central Administration, under Application Management, click Manage Service Applications.
2. On the Manage Service Applications page, click the link for the Excel Services application.
3. On the Manage Excel Services Application page, click User-Defined Function Assemblies, as shown in Figure 4.7, earlier in this chapter.
4. On the User-Defined Functions page, click Add User-Defined Function Assembly.
5. On the Add User-Defined Function Assembly page, the values you enter depends on the location where the assembly is stored.
    - If the assembly is installed in the global assembly cache (GAC), then select that option for the location and enter the strong name of the assembly in the Assembly text box.

- If the assembly is installed in a folder on the server or a file share, select the File Path option and enter the path to the file in the Assembly text box.

6. Select the Assembly Enabled check box to permit the assembly to be loaded by Excel Services.

7. Click OK.

Configuring the PerformancePoint Services Application

PerformancePoint Services is a new service in SharePoint 2010 that includes features previously shipped under the separate product PerformancePoint Server 2007. The service allows business analysts to design and publish charts, graphs, and key performance indicators (KPIs) that display business data in visual form. PerformancePoint Services comes with a dashboard designer that allows business analysts to assemble the data graphics into pages that can show a large amount of information on a single screen.

You can configure the following aspects of PerformancePoint Services:

- Global application settings
- Trusted content locations

Configuring PerformancePoint Services Application Settings

The Application Settings page allows administrators to configure the global settings for PerformancePoint Services. Among these, the most important are the Secure Store Service Application and Unattended Service Account settings. The service needs these values to connect to external sources. To configure the application service settings, use the following steps:

1. From SharePoint 2010 Central Administration, under Application Management, click Manage Service Applications.

2. On the Manage Service Applications page, click the link for the PerformancePoint Services application.

3. On the Manage PerformancePoint Services Application page, click PerformancePoint Services Application Settings.

4. On the PerformancePoint Services Application Settings page, configure the following settings:

Secure Store Service Application PerformancePoint Services uses the Secure Store Service (SSS) to store credentials used to authenticate to data sources. Enter the name of an existing SSS.

Unattended Service Account Click the Edit User button and enter the username and password for the account that will be used for data access.

Comments Select the Enable Comments check box to allow comments on scorecard cells and enter the maximum number of annotated cells per scorecard.

KPI Icon Cache Enter the number of seconds that the cache will be retained. The default of 10 seconds can be lengthened to reduce the graphics that are downloaded with each page refresh. The data underlying the KPIs changes less frequently than the cache timeout.

Data Source Query Time-Out Enter the number of seconds that a data query will wait for a response before it is cancelled. The 300-second default is generally sufficient but may be reduced to increase the responsiveness of pages. However, this may mean that some data does not display.

Remember User Filter Selections For Enter the number of days that user filter selections will be retained. This setting defaults to 90 days, which is generally recommended, but you could reduce it to purge unneeded settings more frequently.

Maximum Members To Load In Filter Tree Enter the number of members to retrieve into a filter of type tree. The default of 5,000 is set to allow a relatively large set of items to be displayed without putting undue load on the SharePoint server and SQL server. This number can be increased if there are sufficient server resources or relatively few users.

Maximum Measures To Load In Select Measure Control Enter the number of measures that can be loaded into a dashboard's Select Measure control. The default is 1,000 items and should be increased only when necessary and if sufficient server resources are available.

Initial Retrieval Limit Enter the number of rows returned when a user clicks Show Details. This setting defaults to 1,000, which can be increased if it does not impact performance.

Maximum Retrieval Limit Enter the maximum number of rows that can be returned or allow Analysis Services to manage the number. The default of 10,000 can be increased to match increases in the Initial Retrieval Limit.

Maximum Number Of Items Enter the maximum number of items (per level) returned to the decomposition tree. The minimum value is 0. The maximum is 1,000,000.

5. Click OK.

Configuring Trusted Content Locations

A trusted content location is a site or list within SharePoint that is allowed to host dashboards and scorecards. The default setting is for all locations to be trusted. This setting can be overridden and only specific locations trusted.

1. From SharePoint 2010 Central Administration, under Application Management, click Manage Service Applications.

2. On the Manage Service Applications page, click the link for the PerformancePoint Services application.

3. On the Manage PerformancePoint Services Application page, click Trusted Content Locations.

4. On the Trusted Content Locations page, select the option Only Specific Locations and click Apply.

5. Click Add Trusted Content Location.

6. On the Edit Trusted Content Location page, enter the full address to the location and select the option that identifies the type of location as a site collection, a site, or a list.

Configuring the Secure Store Service Application

The Secure Store Service (SSS) replaces the Single Sign-On Service from previous versions of SharePoint. It provides an encrypted credential store and brokering service to allow applications to store and retrieve credentials for external data sources and systems in a highly secure manner. A common use for this service is to store the logon accounts and passwords used by other services to connect to external databases.

Configure the Built-in Service Applications

You can configure the following settings of the SSS:

- Generate A New Encryption Key
- Create An Application Definition

Generating a New Secure Store Service Encryption Key

The Secure Store Service Encryption Key is used by SharePoint to encrypt and decrypt credentials stored within the SSS database. In cases where security concerns are high, this key can be rotated periodically to make it more difficult for attackers to crack. To change the key, use the following steps:

1. From SharePoint 2010 Central Administration, under Application Management, click Manage Service Applications.

2. On the Manage Service Applications page, click the link for the Secure Store Service application. A portion of the Secure Store Service page is shown in Figure 4.8.

Figure 4.8: Secure Store Service

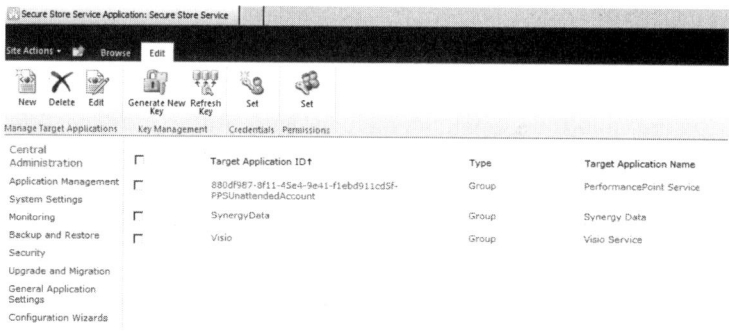

3. From the ribbon, select Generate New Key.

4. Enter a passphrase and confirm it. The passphrase is used to generate a new encryption key and will be required again when you are restoring a Secure Store database.

5. Click OK.

Creating a Secure Store Service Application Definition

Use the following steps to create an entry in the SSS to track a specific set of credentials for one or many users. This set of credentials is called an application definition. Developers will use the application definition to request credentials at runtime.

1. From SharePoint 2010 Central Administration, under Application Management, click Manage Service Applications.

2. On the Manage Service Applications page, click the link for the Secure Store Service application.

3. On the ribbon, click New and enter the following details:

    Target Application ID   You will use this ID whenever an application needs to query the SSS to update or retrieve the specific credentials associated with it. This ID can be any term or phrase that is unique within the SSS applications list.

    Display Name   This value is displayed as a label for the application on the SSS management page and helps to identify the purpose of each application.

    Contact E-mail   Enter an email address for the primary contact for the application.

    Target Application Type   There are two sets of options: Group, which maps all the users in one or more groups to a single set of credentials stored in the SSS database, and Individual, which maps each user to a unique set of credentials stored just for that user.

    For both Individual and Group options, there are two settings: Ticket (the SSS can issue a ticket that can be redeemed by another process to access the same credentials), and Restricted (only code that is Fully Trusted under the .NET Code Access Security model can request credentials).

4. Click Next.

5. On the Credential Fields page, specify the names of the credential storage fields this application will use. For a Windows Active Directory account, leave the Field Type settings at Windows User Name and Windows Password. For a SQL server or other database logon, change the Field Type settings to User Name and Password, respectively. Other field types may be used as needed.

6. Click Next.

7. On the Membership Settings page, enter the users or groups that have Administrative rights on this application. If you selected one of the Group options (see step 3) as the application type, then you must also define the users or groups who can use the credentials to retrieve data into SharePoint.

8. Click OK.

9. For a Group type application, you must also set the User Name and Password values. On the Secure Store Service Application page, check the box next to the application you want to set and, on the ribbon, click Set Credentials.

10. Complete the User Name, Password, and Confirm The Password fields, and then click OK.

Configuring the State Service Application

The State Service in SharePoint 2010 is used by specific services such as InfoPath Forms Services to maintain session information for a user between server requests. The service can be configured through the Farm Configuration Wizard (see "Running the Farm Configuration Wizard," earlier in this chapter) or through PowerShell.

The Enable-SPSessionStateService cmdlet will enable the State Service in a farm. The following example enables the State Service using default values—the database is hosted on the configuration database SQL Server, using Windows Authentication, and with a 60-minute session timeout:

```
Enable-SPSessionStateService -DefaultProvision
```

The following example uses a custom database name, database server name, a session timeout of 120 minutes, and the default Windows Authentication:

```
Enable-SPSessionStateService -DatabaseName "DB_State_Service"
-DatabaseServer "sqlcluster" -SessionTimeout 120
```

Configuring the Visio Graphics Service Application

The Visio Graphics Service allows SharePoint 2010 to load and render a Visio VDW file on the server and display it as a web page to the user. The service also supports dynamic data refresh of external data connections.

The global settings for this application are used to control the amount of server resources that SharePoint can consume when loading and rendering Visio files.

While most of the settings can remain at their default values, the Unattended Service Account must be configured to allow files to be processed:

1. From SharePoint 2010 Central Administration, under Application Management, click Manage Service Applications.

2. On the Manage Service Applications page, click the link for the Visio Graphics Service application.

3. On the Manage Visio Graphics Services Application page, click Global Settings, shown in Figure 4.9.

Figure 4.9: Manage the Visio Graphics Services Application page

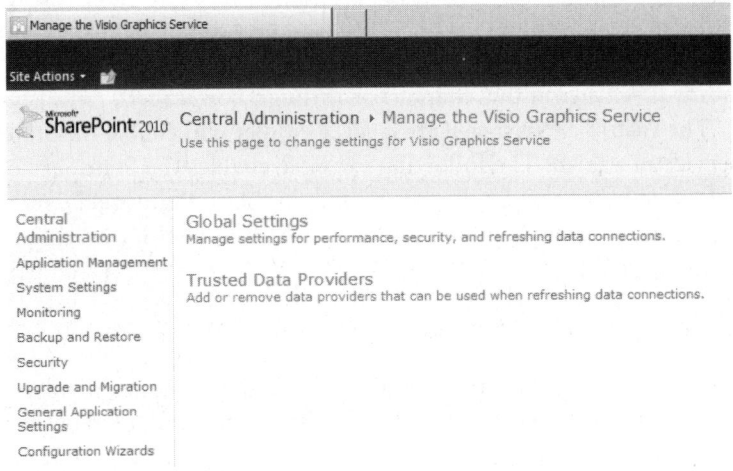

4. On the Global Settings page, configure the following settings:

   Maximum Web Drawing Size   The maximum size in MB (between 1 and 50) of a web drawing that can be rendered. The default value is 5 MB.

   Minimum Cache Age   The minimum number of minutes (between 0 and 34,560) that a web drawing is cached in memory. The default value is 5 minutes.

Maximum Cache Age The number of minutes (between 0 and 34,560) after which cached web drawings are purged. The default value is 60 minutes.

Maximum Recalc Duration The number of seconds (between 10 and 120) before data refresh operations time out. The default value is 60 minutes.

Unattended Service Account – Application ID In order for Visio Services to retrieve data from an external connection, it requires a Secure Store Service Application ID, which must be configured separately. See "Configuring the Secure Store Service Application," earlier in this chapter.

Configuring the Web Analytics Service Application

The Web Analytics Service is responsible for gathering and reporting site usage statistics such as the number of times a page has been viewed and the number of times a search term has been queried.

By default, the Web Analytics Service retains all statistics for 25 months. To reduce the data retention period:

1. From SharePoint 2010 Central Administration, under Application Management, click Manage Service Applications.

2. On the Manage Service Applications page, click the row for the Web Analytics Service application; then on the ribbon, click the Properties link.

3. Change the Data Retention Period value.

4. Click Next, and then click Next again.

Configuring the Word Automation Service Application

The Word Automation Service is designed to allow server-side processing of Word documents without the need to install Word components on the server. The application is multithreaded and scalable; it can be used to convert from one format to another and to perform text operations within documents.

Most of the default settings for the Word Automation Service are suitable for general use. If the service seems to be taking up too many resources on the server, you can adjust the settings lower.

1. From SharePoint 2010 Central Administration, under Application Management, click Manage Service Applications.

2. On the Manage Service Applications page, click the link for the Word Automation Services Application. The page shown in Figure 4.10 appears.

Figure 4.10: Word Automation Services page

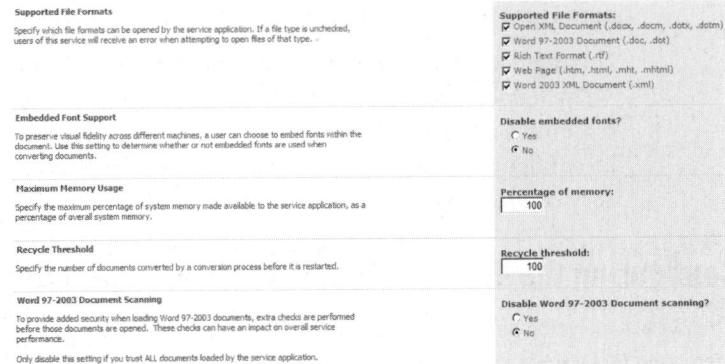

3. On the Word Automation Services page, configure the following settings:

Supported File Formats   Check the box for each file format that will be enabled. All formats are enabled by default.

Disable Embedded Fonts?   Choose whether to disable embedded fonts. Embedded fonts are disabled by default.

Percentage Of Memory   Enter the percentage of memory that can be used by the service. The default setting is 100 percent.

Recycle Threshold   Enter the number of documents that can be converted by a conversion process before it is restarted.

Disable Word 97-2003 Document Scanning?   To improve performance when processing older Word documents, you can choose to disable the automatic security scanning. Unlike the DOCX file format, the older Word format can contain embedded VBA code that could be executed by the Word Automation Service. The security scan prevents the execution of such code. Disabling the security scan may allow malicious code to execute.

Frequency With Which To Start Conversions (Minutes)   Enter the frequency with which groups of conversions are started. The default is 15.

Number Of Conversions To Start (Per Conversion Process)
Enter the number of conversions to start within each group. The default is 300.

Length Of Time Before Conversion Status Is Monitored (Minutes)   The length of time before conversions are monitored and, if necessary, restarted. The default is 5.

Maximum Conversion Attempts   The maximum number of times a conversion is attempted before its status is set to Failed. The default is 2.

4. Click OK.

Configuring the PowerPoint Service Application

The PowerPoint Service Application is new to SharePoint 2010 and supports several new features. As part of the Office Web Applications installation, the PowerPoint Service supports online viewing and editing of PowerPoint files. The service also provides the PowerPoint Broadcast feature, which delivers a PowerPoint presentation in a multicast mode.

To configure the application's settings, follow these steps:

1. From SharePoint 2010 Central Administration, under Application Management, click Manage Service Applications.

2. On the Manage Service Applications page, click the link for the PowerPoint Services Application.

3. On the PowerPoint Services page, configure the following settings:

    Supported File Formats   Check the boxes to enable Open XML Presentation (.pptx) and PowerPoint 97-2003 Presentation (.ppt).

    PowerPoint 97-2003 Presentation Scanning   Check the box to enable the scanning of earlier PowerPoint formats for dangerous content.

Configuring the Word Viewing Service Application

The Word Viewing Service is installed with the Office Web Applications and enables the online viewing and editing of Word documents in SharePoint. To change the settings, follow these steps:

1. From SharePoint 2010 Central Administration, under Application Management, click Manage Service Applications.

2. On the Manage Service Applications page, click the link for the PowerPoint Services Application.

3. On the PowerPoint Services page, configure the following settings:

   Supported File Formats   Check the boxes to enable Open XML Presentation (.docx) and Word 97-2003 Presentation (.doc).

   Disable Embedded Fonts?   Choose whether to disable embedded fonts.

   Disable Word 97-2003 Document Scanning?   To improve performance when processing older Word documents, you can choose to disable the automatic security scanning. Unlike the DOCX file format, the older Word format can contain embedded VBA code that could be executed by the Word Viewing Service. The security scan prevents the execution of such code. Disabling the security scan may allow malicious code to execute.

   Recycle Threshold   Enter the number of documents converted by a conversion process before it is restarted.

   Total Worker Processes   Enter the total number of worker processes dedicated to viewing Word documents. This value can range from 1 to 1,000 but the recommendation is for no more than two worker processes per core processor.

4. Click OK.

Associate Service Applications to Web Applications

Service applications can be connected to one or more web applications to provide the service functionality to site collections and sites. To change the service application associations, use the following steps:

1. From SharePoint 2010 Central Administration, click Application Management.

2. Under Service Applications, click Configure Service Application Associations.

3. Ensure that Web Applications is selected in the View drop-down list.

Associate Service Applications to Web Applications   141

4. Under the Application Proxy Group column, click the service application proxy group you want to edit.

5. In the Configure Service Application Associations dialog box, clear the check boxes to attach or detach service applications from this group. (See Figure 4.11.)

Figure 4.11: The Configure Service Application Associations dialog box

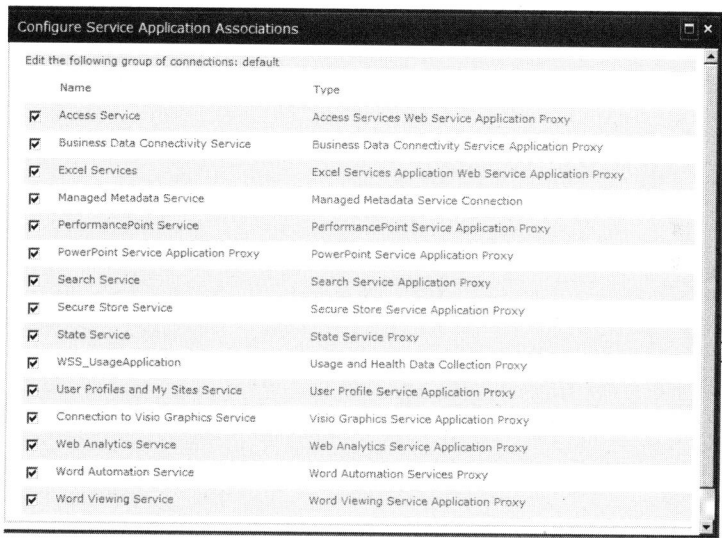

6. Click OK to save the settings.

5
Scaling and High Availability

IN THIS CHAPTER, YOU WILL LEARN TO:

UNDERSTAND FARM TOPOLOGIES (Pages 144 – 150)
- Understanding the Single-Server Farm (Page 145)
- Understanding the Two-Server Farm (Page 145)
- Understanding the Three-Server Farm (Page 146)
- Understanding the Medium-Server Farm (Page 147)
- Understanding the Large Farm (Page 148)

CONFIGURE SERVERS AND SERVICES (Pages 150 – 155)
- Adding and Removing Servers from a Farm (Page 150)
- Managing SharePoint Services (Page 153)

SCALE OUT WEB SERVERS (Pages 156 – 168)
- Configuring Windows-Based NLB (Page 157)
- Using a Hardware-Based Load Balancer (Page 165)
- Running Central Administration on Multiple Servers (Page 166)

SCALE OUT APPLICATION SERVERS (Pages 168 – 182)
- Understanding Cross-Farm Services (Page 169)
- Configuring Cross-Farm Services (Page 170)
- Scaling the Search Service (Page 175)

SCALE OUT DATABASE SERVERS (Pages 182 – 185)
- Adding New SQL Servers (Page 183)
- Scaling Using Database Mirroring (Page 184)
- Scaling Using Clustered SQL Servers (Page 185)

As a 64 bit-only platform, SharePoint does a great job of scaling up to some of the best hardware on the market today. However, scaling out by adding additional servers is usually necessary to achieve your goals, and this is where the greatest flexibility is. This chapter looks at common farm topologies, describes how to configure where services run, and explores how to scale each of the server roles: WFE, application, and database.

Understand Farm Topologies

SharePoint is an enormously flexible platform, allowing you to use many combinations when allocating services across the servers. When you are architecting any system's topology, there are always two principal goals that you should consider: performance and high availability. How responsive does it need to be? How available does it need to be? As much as possible, it's best to quantify these requirements as they become part of your solution's service level agreement (SLA).

Designing the right topology for a SharePoint farm is both an art and a science. The process involves many variables, such as user count, anticipated load per user, stakeholder expectations, business continuity requirements, budget, security, and government regulations—not to mention the ubiquitous CPU, RAM, disk, and network factors.

Despite these complexities, some fairly standard topologies are commonly found in SharePoint farms. They are good starting points for the architectural process. Five such designs are shared in this section.

Fortunately, the implementation of the topology is fairly trivial, once you understand how SharePoint works. Between Central Administration and PowerShell, you can quickly and easily deploy the services as needed.

When designing your farm's topology, bear in mind that farm servers are intended to be in close proximity, usually in the same datacenter. This could mean that multiple farms are needed.

> **NOTE** Before officially selecting the topology, consider staging the different designs and performing various tests, including load and stress testing. That way, you have quantitative, empirical proof that this design will meet your requirements.

Understanding the Single-Server Farm

A single-server farm is one server where all three roles—web front end (WFE), application server, and database server—run on the same machine. This type of farm is usually only found in development or evaluation environments. See Figure 5.1.

Figure 5.1: Single-server farm

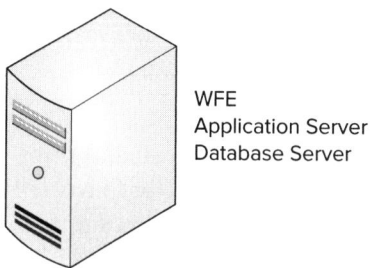

The single-server farm can be a stand-alone farm (as covered in Chapter 1, "Installing SharePoint 2010")—one that can never be scaled out to additional servers. A single-server farm could also be a complete server farm that is running SQL Server locally. Either way, a single-server farm is rarely recommended for a production environment, unless the user count is very small (less than 100) and high availability is not needed.

Understanding the Two-Server Farm

In a two-server farm, one server is the WFE and application server, and the database server is placed on its own dedicated machine. A two-server farm is the smallest size farm that can be easily scaled to larger farms. This makes it a common starting point for new farms that begin as pilots or at the department level but are expected to grow in size.

A dedicated database server increases performance dramatically. With scaled-up hardware, a two-server farm may be able to support as many as 10,000 users. But it does not provide any fault tolerance. See Figure 5.2.

Figure 5.2: Two-server farm

Understanding the Three-Server Farm

In a three-server farm, the database server should be dedicated. A three-server farm can be designed in two primary ways. The options involve where to run the WFE and application server roles. For environments with somewhat heavy web requests that need some fault tolerance, it is common to go with a design like the one in Figure 5.3, with two servers running as a WFE and as an application server. The WFE servers are network load balanced, adding performance and fault tolerance. Application services, in particular query services, can be run on both WFE servers to ensure an even distribution of work.

Figure 5.3: Three-server farm with load balancing

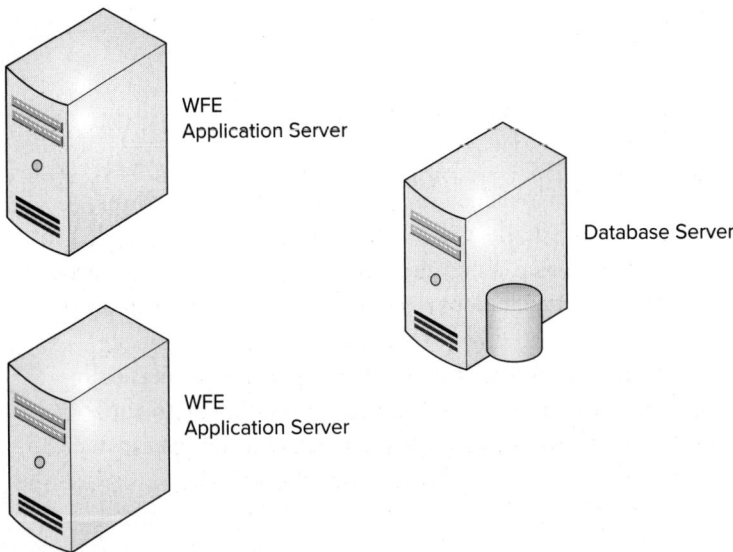

Another option is to separate out the three tiers (WFE, application server, and database server) onto three separate servers, as shown in Figure 5.4. Although this approach is a bit easier to implement than the design with two WFE servers, it is advantageous only if you have heavy application service requests—for instance, Excel Calculation Services—that require a dedicated server. No fault tolerance exists in this design, but fault tolerance can be achieved by adding another WFE, application server, or database server.

Figure 5.4: Three-server farm with dedicated roles

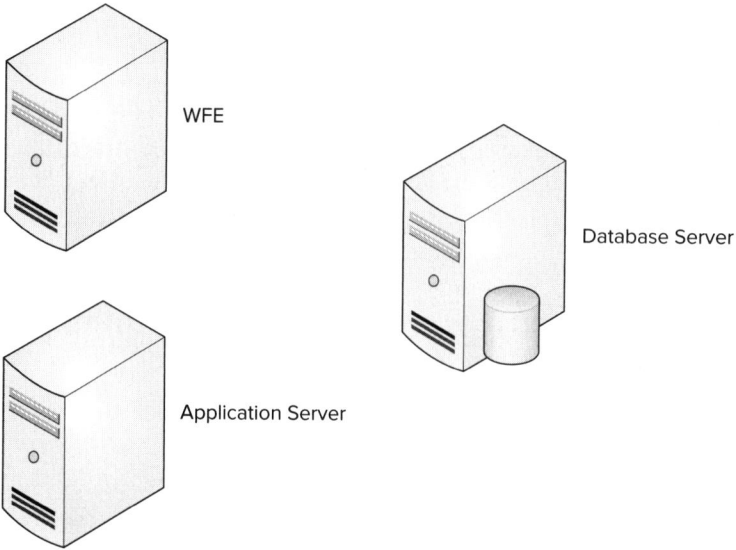

Understanding the Medium-Server Farm

A medium-server farm can exist in many configurations and sizes. In most cases, a medium-server farm uses separate, dedicated servers for each of the three roles: WFE, application server, and database server. How many servers run each role will vary depending on the usage, along with performance and fault tolerance requirements.

Assuming that search is a major component (and it is in most farms), the query and crawl services associated with search are typically put on their own group of servers. You'll learn more about scaling search in the section "Scaling the Search Service" later in this chapter.

Figure 5.5 shows one design for a medium-server farm. A farm of this type can scale up to perhaps as many as 30,000 users, but the most noticeable drawback is the lack of fault tolerance in the database role, making it a single point of failure.

Figure 5.5: Medium-server farm

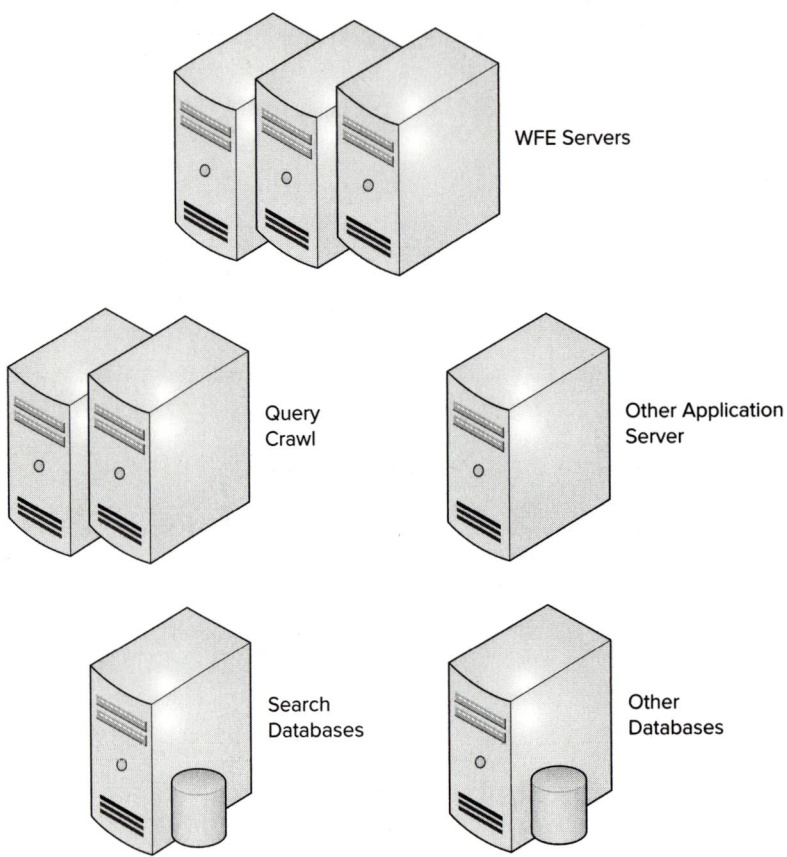

Understanding the Large Farm

A large SharePoint farm extends the concept of the medium-server farm by adding more servers in areas where they are needed. In fact, this need is not usually known when drafting the design on paper. In most cases, a large farm starts out as a small or medium farm and just keeps growing. For example, if heavy Visio Services usage becomes a bottleneck, you can dedicate Visio Services to its own application server.

Again, scaling by adding new servers is done to achieve performance and high-availability goals. You'll learn more details about achieving these two goals for each of these server roles in later sections of this chapter.

> **TIP** If performance is your primary goal, it is best to first scale up the server (such as adding RAM) before scaling out to new servers.

As you scale to a large farm, here are some general guidelines to keep in mind:

- A single WFE can usually handle no more than 10,000 users. For heavy, concurrent users, this number can quickly drop to fewer than 2,000 per WFE.
- For performance reasons, do not allocate more than four WFE servers for each database server.
- For medium or large farms, keep servers dedicated to a single role—that is, do not have servers that are both a WFE and an application server.
- Do not install non-SharePoint-related software, services, or databases on SharePoint servers.
- Keep database servers dedicated to a single farm.
- As much as possible, servers of the same role type—in particular WFE servers that are load balanced or clustered/mirrored SQL servers—should have nearly identical hardware.
- Virtualization is supported by Microsoft across all three roles, but virtualizing database servers has the greatest impact on performance.
- For performance reasons, WFE and application servers should be on the same physical network or virtual local area network (VLAN).
- Keep all servers with like roles on either physical or virtual hardware. For example, if you will have three WFE servers and two

application servers, all three WFE servers should be either physical or virtual.
- Setting up database mirroring or clusters in SQL Server does not increase performance.

> **NOTE** All servers in a farm should be co-located in near proximity, usually in the same datacenter. Whether servers not on the same physical LAN can work together depends on the performance and latency of the network. In most cases the network speed should be at least 1 Gbps with a ping latency of 1 ms or less.

Configure Servers and Services

This section covers how to add and remove servers from the farm and configure services to run on servers. The flexibility of SharePoint's services model allows you to grow a farm from just 2 servers to a large farm with over 20 servers.

Adding and Removing Servers from a Farm

Adding a server to a farm is done just after the SharePoint installation is finished. This process is covered in detail in Chapter 1, but here is a quick recap of the steps:

1. Log into the server using the domain install account.
2. Install prerequisites.
3. Install SharePoint binaries.
4. Apply service packs and/or cumulative updates to match the farm build.
5. Install language packs, if needed.
6. Install any other software components such as Office Web Apps that are running on other servers in the farm.
7. If this server will become a WFE, manually install any custom code that is not deployed by a solution package. To learn more about solution packages, see Chapter 6, "Configuring System Settings."

8. Run the SharePoint 2010 Products Configuration Wizard or `PSConfig.exe` to join an existing farm. Be sure to have the passphrase that you set when creating the farm.

Once the server is added, you are ready to begin configuring services for it. To view all the servers in the farm, go into Central Administration, select System Settings, and click Manage Servers In This Farm. See Figure 5.6.

Figure 5.6: Servers in a farm

Farm Information				
Configuration database version:	14.0.4762.1000			
Configuration database server:	sql.hawmetal.com			
Configuration database name:	Config			

Server	SharePoint Products Installed	Services Running	Status	Remove Server
MAIL.HAWMETAL.COM		Not Configured	No Action Required	Remove Server
RAW-APP1	Microsoft SharePoint Server 2010 Microsoft® Office Web Apps	Microsoft SharePoint Foundation Incoming E-Mail Microsoft SharePoint Foundation Workflow Timer Service SharePoint Server Search	No Action Required	Remove Server
RAW-WFE1	Microsoft SharePoint Server 2010 Microsoft® Office Web Apps	Central Administration Managed Metadata Web Service Microsoft SharePoint Foundation Incoming E-Mail Microsoft SharePoint Foundation Sandboxed Code Service Microsoft SharePoint Foundation Web Application Microsoft SharePoint Foundation Workflow Timer Service Search Query and Site Settings Service Secure Store Service SharePoint Server Search User Profile Service	No Action Required	Remove Server
RAW-WFE2	Microsoft SharePoint Server 2010 Microsoft® Office Web Apps	Microsoft SharePoint Foundation Incoming E-Mail Microsoft SharePoint Foundation Web Application Microsoft SharePoint Foundation Workflow Timer Service Search Query and Site Settings Service SharePoint Server Search	No Action Required	Remove Server
SQL.HAWMETAL.COM		Microsoft SharePoint Foundation Database	No Action Required	Remove Server

NOTE You do not directly add database servers to a farm or remove them from a farm. When you create a database on a different SQL server, SharePoint automatically adds the server and it appears in the list shown in Figure 5.6. You can always recognize a database server since the Services Running column lists the Microsoft SharePoint Foundation Database service. Mail servers that have been configured as outbound SMTP servers are listed as Not Configured. (See mail.hawmetal.com in Figure 5.6 for an example.)

To remove a server from the farm, you should run either the Configuration Wizard or `PSConfig.exe` on that server. Using one of these methods ensures that IIS websites, along with Registry and other local settings on that server, are properly removed.

To remove a server from a farm using the Configuration Wizard:

1. Log into the server using the domain install account.
2. Start the Configuration Wizard (Start ➣ All Programs ➣ Microsoft SharePoint 2010 Products ➣ SharePoint 2010 Products Configuration Wizard).
3. Click Next on the welcome screen.
4. Acknowledge the message that services will be stopped.
5. When prompted, choose Disconnect From This Server Farm, as shown in Figure 5.7.

Figure 5.7: Disconnecting a server from a farm

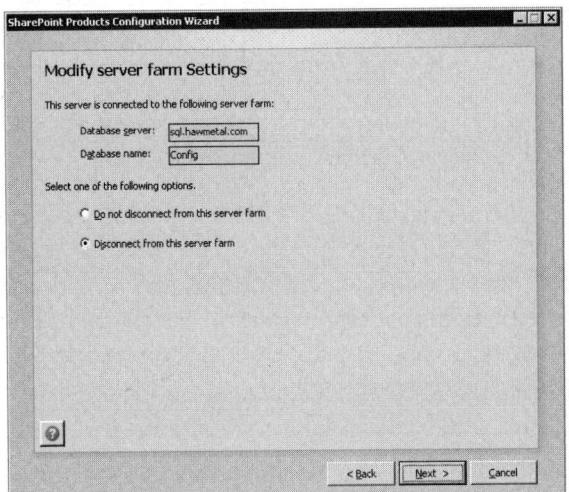

6. Acknowledge the warning and the server is then removed.

If the configuration database is not accessible, you will get an initial error message when trying to remove the server. Despite this, you can still remove the server, but the configuration database is not updated. To update the farm later, click the Remove Server link in the Farm Information table, as shown in Figure 5.6.

The Remove Server link can also be used to forcibly remove a server from a farm if the server is offline (due to a crash, for instance).

To remove a server using PSConfig.exe, follow these steps:

1. Log into the server using the domain install account.
2. Locate PSConfig.exe in the following folder: Program Files\Common Files\Microsoft Shared\Web Server Extensions\14\bin and issue the following command:

   psconfig -cmd configdb -disconnect

Once removed, the server can be rejoined to the farm or joined to a separate farm.

> **NOTE** Removing a server from the farm does not uninstall the SharePoint binaries or any other software from the server. To uninstall SharePoint from a server, open Control Panel and select Add Or Remove Programs.

Managing SharePoint Services

A SharePoint service is similar to a Windows service (in fact, some *are* Windows services) and dictates what role (i.e., WFE or application server) and specific functions a particular server has. The services installed vary depending on whether SharePoint Foundation, SharePoint Server Standard, or SharePoint Server Enterprise has been installed. Other services become available if additional software has been installed. For example, if Office Web Apps or Project Server 2010 is installed on the farm, new services are created.

> **TIP** Do not confuse services with service applications. When you create or delete a service application, the list of services installed is not affected. For example, you will have a Business Data Connectivity service installed whether or not you have created a Business Data Connectivity service application. If you plan on using the Business Data Connectivity service in a farm, you create the service application, associate it to a web application, and then start the service on the server(s) in the farm that should run this service application. Furthermore, not all service applications have a matching SharePoint service. For more information on service applications, see Chapter 4, "Creating Service Applications."

Once a new server joins an existing farm, these three services are automatically started:

- Microsoft SharePoint Foundation Web Application
- Microsoft SharePoint Foundation Workflow Timer Service
- Microsoft SharePoint Foundation Incoming Email

The Microsoft SharePoint Foundation Web Application service tells SharePoint that this server is a WFE. Therefore, by default, any new server added to a farm is assumed to be a WFE. If this server should be a dedicated application server instead, you need to stop this Web Application service, as described in the next section.

For a description of each built-in service and advice on whether it should be run on a WFE or application server, download a SharePoint 2010 topology diagram from the "Topologies for SharePoint Server 2010" page at the Microsoft Download Center:

    www.microsoft.com/downloads/en/details.aspx?FamilyID=fd686cbb-8401-4f25-b65e-3ce7aa7dbeab

Viewing Installed Services

To view the list of installed services from Central Administration, select System Settings and choose Manage Services On Server. Figure 5.8 shows a list of some of the installed services that are part of SharePoint Server Enterprise.

Figure 5.8: Viewing installed SharePoint services

Service	Status	Action
Access Database Service	Stopped	Start
Application Registry Service	Stopped	Start
Business Data Connectivity Service	Stopped	Start
Central Administration	Started	Stop
Claims to Windows Token Service	Stopped	Start
Document Conversions Launcher Service	Stopped	Start
Document Conversions Load Balancer Service	Stopped	Start
Excel Calculation Services	Stopped	Start
Lotus Notes Connector	Stopped	Start
Managed Metadata Web Service	Started	Stop
Microsoft SharePoint Foundation Incoming E-Mail	Started	Stop
Microsoft SharePoint Foundation Sandboxed Code Service	Started	Stop
Microsoft SharePoint Foundation Subscription Settings Service	Stopped	Start
Microsoft SharePoint Foundation Web Application	Started	Stop
Microsoft SharePoint Foundation Workflow Timer Service	Started	Stop

Server: RAW-WFE1   View: Configurable

> **NOTE** If you are not a local Windows administrator on the server that is running Central Administration, you will not have the Manage Services On Server link. Only local administrators who are also farm administrators can view and adjust service settings.

Starting and Stopping a SharePoint Service

The Services On Server screen (Figure 5.8) is used to start and stop a SharePoint service from Central Administration. Here are the steps to start or stop a service:

1. Go to System Settings and select Manage Services On Server.
2. Choose the correct server from the Server drop-down.
3. To start or stop a service, click Start or Stop in the Action column. Depending on the service, you may need to provide additional configuration settings when you start a service.
4. If you are stopping a service, you must confirm the action.

> **WARNING** Although this seems to work just like starting and stopping a Windows service, there is an important distinction. When stopping a SharePoint service, you are not just stopping the service but also removing the service's configuration settings. For example, if you stop the Microsoft SharePoint Foundation Web Application service, IIS websites are removed and local IIS website folders are deleted. Because of this, be sure you stop services carefully and always make sure you have selected the correct server!

Configuring a SharePoint Service

Some services can also be configured from the Services On Server screen. For instance, you can click on Document Conversions Load Balancer Service to set which server the document conversion load balancer runs on. Other services are not configurable and cannot be started or stopped. By default, they are hidden, but you can show them by changing the View drop-down.

Scale Out Web Servers

Scaling out refers to adding additional servers to increase performance, fault tolerance, or both. Scaling out the WFE role is done by using a load balancer. Load balancing works by pooling two or more servers together so that they appear to be, and function as, a single server. When a client request comes in, the load balancer intercepts the request and intelligently routes it to one of the available servers. (See Figure 5.9.) No special software is needed on the client because the load balancing is done on the back end. Load balancing is also transparent to users. Load balancing web servers is an active/active design, meaning that all servers are actively processing requests. This increases both performance and availability. It also simplifies server maintenance since you can pull a server (or node) out of the cluster when applying updates without bringing down the farm.

Figure 5.9: Two-node load-balancing cluster

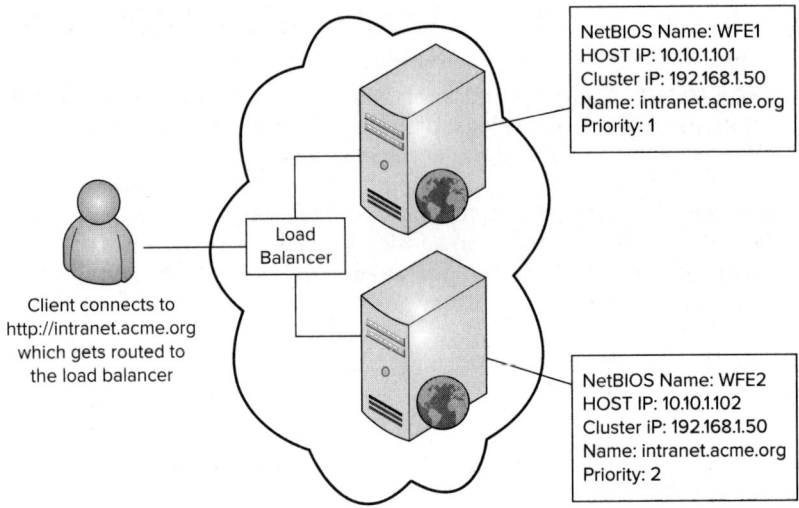

Each node in a load-balancing cluster is a self-contained server and not dependent on any other node. To simplify configuration and ensure a consistent experience for users, it is best to have identical hardware for each server node.

There are two main ways to implement load balancing to scale the WFE role:

- Microsoft's Network Load Balancing (NLB) software built into Windows Server provides basic load balancing. This chapter focuses primarily on Microsoft's NLB solution.
- Hardware or external load balancers run on dedicated devices. While more costly, they usually have more features and deliver better performance.

Configuring Windows-Based NLB

Windows Server has supported NLB for many versions and the software continues to improve. Although NLB will never surpass a hardware load balancer in total features or raw performance, it is a good solution for smaller-sized farms that have simple requirements and limited budgets.

When configuring NLB, it is best to have at least two network interface cards (NICs) in each server, whether physical or virtual. It is technically possible to use a single NIC, but performance can suffer. NICs can be teamed—just be sure to have at least two teams.

When configuring a Windows-based NLB, follow these four primary steps (as detailed in subsequent sections):

1. Configure the network interfaces for each WFE server.
2. Install the Windows NLB software on each WFE.
3. Create the NLB cluster, which adds the first node into the cluster.
4. Add additional nodes to the cluster.

> **NOTE** Do not confuse an NLB cluster with Microsoft Cluster Service, which is used to cluster the operating system. These are completely different technologies that, unfortunately, use the same term.

Configuring WFE Servers

Before you create an NLB cluster and add servers to it, there are some preliminary steps you must complete to prepare the web servers:

1. Get SharePoint installed and have each server join the farm.

2. Since this is a WFE, make sure that the Microsoft SharePoint Foundation Web Application service is running. Other application services can be run, such as Search Query, but they are not managed by NLB. (SharePoint separately handles the load balancing of all application services.) If you choose to run application services on the WFE, each WFE server should run the same set of services.

3. Prepare the NICs. Each card plays a different role:

    Host (Dedicated) Interface Used for normal network communication to other servers on the network. For instance, the WFE queries the database server. Ensure that the host NIC is configured properly with a static IP address.

    Cluster Interface Intended exclusively for NLB traffic. The cluster NIC's IP address and subnet mask will be set when you add the server to the cluster, so this can be left unconfigured for now.

> **TIP** It is useful to rename your network interfaces to something more user-friendly. For example, you can name one **host interface** and the other **cluster interface**. Doing so makes the configuration easier and helps ensure you do not mix them up. You can rename the interfaces on the Network Connections screen found inside Control Panel.

Installing NLB

NLB software and drivers must be added to each WFE server before it can join the cluster. While NLB is built into Windows Server, it's not usually installed by default. Here are the steps to install it:

1. Log in with an administrative account and start Server Manager (Start ➢ All Programs ➢ Administrative Tools ➢ Server Manager).
2. In the navigation panel on the left, click Features.
3. In the right panel, click Add Features.
4. From the list, select Network Load Balancing and click Next.
5. Click Install and wait for the installation to complete. You normally do not have to reboot.

Creating the NLB Cluster

Clusters are created and managed using the Network Load Balancing Manager. This feature exists in both GUI and command-line form (nlb.exe). These steps walk you through creating the cluster by using the GUI:

1. Log in with an administrative account on the server that will become the first node in the cluster.

2. Start Network Load Balancing Manager (Start ➢ All Programs ➢ Administrative Tools ➢ Network Load Balancing Manager).

3. Click Cluster ➢ New.

4. On the Connect page, enter the name of the server you just logged into and click Connect.

5. Under Interfaces Available For Configuring A New Cluster, choose the one that is designated for the cluster, as shown in Figure 5.10. Click Next. If DHCP is enabled on this interface, you will see a warning that it will be turned off.

Figure 5.10: Select the cluster interface

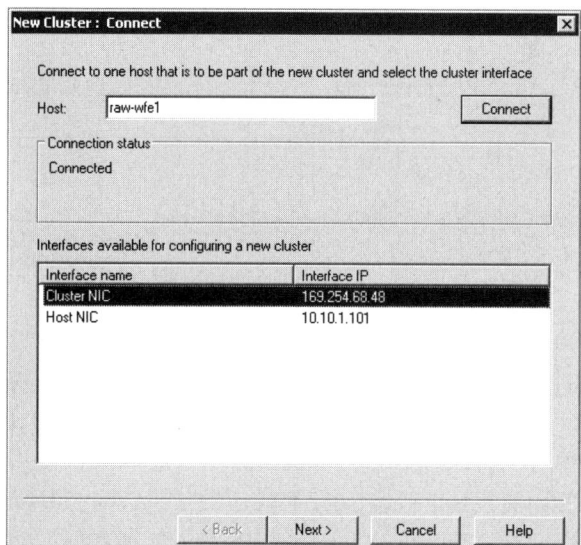

6. On the Host Parameters page, confirm that Priority is set to 1. The priority is a unique number placed on each server in the cluster. The server with the smallest number will receive all incoming requests if a port rule does not exist (you'll create a port rule in a later step).

7. Enter a dedicated IP address for the cluster NIC, as shown in Figure 5.11. This address should be on the same subnet as the cluster address that is assigned in the next step. You need the address to enable communication from one NLB host to the other on the cluster subnet. Click Next.

Figure 5.11: Configuring host parameters

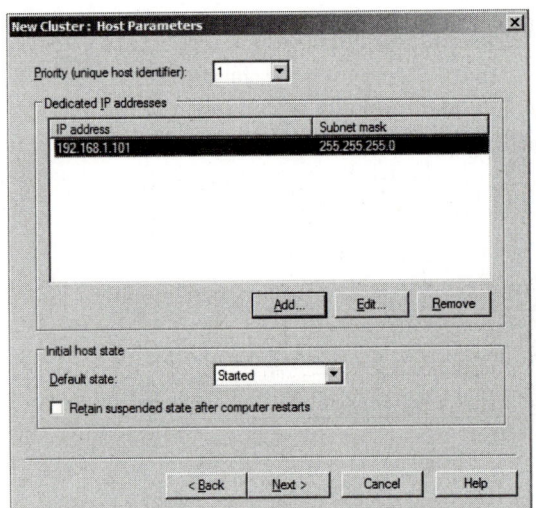

8. On the Cluster IP Addresses page, click Add.

9. Enter the cluster IP address you want to use. You can add multiple addresses for a single cluster. When you're done, it should resemble Figure 5.12. Click Next.

10. On the Cluster Parameters page (Figure 5.13), in the Full Internet Name field, enter the fully qualified domain name for each IP address—for example, `intranet.acme.org`. This name should be

resolvable using Domain Name System (DNS) and match the public URL for the SharePoint web application.

Figure 5.12: Defining cluster IP addresses

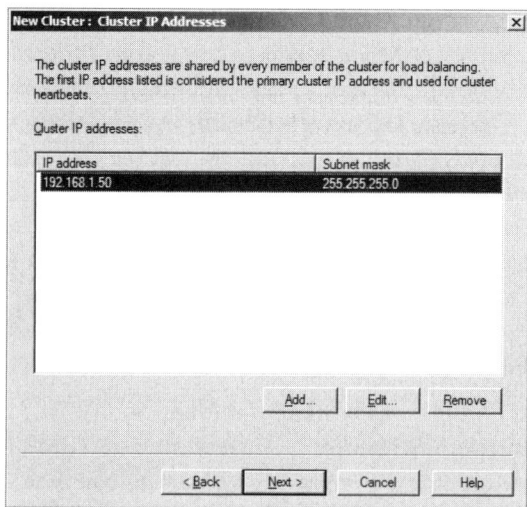

Figure 5.13: Setting cluster parameters

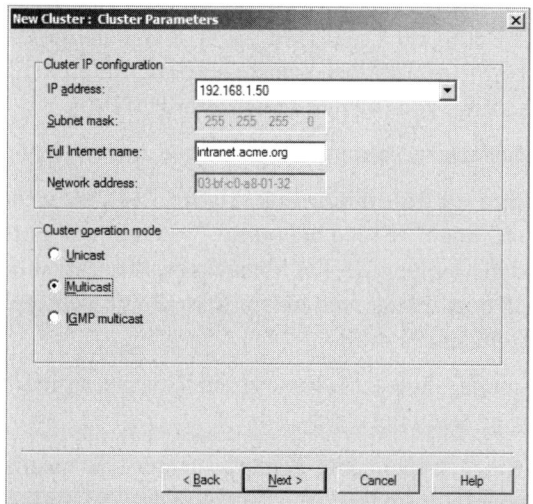

11. Choose the cluster operation mode. You have three choices: Unicast, Multicast, or Internet Group Management Protocol (IGMP) Multicast. Your best choice depends on your network infrastructure; here is a brief summary:

    Unicast   This mode is intended to be simple and is compatible with most routers and switches. It works by replacing the clustered NIC's MAC (media access control) address. However, unicast can create a port-flooding problem with switches. This issue occurs when traffic directed to the cluster goes to all ports on the switch and not just the cluster hosts. This problem can be solved in many ways, but the easiest fix is to place a hub between the WFE servers and the switch. Unicast is not recommended if you're using VMware or if you have only a single NIC. To use Unicast with Hyper-V in Windows Server 2008 R2, make sure that the cluster NIC is configured to allow spoofing of the MAC address.

    Multicast   This mode works by adding a multicast MAC address to the cluster NIC, retaining the card's MAC address. Multicast is compatible with a single network card, but two are recommended for better performance. As with Unicast, port-flooding problems can result when you choose this setting.

    IGMP Multicast   This option solves the port-flooding problem by creating a multicast group membership, thereby filtering traffic to noncluster hosts on the same switch. To use this setting, your switch must support IGMP.

12. Click Next after you've configured the cluster operation mode.
13. In the Add/Edit Port Rule dialog box (Figure 5.14), enter the TCP/UDP ports that should be load balanced. By default, all ports are load balanced in a single rule. For SharePoint, this port should match the TCP port that is used for the SharePoint web application (typically 80 and/or 443).
14. For Filtering mode, choose Multiple Host. This means that load-balanced routing is in effect.
15. For Affinity, Single is the recommended setting. This means that subsequent requests from the same client are directed to the same server. Single affinity is also called sticky sessions. Click OK when you're finished configuring the port rule.

Figure 5.14: Setting up a port rule

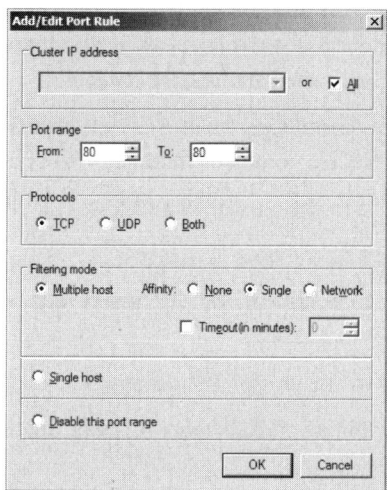

16. Click Finish to create the cluster and configure the first node. This process may take up to a minute to complete. The configuration is shown in the Network Load Balancing Manager log (Figure 5.15). When the process is finished, the status of the host should show as Converged when you select the cluster name (e.g., intranet.acme.org).

Figure 5.15: Cluster with one server node

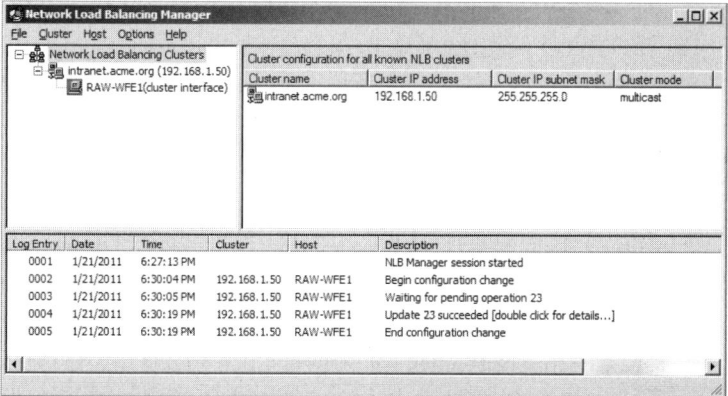

17. Open Control Panel and, on the Network Connections screen, add a default gateway and DNS address to the cluster NIC. The NLB Manager does not add these settings. Now is also a good time to confirm that the IP address settings are correct.

Once the cluster is created, you should perform a variety of tests to ensure everything is working. Here are some combinations to try:

- Ping from an external client to the cluster IP address.
- Ping from an external client to the host IP address.
- Ping from the WFE server to hosts outside the cluster (e.g., the database server).
- Ping from the WFE server to the cluster IP address.
- Test the SharePoint web application to be sure it is still functioning.

Adding Nodes to the Cluster

Adding nodes to the cluster is much easier than creating a cluster. You can add nodes to the cluster from the first server, or you can run NLB Manager on the server to be added. Either way, here are the steps:

1. Start Network Load Balancing Manager.
2. Click Cluster ➢ Connect To Existing and enter the server name that is the first node in the cluster (added in the previous section).
3. Right-click the cluster and select Add Host To Cluster.
4. Enter the server name of the new server you want to add. If you do not have administrative access to this server, you are prompted for credentials.
5. Select the cluster interface on the server and click Next. If DHCP is enabled on this interface, you will get a notice that it will be turned off.
6. Specify the priority for this node.
7. Enter a dedicated IP address for the cluster NIC. This should be on the same subnet as the cluster address but different from other dedicated IP addresses already assigned to other nodes. Click Next.
8. The existing port rules are shown. Click Finish to add the node. This process may take up to a minute to complete. When it finishes, the status of the host should show as Converged. See Figure 5.16.

Figure 5.16: Cluster with two server nodes

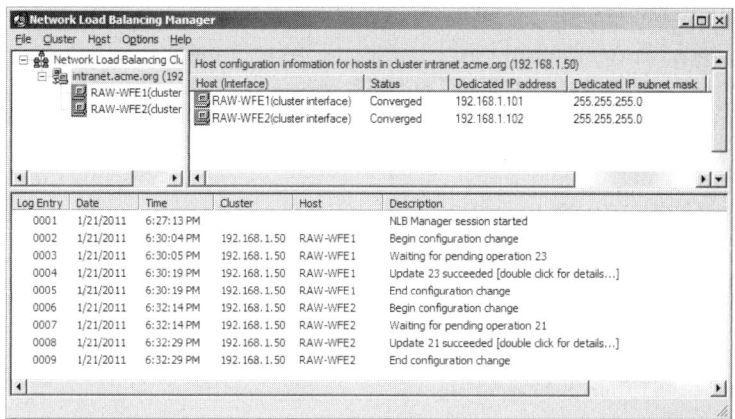

9. Manually add a default gateway and DNS address to the cluster NIC.

Once the host is added, perform the following tests:

- Ping from an external client to the cluster IP address.
- Ping from an external client to the host IP address.
- Ping from WFE server to hosts outside the cluster (e.g., the database server).
- Ping from the WFE server to the cluster IP address.
- Ping from the WFE server to the host IP address of other WFE servers.
- Test the SharePoint web application to be sure it is still functioning.
- For the *real* test, bring down each WFE one by one to be sure the NLB cluster is working correctly.

Using a Hardware-Based Load Balancer

For larger farms or those with more demanding performance requirements, a hardware-based load balancer may be a better solution than Microsoft's built-in NLB. Many vendors provide solutions; F5 and Cisco are two of the leading vendors.

NOTE Microsoft's Forefront Unified Access Gateway (UAG) can also do load balancing. For more information, see www.microsoft.com/uag.

Here are advantages of hardware load balancers compared to Microsoft NLB:

- More intelligent load balancing, in particular, for detecting application layer (HTTP) outages (when, for example, the server is still online, but IIS has stopped)
- Many more options when configuring load-balancing rules
- More scalable and better suited for heavily used applications
- Can often be combined with web accelerator technologies to further improve performance

There are also some disadvantages:

- More costly solution
- May be more complex to configure, requiring specialized knowledge of the product
- Single point of failure if the load balancer doesn't have redundancy

Running Central Administration on Multiple Servers

As a general recommendation, you should run the Central Administration Web Application on more than one server in your farm. This approach gives you added protection in case the primary server is down and you need to do essential maintenance. To add Central Administration to a second server, follow these steps:

1. Log into the server using the domain installer account.
2. Start the Configuration Wizard (Start ➢ All Programs ➢ Microsoft SharePoint 2010 Products ➢ SharePoint 2010 Products Configuration Wizard.
3. Click Next and acknowledge the warning.
4. When prompted, do not disconnect the server from the farm. Click Next.
5. On the Completing page, click the Advanced Settings button.
6. Select the option "Use this machine to host the web site."
7. Click OK.
8. Click Next to apply the changes.

At this point, Central Administration has been configured on this new server. However, there are two related problems. If you launch

Central Administration from the Start menu, it will always go to the first (original) server. SharePoint will also redirect you to the first server if you try to run Central Administration directly by using the URL of the second server in the browser.

To fix the first problem when running Central Administration from the Start menu, follow these steps:

1. Log into the second server and start Registry Editor (Start ➢ Run, and type **regedit**).

2. Navigate to the following key: HKEY_LOCAL_MACHINE ➢ Software ➢ Microsoft ➢ Shared Tools ➢ Web Server Extensions ➢ 14.0 ➢ WSS.

3. Edit the CentralAdministrationURL value and replace it with the http://ServerName:Port address of the second server (for example, http://wfe2:11111).

To fix the second problem where requests are automatically redirected to the first server, you need to edit the public URLs for the Central Administration Web Application. Here are the steps:

1. Start Central Administration.

2. Click System Settings, and then choose Configure Alternate Access Mappings.

3. Under Alternate Access Mapping Collection, select the Central Administration Web Application.

4. Click Edit Public URLs.

5. For any of the other zones, enter the http://ServerName:Port address. Your screen should resemble Figure 5.17.

Figure 5.17: Adding a public URL for Central Administration

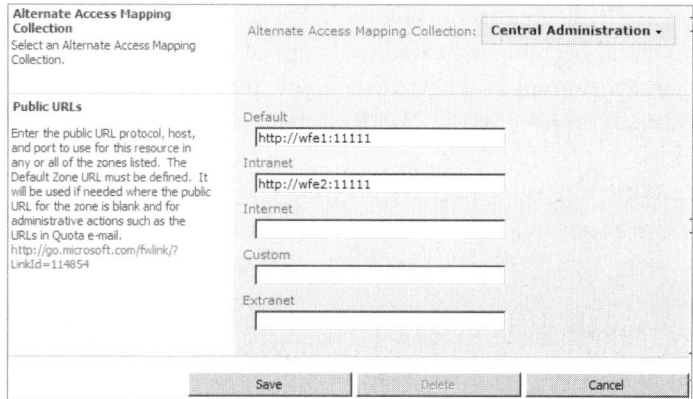

> **WARNING** Adjusting the alternate access mappings in this way will not work if you are using Kerberos authentication on the Central Administration Web Application. See "SharePoint Central Administration: High Availability, Load Balancing, Security & General Recommendations" at www.harbar.net/articles/spca.aspx for a workaround and more details on configuring Central Administration on multiple servers.

Scale Out Application Servers

Scaling the application tier is incredibly flexible when you're working with SharePoint's application services. In the context of this chapter, scaling application services involves these two areas:

- Improving performance and availability by running multiple service instances
- Consuming application services from other farms

Improving performance and availability is easily achieved in a multi-server farm by starting the appropriate services as needed on the farm servers. The load balancing is provided automatically by SharePoint. For example, if two servers are running the Excel Calculation Services service, requests are automatically distributed to both in an active/active design. If one server goes offline, the other server processes all the requests.

As the number of farm servers increases, try to work toward having only dedicated servers for each of the three roles. That is, WFE servers are dedicated to being web application servers; application servers are dedicated to running application services; and, as always, database servers are dedicated to running SQL Server. What the server count is when servers become dedicated will depend on your requirements, but in general this point is reached when you approach the medium-server farm size, as covered in the "Understand Farm Topologies" section earlier.

In addition to providing very scalable application services within one farm, SharePoint supports consuming application services from other farms. How this works and is configured is covered in the next two sections.

Understanding Cross-Farm Services

While a single farm can scale to support tens of thousands of users, it is not always practical to deploy everything in just a single farm. Recall that all farm servers must be in close proximity, usually in one datacenter. For multinational firms that have large teams located around the globe, one farm is not feasible. Many opt for deploying a farm in each major region. Some of the benefits include faster performance, improved business continuity, less bandwidth consumed, and the ability to decentralize farm administration tasks.

When multiple farms are deployed, there is often a need to share application services among farms. For example, all farms must use a single User Profile service application. SharePoint supports cross-farm services, which enables one farm to call into services made available by another farm. However, this feature is not supported for all service applications. The following is a list of built-in service applications that can be shared cross-farm (all others can only be used in a single farm):

- Business Data Connectivity
- Search
- Managed Metadata
- Secure Store
- User Profile
- Web Analytics

The farm that is making a service available is called the publishing farm. The farm that is requesting service is called the consuming farm. One farm can be both a publishing farm and a consuming farm, just not on the same service application.

> **NOTE** A valid topology for environments with multiple farms is to have one farm that is dedicated to providing one or more service applications to other farms. For example, to implement an enterprise-wide search solution, a dedicated search farm can be deployed that publishes search services to multiple consuming farms.

Configuring Cross-Farm Services

There are four primary steps to enable and configure cross-farm services:

1. Configure a trust relationship between farms.
2. Configure a publishing farm.
3. Publish a service application.
4. Consume a service application.

All of these steps can be configured using PowerShell, and some of them must be done using PowerShell. Since this is not something that is usually scripted, those steps that can be done using Central Administration are shown that way.

Configuring a Trust Relationship Between Farms

Before any service applications can be published, a trust relationship must be established between the publishing and consuming farm. Despite the term "trust," do not confuse this with an Active Directory (AD) trust relationship. The trust relationship between farms is specific to SharePoint, and farms in separate AD domains or forests can trust each other. However, some service applications, such as User Profile, also require an AD domain-level trust relationship to be in place. For more details on AD trust relationships, see the article "Share Service Applications Across Farms" at http://technet.microsoft.com/en-us/library/ff621100.aspx

To create a relationship between publisher and consumer, root certificates on each farm must be exchanged with each other. Also, the Security Token Service (STS) certificate from the consuming farm must be installed on the publishing farm. Doing so allows requests to be authenticated and passed securely between farms.

Some of these steps of this task require PowerShell and some can be done with Central Administration. In the steps that follow, Central Administration is shown where it can be used. When using PowerShell, the command can be run from any server in the farm.

1. On the consuming farm, export the root certificate from a server. Here is the PowerShell script:

    ```
    $rootCert = (Get-SPCertificateAuthority).RootCertificate
    $rootCert.Export("Cert") | ↵
    Set-Content <C:\ConsumingRoot.cer> -Encoding byte
    ```

    Replace <C:\ConsumingRoot.cer> with the filename path to where you want the file saved.

2. On the consuming farm, export the STS certificate using the following PowerShell script:

```
$stsCert = (Get-SPSecurityTokenServiceConfig).
LocalLoginProvider.SigningCertificate
$stsCert.Export("Cert") |
Set-Content <C:\ConsumingSTS.cer> -Encoding byte
```

3. On the publishing farm, export the root certificate using the following PowerShell script:

```
$rootCert = (Get-SPCertificateAuthority).RootCertificate
$rootCert.Export("Cert") |
Set-Content <C:\PublishingRoot.cer> -Encoding byte
```

4. Copy these files so that a server on the publishing farm has the two consuming farm certificates, and one server on the consuming farm has the one publishing farm certificate.

5. On the publishing farm, import the two certificates from the consuming farm. In Central Administration, click Security, then click Manage Trust.

6. In the ribbon, click New.

7. The Establish Trust Relationship dialog box appears (Figure 5.18). For Name, enter a friendly name for the consuming farm (e.g., Europe Consumer).

Figure 5.18: Create a trust relationship on the publishing farm

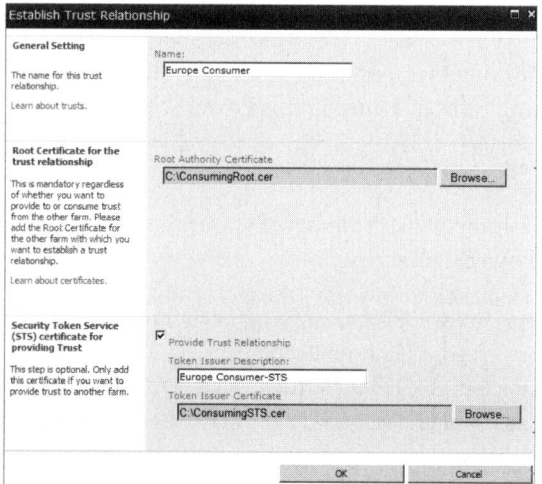

8. For Root Authority Certificate, select the root certificate file from the consuming farm (i.e., `ConsumingRoot.cer`).

9. For Token Issuer Description, enter a friendly name for the consuming farm STS (e.g., Europe Consumer-STS).

10. For Token Issuer Certificate, select the STS certificate from the consumer farm (i.e., `ConsumingSTS.cer`).

11. Click OK to save.

12. On the consuming farm, import the root certificate from the publishing farm. In Central Administration, click Security, then click Manage Trust.

13. In the ribbon, click New.

14. For Name, enter a friendly name for the publishing farm (e.g., US Publisher).

15. For Root Authority Certificate, select the root certificate file from the publishing farm (i.e., `PublishingRoot.cer`).

16. Click OK to save.

Configuring a Publishing Farm

The next step is to grant permissions on the consuming farm. The first permission that must be granted is to the "Application Discovery and Load Balancer Service Application," aka the topology service. Doing so allows the consuming farm to request services from the publishing farm. The second permission grants permission to the specific application service.

Here are the steps and corresponding PowerShell code:

1. On the consuming farm, obtain the globally unique ID (GUID) of the consuming farm by running this PowerShell script:

   ```
   Get-SPFarm | Select id
   ```

2. On the publishing farm, grant permissions to the consumer farm. Here is the PowerShell script:

   ```
   $security = Get-SPTopologyServiceApplication | ↵
   Get-SPServiceApplicationSecurity
   $claim = (Get-SPClaimProvider System).ClaimProvider
   $principal = New-SPClaimsPrincipal -ClaimType ↵
   ```

```
http://schemas.microsoft.com/sharepoint/2009/08/ ↵
claims/farmid -ClaimProvider $claim ↵
-ClaimValue <Farm GUID>
Grant-SPObjectSecurity -Identity $security ↵
-Principal $principal -Rights "Full Control"
Get-SPTopologyServiceApplication | ↵
Set-SPServiceApplicationSecurity -ObjectSecurity ↵
$security
```

Replace <Farm GUID> with the GUID you obtained in step 1.

3. Grant application service-specific permissions to the consumer farm. The script for this is almost exactly the same as the script used in the previous step, but does vary slightly depending on the service application. Here is a sample script for granting permissions to the Managed Metadata Service application:

```
$security = Get-SPMetadataServiceApplication ↵
<"Metadata Service Application Name"> | ↵
Get-SPServiceApplicationSecurity
$claim = (Get-SPClaimProvider System).ClaimProvider
$principal = New-SPClaimsPrincipal -ClaimType ↵
"http://schemas.microsoft.com/sharepoint/2009/08/ ↵
claims/farmid" -ClaimProvider $claim -ClaimValue ↵
<Farm GUID>
Grant-SPObjectSecurity -Identity $security ↵
-Principal $principal -Rights ↵
"Read Access to Term Store"
Get-SPMetadataServiceApplication ↵
<"Metadata Service Application Name"> | ↵
Set-SPServiceApplicationSecurity -ObjectSecurity ↵
$security
```

4. Replace <Farm GUID> with the GUID obtained in step 1.

5. Replace <"Metadata Service Application Name"> with the name of the service application.

See the article "Set Permission to a Published Service Application" located at http://technet.microsoft.com/en-us/library/ff700211.aspx for more information and examples on how to configure permissions for other service applications.

Publishing a Service Application

Cross-farm service applications communicate via Windows Communications Foundation (WCF)-based web services. The web service can be configured to use either HTTP or HTTPS connections, and this is defined on the publishing farm when the service is enabled for publishing.

Here is how to publish a service application using Central Administration on the publishing farm:

1. Click Application Management, then select Manage Service Applications.
2. Highlight the desired service application and click the Publish button in the ribbon.
3. Set the connection type, either HTTP or HTTPS.
4. Click the check box to publish this service application to other farms.
5. Copy the published URL into the clipboard or to a temporary text file. (You will use this URL on the consuming farm, as described in the next section.)
6. Optionally, enter a description and information URL to provide guidance to the farm administrator on the consuming farm.
7. Click OK to save.

> **NOTE** The published URL (technically a uniform resource name or URN) contains the path to the topology web service for one server on the publishing farm. This creates a single point of failure if this server is down. To make this service fault tolerant, see the article "Load Balancing the SharePoint 2010 Topology Service" located on the "Beside the Point" blog at http://blogs.msdn.com/b/besidethepoint/archive/2010/12/08/load-balancing-the-sharepoint-2010-topology-service.aspx.

Consuming a Service Application

Consuming a service application can be done with Central Administration on the consuming farm. Here are the steps:

1. Click Application Management, and then select Manage Service Applications.

2. In the ribbon, click Connect and then select the appropriate service application.

3. In the pop-up dialog box, enter the published URL that you captured when publishing the service application (described in the previous section).

4. Click OK to save. A new service application connection entry is now shown on the consuming farm.

5. If necessary, add entries in the firewall to allow traffic through the designated TCP port (by default, 32,844).

Scaling the Search Service

Scaling the search application role is handled somewhat differently than scaling other application services due to the search engine's architecture. The degree of scalability depends on which search application engine is used. Microsoft makes five different search applications that can be used in SharePoint:

- SharePoint Foundation Search
- Microsoft Search Server 2010 Express
- Microsoft Search Server 2010
- SharePoint Server 2010 Search
- FAST Search Server 2010 for SharePoint

To learn more about the differences between each of these products, download the PDF document "Search Model 1 of 4 - Search Technologies from http://go.microsoft.com/fwlink/?LinkID=167733.

In this section, the focus is on SharePoint Server 2010 Search, which has the ability to scale up to 100 million search items.

Understanding Search Scalability

The search engine in SharePoint Server 2010 is very flexible, and while it may be a bit confusing when you're first learning the moving parts, once you do, the configuration of the services is quite simple.

The search architecture can be divided into two parts:

Crawler The crawler is responsible for reading the items from each content source, extracting keywords and metadata, and storing them to make the index. The crawler runs based on defined crawl schedules.

Query Service The Query service searches this index when a search query is issued and returns matching items to clients.

To learn more about the basics of configuring the search service, see Chapter 8, "Configuring the Search Service" and Chapter 9, "Configuring Search Scopes and Search Results."

Scaling Crawler Services

SharePoint's crawler is very flexible. It has an active/active design where multiple application servers crawl simultaneously. This design delivers faster performance (i.e., crawling content in less time) and fault tolerance, something not available in previous versions of SharePoint. Crawlers in SharePoint 2010 are stateless, which refers to two different aspects of their behavior:

- Index files are not stored locally on the crawl server. Instead, index files are delivered directly to query server(s).
- A crawl database is used to log what has been crawled. This allows multiple crawl servers to remain in sync.

Scaling crawlers can be done by creating multiple crawl components and crawl databases. Each crawl component is an application server participating in crawling. Creating another crawl database is done when database contention becomes a bottleneck. Here are guidelines you should follow when configuring the crawler:

- Avoid having more than 25 million items per crawl database.
- Avoid having more than 10 crawl databases per search application.
- There should be at least 4 CPU cores on each server where a crawl component is running.
- Avoid having more than 16 crawl components in a single Search Service Application.

Here are the steps to create a new crawl component using Central Administration:

1. Go to the search topology screen. (Central Administration, click Application Management, and then click Manage Service

Scale Out Application Servers

Applications. Click the search service application you want to configure.)

2. Click the Modify button under Search Application Topology.
3. Click New ➤ Crawl Component to display the Add Crawl Component window shown in Figure 5.19.

Figure 5.19: Creating a new crawl component

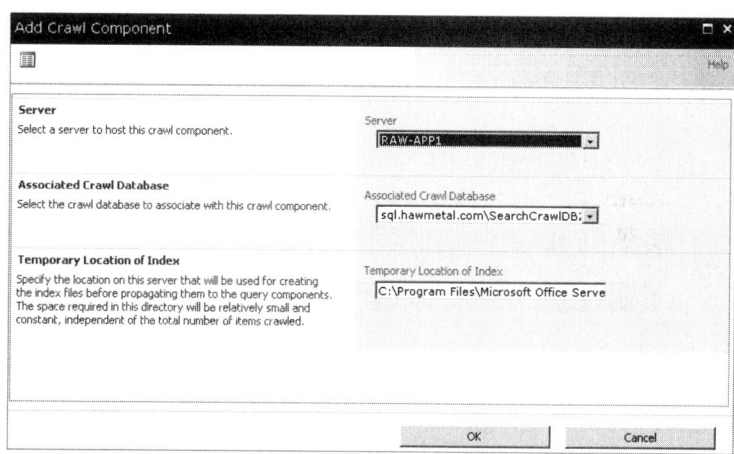

4. Select the application server to associate to this crawl component.
5. Select the crawl database to associate to this crawl component. Multiple crawl components can use a single crawl database, and a basic guideline is to have two crawl components per crawl database.
6. Optionally, for Temporary Location Of Index, change the local path. This is used to cache small portions of the index as it is being built. The default path is on the C: drive and only needs to be changed if space on this drive is very limited.
7. Click OK to save. This modification is now registered as a pending change. A pending change allows you to make multiple changes and apply them at one time.
8. To apply all changes, click the Apply Topology Changes button.

> **NOTE** To avoid unintended outages, you should apply search application topology changes during scheduled downtime.

To create a new crawl database, follow these steps:

1. Go to the search topology screen. (Central Administration, click Application Management, and then click Manage Service Applications. Click the search service application you want to configure.)
2. Click the Modify button under Search Application Topology.
3. Click New ➤ Crawl Database to display the Add Crawl Database window shown in Figure 5.20.

Figure 5.20: Creating a new crawl database

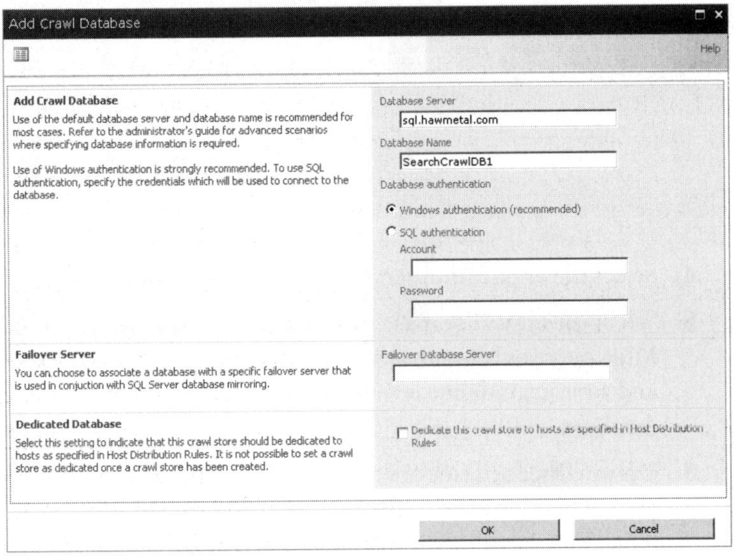

4. Specify the database server and name. This works the same way as creating any new database.
5. For Database Authentication, specify whether a Windows-authenticated (recommended) or SQL-authenticated login should be used when SharePoint queries this database.

6. Optionally, specify a failover server. This topic is covered in more detail in the "Scaling Using Database Mirroring" section later in this chapter.

7. Optionally, select the check box to specify that this will be a dedicated database—that is, this database will only be used for content from servers defined in host distribution rules.

    A host distribution rule (introduced in Chapter 8) allows you to designate specific crawl components when crawling specific content. For example, you may wish to dedicate the crawling of a large file server to a single crawl component.

8. Once a crawl database has been flagged as dedicated, you can create a new host distribution rule.

Scaling Query Services

SharePoint's query engine can be scaled in two primary ways:

Creating Multiple Query Components A query component runs on a WFE or application server. The component has a local copy of an index partition, which is searched when a query request is received. Having multiple query components for an index partition allows separate query requests to be load balanced across multiple servers. This design is called using query component mirrors.

Creating Multiple Index Partitions Having multiple query partitions can also optimize search requests. As introduced in Chapter 8, an index partition is a subset of the total index. Each index partition is associated with a separate query component. For example, if three index partitions exist, you have at least three separate query components and these components can run on three different servers. When a search request comes in, it is sent to three servers simultaneously, each component searching its own index partition. The results are then aggregated together. This design reduces the total time needed to process a search request.

To summarize, there is a one-to-many relationship between index partitions and query components. So, each index partition can be associated with multiple query components, but each query component is associated with only one index partition.

SharePoint also uses another search database called the *property database*. It is considered part of the index and stores metadata properties and item security details. Property databases are populated by crawl components when creating the index and read by query components when processing a search request. SharePoint supports multiple property databases. The property database is set when creating an index partition. Multiple index partitions can share the same property database.

Follow these guidelines when scaling query services:

- Use one index partition for each 10 million items crawled.
- Avoid having more than 10 index partitions per search application.
- SharePoint automatically distributes index items among the available index partitions. This distribution is not configurable.
- Avoid having more than 25 million items per each property database.

When you create a new index partition, you also create a new query component. Here are the steps:

1. Go to the search topology screen. (Central Administration, click Application Management, and then click Manage Service Applications. Click the search service application you want to configure.)
2. Click the Modify button under Search Application Topology.
3. Click New ➢ Index Partition And Query Component to display the Add Query Component window shown in Figure 5.21.

Figure 5.21: Creating a new query component

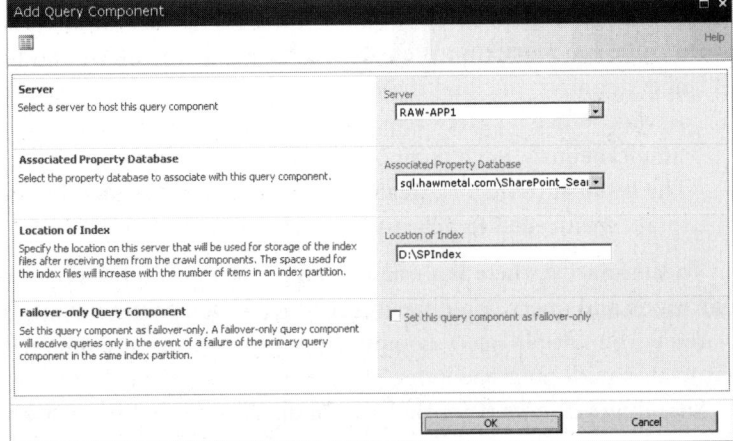

4. Select the application or WFE server you want to host this query component.

5. Select the property database.

6. In the Location Of Index section, select where the file system portion of the index will be stored. This path must be a local one. If possible, store the file system portion of the index on a drive other than C: for space and performance reasons.

> **NOTE** To estimate the amount of disk space needed, take the total amount of content that is being indexed, divide this amount by the number of index partitions, and then multiply by 0.035. For example, if you are indexing 500 GB of content and have two index partitions, the estimated amount of space is 8.75 GB (500 GB ÷ 2 × 0.035).

7. Optionally, set this component to be a failover query component. A failover query component uses an active/passive design, which means the failover server receives requests only if the primary query component is down. This option is not normally enabled when you're creating a new query component.

8. Click OK to save. The new query component is now registered as a pending change.

Adding an additional query component mirror to an existing index partition improves query performance and fault tolerance. Here are the steps:

1. Go to the search topology screen. (Central Administration, click Application Management, and then click Manage Service Applications. Click the search service application you want to configure.)

2. Click the Modify button under Search Application Topology.

3. For the desired index partition, select any of the existing query components and choose Add Mirror from the context menu. See Figure 5.22.

Figure 5.22: Creating a query component mirror

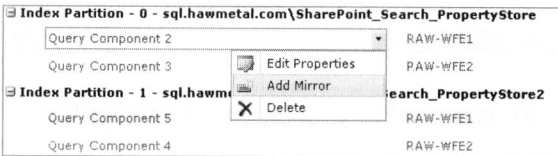

4. Select the application or WFE server you want to host this query component.

5. Select where the file system portion of the index will be stored.

6. Optionally, set this component to be a failover query component. If set as a failover query component, this server processes a query request only if other query components for the same index partition are offline. This arrangement doesn't improve performance and only adds fault tolerance.

7. Click OK to save. This query component mirror is now registered as a pending change.

To add a new property database, follow these steps:

1. Access the search topology. (Central Administration, click Application Management, and then click Manage Service Applications. Click the search service application you want to configure.)

2. Click the Modify button under Search Application Topology.

3. Click New ➢ Property Database.

4. Specify the database server and name as you would when creating any new database.

5. Click OK to save. This new property database is now registered as a pending change.

For more details on scaling search and several sample scenarios, see an excellent three-part series on the blog "A Static State." The series starts here:
www.astaticstate.com/2010/12/sharepoint-2010-search-architecture.html

Scale Out Database Servers

Any system is only as strong as its weakest link. In a SharePoint farm, the database role is usually the most common performance bottleneck. Furthermore, content databases store the data most critical to the users. These two reasons alone justify the importance of focusing on the database role to achieve greater performance and fault tolerance. Scaling the database also increases the total storage potential of the SharePoint farm.

Each of the sections that follow delivers at least one of these three goals: increasing performance, increasing fault tolerance, and increasing total storage space. When scaling, always keep your requirements in mind to ensure that you address the most important need. Whereas SQL Server Standard Edition can address all these goals, SQL Server Enterprise Edition is the most scalable and best performing.

Adding New SQL Servers

You can add new SQL servers to SharePoint by specifying a different server name when you're creating a new content or application service database. This approach sounds simple, but you should have a carefully mapped-out strategy of database server usage to minimize maintenance and recovery. For example, you might choose to store all search databases on one SQL server, whereas content, configuration, and other service databases are on a second server.

For any new SQL server that you add, you must make sure that the farm account (introduced in Chapter 1) has been granted the dbcreator and securityadmin server role permissions. If you'll be using Windows Authentication to connect to the SQL server (specified when you're creating the database), the database server must be in the same AD domain or in a trusted domain as other farm servers.

When adding new SQL servers, follow these guidelines:

- For production environments, we strongly recommend that you keep SQL servers dedicated to a single SharePoint farm.
- A typical ratio of WFE-to-database servers is about 4:1.
- Search databases are both read and write intensive with crawler and query activities. As the farm grows to the medium size and beyond, consider having a dedicated SQL server for your search databases.

Here are guidelines for optimizing databases (these tasks are usually done by the SQL database administrator):

- Separate database and log files onto separate physical disks or LUNs (logical unit numbers).
- For large and active databases, including tempdb, add secondary data files to the PRIMARY file group and spread these files across separate physical disks or LUNs. In general, the number of data files should match the number of CPU cores for the server.

- If disk space exists, presize databases that are expected to grow large. If the extra space is not used, the database can be shrunk.
- Have your database administrators (DBAs) set up a database maintenance plan for the server. The most important task (assuming backups are handled separately) is to check database integrity.
- A storage area network (SAN) is usually faster than direct attached storage (DAS).
- When using a SAN, consult your hardware storage vendor for optimal configuration settings.

For more guidance on scaling database servers including estimating the amount of space needed for database servers, see the article "Storage and SQL Server Capacity Planning and Configuration" at `http://technet.microsoft.com/en-us/library/cc298801.aspx`.

Scaling Using Database Mirroring

Database mirroring is an active/passive design that adds fault tolerance to one or more databases. Active/passive means that only the active server is responding to live requests; the passive server takes over when the active server fails. Hence, mirroring does not increase performance and, depending on the configuration, adds a small degree of overhead.

Mirroring requires at least two SQL server instances, which should be on separate servers. It works by applying transactions (the changes recorded by SQL Server) from the primary database to its mirrored copy running on another server.

Mirroring is configured at the database level, meaning you can choose which databases to mirror. Implementing database mirroring is done inside SQL Server and should be done by qualified DBAs.

SharePoint can automatically redirect requests to the mirror if the primary database is unavailable. SharePoint calls the mirror a failover server. A failover server can be configured when you're creating or editing content or application service databases. Figure 5.23 shows the failover server settings in the Add Content Database window.

Figure 5.23: Configuring a failover database server

Failover Server	Failover Database Server
You can choose to associate a database with a specific failover server that is used in conjuction with SQL Server database mirroring.	

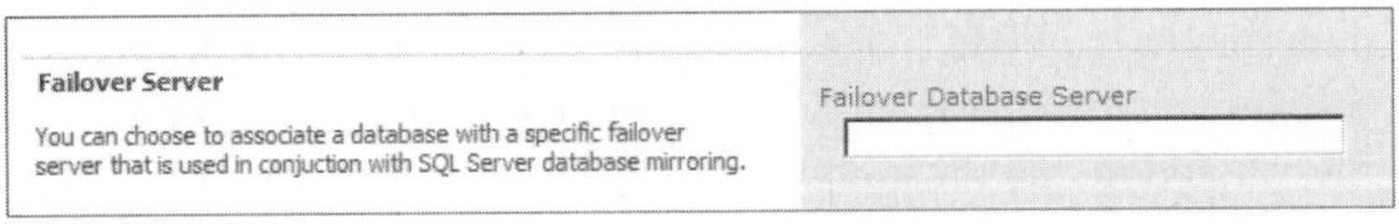

> **NOTE** The failover server settings can also be specified on existing SharePoint databases, including the configuration database, using PowerShell. For more information, see the blog "Setting a SharePoint 2010 Config DB Failover Server with PowerShell" at `www.toddklindt.com/blog/Lists/Posts/Post.aspx?ID=202`.

When a primary database (called the *principal*) or its server goes down, it must be failed over to the mirror database for SharePoint to function. In SQL Server, this can be done automatically by using a third SQL server called the witness server, or it can be done manually by a DBA. For failover to work properly, make sure that SharePoint's farm account and application pool accounts have login permissions on the mirrored server. For information on how to mirror SQL databases, see the article "How to: Configure a Database Mirroring Session (SQL Server Management Studio)" at `http://msdn.microsoft.com/en-us/library/ms188712.aspx`.

Scaling Using Clustered SQL Servers

Like mirroring, clustering a SQL server is designed to increase fault tolerance. With clustering, you have two or more identical servers that appear as one server to database clients (like SharePoint). Unlike mirroring, clustering is done at the server level so it's a more holistic, high-availability solution. SQL Server clustering is an active/passive design and does not increase performance. SQL Server clustering is built on top of clustering at the operating system level (called Microsoft Cluster Service). With SQL Server 2008 Enterprise Edition, you can have up to 16 cluster nodes, whereas with Standard Edition, you can only have 2. In either case, you still only have one active node per SQL instance.

SQL Server clustering is done entirely at the database server and SharePoint is blissfully unaware of it—no SharePoint configuration is needed! Properly implementing a SQL Server cluster is a complex process and should be done by a qualified DBA and storage experts. For more information on clustering, see the article "How to: Create a New SQL Server Failover Cluster (Setup)" at `http://msdn.microsoft.com/en-us/library/ms179530.aspx`.

PART II
Configuring SharePoint 2010

IN THIS PART

CHAPTER 6: Configuring System Settings............................189

CHAPTER 7: Configuring the User Profiles and My Sites Services....221

CHAPTER 8: Configuring the Search Service......................255

CHAPTER 9: Configuring Search Scopes and Search Results.........283

CHAPTER 10: Configuring Document Management....................311

CHAPTER 11: Configuring the Managed Metadata Service...........333

CHAPTER 12: Configuring Records Management....................361

CHAPTER 13: Configuring Web Content Management
and Publishing......................................391

6
Configuring System Settings

IN THIS CHAPTER, YOU WILL LEARN TO:

▶ **MANAGE CONTENT DATABASES** (Pages 190 – 196)
- Adding a Content Database (Page 190)
- Removing a Content Database (Page 193)
- Configuring a Content Database (Page 194)
- Moving a Content Database (Page 196)

▶ **MANAGE EMAIL AND TEXT MESSAGES (SMS)** (Pages 197 – 205)
- Configuring Incoming Email (Page 197)
- Configuring Outgoing Email (Page 203)
- Configuring SMS Messaging (Page 204)

▶ **MANAGE SOLUTIONS** (Pages 206 – 215)
- Managing Farm Solutions (Page 206)
- Managing User Solutions (Page 211)

▶ **MANAGE FEATURES** (Pages 215 – 219)
- Activating and Deactivating Features (Page 216)
- Using PowerShell to Manage Features (Page 218)

This chapter covers additional administrator tasks that apply to the farm or web application. Building on the introduction given in Chapter 3, "Creating and Managing Site Collections," this chapter delves deeper into managing content databases. We'll then cover how to configure incoming and outgoing messaging. The two sections on solutions and features cover tasks relating to the deployment and management of custom code.

Manage Content Databases

A content database is the storage container for site collections. As covered in Chapter 3, a site collection is stored in its entirety within a single content database. A content database can hold one or more site collections.

Content databases are powerful, but managing them is easy. All the main operations, such as adding, removing, and configuring content databases, are possible using both Central Administration and PowerShell.

Adding a Content Database

Here are reasons for needing to add a new content database:

- Creating a new web application
- Scaling out to a new SQL server, as covered in Chapter 5, "Scaling and High Availability"
- Segregating certain site collections for organizational, security, or regulation purposes
- Controlling the size of content databases

> **NOTE** When you're creating a new content database from Central Administration, it is the farm account that issues the create database request to the SQL server. When creating a content database on a different SQL server, be sure that the farm account (described in Chapter 1, "Installing SharePoint 2010") has both the dbcreator and the securityadmin server role permissions on the SQL server.

Creating a Content Database Using Central Administration

Creating a content database from Central Administration is a simple process. Here are the steps:

1. Start Central Administration (Start ➢ All Programs ➢ Microsoft SharePoint 2010 Products ➢ SharePoint 2010 Central Administration).
2. In the Application Management section, click Manage Content Databases.
3. Select the web application to which you want to add a content database.
4. The list of content databases for this web application appears. Click Add A Content Database.

    The interface for creating a content database, shown in Figure 6.1, should look familiar. It's almost exactly the same as the one you use when you're creating a new web application, as covered in Chapter 2, "Creating and Managing Web Applications."

Figure 6.1: Creating a content database

Web Application	
Select a web application.	Web Application: http://portal.synergy.com/ ▼

Database Name and Authentication	

Use of the default database server and database name is recommended for most cases. Refer to the administrator's guide for advanced scenarios where specifying database information is required.
 	
Use of Windows authentication is strongly recommended. To use SQL authentication, specify the credentials which will be used to connect to the database.
	Database Server
	sqlcluster.synergy.com
	Database Name
	WSS_Content
	Database authentication
	⊙ Windows authentication (recommended)
	○ SQL authentication
	   Account
	   [ ]
	   Password
	   [ ]

Failover Server	
You can choose to associate a database with a specific failover server that is used in conjuction with SQL Server database mirroring.	Failover Database Server [ ]

Search Server	
	Search service is provided by: SharePoint Server Search

Database Capacity Settings	
Specify capacity settings for this database.	Number of sites before a warning event is generated 9000 Maximum number of sites that can be created in this database 15000

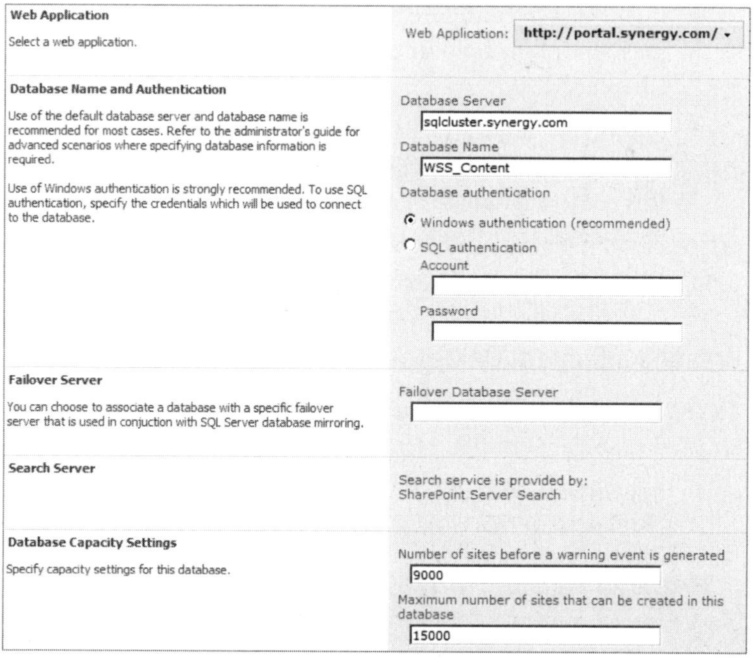

5. Specify the name of the database server or the name of a SQL alias that has been created. Any name that can resolve to the correct IP address can be used. If you are connecting to a named SQL instance, specify the name using the *servername\instance* name syntax.

6. Provide the database name. It's best to consistently follow an intuitive database naming convention for all content databases. If the database name does not exist, it will be created. If the database already exists, SharePoint attempts to mount it.

> **NOTE** Using this process to mount an existing content database can be useful, but there are caveats. The database must be for SharePoint 2010 and should match the build (the full version of the farm, e.g., 14.0.4762.1000) of the current farm. If the database build is newer than the current farm, the database cannot be mounted. If the database is older, it is best to mount using PowerShell, as covered later in this section.

7. Choose the database authentication method that the application pool account should use when it connects to this SQL server.

8. If you plan to configure this database for database mirroring, enter the name of the failover database server. (Mirroring is covered in Chapter 5.)

9. Optionally, adjust the database capacity settings. These numbers set limits on the number of site collections that can be stored in this content database and are also used to determine which content database will be used when creating a new site collection.

10. Click OK to create the content database.

Creating a Content Database Using PowerShell

To create a content database using PowerShell, use the New-SPContentDatabase cmdlet. Here is the basic syntax:

```
New-SPContentDatabase -Name <DatabaseName>
-WebApplication <URL> -DatabaseServer <ServerName>
```

Here is an example:

```
New-SPContentDatabase -Name IT_Content -WebApplication
http://intranet -DatabaseServer sqlcluster.acme.org
```

> **NOTE** When you're creating a content database using PowerShell, the Windows account you've logged in as is connecting to the SQL server and creating the database. Be sure this account has dbcreator and securityadmin server role permissions on the SQL server.

To mount an existing database, use the `Mount-SPContentDatabase` cmdlet. This is the preferred form to use if the database is from an older build or version (including SharePoint 2007 SP2 or later) and needs to be upgraded.

Removing a Content Database

Removing a content database dismounts or disconnects it from a web application. When using Central Administration to remove, the database is simply dismounted from SharePoint but remains online and intact inside SQL server. This allows you to mount the database again using the steps just covered in the previous section.

When a content database is removed, all site collections inside the database become inaccessible.

Here are the steps to dismount a content database using Central Administration:

1. In the Application Management section, click Manage Content Databases.
2. Select the correct web application.
3. The list of content databases for this web application appears. Click the database you wish to dismount.
4. Details for this content database are shown. Near the bottom of the window, click Remove Content Database.
5. Click OK.

Content databases can be removed using PowerShell in two ways:

- To just dismount the database from SharePoint, keeping the database intact, use the `Dismount-SPContentDatabase` cmdlet.
- To dismount and delete the content database from the SQL server, use `Remove-SPContentDatabase`.

Configuring a Content Database

To configure the settings of a content database using Central Administration, follow these steps:

1. In the Application Management section, click Manage Content Databases.
2. Select the correct web application.
3. The list of content databases for this web application appears. Click the database you want to configure.
4. View and change configuration options as desired. Click OK to save your changes.

The information and settings in the configuration dialog box are as follows:

Database Information   This section shows the database server, name, and authentication type. It also specifies whether the database is read-only. The only setting you can change is database status. This setting controls whether this content database can be used when storing new or restored site collections. The status of *Ready* means that this database can be used to store new or restored site collections. The status of *Offline* means that it cannot be used when storing new or restored site collections. More details on how you can use the database status setting to manage your site collection placement are covered in Chapter 3.

> **NOTE**   Adjusting the database status is a useful feature, but the on-screen wording here is confusing. Contrary to how it sounds, *Offline* does not mean to disconnect or take the database down. Furthermore, the *Ready* and *Offline* terms are not used consistently. When you are viewing the list of content databases for a web application, a database that is ready is displayed as *Started*; a database that is offline is displayed as *Stopped*. Remember the concept and don't let these terms confuse you.

Database Versioning And Upgrade   Note the details on the database version and build. Although there is nothing to adjust here, knowing this build is useful when you are performing an upgrade from SharePoint 2007. The Current SharePoint Database Schema is the current build for this content database. The Maximum SharePoint Database Schema version is the current build for the farm. When these numbers match, you know that your content database build matches the farm build, which is what you want. More details are covered in the next section.

Failover Server Set the server name for an alternate SQL server if you are mirroring this database. If SharePoint cannot connect to the primary server, it will attempt to connect to this failover server. For more details on this topic, see Chapter 5.

Database Capacity Settings This controls how many site collections can be stored in this content database. You can adjust both the warning and maximum levels. These numbers are also used to determine which content database to use when creating a new site collection.

Search Server This setting is only applicable if you are using the SharePoint Foundation (SPF) Search service. If you are using SharePoint Server (SPS) and are using a Search service application, this setting does not apply.

Preferred Server For Timer Jobs If you are running timer jobs associated with this content database, specify the WFE or application server in the Preferred Server For Timer Jobs drop-down menu.

A content database's settings can also be adjusted using PowerShell. The primary command is Set-SPContentDatabase. Here is the basic syntax:

```
Set-SPContentDatabase <DatabaseName>
[-Status <Online | Offline>] [-WarningSiteCount <number>]
[-MaxSiteCount <number>]
```

> **TIP** To learn more about the different parameter values that you can employ, use the following PowerShell cmdlet: Get-Help Set-SPContentDatabase -detailed

This example adjusts the warning and maximum site collection counts for all online content databases for a web application:

```
Get-SPContentDatabase -WebApplication http://intranet |
Set-SPContentDatabase -WarningSiteCount 5 -MaxSiteCount 10
```

> **WARNING** You will encounter a bug in the release-to-manufacturing (RTM) version of SharePoint 2010 when adjusting the database status to offline using PowerShell. When you use this command, the status correctly goes to offline. But when viewing the status from Central Administration, it shows *Error*. The database is completely healthy and properly offline, so the display is incorrect. However, it is disconcerting, so you may prefer to use Central Administration when adjusting this setting.

Moving a Content Database

A content database can be moved from one SQL server to another, but there is not a single operation in SharePoint to do this. Here is an overview of the steps you must perform:

1. Disable scheduled timer jobs or search crawls associated with the web application in which the content database is used.

2. Dismount the content database from SharePoint, as covered previously in the "Removing a Content Database" section.

3. Back up the content database from the source SQL server and restore it on the destination SQL server.

   A faster but more complex alternative is to detach the database from the SQL server, manually copy over all database files (MDF, LDF, NDF) to the destination SQL server, and then reattach.

4. Mount the content database to SharePoint using the new SQL server name, as explained earlier in the "Adding a Content Database" section.

5. Re-enable timer jobs that were disabled and resume any search crawls.

Steps 1 and 5 are optional but recommended for production environments. To simplify the effort, you can use PowerShell to script these two steps. For more information on moving content databases, see the article "Move Content Databases (SPF 2010)" at http://technet.microsoft.com/en-us/library/cc287899.aspx.

Manage Email and Text Messages (SMS)

SharePoint can integrate with email platforms, enabling you to either send email messages with attachments to SharePoint, or receive email and Short Message Service (SMS) text notifications from SharePoint.

Configuring Incoming Email

If you set up incoming email, SharePoint can process and store email messages in a list or library. It is a useful feature that can be used for messages originating from internal or external users. For example, a company can use the hr@sharepoint.acme.org email address to store resumes from interested job applicants in a designed HR document library.

When storing messages in a document library, you have some control over how the message is stored, in particular over how the attachment is saved. You can also restrict who has permissions to email the list or library.

To use incoming email in SharePoint, you must have the SMTP (Simple Mail Transport Protocol) service running on at least one server in the farm.

Configuring incoming email involves four main steps. These are covered in the four following sections:

1. Enabling incoming email.
2. Installing SMTP service.
3. Configuring Exchange or another messaging server to forward messages. This chapter assumes that you are using Exchange Server but other messaging systems can be used.
4. Configuring list and libraries to receive email.

Enabling Incoming Email

To enable incoming email, follow these steps:

1. Start Central Administration.
2. Click System Settings and then select Configure Incoming Email Settings. You are presented with the page shown in Figure 6.2.

Figure 6.2: Enabling incoming email

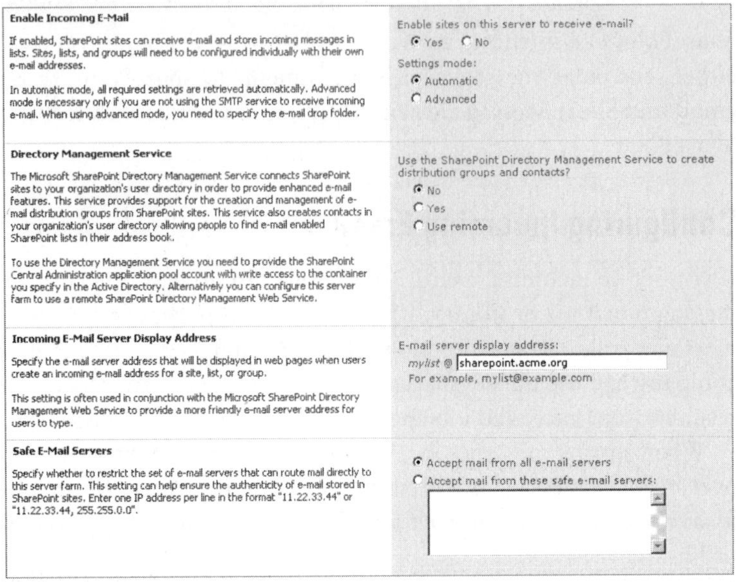

Enable Incoming E-Mail
If enabled, SharePoint sites can receive e-mail and store incoming messages in lists. Sites, lists, and groups will need to be configured individually with their own e-mail addresses.

In automatic mode, all required settings are retrieved automatically. Advanced mode is necessary only if you are not using the SMTP service to receive incoming e-mail. When using advanced mode, you need to specify the e-mail drop folder.

Enable sites on this server to receive e-mail?
- ○ Yes ○ No

Settings mode:
- ● Automatic
- ○ Advanced

Directory Management Service
The Microsoft SharePoint Directory Management Service connects SharePoint sites to your organization's user directory in order to provide enhanced e-mail features. This service provides support for the creation and management of e-mail distribution groups from SharePoint sites. This service also creates contacts in your organization's user directory allowing people to find e-mail enabled SharePoint lists in their address book.

To use the Directory Management Service you need to provide the SharePoint Central Administration application pool account with write access to the container you specify in the Active Directory. Alternatively you can configure this server farm to use a remote SharePoint Directory Management Web Service.

Use the SharePoint Directory Management Service to create distribution groups and contacts?
- ○ No
- ○ Yes
- ○ Use remote

Incoming E-Mail Server Display Address
Specify the e-mail server address that will be displayed in web pages when users create an incoming e-mail address for a site, list, or group.

This setting is often used in conjunction with the Microsoft SharePoint Directory Management Web Service to provide a more friendly e-mail server address for users to type.

E-mail server display address:
mylist @ [sharepoint.acme.org]
For example, mylist@example.com

Safe E-Mail Servers
Specify whether to restrict the set of e-mail servers that can route mail directly to this server farm. This setting can help ensure the authenticity of e-mail stored in SharePoint sites. Enter one IP address per line in the format "11.22.33.44" or "11.22.33.44, 255.255.0.0".

- ● Accept mail from all e-mail servers
- ○ Accept mail from these safe e-mail servers:

NOTE If you are not a local Windows administrator on the server that is running Central Administration, you will not have the incoming email settings link. Only local administrators who are also farm administrators can enable incoming email.

---

3. In the Enable Incoming E-Mail section, choose Yes to enable sites on this farm to receive email.

4. For Settings Mode, in most cases you will pick Automatic, which is the most common choice. This setting tells SharePoint to work with a locally installed SMTP server.

5. Specify whether you want to use Directory Management Service to automatically create contacts and maintain distribution lists within your Exchange global address list (GAL). This feature is useful as it allows any list or library that is email enabled to be automatically published in the GAL. The drawback, however, is that server administrators have no control over what contact name is used, and an inappropriate name could be easily

published into the address list for all to see. More details on configuring this service are available in the article "Configure Incoming E-mail (SPF 2010)" at http://technet.microsoft.com/en-us/library/cc287879.aspx.

6. In the Incoming E-mail Server Display Address section, choose the domain name you want to use for email. To simplify the routing of mail from Exchange or another messaging system, prefix this entry with a subdomain name. For example, if the regular domain is acme.org, use a name like **sharepoint.acme.org**.

7. Optionally, in the Safe E-mail Servers section, enter one or more IP addresses of the Exchange or other messaging server(s) that will be forwarding email to SharePoint. Doing so helps prevents unauthorized SMTP servers from delivering mail to SharePoint.

8. Click OK to save changes.

Installing and Configuring SMTP Service

SharePoint's incoming email engine uses a local SMTP service to receive messages from an external messaging system such as Exchange. The SMTP service does very little—it simply writes the message into a drop folder where a timer job can pick it up and store the message in the correct list or library.

You need at least one SMTP service to use incoming email. For redundancy, you can add multiple SMTP servers, but you need to separately configure load balancing. This section only covers how to configure a single server.

To install the SMTP service for incoming email, follow these steps:

1. Choose one of the WFE or application servers to become the SMTP server.

2. Log into the server as a local administrator and run Server Manager.

3. In the left navigation panel, click Features.

4. In the right panel, click Add Features.

5. In the list of features, select SMTP Server.

6. The SMTP Server feature requires ODBC Logging and SMTP Server Tools to be installed. If these components are not installed already, you will be prompted to add them.

7. Click Next three times and then click Install.

Once the SMTP service is installed, you must change the local domain name so that the service recognizes incoming messages. Here are the steps:

1. Start Internet Information Services (IIS) 6.0 Manager (Start ➤ Administrative Tools ➤ IIS 6.0 Manager).

2. In the navigation panel on the left, expand down through the server name and the SMTP virtual server listed.

3. Click Domains and a default domain should be listed in the right panel.

4. Right-click this default domain name entry (initially configured as the fully qualified domain name for this server) and select Rename.

5. Type the domain name that you specified when enabling incoming email in the previous section—for example, **sharepoint.acme.org**.

Configuring Exchange to Forward Messages

You can configure Exchange to forward appropriate messages to the SharePoint SMTP server. Technically, you are not required to use Exchange or any other email system to forward messages to SharePoint. However, it is a best practice to route SharePoint's messages through an external system first. The primary advantage is to make use of features such as spam filtering and antivirus protection.

> **TIP** If you don't intend to route SharePoint's messages through an external system, then at this point you just need to create an MX record in the authoritative DNS zone for your email domain name that SharePoint is configured to use. This record points to the fully-qualified domain name (FQDN) of the SharePoint(s) running SMTP services (e.g., **sharepoint.acme.org**).

If you use Exchange as the external system, Exchange receives all incoming messages. Messages that should go to SharePoint are routed via a send connector to your SharePoint SMTP sever. The steps that follow assume you are using Exchange 2010, but the process is similar for previous versions.

1. In Exchange Management Console, expand through Organization Configuration and select Hub Transport.

2. In the Actions pane, click New Send Connector. A wizard is launched.

3. Give the connector an intuitive name such as **SharePoint**.
4. For Address Space, click Add. In the dialog box, enter the domain name that SharePoint is configured to use (e.g., `sharepoint.acme.org`).
5. For Network Settings, select Route Mail Through The Following Smart Hosts and click Add.
6. Enter either the IP address of the SMTP server or the FQDN that directs Exchange to SharePoint's SMTP server.
7. For Smart Host Authentication, accept the default of None.
8. For Source Server, ensure that your Exchange Server name is listed.

The final settings should resemble those in the summary screen shown in Figure 6.3.

Figure 6.3: Configuring a New Send Connector

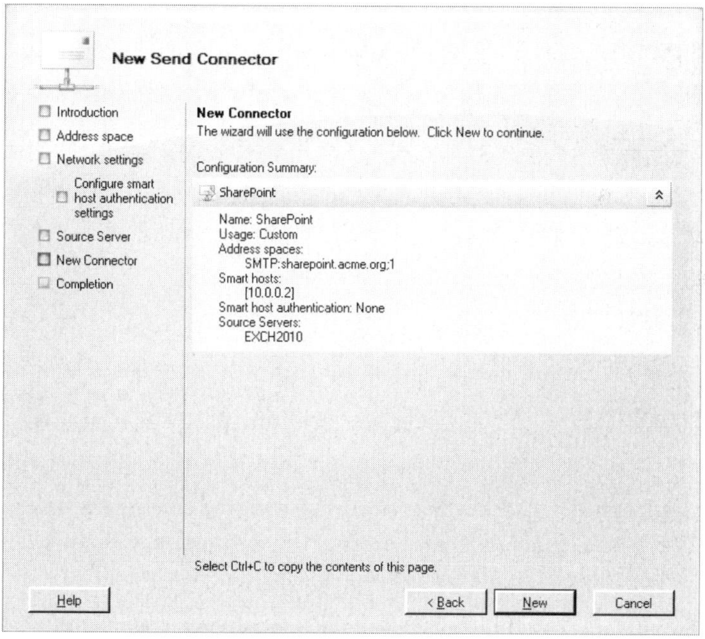

Configuring a Library to Receive Email

The final step in setting up incoming email is configuring which lists and libraries will receive incoming email.

All libraries can be configured to receive incoming email, but not all lists can. For example, tasks, contacts, and custom lists do not support incoming email.

To configure a list or library to use incoming email, follow these steps:

1. Navigate to the list or library.
2. Above the ribbon, click the List or Library tab.
3. Click the List Settings or Library Settings button in the ribbon.
4. In the Communications category, click Incoming Email Settings. (If you do not see this link, either incoming email was not enabled or this list does not support incoming email.) You are presented with the screen shown in Figure 6.4.

Figure 6.4: Enabling a library to receive incoming email

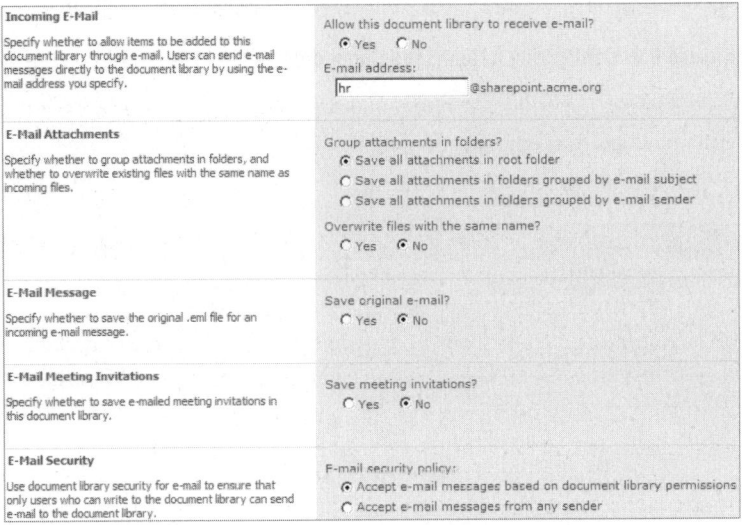

5. Configure the list or library as needed, including adding the name portion of the email address. For lists, the settings vary slightly from those shown in Figure 6.4, depending on the type of list.
6. Optionally, set the email security policy to control who can send email to this list or library. By default, only users that have Contribute permissions are able to send email to the list or library. (This is the setting labeled "Accept e-mail messages based on document library permissions.")

NOTE Another optional step is to create either an AD contact or an Exchange recipient. This helps users find this account when browsing the GAL. This is not required if users are entering the email address directly, or if the email address is included in a distribution list that users will be using instead.

Configuring Outgoing Email

Outgoing email is used by SharePoint for numerous reasons, including alerts and other notifications, such as those sent when a disk space quota is reached or when new access has been granted to a user. Configuring outgoing email is easy. All that is needed is to specify which SMTP server will deliver the messages. However, you must remember two important details about configuring outgoing email:

- Outgoing email can be configured on the farm as a whole or on individual web applications. If you configure outgoing email for both, the web application setting will override the farm setting. Configuring it for a web application is useful if you want that application to be able to send messages in a different language.

- SharePoint is not able to authenticate to the SMTP server when sending email. That means that the receiving SMTP server (e.g., an Exchange Server) must be configured to allow messages from anonymous users. If this presents a security problem, you can install a local SMTP server. You then configure SharePoint to send messages to this server which are then forwarded (using authentication) to your destination SMTP server.

To configure outgoing email using Central Administration, follow these steps:

1. To configure outgoing email at the farm level, click System Settings, and then select Configure Outgoing Email Settings.

    To configure outgoing email at the web application level, click Application Management, and then choose Manage Web Applications. Select the web application and in the ribbon, select General Settings ➢ Outgoing Email.

    You are presented with the screen shown in Figure 6.5.

Figure 6.5: Configuring outgoing email

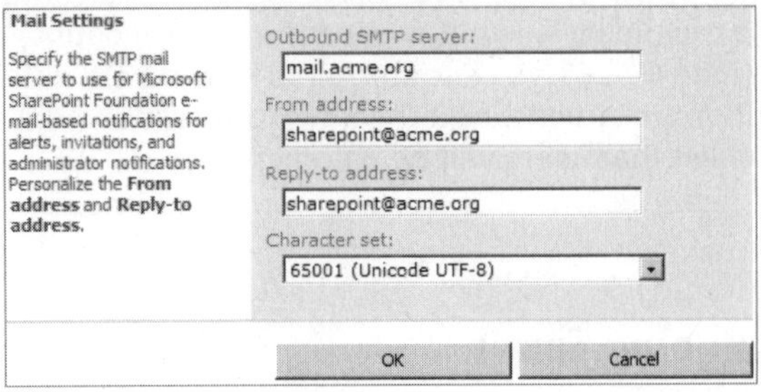

```
Mail Settings                Outbound SMTP server:
Specify the SMTP mail        [mail.acme.org              ]
server to use for Microsoft
SharePoint Foundation e-     From address:
mail-based notifications for [sharepoint@acme.org        ]
alerts, invitations, and
administrator notifications. Reply-to address:
Personalize the From         [sharepoint@acme.org        ]
address and Reply-to
address.                     Character set:
                             [65001 (Unicode UTF-8)    ▼]

                                  [   OK   ]   [ Cancel ]
```

2. Specify the name of the SMTP server to be used. If you require a fault-tolerant design, ensure this host is configured to use load balancing.

3. Provide the From Address. This does not need to be a real address; it's simply used as the From field for each SMTP message.

4. Provide the Reply-To Address. Again, this does not need to be a real address.

5. Optionally adjust the language (Character Set) for messages to be sent.

6. Click OK.

Configuring SMS Messaging

In addition to email alerts, SharePoint supports SMS for the texting generation. To use SMS, you must first sign up with a hosting provider that supports Office Mobile Service (OMS). You can quickly find many such providers by going to http://messaging.office.microsoft.com/HostingProviders.aspx?src=014&lc=1033.

When an SMS message needs to be sent, SharePoint contacts the hosting provider via a secure web service call. To encrypt message contents, the provider must support Secure Sockets Layer (SSL).

To configure SMS messaging using Central Administration, follow these steps:

1. To configure SMS messages at the farm level, click System Settings and then choose Configure Mobile Account.

   To configure SMS messages at the web application level, click Application Management and then click Manage Web Applications. Select the web application and in the ribbon, choose General Settings ➤ Mobile Account.

Manage Email and Text Messages (SMS)

You are presented with the screen shown in Figure 6.6.

Figure 6.6: Configuring SMS service settings

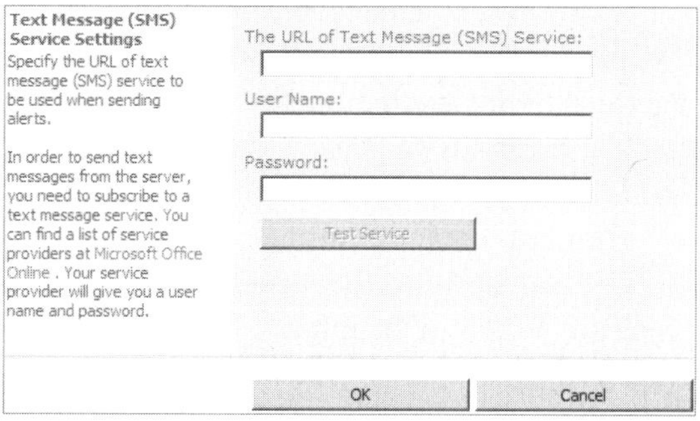

2. For the URL, enter in the external web service URL given to you by the OMS hosting provider.
3. Enter the User Name and Password for your subscription.
4. Click OK to save.

NOTE If the SSL certificate used by the hosting provider is not from a trusted certificate authority (CA), you will need to download and install the certificate in to the trusted root CA store on each WFE server.

Now that SMS messaging is configured, users can optionally choose to receive certain alerts via SMS. Here is how a user configures it:

1. Navigate to the list or library.
2. Above the ribbon, click the List or Library tab.
3. Click the Alert Me button in the ribbon and choose "Set alert on this library."
4. In the dialog box shown in Figure 6.7, enter the mobile number to use for sending the alert.

Figure 6.7: Configuring delivery of alerts via SMS message

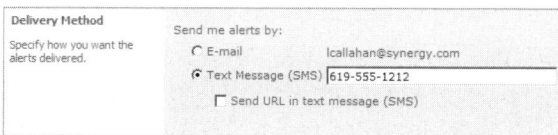

Manage Solutions

SharePoint is an extensible platform that allows developers and third-party software vendors to integrate custom applications into the product. In fact, the sole focus of many companies is to sell products that build on top of SharePoint. This makes SharePoint much more flexible as a base product.

Deploying custom code manually to SharePoint is a risky and burdensome task. You typically need to copy files manually to multiple servers, edit web.config files, and manually make UI changes. And that's not all—when new servers are added to the farm, these changes need to be applied all over again. When performing a disaster recovery or an upgrade, you may also need to re-apply the custom changes.

Fortunately, SharePoint is able to automate all of this manual effort, making it a simple and painless experience. The way SharePoint does this is through something called a SharePoint solution package. A solution package is a file that contains all the files to deploy. It also contains the deployment instructions.

A solution package has the extension .wsp (WSS Solution Package) and is just a Windows Cabinet file in disguise. Deploying custom code using a solution package is not just a best practice—it should be a required practice, especially for code that is written by an internal team of developers.

> **NOTE** In some cases, custom code may come in the form of a Windows Installer file (with the extension .msi). This is also an acceptable form of deploying code since it is also automated. However, there is a distinct advantage to using a solution package, especially when adding or replacing servers in the farm, because the solution package is automatically deployed when needed without any intervention.

Managing Farm Solutions

As a SharePoint administrator, you do not need to know how to create a solution package—you just need to know how to deploy one. When you're working with solution packages, there are four steps to the solution package life cycle:

- Add
- Deploy

- Retract
- Remove

Most of these steps can be done with Central Administration, and all of them can be done using PowerShell. Each step is covered in the subsequent sections.

Adding a Solution Package

Adding a solution package is easy, but it cannot be done using Central Administration. It's the only one of the four life-cycle steps that requires PowerShell. Adding a solution package places the WSP file into the solution store, which resides in the configuration database and is used to keep track of all custom enhancements to SharePoint. Think of this step as getting the solution package ready to deploy.

To add a solution package to the store, you need to use PowerShell from one of the WFE servers. Here is the syntax:

```
Add-SPSolution <LiteralPath>
```

Here is an example of how it is used:

```
Add-SPSolution c:\temp\BIWebParts.wsp
```

That's it. The solution package is now ready to be deployed.

Deploying a Solution Package

Deploying a solution package is where the actual installation is done. This involves copying code files to locations like the global assembly cache (GAC) or the SharePoint root (aka "14 Hive"). Changes to web.config can also be made. Remember, you're not doing the actual installation—you're just telling SharePoint to deploy for you.

If the solution package contains custom features (covered in the "Manage Features" section later in this chapter), they are automatically installed. Deployment is done automatically for each WFE server in the farm.

Before a package can be deployed, it must be added to the solution store (see the previous section).

A solution package can be deployed using Central Administration or PowerShell. For some solution packages, you have the option of deploying to one or more individual web applications rather than to the whole farm. This flexibility allows you to scope the custom code to specific web applications. Other solution packages are always deployed to the whole farm. This is called a global solution. Which option you have depends on how the package was put together and where it deploys code.

Here are the steps to deploy a solution package using Central Administration:

1. Click System Settings, and then select Manage Farm Solutions. You are presented with the solution store, as shown in Figure 6.8. On newly-created farms, this list is empty.

Figure 6.8: Solution packages in the solution store

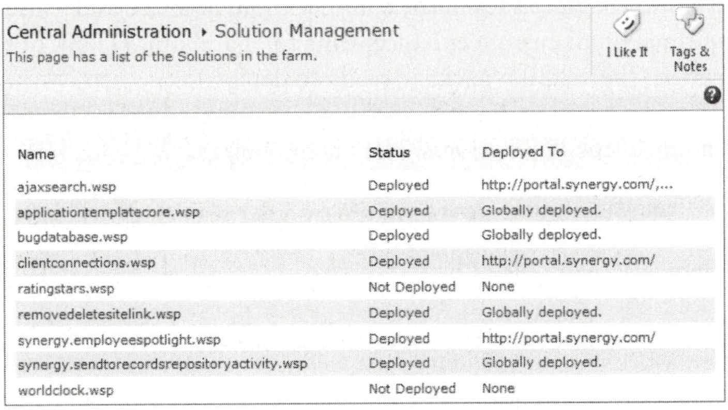
Central Administration ▸ Solution Management
This page has a list of the Solutions in the farm.
I Like It
Tags & Notes
Name
Status
Deployed To
ajaxsearch.wsp
Deployed
http://portal.synergy.com/,...
applicationtemplatecore.wsp
Deployed
Globally deployed.
bugdatabase.wsp
Deployed
Globally deployed.
clientconnections.wsp
Deployed
http://portal.synergy.com/
ratingstars.wsp
Not Deployed
None
removedeletesitelink.wsp
Deployed
Globally deployed.
synergy.employeespotlight.wsp
Deployed
http://portal.synergy.com/
synergy.sendtorecordsrepositoryactivity.wsp
Deployed
Globally deployed.
worldclock.wsp
Not Deployed
None

2. Click on the WSP package filename you want to deploy. You see the screen shown in Figure 6.9. This screen displays the current status of the solution package along with where it has been deployed.

Figure 6.9: Status of this solution package

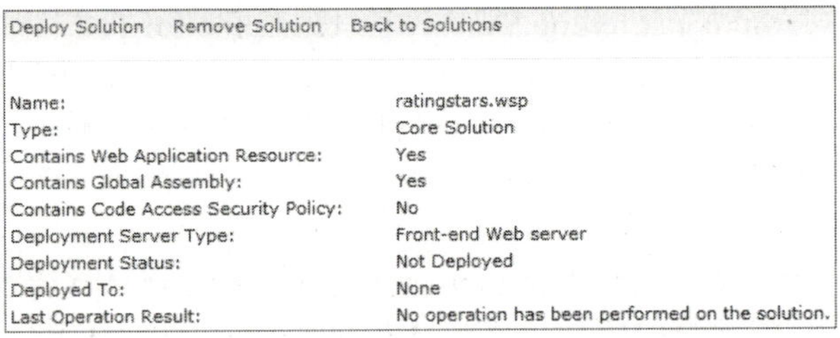
Deploy Solution
Remove Solution
Back to Solutions
Name:
ratingstars.wsp
Type:
Core Solution
Contains Web Application Resource:
Yes
Contains Global Assembly:
Yes
Contains Code Access Security Policy:
No
Deployment Server Type:
Front-end Web server
Deployment Status:
Not Deployed
Deployed To:
None
Last Operation Result:
No operation has been performed on the solution.

3. To deploy this package, click the Deploy Solution link. You are now taken to the screen shown in Figure 6.10.

Figure 6.10: Deploying a solution package

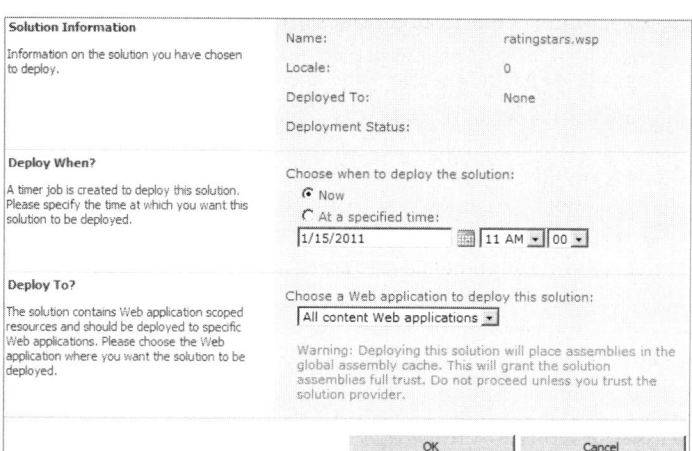

4. If this package supports web application-specific deployment, choose the web application in the Deploy To section, as shown in Figure 6.10. If this solution package is placing code into the GAC, you will see a red warning. For security reasons, only code that is from known and trusted sources should be deployed into the GAC.

5. Optionally, specify a time when this package should be deployed in the Deploy When section.

6. Click OK to run or schedule the deployment.

NOTE When deploying and retracting a solution package, the application pool for the web application is recycled. This process causes a momentary outage while a new pool is started and warmed up. This outage is one reason why you might want to schedule the deployment to occur after hours.

When you deploy solutions, a timer job is created on each WFE server. If you specify that a package is to be deployed now, it may take a minute or so for the deployment to finish.

NOTE As soon as the deployment finishes, you should do a basic test of the web application to ensure that its pages still display. This applies whether you scheduled the deployment to take place now or later. Do not schedule the deployment for 2 A.M. if no one is there to confirm that the deployment succeeded.

To deploy a solution package using PowerShell, use the `Install-SPSolution` cmdlet. Here is the basic syntax:

```
Install-SPSolution <package name> [-WebApplication <URL>]
[-GACDeployment] [-confirm]
```

Here is a sample form:

```
Install-SPSolution biwebparts.wsp -WebApplication
http://intranet -GACDeployment
```

The `-GACDeployment` switch must be used if code is deployed into the GAC.

Retracting a Solution Package

Retracting a solution package uninstalls a deployed solution package from one or more web applications. You retract a solution package when you are no longer using it, or if you need to deploy a newer version. Solution packages must be deployed before they can be retracted. Retracting can be done from Central Administration or PowerShell. Here are the steps when using Central Administration:

1. Click System Settings, and then select Manage Farm Solutions.
2. Select the WSP package you wish to retract.
3. Click Retract Solution.
4. If this solution was deployed to an individual web application, select the web application. For a global solution, you won't have this option.
5. Optionally, choose a time for the retraction to take place.
6. Click OK.

To retract a solution package using PowerShell, use the `Uninstall-SPSolution` cmdlet. Here is the basic syntax:

```
Uninstall-SPSolution <package name>
[-WebApplication <URL>] [-confirm]
```

Here is a sample uninstall script that retracts this solution from one web application and suppresses the confirmation prompt:

```
Uninstall-SPSolution biwebparts.wsp -WebApplication
http://intranet -confirm:$false
```

Removing a Solution Package

The fourth step in the life cycle is to remove a solution package. As you can guess, it removes the WSP solution package from the store. In most cases, you should make sure that the package has been retracted from all web applications prior to removal.

To remove a solution package using Central Administration, follow these steps:

1. Click System Settings, and then select Manage Farm Solutions.
2. Select the WSP package you wish to remove.
3. Click Remove Solution and confirm the action.

To remove a solution using PowerShell, use the `Remove-SPSolution` cmdlet. Here is the basic syntax:

```
Remove-SPSolution <package name> [-confirm] [-force]
```

The optional -force parameter is useful for removing a package that is still installed. This parameter should only be used to remove packages that are in an error state and cannot be properly retracted.

> **NOTE** The Install-SPSolution and Uninstall-SPSolution cmdlets use timer jobs for the actual work. When running multiple SPSolution commands using a PowerShell script, the command processor does not wait for these timer jobs to complete before continuing to the next line of the script. This can cause problems, for example, if you have a script that runs both Uninstall-SPSolution and Remove-SPSolution in succession. The Remove-SPSolution cmdlet produces an error if the uninstall hasn't finished yet. You can work around this issue by using a Start-Sleep cmdlet in between. For those who need a more intelligent script, see the article "Deploying SharePoint 2010 Solution Packages Using PowerShell" on the SharePoint Automation blog at http://blog.falchionconsulting.com/index.php/2010/06/deploying-sharepoint-2010-solution-packages-using-powershell/.

Managing User Solutions

User solutions, also called sandboxed solutions, are introduced in Chapter 3, which covers how a site collection administrator can upload and activate a user solution for a single site collection. This section focuses on how the farm administrator can manage user solutions across the farm.

A user solution package is nearly identical to a farm solution. The contents of the WSP package are the same, but there are restrictions on what a user solution can do and differences in how the code is run. User solutions are designed so that the potential risk of running custom code is mitigated. For example, if a faulty web part is deployed from a user solution and added to a web page, only the web part itself is broken but the page still displays. If this same web part is deployed as a farm solution, it can prevent the whole page from displaying, or, worse-yet, cause farm-wide problems.

Both built-in SharePoint code and custom code from farm solutions together run inside the application pool for the web application. Code from user solutions, however, runs in a separate process, which protects SharePoint from potentially harmful code. This separate process and its security settings constitute the sandbox.

Configuring Load Balancing for Sandboxed Code

Before code originating inside user solutions can be run, the Microsoft SPF Sandboxed Code Service must be running on at least one server in the farm. To start this service from Central Administration, follow these steps:

1. Click System Settings, and then click Manage Services On Server.
2. Choose the correct server.
3. For the Microsoft SPF Sandboxed Code Service, click Start.

As a farm administrator, you have control over which WFE(s) or application server(s) are able to run this type of code. When configuring these load balancing settings, you have two primary options:

- All sandboxed code runs on the same machine as a request. This is the most efficient option, but it requires that all of the WFE servers have the sandboxed code service running. This approach works well if you have a small farm or do not use many user solutions.

- Requests to run sandboxed code are routed by solution affinity. This choice tells SharePoint to direct requests only to those servers that are running the sandboxed code service. This option gives you more flexibility in choosing which servers are used. It's also better if you have several user solutions or if the code running in user solutions is resource heavy.

To configure these load balancing settings from Central Administration, follow these steps:

1. Click System Settings, and then select Manage User Solutions.
2. In the Load Balancing setting, select one of these two choices as shown in Figure 6.11.
3. Click OK to save the settings.

Figure 6.11: Configuring load balancing for user solutions

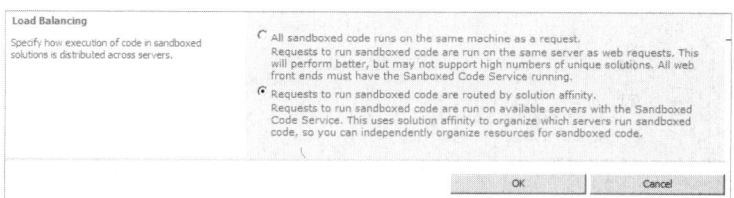

TIP A common problem when working with sandboxed solutions is this error: "The sandboxed code execution request was refused because the Sandboxed Code Host Service was too busy to handle the request." For some troubleshooting guidance on this problem, see the SharePoint Developer Team Blog at http://bit.ly/eftSoH.

Adjusting How Quota Points Are Calculated

In addition to a disk space quota, a site collection has a resource quota on the usage of user solutions. The quota prevents excessive use from certain site collections and also opens opportunities for chargeback based on resource usage. Resource usage is calculated by looking at counters, such as CPU and memory. SharePoint attempts to normalize each counter's usage by translating it into a point count. The total point count for all counters for all user solutions in a site collection becomes the resource usage for the day. Thus, user solution quotas are based on daily usage. Once the usage for the day is reached, no more user solution code can run until SharePoint resets the count via the Solution Daily Resource Usage Update timer job.

As a farm administrator, you can adjust how these quota points are calculated. For example, if CPU is limited, you can make CPU usage more "expensive." Or if RAM is abundant, you can make memory usage "cheaper." These counters can only be adjusted by using PowerShell. Changes to these counters apply to the farm as a whole, so the calculation rules apply the same to all site collections.

To view all the counters, you can run this short script.:

```
[Microsoft.SharePoint.Administration.SPUserCodeService]
::Local.ResourceMeasures | Select Name,ResourcesPerPoint
```

Figure 6.12: Resource quota calculation settings

```
PS C:\> [Microsoft.SharePoint.Administration.SPUserCodeService]::Local.ResourceM
easures | Select Name, ResourcesPerPoint

Name                                    ResourcesPerPoint
AbnormalProcessTerminationCount                         1
CPUExecutionTime                                      200
CriticalExceptionCount                                 10
IdlePercentProcessorTime                              100
InvocationCount                                       100
PercentProcessorTime                                   85
ProcessCPUCycles                              100000000000
ProcessHandleCount                                  10000
ProcessIOBytes                                   10000000
ProcessThreadCount                                  10000
ProcessVirtualBytes                            1000000000
SharePointDatabaseQueryCount                          400
SharePointDatabaseQueryTime                            20
UnhandledExceptionCount                                50
UnresponsiveprocessCount                                2

PS C:\>
```

The default settings for a farm are shown in Figure 6.12.

To make CPU execution time "less expensive," just increase this number. The default value is 200, and the following script increases it to 400:

```
$cpu=[Microsoft.SharePoint.Administration.
SPUserCodeService]::Local.ResourceMeasures |
where {$_.Name -eq "CPUExecutionTime"}
$cpu.ResourcesPerPoint = 400
$cpu.Update()
```

With this new setting, 400 units of CPUExecutionTime now equals one point. Similarly, to make CPUExecutionTime more expensive, use a smaller number. Other counters work in the same way.

> **TIP** Until you know what your real needs are, you should not arbitrarily change quota point numbers.

Timer jobs (Solution Resource Usage Log Processing and Solution Resource Usage Update) are used to calculate the points. Any changes made to the counters may take up to 15 minutes for the updated totals to be reflected in each site collection.

Manage Features

A feature is a type of enhancement that can be plugged into SharePoint. Custom features can be written by developers, but SharePoint itself is built on features as well. For example, many of the capabilities found in SPS are implemented as features that aren't present in SPF. This makes sense since SPS adds many enhancements on top of SPF.

Features can be used for many types of functionality, such as adding or removing menu commands, creating lists, creating content types, even altering the SharePoint interface using custom ASP.NET controls.

Each SharePoint feature has a defined scope. The scope gives users flexibility in determining where the enhancement is used. Four scopes are available:

- Website
- Site collection
- Web application
- Farm

For example, take a custom feature that adds a new command to the Site Actions menu. If this feature is scoped to a single website, then only designated websites will have this new command. If this feature is scoped to a site collection, then every website in designated site collections have this new menu command. If this feature is scoped to a web application, then every website in every site collection in designated web applications have this new menu command.

Before a feature can be used, it must be installed. In most cases, a solution package is used to automate the installation of features. By default, when a solution package is deployed, any features that are part of the package are also installed.

Once a feature is installed, it must be activated in order to be used. This is covered next.

> **NOTE** It's easy to get solutions and features mixed up. Remember, the solution deploys custom code. The feature is just a form of custom code. So, when deploying a solution, a feature may also be deployed. Specifically, the solution copies the feature's files to each WFE server in your farm. It also installs the feature so that it becomes registered with SharePoint.

Activating and Deactivating Features

When a feature is activated, it becomes usable for one or more websites, depending on the feature's scope. A web-scoped feature that is activated within a website becomes available in just that website. A site collection-scoped feature that is activated becomes available for all websites in that site collection. You must activate a feature at a level that matches the feature's scope. In other words, a feature that is scoped to a website cannot be activated for a site collection, and vice versa. The scope is set by the developer inside the feature and cannot be changed. Deactivating a feature allows you to turn off a feature that was previously activated.

SharePoint's UI provides four screens where features can be activated or deactivated. Each screen corresponds to one of the scopes: website, site collection, web application, and farm. When a feature is activated or deactivated, it is done immediately.

This section provides the specific steps to activate or deactivate features for each scope. Features can also be managed using PowerShell, as is discussed in "Using PowerShell to Manage Features," later in this chapter.

In terms of activating and deactivating features, all the scopes work the same way: You are presented with a list of features, and you click the Activate or Deactivate button for the feature you want to control. If you deactivate a feature, you must confirm the action.

> **Website Features** Features that are scoped to the website level are the most granular. Deploying features to specific websites gives you precise control over which websites use the features. By default, only hierarchy managers, site owners, or site collection administrators are able to activate or deactivate features for a website. Here are the steps:
>
> 1. Click Site Actions ➤ Site Settings.
> 2. In the Site Actions category, click Manage Site Features.
>
> A list of website features is shown in Figure 6.13.

Figure 6.13: Activating and deactivating features at the website level

Name		Status
Content Organizer Create metadata based rules that move content submitted to this site to the correct library or folder.	Activate	
E-mail Integration with Content Organizer Enable a site's content organizer to accept and organize email messages. This feature should be used only in a highly managed store, like a Records Center.	Activate	
Group Work Lists Provides Calendars with added functionality for team and resource scheduling.	Activate	
Hold and eDiscovery This feature is used to track external actions like litigations, investigations, or audits that require you to suspend the disposition of documents.	Activate	
Metadata Navigation and Filtering Provides each list in the site with a settings pages for configuring that list to use metadata tree view hierarchies and filter controls to improve navigation and filtering of the contained items.	Activate	
Offline Synchronization for External Lists Enables offline synchronization for external lists with Outlook and SharePoint Workspace.	Deactivate	Active

Site Collection Features Many types of features, including built-in features, are scoped to the site collection level. It is common to see web parts, master pages, page layouts, content types, and others made available by activating a site collection-scoped feature. For example, by activating a feature, you create a new web part definition in the Web Parts gallery (introduced in Chapter 3).

In general, an activated site collection feature applies to all websites in the site collection. Only site collection administrators are able to activate or deactivate features for a site collection. Here are the steps:

1. Access the top-level website for a site collection.
2. Click Site Actions ➢ Site Settings.
3. In the Site Collection Administration category, click Site Collection Features.

TIP If you can't find the feature you want, be sure you are looking at the right screen. In some cases, you may not know the feature scope, so if you can't find it for one scope, check the other ones. Remember site collection-scoped features are different from website-scoped ones.

Web Application Features Web application-scoped features can be activated and deactivated by using Central Administration. Here are the steps:

1. Click Application Management, then choose Manage Web Applications.
2. Highlight the desired web application.
3. In the ribbon, click the Manage Features button.

Farm Features Farm features have the widest scope—they apply to the whole farm. Be very careful about deactivating farm-scope features, in particular built-in ones, as they have a big impact.

To activate and deactivate farm-scoped features using Central Administration, click System Settings and then click Manage Farm Features.

Using PowerShell to Manage Features

PowerShell gives administrators complete control over managing features. The biggest advantage to using PowerShell is the ability to automate the activation or deactivation of features across a wide number of websites or site collections. Five cmdlets are available when working with features from PowerShell:

`Get-SPFeature` Returns information about features installed into SharePoint. Information for both built-in and custom features is returned. You can optionally specify a scope to filter the features to those of a certain scope. Here is the basic syntax:

```
Get-SPFeature [-Web | -Site | -WebApplication | -Farm]
```

`Install-SPFeature` Used to manually install a feature. This cmdlet is not typically used by administrators because installation is automated when you deploy a solution package.

`Enable-SPFeature` Used to activate a feature. Here is the basic syntax:

```
Enable-SPFeature <FeatureName> -Url <URL>
```

FeatureName is the name of the folder where the feature is stored. Each feature must have a unique folder located here: `Program`

Files\Common Files\Microsoft Shared\Web Server Extensions\14\
TEMPLATE\FEATURES.

This example activates a feature for the finance site collection:

    Enable-SPFeature BIWebParts -Url ↵
    http://intranet/sites/finance

This example activates a feature for all site collections in the intranet web application:

    Get-SPSiteAdministration http://intranet/* -Limit all ↵
    | ForEach-Object {Enable-SPFeature EmployeeSpotlight ↵
    -url $_.Url}

Disable-SPFeature   Used to deactivate a feature. It works the same as Enable-SPFeature.

Uninstall-SPFeature   Used to manually uninstall a feature.

7

Configuring the User Profiles and My Sites Services

IN THIS CHAPTER, YOU WILL LEARN TO:

▶ **CONFIGURE THE USER PROFILE SERVICE APPLICATION** (Pages 223 – 233)

- Configuring Accounts and Permissions (Page 224)
- Preparing the Farm for Supporting My Sites (Page 225)
- Creating the User Profile Service Application (Page 228)
- Starting the User Profile Services (Page 232)

▶ **CONFIGURE USER PROFILE PROPERTIES** (Pages 233 – 238)

- Configuring a Property for Import (Page 233)
- Configuring a Property for Export (Page 235)
- Creating a Custom Property Mapping (Page 236)

▶ **CONFIGURE USER PROFILE SYNCHRONIZATION** (Pages 238 – 244)

- Creating a Synchronization Connection (Page 238)
- Performing Synchronization (Page 241)
- Configuring Synchronization Settings (Page 242)
- Editing Connection Filters (Page 243)

▶ **MANAGE USER PROFILES** (Pages 244 – 246)

- Viewing Profiles and Editing a Profile (Page 244)
- Creating a New Profile (Page 245)
- Deleting a Profile (Page 245)

▶ **CONFIGURE AUDIENCES** (Pages 246 – 249)

- Creating an Audience (Page 246)
- Editing an Audience (Page 248)

- Deleting an Audience (Page 248)
- Scheduling Audience Compilation (Page 249)

CONFIGURE MY SITES AND SOCIAL NETWORKING (Pages 249 – 254)

- Setting Up My Sites (Page 250)
- Configuring Trusted Host Locations (Page 252)
- Configuring Personalization Site Links (Page 253)
- Publishing Links to Office Client Applications (Page 254)

This chapter discusses the purpose and configuration of the SharePoint 2010 User Profile service. The User Profile service is responsible for providing social networking and content targeting capabilities. Using these features, organizations can empower users to share personal information with other users in a secure and supported environment. SharePoint 2010 offers many of the same tools for exchanging informal and personal information that public sites such as Facebook and LinkedIn do and offers the added benefit of integration with team site libraries and lists as well as enterprise search results.

Configure the User Profile Service Application

Public social networking sites such as Facebook and LinkedIn have gained popularity because they allow an open and relatively unstructured form of communication that encourages users to share ideas and insights. Some organizations have begun to see the value in this type of interaction and have started endorsing the use of some of these technologies during the workday as part of their corporate communications strategy. While public Internet sites are suitable in some cases, most organizations require that information relating to their business be kept within a closed environment that can be monitored and controlled.

With My Sites, organizations can give employees a personal SharePoint site where they can store and share documents, pictures, and other details that don't belong in departmental team sites. More importantly, users have complete control over the security and exposure given to this information, allowing them to exchange confidential information with select sets of users.

We need to be clear that there is a difference between personal information and private details and that corporate social networking is not necessarily intended for both. An employee may feel comfortable sharing something personal, such as a hobby or a book recommendation, with others in the workplace but not want to share something private like their birthday or cell phone number.

SharePoint 2010 allows organizations to import employee details from Active Directory and other data sources, to present this information as user profiles, and to set policies on who is allowed to see which data. Users can update some of their own profile details and control the amount of information they want to share.

One of the advantages of storing many details about employees in their user profiles is that these details can be used to create custom *audiences* that content publishers can use to target information to groups of users. Audiences can be based on details such as a staff member's office location or a code stored in their position title and then used to show or hide pages in a site based on which audience a user belongs to.

The following steps are required to deploy the User Profile service application:

1. Configure accounts and permissions to prepare for synchronization of the User Profile service.
2. Set up the User Profile service application.
3. Start the User Profile service.
4. Set up and perform synchronization.

This section describes the first three tasks in detail. Synchronization is covered in "Configure User Profile Synchronization," later in this chapter.

Configuring Accounts and Permissions

The User Profile service manages data by synchronizing with Active Directory or another data source. This service requires specific permissions to be in place in order to perform synchronization. Some of these permissions must be configured before you attempt to perform synchronization.

SharePoint 2010 Farm Account This is the identity account of the SharePoint Central Administration application pool and must be made a member of the local Administrators group on the synchronization server. The account must also have the Log On Locally right on the synchronization server. (Instructions for selecting the synchronization server are in the section "Creating the User Profile Service Application," later in this chapter.)

When the Forefront Identity Manager (FIM) services start, they will automatically adopt this account as their service account. Once the configuration process is complete, the permission can be removed.

Synchronization Account In preparation for configuring the User Profile service, you must create an Active Directory account, or choose an existing one, to be the synchronization account. The synchronization account is used by the service to connect to Active

Directory or another data source to import user details into the profiles. Following the principle of least privilege, we recommend creating a separate account. This account must then be granted at least the Replicating Directory Changes right. If you intend to replicate content back into Active Directory, it must also have the Create Child Objects right.

To configure these permissions:

1. Log onto the Active Directory Domain Controller and open Active Directory Users And Computers.
2. Right-click the domain and then click Delegate Control.
3. In the Delegation Of Control wizard, click Next.
4. On the Users Or Groups page, click Add.
5. Enter the name of the synchronization account, click Check Names, and then click OK.
6. Click Next.
7. On the Tasks To Delegate page, select Create A Custom Task To Delegate, and then click Next.
8. On the Active Directory Object Type page, select "This folder, existing objects in this folder, and creation of new objects in this folder," and then click Next.
9. On the Permissions page, check the boxes next to Write, Create All Child Objects, and Replicating Directory Changes; then click Next.
10. Click Finish.

Preparing the Farm for Supporting My Sites

As part of the configuration of the User Profile service application, several steps need to be performed to prepare the farm for supporting My Sites. You need to perform the following steps in order:

1. Create or select a web application to host My Sites.
2. Create the managed paths for My Sites.
3. Create a My Site host.
4. Set up self-service site creation.

Creating or Using an Existing Web Application

Each My Site will be created as a separate site collection in a specific web application. While SharePoint can be configured to create My Sites in almost any web application, it is a best practice to create a dedicated web application to hold the My Sites content. This separate web application will automatically have a dedicated database to keep the My Sites content distinct from other site content. It will also allow farm administrators to configure settings and policies at the web application level to apply only to the My Sites web application.

There is nothing unique in the way that a web application is created for use by My Sites as compared to other web applications created for intranet purposes—except for the URL used. We recommend that the URL be one that is distinctive and recognizable by users, for example, http://mysites.company.com. For the steps to create a new web application, see Chapter 2, "Creating and Managing Web Applications."

Creating the Managed Paths

Managed paths allow web applications to support multiple site collections under a common root URL. In the case of My Sites, SharePoint requires that two managed paths be created:

Explicit Managed Path This path is used for the My Site Host site collection. The My Site Host managed path is a dedicated site collection that is the entry point for all users to the My Sites.

Wildcard Managed Path This path is used for all the user site collections. The wildcard managed path will allow multiple new My Site site collections to be created under the My Site Host managed path without conflicting with any other URLs.

For more details on managed paths, see Chapter 3, "Creating and Managing Site Collections."

To create the My Site managed paths, perform the following steps:

1. From SharePoint 2010 Central Administration, under Application Management, click Manage Web Applications.
2. Click the row for the web application created to hold the My Sites.
3. From the ribbon, click the Managed Paths button. Notice that there is already a managed path called (root), which is

automatically created with an Explicit inclusion. This path can be used as the path for the My Site Host or a new path can be created. To create a new host site path, in the Path box enter the name of the relative URL, such as my, and from the Type drop-down, select Explicit Inclusion. Then click Add Path.

4. In the Path box, enter the name of the relative URL to be used as the root for all user site collections, such as **personal**, and, under the Type drop-down, select Wildcard Inclusion. Then click Add Path.

5. Click OK.

Creating a My Site Host

The My Site Host site collection serves as the "landing page" for all users browsing to their My Site and also supports the automatic redirect that creates a new My Site for a user who does not have one already.
To create the My Site Host site, follow these steps:

1. From SharePoint 2010 Central Administration, under Application Management, click Create Site Collections.

2. From the Web Application drop-down menu, select the My Site web application you created earlier.

3. In the Title box, enter a title, such as **My Sites**, which will appear to users. In the Description box, enter the purpose of this site.

4. In the Web Site Address drop-down list, select the path created in the previous section as the Explicit inclusion for the My Site host. By default, the URL root (/) will be selected.

5. In the Template Selection section, click the Enterprise tab, and then select My Site Host.

6. In the Primary Site Collection Administrator box, enter the username for the user who will be the site collection administrator; use the pattern *domain\username*.

7. Click OK.

Setting Up Self-Service Site Creation

Once the My Site hosts site has been created, Self-Service Site Creation must be enabled on the My Sites web application. Normally, the only way to create a new site collection is for a farm administrator to create it from within Central Administration. But this would be an impractical way of creating site collections for every user. When Self-Service Site Creation is turned on, users receive the right to create a site collection on their own in the My Site web application and are automatically designated as the site collection administrator of their new site collection. Users don't need to know anything about this right because SharePoint handles all the processing for them when they navigate to their My Site for the first time.

To enable Self-Service Site Creation, perform the following steps:

1. From SharePoint 2010 Central Administration, under Application Management, click Manage Web Applications.
2. Click the row for the web application created to hold the My Sites.
3. From the ribbon, click the Self-Service Site Creation button.
4. Click the On option and click OK.

NOTE Enabling Self-Service Site Creation has the side effect that any user with permission to create a My Site will also be able to navigate to a page exposed by this feature at the relative address _layouts/scsignup.aspx under the My Site host and create an additional site collection. The good news is, there is no link to this page published anywhere in the site, so most users will never find it. The bad news is, there is no way of restricting access to this page, short of renaming the file itself.

Creating the User Profile Service Application

To support all the social networking features of SharePoint 2010, the farm requires that at least one User Profile service application be created.

You must create this application *before* you start the User Profile service and the User Profile Synchronization service.

The SharePoint 2010 User Profile service makes use of two FIM services. This fact makes its configuration and operations distinctly different from those of SharePoint 2007. The services are exposed in Central Administration under Services On Server. They are called the User Profile service and the User Profile Synchronization service.

> **TIP** If you run into problems following the steps in this section and services fail to provision correctly, don't panic. This is actually a common experience with the RTM version of the product. Simply stop the User Profile service on the server, delete the service application and any databases created, and try again. In many cases, the same steps will work on the second try. For more information on creating and deleting service applications, refer to Chapter 4, "Creating Service Applications."

The following steps assume that the My Site host site and managed path have already been created. The steps for creating them are found earlier in this section.

1. From SharePoint 2010 Central Administration, under Application Management, click Manage Service Applications.
2. From the ribbon, click the New menu and select User Profile Service Application.
3. At the top of the dialog box, enter a unique name for this service as you want it to appear in the Service Applications list.
4. In the Application Pool section, you need to either choose an existing application pool or create a new one. If you choose to create a new application pool, enter a unique name for the pool; then, in the Configurable field, either select an existing managed account or click Register New Managed Account to create a new one. (We don't recommend that you use predefined accounts for production installations.)

   The application pool serves as the process space for executing the operations of the service. While it is not necessary to create a dedicated application pool for the User Profile service, it is considered a best practice and provides better isolation and security.
5. In the Profile Database section, enter the name of the SQL server where the database will be created and the name of the database you want to create, as shown in Figure 7.1. Then either select Windows Authentication to use the application pool account to access the database, or enter specific SQL Server logon credentials if Windows Authentication to the SQL server is blocked. Enter the name of the failover database server if you are implementing fault tolerance through database mirroring.

The Profile database holds the details about all the users and organizations imported from Active Directory.

Figure 7.1: Profile database settings

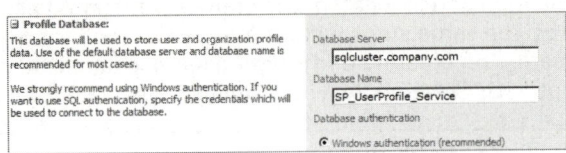

6. In the Synchronization Database section, enter the name of the SQL server where the database will be created and the name of the database you want to create, as shown in Figure 7.2. Then provide authentication and fault tolerance settings, as in step 5. The Synchronization database holds the configuration and processing details for connections to Active Directory and other data sources.

Figure 7.2: Synchronization database settings

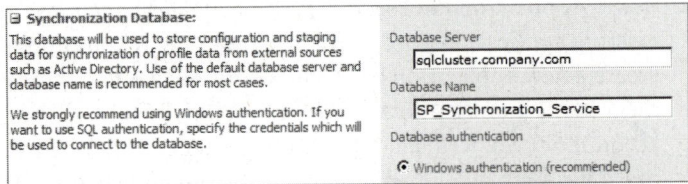

7. In the Social Tagging Database section, enter the name of the SQL server where the database will be created and the name of the database you want to create, as shown in Figure 7.3. Then provide authentication and fault tolerance settings, as in step 5. The Social Tagging database holds the tags (enterprise keywords) and personal notes entered by users and made available through their user profile.

Figure 7.3: Social Tagging database settings

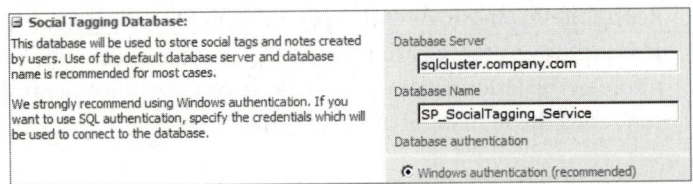

8. From the Profile Synchronization Instance drop-down list, select the SharePoint server that will execute the profile synchronization processing. While not a very intensive process in itself, the synchronization should be run on a machine that will not be heavily engaged in other processes at the scheduled synchronization time.

9. In the My Site Host URL box, shown in Figure 7.4, enter the fully qualified URL to the site collection that has been created using the My Site Host site template. See the "Creating a My Site Host" section earlier in this chapter for more details.

Figure 7.4: My Site Host URL and My Site Managed Path settings

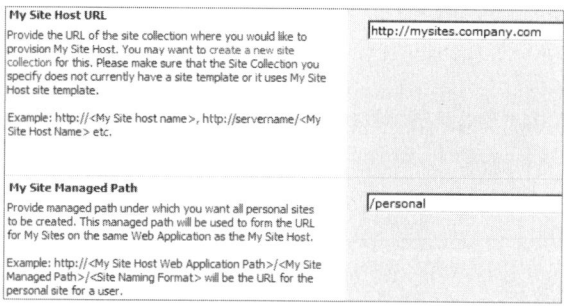

10. In the My Site Managed Path box, shown in Figure 7.4, enter the managed path that has been created for provisioning new My Sites under the "Creating a My Site Host" section.

11. In the Site Naming Format section, choose the format for the site name that will be created for each user. For details on the formats, see "Setting Up My Sites," later in this chapter.

12. The Default Proxy Group setting specifies whether this service will automatically be part of the group of services assigned to all web applications or whether this service will be created independently. If the service is created independently, it must be assigned manually through a custom association. In most cases, when you only plan to have one User Profile service, it is appropriate to leave the default value set to Yes to include it in the Default Proxy Group.

13. Click Create to create the User Profile service application.

Starting the User Profile Services

Starting the User Profile service in Central Administration also starts the corresponding Windows services on the synchronization server.

1. From SharePoint 2010 Central Administration, under System Settings, click Manage Services On Server.
2. From the Server drop-down, select Change Server and set it to the synchronization server selected in step 8 in the previous exercise.
3. Next to User Profile Service, click Start under the Action column.
4. Next to User Profile Synchronization Service, click Start under the Action column. The service startup screen appears, as shown in Figure 7.5.

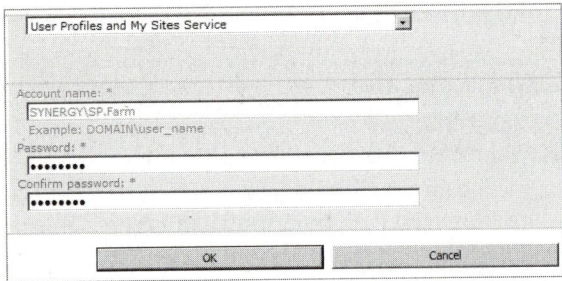

Figure 7.5: User Profile Synchronization Service startup screen

5. Select the User Profile service application that you created in the previous exercise.
6. Enter the password for the farm account, and then confirm the password.
7. Click OK.

The User Profile Synchronization Service status will change to Starting and will remain so for up to 15 minutes as the FIM service is configured. Once it is completed, the status will change to Started. To confirm that the services are fully configured:

1. Open the Services applet under Administrative Tools on the synchronization server.

2. Locate the Forefront Identity Manager Service and the Forefront Identity Manager Synchronization Service.

3. Confirm the following for both services:
   - They have the status of Started.
   - They have been configured to start automatically.
   - They have their logon account set to the farm account.

4. As a final step to prepare for configuring a synchronization connection, restart IIS by opening a command prompt and typing **IISRESET**.

Configure User Profile Properties

SharePoint 2010 supports customizing the details about users that are imported into user profiles by modifying the properties defined by the User Profile service. If your organization has created custom attributes in Active Directory, those attributes can be mapped onto custom properties in the user profile and imported along with the built-in attributes. SharePoint 2010 also supports the new capability of exporting property values from the user profile to update the attributes in Active Directory.

Configuring a Property for Import

You may need to modify the import settings of an existing property to change the attribute that the data is drawn from or to have it import from a different synchronization connection. To change the way that data is imported into an existing profile property, do the following:

1. From SharePoint 2010 Central Administration, under Application Management, click Manage Service Applications.

2. On the Manage Service Applications page, click the User Profile Service Application link.

3. From the Manage Profile Service page, shown partially in Figure 7.6, under the People section, click Manage User Properties.

Figure 7.6: Manage Profile Service commands

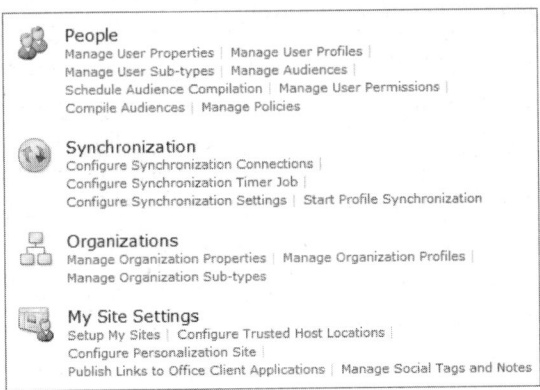

On the Manage User Properties page, the Property Name entry in the left column is the name that users see when they view a profile. The Mapped Attribute value is the Active Directory attribute that is being imported.

4. In the properties list, locate a property to configure and from the property's context menu, select Edit. For example, the Mobile Phone property is not mapped to an Active Directory property by default.

5. In the Add New Mapping section, select the Source Data Connection (for more information on connections, see "Configure User Profile Synchronization," later in this chapter).

6. Select the attribute you want to import from. For example, the Mobile Phone property could be mapped to the Active Directory attribute labeled `mobile`, as shown in Figure 7.7.

Figure 7.7: Configuring import mapping

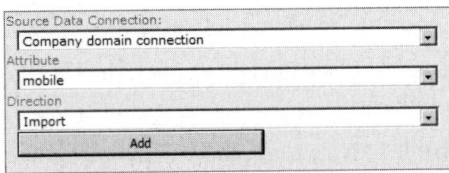

7. For the Direction option, select Import.
8. Click Add.

Configuring a Property for Export

You may want to export a property value from SharePoint 2010 into Active Directory to take advantage of details that users have modified in their profiles. For example, users can update the Picture property in their SharePoint profile but they normally have no access to this property in Active Directory. The Picture property is also designed specifically to be exported from SharePoint to Active Directory. To configure data to be exported from an existing Profile property, do the following:

1. From SharePoint 2010 Central Administration, under Application Management, click Manage Service Applications.

2. On the Manage Service Applications page, click the User Profile Service Application link.

3. From the Manage Profile Service page, shown partially in Figure 7.6, under the People section, click Manage User Properties.

4. In the properties list, locate a property to configure and from the property's context menu, select Edit. For example, the Picture property is not configured for export by default, as shown in Figure 7.8.

Figure 7.8: Editing a profile property

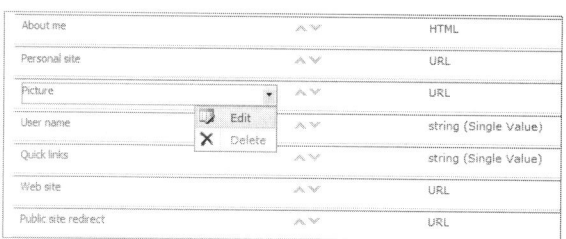

5. In the Add New Mapping section, select the Source Data Connection (for more information on connections, see "Configure User Profile Synchronization," later in this chapter).

6. Select the attribute you want to import from. For example, the Picture property is designed to be mapped to the Active Directory `thumbnailPhoto` attribute.

7. For the Direction option, select Export.

8. Click OK.

Creating a Custom Property Mapping

You can create a completely new property for the user profile. For example, a company might store a staff member's employee ID in a custom attribute in Active Directory and might want to import this value into the user profiles. A new custom property can be created to hold the value.

To create a new property:

1. From SharePoint 2010 Central Administration, under Application Management, click Manage Service Applications.
2. On the Manage Service Applications page, click the User Profile Service Application link.
3. From the Manage Profile Service page, shown partially in Figure 7.5, under the People section, click Manage User Properties.
4. On the toolbar, click New Property.
5. In the Name box, enter an internal name for the property. This value is used by the User Profile service and cannot be changed once it is created.
6. In the Display Name box, enter a name for the property that users will see.
7. From the Type drop-down list, select the data type for the property and the length, if appropriate. Most of the types represent simple data types with no configuration options beyond the length. Selecting a String data type allows for the option to select a *term set* (new to SharePoint 2010) to use as the source for the values that users can enter into this property. For more details on term sets, see Chapter 11, "Configuring the Managed Metadata Service."
8. The Default User Profile Subtype check box, selected by default, is the most commonly used option. If you intend to configure different sets of properties for different groups of users, then deselect this option to dissociate the property from the default subtype.
9. Enter a description to explain the purpose of this property.
10. In the Policy Settings section, choose whether data for this property will be Required, Optional, or Disabled. The Disabled setting will hide the property from users and only allow it to

be edited by the User Profile service administrator. Also choose the default privacy of this property, which indicates who can see it in the user's profile. The options are Only Me, My Manager, My Team, My Colleagues, or Everyone. To allow users to change the privacy setting, select the User Can Override check box.

11. In the Edit Setting section, select "Allow users to edit values for this property" to permit users to update this property. Generally, users should only be allowed to edit properties that are configured as an export mapping or are not mapped to an Active Directory attribute. The reason is that those configured for import will be overwritten with values from Active Directory each time synchronization occurs.

12. In the Display Settings section, check the appropriate visibility options:

    - Show in the profile properties section of the user's profile page
    - Show on the Edit Details page
    - Show updates to the property in newsfeeds

13. In the Search Settings section, select the options that affect how the property is indexed by SharePoint Search:

    Alias Allows SharePoint to recognize the value as equivalent to the username and account name for searching purposes.

    Indexed Allows this property to be indexed. That way, the SharePoint crawler can read the values of this property and incorporate it into search results.

14. Check the Property Mapping For Synchronization section; it displays any existing mappings between this property and Active Directory attributes and allows mappings to be removed if necessary.

15. In the Add New Mapping section, select the Source Data Connection (for more information on connections, see the next section, "Configure User Profile Synchronization").

16. Select the attribute you want to import from or export to.

17. For the Direction option, select either Import, to bring values into the user profile from the data source, or Export, to push values

from the user profile into the data source. In most cases, when you are intending to display values stored in Active Directory, you would select Import.

18. Click OK.

Configure User Profile Synchronization

The process of profile synchronization allows SharePoint 2010 to both import data from external sources and export data to those same sources. Not all data can be both imported and exported since restrictions exist based on the type of data and the data source itself. SharePoint 2010 can synchronize over one or more connections, and each connection can communicate with a different data source. SharePoint 2010 supports connections to Active Directory domains; Business Data Connectivity (BDC), which is also now referred to as Business Connectivity Services (BCS) in SharePoint 2010; IBM Tivoli Directory Server (ITDS); Novell eDirectory; or Sun Java System Directory Server. Through the BDC connection, SharePoint can import data from any Open Database Connectivity (ODBC) database or web service, allowing SharePoint profiles to include data from most legacy human resources systems.

There are two steps to synchronization:

1. Creating a synchronization connection
2. Performing a profile data import

The following sections describe how to perform these steps.

Creating a Synchronization Connection

Before you start a profile data import, you need to create at least one synchronization connection. To create a connection, perform the following steps:

1. From SharePoint 2010 Central Administration, under Application Management, click Manage Service Applications.
2. On the Manage Service Applications page, click the User Profile Service Application link.
3. On the Manage Profile Service page, under the Synchronization section, click Configure Synchronization Connections. The

Configure User Profile Synchronization

Synchronization Connections page, shown partially in Figure 7.9, is displayed.

Figure 7.9: Synchronization Connections page

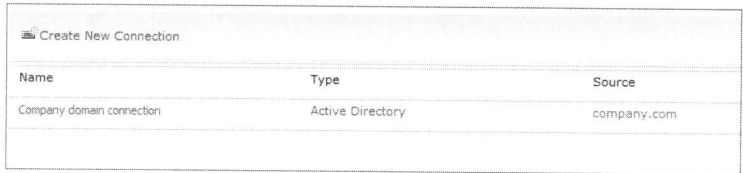

4. Click Create New Connection. The Add New Synchronization Connection page, shown in Figure 7.10, is displayed.

Figure 7.10: Add New Synchronization Connection page

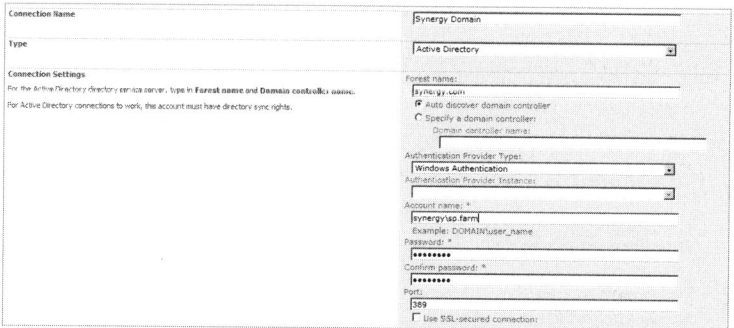

5. In the Connection Name box, enter a descriptive name for this connection.
6. From the Type drop-down list, select the type of data source you want to connect to.
7. In the Connection Settings section, enter the reference to the source of the data. In the case of an Active Directory connection, enter the full name of the forest. In the case of a BDC connection, enter or browse for the external content type. For all other connections, enter the name of the server.
8. In most cases it is preferable to allow SharePoint to autodiscover the domain controller. However, if this fails you can enter the name of a specific domain controller to synchronize with.

9. For Authentication Provider Type, specify the type of authentication for this connection: Active Directory, Forms Authentication, or Trusted Claims Provider Authentication.

10. In the Account Name box, enter the domain account name of the user profile synchronization account that was previously granted permissions on Active Directory. Enter the password and then confirm it.

11. In most cases, the default port of 389 is appropriate as most of the connections will be LDAP queries and the default port for the LDAP protocol is 389. If you need to specify a different port, do so.

12. If this connection needs to be secured, then select the Use SSL-Secured Connection check box. (Checking this box will require additional steps on the data source side to configure the digital certificate. These steps are outside the scope of this book.)

13. Click the Populate Containers button. This step will execute a query against the data source using the credentials provided. If the query is successful, the box will display all the organizational units (OUs) in the Active Directory domain, as shown in Figure 7.11.

Figure 7.11: Populate Containers list

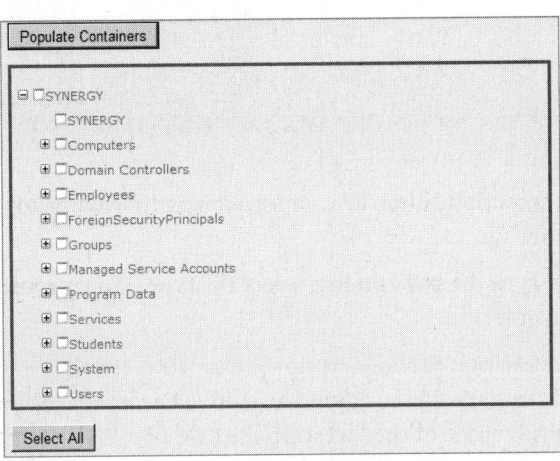

14. Check the boxes next to the OUs that contain accounts that should be imported, and click OK.

> **NOTE** If the synchronization connection appears to save correctly but does not display in the list on the Synchronization Connections page, then run the `IISRESET` command on the synchronization server (open a command prompt and type `IISRESET`) and refresh the page to make it display.

15. Once the connection is created, perform a full synchronization. (For instructions, see the next section, "Performing Synchronization.")

Performing Synchronization

Profile synchronization is required to import accounts from a data source into user profiles. Either a full or an incremental synchronization can be performed manually. You can schedule an incremental synchronization to import profiles on a regular basis.

Synchronizing Manually

A full synchronization imports all content from the data source and overwrites the current profiles. An incremental synchronization only imports changes to the existing profile data.

To manually start profile synchronization:

1. From SharePoint 2010 Central Administration, under Application Management, click Manage Service Applications.
2. On the Manage Service Applications page, click the User Profile Service Application link.
3. On the Manage Profile Service page, under the Synchronization section, click Start Profile Synchronization.
4. Select the option Start Incremental Synchronization or Start Full Synchronization.
5. Click OK.

On the Manage Profile Service page, the Profile Synchronization Status will change to Synchronizing and will show a Stop link to cancel the current synchronization.

Setting Up a Synchronization Schedule

Incremental synchronization can be scheduled to import profiles on a regular basis. The frequency with which you perform an import will depend on the type of data source, the number of accounts being imported, and how frequently changes to the data occur. As a general rule, at least a once-daily profile import is recommended and is configured by default in the timer job setting.

To change the frequency of incremental synchronization:

1. From SharePoint 2010 Central Administration, under Application Management, click Manage Service Applications.

2. On the Manage Service Applications page, click the User Profile Service Application link.

3. On the Manage Profile Service page, under the Synchronization section, click Configure Synchronization Timer Job.

4. Select the option for the import to recur at an interval of Minutes, Hourly, Daily, Weekly, or Monthly and set the appropriate interval value. For the Daily, Weekly, and Monthly intervals you can set a specific start time. For the others, you set a number of minutes or minutes past the hour to start.

5. Click OK.

Configuring Synchronization Settings

There are a number of general settings that affect the synchronization process. You can:

- Synchronize either users only, or both users and groups
- Choose whether to import existing BCS connections
- Set up an external identity manager

To configure synchronization settings, perform the following steps:

1. From SharePoint 2010 Central Administration, under Application Management, click Manage Service Applications.

2. On the Manage Service Applications page, click the User Profile Service Application link.

3. On the Manage Profile Service page, under the Synchronization section, click Configure Synchronization Settings.

4. In the Synchronization Entities section, shown in Figure 7.12, choose what you want to synchronize. Users And Groups synchronizes all objects; Users Only minimizes the number of accounts imported.

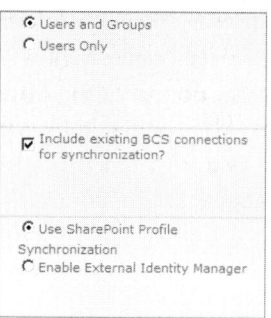

Figure 7.12: Configuring synchronization settings

5. In the Synchronize BCS Connections section, the box labeled "Include existing BCS connections for synchronization?" is checked by default. To avoid importing BCS data during synchronization, uncheck the box.

6. The External Identity Manager section allows you to elect to replace the built-in SharePoint FIM services with a separate component to perform the synchronization with data sources. The most commonly used external identity manager is Microsoft Forefront Identity Manager 2010, available as a separate product. To use this approach, click the option Enable External Identity Manager.

7. Click OK.

Editing Connection Filters

Connection filters allow you to restrict the number of users or groups retrieved from a data source by applying excluding criteria to the query. For example, the default setting in SharePoint 2010 will import all user and group accounts from Active Directory, including accounts that are marked as Disabled. This may not be appropriate if the disabled accounts represent users who have left the company or been fired. Adding a filter will allow these accounts to be excluded. To edit the filters for an existing connection, perform the following steps:

1. From SharePoint 2010 Central Administration, under Application Management, click Manage Service Applications.

2. On the Manage Service Applications page, click the User Profile Service Application link.

3. On the Manage Profile Service page, under the Synchronization section, click Configure Synchronization Connections.

4. On the Synchronization Connections page, click the context menu for the connection to edit and select Edit Connection Filters.

5. In the Exclusion Filters For Users section (shown in Figure 7.13) or in the Exclusion Filters For Groups section, click the Attribute drop-down list and select the property you want to apply a filter on.

Figure 7.13: Exclusion Filters For Users settings

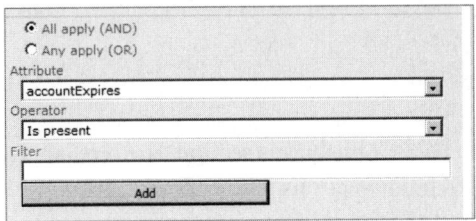

6. Select the correct operator. Depending on which operator you pick, you might need to enter a criteria value in the Filter box.

7. Click the Add button.

Manage User Profiles

After a successful profile synchronization, it may be necessary to view and edit the resulting user profiles. This is commonly done to review and make temporary changes to profiles in between synchronizations. However, it may also be necessary to update profile properties that users should not be updating themselves.

Viewing Profiles and Editing a Profile

It is useful to be able to review the profiles after they have been imported and to be able to manually update the details in each profile.

To view and edit a profile, perform the following steps:

1. From SharePoint 2010 Central Administration, under Application Management, click Manage Service Applications.

2. On the Manage Service Applications page, click the User Profile Service Application link.

3. On the Manage Profile Service page, click Manage User Profiles.

4. In the Find Profiles box, enter all or part of a profile name to search for, and then click Find.

5. Hover over the profile you want to view and, from the context menu, select Edit My Profile.

6. Change the values you wish to update and click Save And Close.

Creating a New Profile

Normally, profiles are created automatically through the synchronization process. It may be necessary in some cases to create a profile manually for accounts that are not included in the import.

To create a profile, follow these steps:

1. From SharePoint 2010 Central Administration, under Application Management, click Manage Service Applications.

2. On the Manage Service Applications page, click the User Profile Service Application link.

3. On the Manage Profile Service page, click Manage User Profiles.

4. Click New Profile and fill in the required fields.

NOTE Fields that are mapped to Active Directory attributes will be overwritten during the next synchronization.

5. Click Save And Close.

Deleting a Profile

To immediately delete a profile that should no longer be displayed, perform the following steps:

1. From SharePoint 2010 Central Administration, under Application Management, click Manage Service Applications.

2. On the Manage Service Applications page, click the User Profile Service Application link.

3. On the Manage Profile Service page, click Manage User Profiles.

4. In the Find Profiles box, enter all or part of a profile name to search for, and then click Find.

5. Hover over the profile you want to view and, from the context menu, select Delete.

6. Click OK.

Configure Audiences

Perhaps contrary to the common opinion, the biggest challenge for managing content in SharePoint is not how to display more information to users, but how to display less. SharePoint 2010 is scalable to millions of documents, pages, or items per library or list and the average user is only interested in browsing a few of them at any given time. While there are extensive filtering and grouping capabilities available in lists and libraries, limited options exist for building views that dynamically change the display for each user.

Audiences in SharePoint 2010 are used to display specific sets of content to a group of users most likely to be interested in that content, and to hide content that they are not interested in. Here are some ways an audience can be used:

- Filter the pages displayed in a Content Query web part to reduce the items that users need to read.

- Hide and show different web parts on a page to optimize the use of the page real estate.

- Change the set of global navigation menu links that users see to avoid cluttering the navigation experience.

Creating an Audience

Built-in audiences are available to site administrators that are based on either Active Directory security groups or on SharePoint site groups. However, the most powerful type of audience is a *global audience* created within the User Profile service application. This type of audience can make full use of all profile properties and can be used across site collections. A global audience is generated by defining a set of one or more business rules with specific criteria identifying which users or groups will belong to the audience. The audience is then compiled to create the resulting set of users.

To create a global audience:

1. From SharePoint 2010 Central Administration, under Application Management, click Manage Service Applications.

2. On the Manage Service Applications page, click the User Profile Service Application link.
3. On the Manage Profile Service page, under the People section, click Manage Audiences.
4. On the View Audiences page, click New Audience.
5. In the Name box, shown in Figure 7.14, enter a display name for this audience and in the Description box, enter some explanatory details.

Figure 7.14: Settings for create an audience

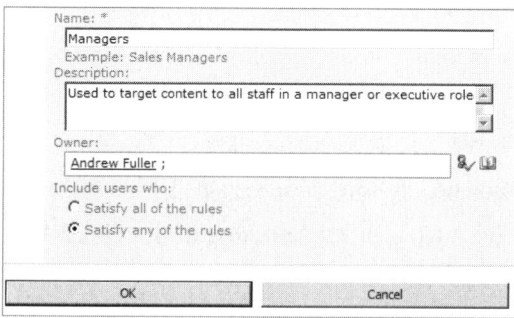

6. In the Owner field, enter the account name of the user who will be responsible for maintaining this audience.
7. Under the Include Users Who setting, select whether a user will be included in the audience only if they satisfy all of the rules (an AND relationship) or if they satisfy any of the rules (an OR relationship).
8. Click OK.
9. On the Add Audience Rule page (shown in Figure 7.15), under Select one of the following, select either User or Property to build the criteria on.

Figure 7.15: Add Audience Rule settings

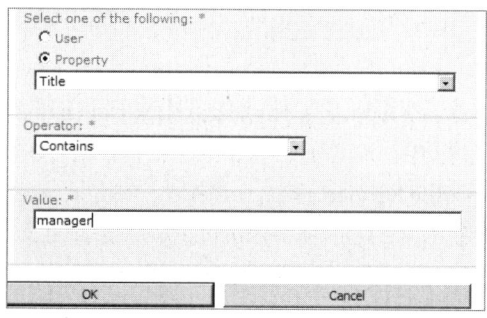

- If you select User, you can then select users based on who their manager is (the Reports Under setting) or which Active Directory group they belong to (the Member Of setting).
- If you select Property, you can then choose one of the user profile properties, a value, and an operator (=, Contains, <>, Not Contains) to use as a criterion.

10. Once the audience is defined, it will need to be compiled. On the View Audience Properties page, click Compile Audience. The Number Of Members value displayed on the page should change to show the compiled total of users in the audience.
11. To view the users in an audience, click the View Membership link.

Editing an Audience

To edit an existing audience, follow these steps:

1. From SharePoint 2010 Central Administration, under Application Management, click Manage Service Applications.
2. On the Manage Service Applications page, click the User Profile Service Application link.
3. On the Manage Profile Service page, under the People section, click Manage Audiences.
4. On the View Audiences page, click the context menu of the audience you want to edit and select View Properties.
5. On the View Audience Properties page, you can edit individual rules or click Edit Audience to modify the audience name or description.

Deleting an Audience

To delete an existing audience, perform the following steps:

1. From SharePoint 2010 Central Administration, under Application Management, click Manage Service Applications.
2. On the Manage Service Applications page, click the User Profile Service Application link.
3. On the Manage Profile Service page, under the People section, click Manage Audiences.

4. On the View Audiences page, click the context menu of the audience you want to edit and click Delete.

5. Click OK to confirm.

Scheduling Audience Compilation

Since audience membership is tied to profile properties, it is important to schedule audience compilation to occur *after* profile synchronization so that the most current profile data is available. We recommend that audiences be recompiled at least once a week, but you may do so as often as once a day.

To modify the compilation schedule, perform these steps:

1. From SharePoint 2010 Central Administration, under Application Management, click Manage Service Applications.

2. On the Manage Service Applications page, click the User Profile Service Application link.

3. From the Manage Profile Service page, under the People section, click Schedule Audience Compilation.

4. On the Specify Compilation Schedule page, shown in Figure 7.16, set the date and time for compilation. Remember to schedule compilation to take place *after* the estimated end time of the profile synchronization job.

Figure 7.16: Specifying a compilation schedule

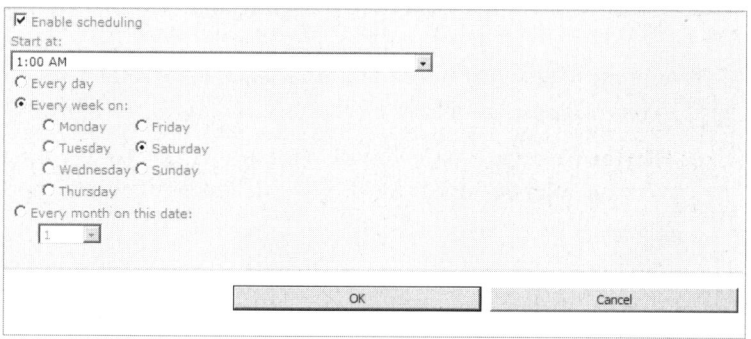

Configure My Sites and Social Networking

The purpose of a My Site is to provide users with a personal space, similar to their Windows desktop, where they can store content and manage it conveniently. Unlike a user's desktop, the contents of a My Site can be shared with other users either in whole or in part, depending on the owner's preference. My Sites can be viewed in much the same way as the thumbtack board in a user's cubicle; they are a means for users to manage information that is important to them but that doesn't fit into any of the formal sites created for departments or projects.

Since all My Sites are indexed along with other content in SharePoint, any information that users choose to share with others will be discoverable. In addition, every My Site allows users to create a personal blog through which they can share ideas and information with others in the organization. Users can explore all of the capabilities of SharePoint sites through their My Site without requiring additional permissions on any of the more formally controlled sites elsewhere in SharePoint.

Setting Up My Sites

Some of the My Sites configuration details are set up during the creation of the User Profiles service application discussed earlier. Other settings must be configured later, under the Setup My Sites link. In preparation for this configuration task, you will need to have at least one site configured using the Enterprise Search Center template. This site will be linked into each user's My Site and allow users to perform enterprise searches directly by having their query redirected to the Enterprise Search Center you configured.

To set up My Sites, do the following:

1. From SharePoint 2010 Central Administration, under Application Management, click Manage Service Applications.

2. On the Manage Service Applications page, click the User Profile Service Application link.

3. On the Manage Profile Service page, under the My Site Settings section, click Setup My Sites. The My Site Settings page opens.

4. In the Preferred Search Center section, shown in Figure 7.17, enter the URL to the site created earlier based on the Enterprise Search Center site template. Include the full path to the pages library—for example, http://portal.synergy.com/search/pages. Select the search scope to be used for finding people (it defaults to People) and the scope to be used for content search (it defaults to All Sites).

Figure 7.17: Preferred Search Center

5. The My Site Host Location section, shown in Figure 7.18, is for specifying the site that was created using the My Site Host template (discussed earlier in the chapter). Enter that same URL here.

Figure 7.18: My Site Host Location

6. In the Personal Site Location section, shown in Figure 7.19, enter the managed path that was created previously to use as the root for all My Site site collections. Both "personal" and "my/personal" are common examples.

Figure 7.19: Personal Site Location

7. In the Site Naming Format section, shown in Figure 7.20, choose the pattern for SharePoint to use to name each new My Site as it is created. The first option, "User name (do not resolve conflicts)," provides a simple format for single-domain environments. For example, Andrew Fuller's My Site URL would become /afuller. The second option, "User name (resolve conflicts by using domain_username," is useful when there are trusted domains where two users could have the same account name and you want to eliminate conflicts only when they arise. For example, if Andrew Fuller's My Site URL already existed at /afuller, and then Adam Fuller from the CORP domain also created a My Site, Adam's

URL would be /corp_afuller. The final option, "Domain and user name (will not have conflicts)," simply enforces the pattern of *domain_accountname* for all users regardless of conflicts.

Figure 7.20: Site Naming Format

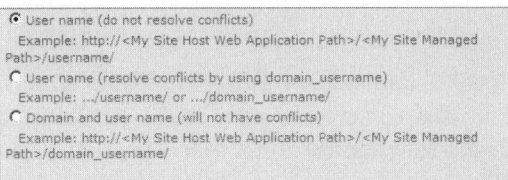

> **TIP** There is still a risk of name conflicts occurring when a My Site is created if a user has left the organization and their account has been deleted but their My Site still exists. If a new user account is created with the same name, then the new user won't be able to create a new My Site but also won't be able to access the old user's My Site due to lack of permissions. The solution is to delete the old user's My Site, which will immediately allow the new user to create their own My Site using the same name.

8. If you have installed multiple language packs on the server, you will see an option labeled "Allow users to choose the language of their personal site." Check the box to allow users to make this selection, or uncheck it to disallow changes.

9. The Read Permission Level section controls which groups will be allowed to read content stored in each user's Shared Documents and Shared Pictures libraries. By default, all authenticated users are granted read rights.

10. In the My Site E-Mail Notifications section, enter an email address or a dummy email address that will become the "from" address for My Site email notifications. The address is not verified, so it does not need to be real.

11. Click OK.

Configuring Trusted Host Locations

In an organization that has multiple divisions or subsidiaries requiring their own separate SharePoint environments, there may be a requirement for multiple User Profile service applications. While each of these applications may have its own separate My Sites web application, it may be more efficient to consolidate all the My Sites under one or more centralized URLs. The Trusted My Site host location is a set of URLs that represent My Site locations that can be used by more than one User Profile service application. This ensures that users have consistent access to a single My Site even if they access their My Site from different web applications connected to different User Profile service applications.

1. From SharePoint 2010 Central Administration, under Application Management, click Manage Service Applications.
2. On the Manage Service Applications page, click the User Profile Service Application link.
3. On the Manage Profile Service page, click Configure Trusted Host Locations.
4. Click New Link to create a new entry.
5. In the URL box, enter the address of the My Site location.
6. In the Description box, enter the explanation of the purpose for this address.
7. Optionally, enter a target audience for this location.
8. Click OK.

Configuring Personalization Site Links

Personalization site links are used to provide users in My Sites with additional menu links that can direct them to other sites of interest. The links appear in the menu bar at the top of the My Site, as shown by the example of the HR Info Center link in Figure 7.21.

Figure 7.21: Personalized site link in a My Site

To set up personalization site links, follow these steps:

1. From SharePoint 2010 Central Administration, under Application Management, click Manage Service Applications.

2. On the Manage Service Applications page, click the User Profile Service Application link.

3. On the Manage Profile Service page, click Configure Personalization Site.

4. In the URL box, enter the address of the site you want to link to.

5. In the Description box, enter the display text for the link.

6. In the Owner box, provide the account of the user who will manage this link. This is generally the user who is responsible for the site that the link connects to.

7. Optionally, select a target audience for this link.

8. Click OK.

Publishing Links to Office Client Applications

To assist users in knowing where to find and save files in SharePoint, administrators can provide users with shortcut links to the preferred locations. These links show up in the user's Office application File Open and Save As dialog boxes, under the Favorites link heading in a category labeled SharePoint Sites.

1. From SharePoint 2010 Central Administration, under Application Management, click Manage Service Applications.

2. On the Manage Service Applications page, click the User Profile Service Application link.

3. On the Manage Profile Service page, click Publish Links To Office Client Applications.

4. On the Published Links To Office Client Applications page, click New Link.

5. In the URL box, enter the address of the location where users will be able to open or save documents.

6. In the Description box, enter a name for this location.

7. Select the descriptive type of the location that this link connects to.

8. Optionally, select a target audience for this link.

9. Click OK.

8
Configuring the Search Service

IN THIS CHAPTER, YOU WILL LEARN TO:

▶ **CONFIGURE THE SEARCH SERVICE APPLICATION** (Pages 257–262)
- Configuring the Search Service Accounts (Page 257)
- Configuring the SharePoint Foundation Search Service (Page 258)
- Creating the SharePoint Search Service (Page 260)

▶ **CONFIGURE CRAWLER IMPACT RULES** (Pages 262–263)

▶ **CONFIGURE FARM SEARCH ADMINISTRATION** (Pages 263–267)
- Configuring Farm-Level Search Settings (Page 265)
- Configuring Search Topology (Page 265)

▶ **CREATE A NEW CONTENT SOURCE** (Pages 267–270)
- Creating a New Content Source (Page 267)
- Types of Content Sources (Page 269)

▶ **MANAGE CRAWLS** (Pages 271–276)
- Managing Crawl Schedules (Page 271)
- Managing Crawl Rules (Page 273)
- Viewing the Crawl Log (Page 275)

▶ **DEFINE SERVER NAME MAPPINGS** (Page 276)

▶ **CONFIGURE DATABASES AND HOST DISTRIBUTION RULES** (Pages 277–278)
- Creating Additional Crawl Databases (Page 277)
- Creating a Host Distribution Rule (Page 277)

▶ **CONFIGURE IFILTERS AND FILE TYPES** (Pages 278 – 280)
- Understanding IFilters and File Formats (Page 278)
- Installing IFilters (Page 279)
- Editing File Types (Page 279)
- Configuring File Icons (Page 280)

▶ **RESET THE INDEX** (Pages 280 – 281)

▶ **UNDERSTAND FAST FOR SHAREPOINT 2010** (Pages 281 – 282)

This chapter focuses on the setup and configuration of the Enterprise Search functionality that is part of SharePoint Server 2010. We will also discuss configuring the related SharePoint Foundation Search Service. SharePoint 2010 also supports integration with the FAST for SharePoint 2010 server product (licensed and installed separately from SharePoint). FAST is not covered in detail, but we will briefly discuss how it compares with the SharePoint 2010 server search.

Configure the Search Service Application

A powerful feature of SharePoint 2010 is its enterprise search capabilities. The term enterprise search refers not to the edition of SharePoint that hosts it but to the ability of the service to index and support searching of all content in an organization's network (i.e., the enterprise).

As the quantity of digital content tracked and stored by organizations continues to grow, workers spend more time searching for content. A 2006 study by International Data Corporation (IDC) estimated that users may spend an average of 48 percent of their time searching for and analyzing information. The purpose of enterprise search software is to minimize this effort by allowing users to reliably search all the content that they have access to, using a single tool. SharePoint 2010 provides this service through its ability to index content stored in a variety of formats and locations in the network and compile a single index that users can search.

Setting up the enterprise search service involves the following steps:

1. Configuring the accounts that will be used by the search service
2. Configuring the SharePoint Foundation Search Service
3. Creating the SharePoint Search Service

Configuring the Search Service Accounts

Before you create the service application itself, it is important to configure the accounts that will be used by the service. We generally recommend that you create at least two dedicated service accounts for search, but you might need to create as many as four or even more if multiple search service applications are created.

An important point to remember is that the content crawler account is not maintained in SharePoint as a managed account. One of the features of managed accounts is that a farm administrator can configure the account to automatically change its password to meet password expiration policies. However, the content crawler account's credentials are stored separately from the managed accounts. If the content crawler setting uses an account that is also a managed account, and then if the account automatically changes its password, the account will not be usable by the crawler to conduct crawls until the password is manually reset in the search service.

Table 8.1 lists the Active Directory domain accounts that you should create before implementing the search service. The table also indicates which ones should be registered as SharePoint managed accounts (for more details on creating managed accounts, see Chapter 12, "Configuring Records Management").

Table 8.1: Search service accounts

Account	Purpose	Managed Account?
Search Service	Windows service account shared by all search service applications	Yes
Search Admin Web Service Application Pool	Assigned to the Search Administration Web Service for Search Service when it is created	Yes
Search Query and Site Settings Web Service Application Pool	Supports search queries and settings change at the site collection level	Yes
Crawler Account	Used for authenticating to the content being crawled	No

Configuring the SharePoint Foundation Search Service

In an installation of SharePoint Foundation, the SharePoint Foundation Search Service performs all the indexing and search functions for the farm. However, in a SharePoint Server installation, the SharePoint Foundation Search service is deprecated to indexing only the help files for the application. If you want to be able to search the help system in SharePoint, then you need to configure this service. To do so, follow these steps:

1. From SharePoint 2010 Central Administration, under System Settings, click Manage Services On Server.

2. Locate the SharePoint Foundation Search Service and, under the Action column, click Start.
3. In the Service Account drop-down, select the managed account you want to use for this service, as shown in Figure 8.1.

Figure 8.1: SharePoint Foundation Service Account settings

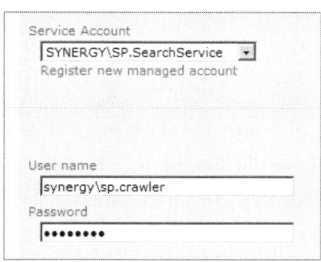

4. In the Content Access Account text boxes, enter the domain username and password for the account that will be used for content crawling, as shown in Figure 8.1.
5. In the Database Server text box, enter the name of the SQL server that will host the search database. In the Database Name text box, enter a name for the search database, as shown in Figure 8.2.

Figure 8.2: SharePoint Foundation Service Search Database settings

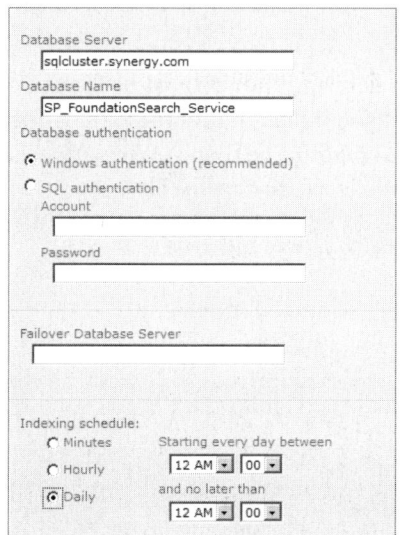

6. In the Indexing Schedule section, select the frequency for crawling the content. If this service is running in a farm that also hosts the full SharePoint Search Service, it will only be crawling the help files, which are not likely to change. Therefore, a frequency of once per day would be sufficient.

7. Click Start.

> **NOTE** Once the service has started, the name will change to SharePoint Foundation Help Search.

In a farm that is running only SharePoint Foundation, you would next select the SharePoint Foundation Search server for each content database by configuring the content database properties. This step isn't necessary when the farm is installed with SharePoint Server Standard or Enterprise edition.

Creating the SharePoint Search Service

Following creation of the appropriate search accounts, it is time to create the search service application. This service is somewhat sensitive to the sequence in which it is installed and configured, so it is important to perform the steps in the correct order:

1. From SharePoint 2010 Central Administration, under Application Management, click Manage Service Applications.

2. From the ribbon, click the New menu and select Search Service Application.

3. In the Name box, enter a descriptive display name for this service, as shown in Figure 8.3. If you intend to host more than one search service, it is a good idea to refer to the scope of the service in the name, for example, **Search Service—Europe Division**.

Figure 8.3: Creating a new search service application

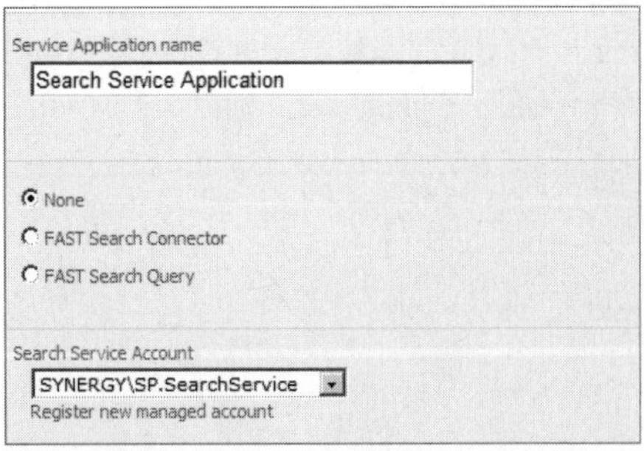

Configure the Search Service Application 261

4. For a server farm that is not using the FAST search component, you can leave FAST Service Application set to None. For the other settings, see the Microsoft documentation on FAST.

5. In the Search Service Account drop-down, select the managed account you want to use for this service.

6. In the Application Pool For Search Admin Web Service section, either select an existing application pool or enter the credentials to create a new one, as shown in Figure 8.4. We recommend that you have a separate application pool for your search service accounts.

Figure 8.4: Application Pool For Search Admin Web Service settings

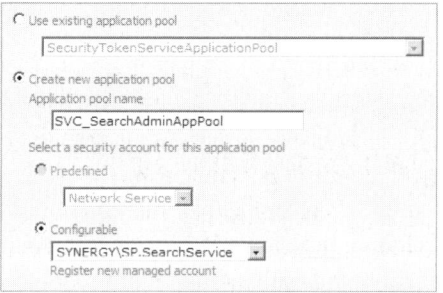

7. In the Application Pool For Search Query And Site Settings Web Service section, either select an existing application pool or enter the credentials to create a new one, as shown in Figure 8.5. It is an acceptable practice to use the same application pool for both the Search Admin Web Service and the Search Query and Site Settings Web Service.

Figure 8.5: Application Pool For Search Query And Site Settings Web Service settings

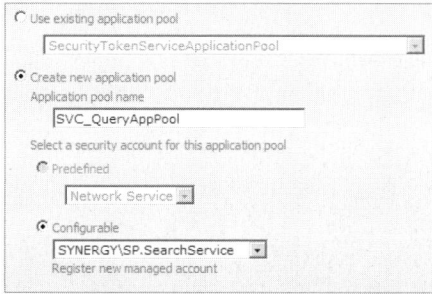

8. Click OK.

Once the search service configuration completes, return to the Services On Server page and confirm that the SharePoint Search Service is started. The configuration process creates two entries in the Service Applications list. One of these is the search service application that you just configured. The other is named WSS_UsageApplication, which supports the Usage and Health Data Collection Service.

Configure Crawler Impact Rules

At the SharePoint farm level, the crawler impact rules can be used to modify the effect that search has on the sites it is crawling.

Crawler impact rules are policies that allow administrators to constrain the volume of requests that SharePoint makes to a particular site or server. The purpose of these rules is to throttle the number of requests for pages and documents that SharePoint makes to a server to match the rate at which the server can respond. For example, if the SharePoint server is more powerful than the target server that it is crawling, it might request pages faster than the target can respond. This can choke the target and cause unanswered requests to queue up on the SharePoint server, reducing overall performance. By reducing the number of simultaneous requests that the SharePoint server makes, you can improve the performance of both systems.

To add a crawler impact rule, do the following:

1. From SharePoint 2010 Central Administration, click General Application Settings.

2. Under Search, click Crawler Impact Rules.

3. Click Add Rule.

4. In the Site text box, shown in Figure 8.6, enter the name of the site or server that is being crawled without the protocol prefix. For example, enter **http://accounting.synergy.com**.

Figure 8.6: Add Crawler Impact Rule

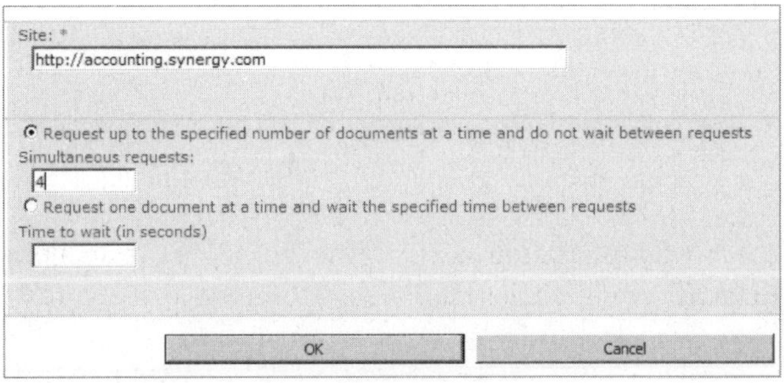

5. Enter the number of simultaneous requests that SharePoint will make to the server. It is generally not necessary to increase the number above the default of 8 unless the target that is being crawled can respond quickly enough to answer all the requests at once. In that case, a higher setting could reduce the crawl duration. In most cases, a crawl rule is used to reduce the number of requests even to the point of only one at a time if that is all the target server can handle.

6. Click OK.

Configure Farm Search Administration

The SharePoint Search Service is installed with its own administrative pages, which can be accessed from the Service Applications list. To open search administration, do the following:

1. From SharePoint 2010 Central Administration, under Application Management, click Manage Service Applications.

2. Click the link representing your search application, or click the row that the application is on and click the Manage button on the toolbar.

3. The Search Administration screen opens, as shown in Figure 8.7.

Figure 8.7: Search Administration screen

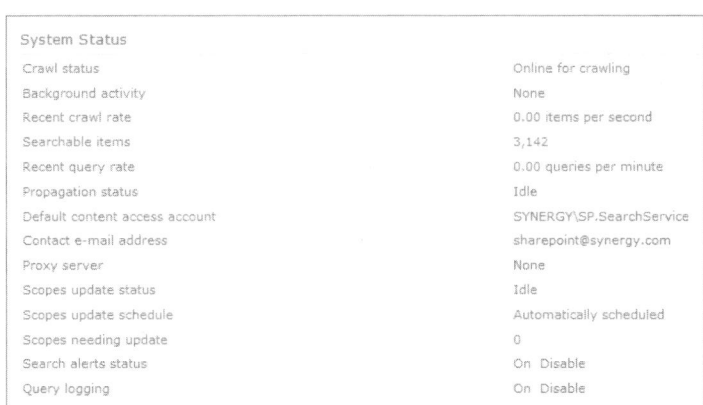

The Search Administration screen provides links to the majority of the configuration commands that are used to manage the search service.

The main page lists a number of key measurements and settings. The following list describes some of the settings:

Crawl Status   Indicates whether the crawler is currently online and active.

Background Activity   Indicates how actively SharePoint is using resources in the background.

Recent Crawl Rate   Lists the number of content crawl requests processed per second. This is a good indicator of the crawler's performance.

Searchable Items   Includes the number of items that have been crawled and indexed.

Recent Query Rate   Indicates the number of search responses returned to users. This is a good indicator of the query service's performance.

Propagation Status   Indicates whether index items are currently being copied from the crawler to the query servers. Problems with propagation would be indicated here.

Default Content Access Account   Specifies the domain account that is configured to index the content on the network.

Contact E-mail Address   Contains an address that is passed to websites that are crawled in case the crawler causes problems during the crawl.

Proxy Server   Indicates the identity of the proxy server configured to allow the crawler to access content.

Scopes Update Status   Indicates whether any search scopes are currently being recalculated by the search service.

Scopes Update Schedule   Indicates whether refreshing of search scopes is handled by an automated timer job or must be run manually. The default is set to Automatically Scheduled. To change to On Demand, click the link for the current setting and select the option On Demand Updates Only.

Scopes Needing Update   Indicates the number of search scopes waiting to be updated.

Search Alerts Status   Specifies whether search alerts are turned on.

Query Logging   Indicates whether user search queries are being logged.

Configuring Farm-Level Search Settings

To access the farm-level search settings, from the Search Administration screen, click Farm Search Administration. The page is shown in Figure 8.8.

Figure 8.8: Farm Search Administration

Farm-Level Search Settings	
Proxy server	None
Time-out (seconds)	60, 60
Ignore SSL warnings	No

Search Service Applications	
Name	Modify Topology
Search Service	Modify Topology

The following settings can be configured:

Proxy Server   Configure this setting if the crawler needs to go through a proxy server to reach the Internet or a target network that it needs to crawl. Include the address and the port number of the server. There is an option to apply these settings to federated queries as well. Federated search queries are explained in Chapter 9, "Configuring Search Scopes and Search Results."

Connection Time-Out Settings   The default of 60 seconds is usually appropriate but may be lengthened if slow links are causing crawl failures.

Ignore SSL Certificate Name Warnings   Check this option if the sites being crawled might be using a nontrusted SSL certificate such as one generated by using Microsoft Certificate Server for internal purposes.

Configuring Search Topology

The Modify Topology link in the Search Service Applications section opens the page shown in Figure 8.9, showing the current arrangement of crawler and query servers. Considerations of scalability through the use of additional components are discussed in Chapter 5, "Scaling and High Availability."

Figure 8.9: Search Topology page

Category	Server Name
⊟ **Admin**	
Administration Component	SPSERVER
⊟ **Crawl - sqlcluster.synergy.com\Search_Service_CrawlStoreDB_3934f609b9274539a30616195f046c29**	
Crawl Component 0	SPSERVER
⊟ **Databases**	
Administration Database : Search_Service_DB_3b10e9cad5ba47d0aed303c86486d9d8	SQLCLUSTER.SYNERGY.COM
Crawl Database : Search_Service_CrawlStoreDB_3934f609b9274539a30616195f046c29	SQLCLUSTER.SYNERGY.COM
Property Database : Search_Service_PropertyStoreDB_702c106b66004711ae1a34eac6582d00	SQLCLUSTER.SYNERGY.COM
⊟ **Index Partition - 0 - sqlcluster.synergy.com\Search_Service_PropertyStoreDB_702c106b66004711ae1**	
Query Component 0	SPSERVER

Here's what each of the sections displayed means and how they relate to the search service:

Admin This section hosts the Administration component, which is responsible for configuring and managing the other components listed on the page. This component also initiates crawls according to the content source crawl schedules and assigns crawlers to these tasks. In addition, the database created for this component during the setup of the search service stores all the configuration details for the search topology. If the server hosting this service is offline, then changes cannot be made to the settings on the Topology screen.

Crawl This section lists components that retrieve content from the network and index it for the search service. In SharePoint 2010, the crawl component is stateless and does not hold a copy of the indexed content. Instead, it tracks which pages have been crawled and sends the index update to the query components. The crawl component also extracts metadata from the content and stores it in the designated crawl database.

Databases This section lists all the databases that are associated with the search service. The Administration database is used by the Administration component. The Crawl database is used by the Crawl component to store the record of content that has been crawled along with the date/time stamp of when it was last crawled. The Property database is used by both the Crawl and Query components to track metadata that is extracted from the indexed content.

Index Partitions Index partitions are used to divide an index into multiple segments that can be distributed to separate query servers.

These divisions can reduce the size of the index and reduce the time it takes to search and retrieve results. For optimum benefit, each partition should be placed on a separate server. Index partitions can also be mirrored to separate servers so that if the primary query server fails, the server hosting the mirror can service queries.

Create a New Content Source

Content sources track the locations of content that you want indexed for search. SharePoint 2010 creates a default content source for indexing all the content stored inside SharePoint. If you want to search any other content stored on the network, you will need to create additional content sources to index.

A content source can reference more than one start address, but each start address must be of the same type—that is, SharePoint must use the same protocol for accessing all the addresses. Content sources are crawled based on a schedule configured for each content source. All of the addresses in the content source are crawled under the same schedule.

The decision to create a new content source is therefore based on two primary criteria: the protocol of the content address and the schedule that will be applied. You will need to create a new content source if the address you want to crawl uses a different protocol than the existing content sources. Likewise, you will need to create a new content source if you want to crawl the address on a different schedule from the existing content sources.

The setup of the search service automatically creates the Local SharePoint Sites content source that holds addresses to all the SharePoint web applications. This content source can be modified by moving some or all of the content addresses into different content sources. SharePoint automatically grants the default content access account permissions on these addresses through the Policy for Web Applications feature.

Creating a New Content Source

SharePoint 2010 has a recommended limit of 50 content sources per search service. While it is possible to exceed this limit, there may be problems with scalability as the number of content sources increases.

When a content source is crawled, SharePoint will index all the start addresses listed in the content source. As more addresses are added to a content source, the crawl takes longer. Adding more content sources will reduce the crawl time for each and allow for portions of an address to be crawled on different schedules.

Regardless of the type of content that is being crawled, the content crawler account must be granted full read permissions on all the content to be indexed.

To add a new content source, do the following:

1. From the Search Administration page, click Content Sources.
2. On the Manage Content Sources page, click New Content Source.
3. On the New Content Source page, shown in Figure 8.10, enter a name for the content source that describes the content that will be crawled.

Figure 8.10: Add Content Source page (partial)

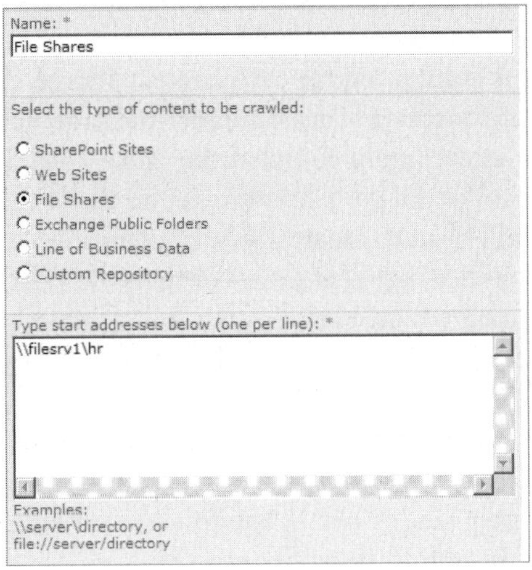

4. Under the Content Source Type section, select the option for the protocol or type of content that will be included. While some types may sound similar to each other, such as SharePoint Sites and Web Sites, there are differences in the way that the content is treated. These differences will be discussed in the next section, "Types of Content Sources."
5. Under Start Addresses, enter the addresses of all content locations that will be included in this content source.

6. In the Crawl Settings section, elect to crawl all content under the start address or only the portion of the content specified by the start address. This option allows you to set up different crawl schedules for different subsites or subfolders of content so that some portions of the content can be crawled more frequently.

7. Under Crawl Schedules, shown in Figure 8.11, it is necessary to select an existing schedule or create a new one in order for index crawls to occur. For more details on crawl schedules, see the section, "Managing Crawl Schedules," later in this section.

Figure 8.11: Setting crawl schedules

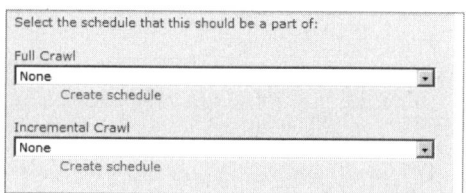

8. Under Content Source Priority, designate which content sources will be ranked higher in the crawl queue. Higher-ranked sources are given priority if multiple crawls are running at the same time. You might want to configure these settings if an important set of content is not being indexed in a timely manner because other crawls are slowing down the indexing process.

9. Check the Start Full Crawl option if this content source should be available immediately to the farm.

10. Click OK.

Types of Content Sources

The following are the types of content sources that SharePoint can crawl:

SharePoint Content Sources A SharePoint content source can be used to index sites in farms that are running SharePoint 2010 (including SharePoint Foundation), SharePoint 2007 including WSS 3.0, or SharePoint 2003 including WSS 2.0. The sites can be located either in the local farm or in a separate farm, as long as the content access account is granted permissions to the sites.

Note that SharePoint 2010 cannot automatically identify all site collections hosted in earlier versions of SharePoint, so each site collection start address will have to be added separately.

SharePoint is able to read the security descriptors on all SharePoint content for use in filtering search queries by users.

Website Content Sources   This content source is used to index any HTTP or HTTPS website regardless of the technology used by its host. With this type of content, SharePoint does not read the security settings on the pages, so all content will be searchable by all users. With this type of content source, you have the option of crawling the entire site or only the first page of the site, or you can specify a page depth and hop count from the start page, as shown in Figure 8.12.

Figure 8.12: Website content source crawl settings

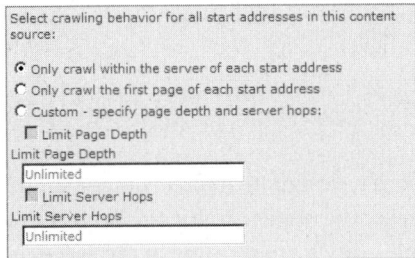

File Share Content Sources   The file share content source allows indexing of any Windows server shared folder and all its contents. SharePoint automatically indexes all the security descriptors on this type of source and filters the search results for users accordingly.

Exchange Public Folder Content Sources   This content source is used to index document, calendars, and other types of public folders hosted in an Exchange server. This source type does expose security information to SharePoint for use in filtering content.

Line-of-Business Data Content Sources   This content source is used to index external data accessed through Business Connectivity Services (BCS). The data sources must be configured to support indexing before the content source can be configured.

Custom Repository Content Sources   Custom repositories represent any additional content source type installed on the server such as third-party connectors for document management systems and non-Windows servers.

Manage Crawls

SharePoint 2010 builds indexes of content sources. The indexing process is called a *crawl*. Crawls occur on specific schedules and run according to crawl rules that you set up. You can view the crawl logs to determine whether indexing is working properly.

Managing Crawl Schedules

SharePoint 2010 indexes content sources based on scheduled crawl cycles. The crawl cycles must be configured as part of the setup of a content source. SharePoint 2010 can conduct two types of crawl:

Full Crawl A full crawl indexes all content in the content source. A full crawl is required when you index a content source for the first time in order to completely discover and capture all the content. Full crawls are not required thereafter except under specific circumstances such as the following:

- Changes to a search component, such as installing a new IFilter
- Modification to managed properties
- Updates to crawl rules
- Change to the default content access account
- Incremental crawls keep missing content changes

Many organizations schedule a full crawl on a periodic basis such as once a week or once a month to ensure that these issues are automatically covered. However, a full crawl of all content may take a long time and might need to be scheduled to occur during weekends or nonpeak hours.

Incremental Crawl Incremental crawls are used to update content on a regular basis after an initial full crawl has been done. If an incremental crawl is initiated before a full crawl has been performed, then SharePoint 2010 will automatically initiate a full crawl of the content source instead. Incremental crawls are much more efficient and faster than full crawls because they only update the index with additions, deletions, or changes to the content.

For incremental crawls of SharePoint 2010 sites in the farm, the search service is able to read the change log kept in each of the content databases and only crawls the content that has specifically changed. This produces very fast and efficient crawls. For all other content sources, the incremental crawl checks the date/time stamp of each item in the content source to determine if it has changed since the last crawl. It then indexes only the content that has changed.

Crawls are scheduled based on the frequency with which the content changes and therefore needs to be indexed. Crawl schedules are also based on the size of the content source and the length of time that it takes to complete a crawl. A large content source might take 4 hours to crawl; this crawl could be scheduled to run every 4 hours if necessary. A smaller content source may only take 15 minutes to crawl and can be scheduled much more frequently. Some very large content sources may take days to be crawled; such a crawl might be scheduled on a monthly basis.

To create a new crawl schedule:

1. From the Edit Content Source page, click the Create Schedule link.

2. On the Manage Schedules page, shown in Figure 8.13, choose to schedule the crawl on a daily, weekly, or monthly basis and have crawls conducted at periodic intervals within each day that is designated for crawling.

Figure 8.13: Manage Schedules page

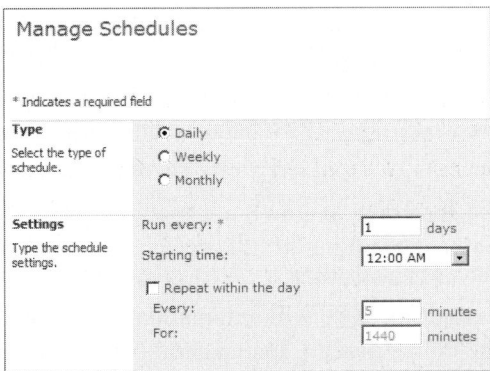

3. Choose whether you want the crawl to run at intervals within each day.

4. Click OK.

Managing Crawl Rules

Crawl rules are a means of adjusting the way that SharePoint crawls a particular content location without altering the content source addresses. One example of a crawl rule would be to exclude a subsite or subfolder from being indexed. Another example would be to specify an alternate account for crawling a particular server URL where the default content access account does not have permissions.

Viewing, Adding, and Testing Crawl Rules

To view all crawl rules and add new ones, from the Search Administration page, click Crawl Rules. (See Figure 8.7, earlier in this chapter.) The Manage Crawl Rules page opens, as shown in Figure 8.14.

Figure 8.14: Manage Crawl Rules page

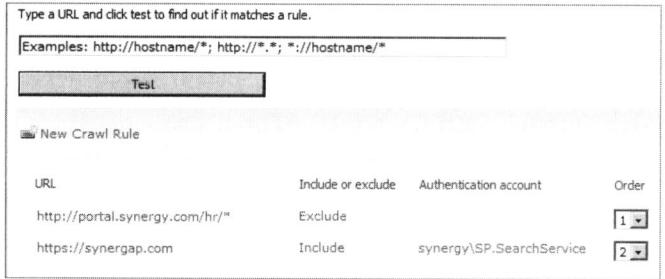

Crawl rules will be applied to content in the order that they are set in the crawl rules list. Use the Order column to change the order of the rules. To determine if a crawl rule will apply to a particular site or folder, enter the address in the text box at the top of the page and click the Test button. As shown in Figure 8.14, the result will indicate how the address will be treated and which crawl rule will apply to it.

Creating a Crawl Rule

To create a crawl rule, follow these steps:

1. Click New Crawl Rule on the Manage Crawl Rules page.
2. On the Add Crawl Rule page, shown in Figure 8.15, enter an address in the Path box.

Figure 8.15: Add Crawl Rule page

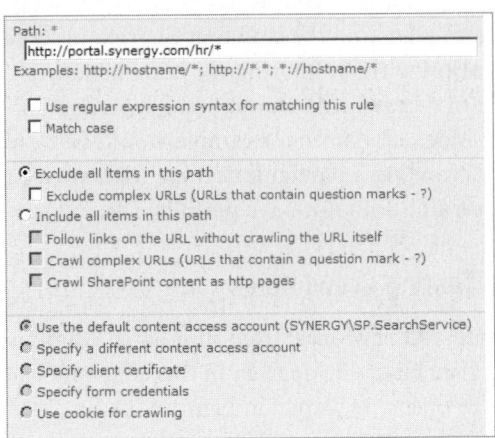

You can use the wildcard character (*) to specify ranges of content to affect. Here are two examples:

- The path http://portal.synergy.com/hr/* applies to any URL underneath the hr location.
- The path *://*.htm applies to all files with the .htm file extension.

3. In the Crawl Configuration section, select one of the following:

- Exclude All Items In This Path prevents all items in the path from being indexed.
- Include All Items In This Path allows special treatment of the items in the path. If you choose this, you can check one or more of the following options: "Follow links on the URL without crawling the URL itself" is useful for crawling site map pages without having them appear in search results. "Crawl complex URLs" is useful for crawling pages that use query strings to pass parameters or filter values. "Crawl SharePoint content as HTTP pages" causes all content under the path to appear in search results regardless of the item permissions on the pages.

4. Choose the authentication model that the crawl rule will use. The options are as follows:

- Specify A Different Content Access Account allows you to enter an alternate Windows domain account to connect to locations that the default content access account does not have permissions to.

- Specify Client Certificate can be used to associate a digital certificate that can be passed to a server for authentication.
- Specify Form Credentials is a necessary option when indexing a website that requires a login through a web page rather than a Windows prompt.
- Use Cookie For Crawling allows the selection of a cached or prerendered cookie to pass through to a Forms-authenticated website.

5. Click OK.

Viewing the Crawl Log

The crawl log tracks the history of every content indexing operation and the results of every content item request. By reviewing the crawl log, you can determine whether indexing is succeeding for all the content targeted and where it may be encountering problems. The log will report whether a location is inaccessible due to permissions issues, if a URL is excluded due to a crawl rule, or if content has been removed because it cannot be found by the indexer.

Because of the importance of monitoring the health of the index, we strongly recommend that you review the crawl log on a regular basis. To view the crawl log, do the following:

1. From the Search Administration page, click Crawl Log.

2. On the Crawl Log page, click one of the five views at the top of the page to filter the log entries. The views are Content Source, Host Name, URL, Crawl History, and Error Message.

The Content Source and Host Name views display the totals for the primary types of results:

Successes Indicates the total number of items that were crawled successfully without any issues.

Warnings Indicates the count of items that could not be crawled due to configuration settings such as the site being marked as excluded from search.

Errors Summarizes the items that could not be indexed due to some failure such as an "access denied" response from the server.

Deletes Indicates items that were not found during the last crawl and were removed from the index.

Top Level Errors Indicates the errors totaled separately because an error in accessing the root of an address typically prevents crawling of any part of the address.

Define Server Name Mappings

Server name mappings are used to alter the way that search results derived from websites and file share content are displayed to users when they search. This feature allows a specific server name or hostname to map to any other name. The substitute name is presented as the valid address to the documents or pages.

For an example of a server name mapping, assume that users access content though a proprietary web login at the address https://forms.synergy.com, and that SharePoint cannot authenticate to this address. A separate URL is exposed for SharePoint to crawl the content via Windows authentication at the address http://ntlm.synergy.com. Since users need to see search results that direct them to their normal web address, server name mapping can be configured to replace the http://ntlm.synergy.com address with the https://forms.synergy.com address in search results.

To create a new server name mapping, do the following:

1. From the Search Administration page, click Server Name Mappings.
2. Click New Mapping.
3. In the Address In Index text box, enter the address to replace, including the protocol prefix.
4. In the Address In Search Results text box, enter the substitute address, including the protocol prefix.
5. Click OK.

After adding a new mapping, you will need to perform a full crawl of the content to apply the changes. Be careful not to apply server name mappings that may conflict with alternate access mappings (AAMs). (see Chapter 2, "Creating and Managing Web Applications") defined elsewhere, because the server name mappings might overwrite the AAMs.

Configure Databases and Host Distribution Rules

When SharePoint indexes content, it stores the addresses it has crawled and the status result along with additional tracking details in one of the available crawl databases in the farm. By default, SharePoint load-balances the distribution of these crawl entries between databases according to an internal analysis of the quantity of items that are being crawled under a given hostname. This database usage can be overridden via Host Distribution Rules.

Creating Additional Crawl Databases

The crawl database is used by SharePoint to track the content addresses, crawl schedules, and crawl history for content indexed by the search service. In large-scale indexing scenarios, the volume of content being crawled can result in a great many read and write operations to the crawl database. Contention issues may arise between crawlers accessing this data. To eliminate bottlenecks, you can create additional crawl databases to provide load balancing.

To add a new crawl database, follow these steps:

1. From the Search Administration page, under the Search Application Topology section, click the Modify button.
2. On the Manage Search Topology page, click New, and then click Crawl Database.
3. In the Add Crawl Database section, enter the name of the database server and the database name.
4. Click OK.
5. On the Manage Search Topology page, click Apply Topology Changes.

Creating a Host Distribution Rule

Normally, SharePoint 2010 identifies the most appropriate crawl database to use to store the crawl results for a given server that is being crawled. In some cases, the distribution that SharePoint creates may not be best for your needs. In these cases, you can manually associate specific server hostnames with specific crawl databases. To set up a host distribution rule, do the following:

1. From the Search Administration page, click Host Distribution Rules.
2. On the Host Distribution Rules page, click Add Distribution Rule.
3. In the Hostname field, enter the name of the content server for which the crawl results should be associated with a different database.
4. In the Select Crawl Database drop-down, select the database to use.
5. Click OK.
6. On the Host Distribution Rules page, click Apply Changes.
7. Click OK to commit the rule.

Configure IFilters and File Types

In order for SharePoint to index a particular type of content, it must be able to load and process the file format of the page or document. SharePoint comes with the ability to index most standard file types, including all Office formats, text, XML, and—new to SharePoint 2010—both TIF and Zip files. At times, it is necessary to expand or adjust the list of formats that SharePoint can index by installing new IFilters and registering the new file types.

Understanding IFilters and File Formats

When SharePoint processes an address in a content source, it performs two tests on each file that it finds to determine whether it is able to index it:

1. SharePoint checks the extension of the content file against the list of permitted file types.
2. If the file extension is in the allowed list, SharePoint ensures that the appropriate IFilter has been installed on the crawler.

An IFilter is essentially a file-reading utility that the crawler uses to open a file of a particular type and extract the text contents while stripping away any formatting characters that are irrelevant to search. SharePoint comes with several IFilters, but others, such as the IFilter for the PDF file format, must be installed separately.

> **NOTE** Adobe provides a free 64-bit PDF IFilter. However, IFilter version 9, the version available as of this writing, is known to have performance issues and is not recommended for production SharePoint installations. Commercial vendors including Foxit and PDFlib offer PDF IFilters for SharePoint 2010 that have better performance and support.

Installing IFilters

Commercial IFilters designed for SharePoint 2010 are available for most of the commonly used file types in the industry today.

Typically, the installation of an IFilter is simple and straightforward. The process may differ slightly depending on the vendor, but it will look something like this:

1. On each SharePoint server that will perform the crawl role in the farm, run the IFilter setup file provided by the vendor.

2. Restart the World Wide Web Publishing Service under the Services applet located under Administrative Tools on the SharePoint crawler.

Editing File Types

Once you have installed the correct IFilter, you must configure SharePoint to recognize the file extensions that are associated with the file type. To register a new file extension, do the following:

1. From the Search Administration page, click File Types.
2. Click New File Type.
3. Enter the extension of the file type that will be indexed (without the period at the front).
4. Click OK.

Once both the IFilter is installed and the file type is registered, perform a full crawl to index the files of that type.

Configuring File Icons

While it is sufficient to configure only the IFilter and the file type in order for content to be indexed, it is useful to users to see the appropriate icon next to the item in search results. The icons should be in GIF format and no more than 16 × 16 pixels in dimension at 96 DPI. To register a new file type icon, do the following:

1. Copy the icon to the `C:\Program Files\Common Files\Microsoft Shared\Web Server Extensions\14\TEMPLATE\IMAGES` folder.

2. Open the `C:\Program Files\Common Files\Microsoft Shared\Web Server Extensions\14\TEMPLATE\XML\DOCICON.XML` file in Notepad or another text editor.

3. Add a row to the `<ByExtension>` section of the file using the format `<Mapping Key="`*three_letter_extension*`" Value="`*image_name.gif*`" />` and changing the extension and image name as appropriate. For example, you might add the following to register an icon for PDF files:

    ```
    <Mapping Key="pdf" Value="icpdf.gif" />
    ```

4. Save and close the file.

Reset the Index

In some cases, problems will arise with the index compiled by SharePoint 2010 that cannot be solved through normal means. For example, a particular item may have been deleted from the site but still appears in the index results despite numerous crawls. Or you might have unexplained errors appearing in the crawl log when you're trying to index specific content. In cases like these, the solution may simply be to delete the index and start again with a fresh full crawl. You might also want to use this approach when you have a large amount of content referenced by your index and you need to perform a full crawl. A full crawl conducted after deleting the index often runs significantly faster than a full crawl against an existing index.

To delete the existing index and start a new index build, you first use the Index Reset command and then perform a full crawl.

> **WARNING** Once the index has been reset, user search queries will no longer return results. It is a good idea to plan resetting the index for a weekend or a period of time when search will not be needed.

To reset the index, do the following:

1. From the Search Administration page, click Index Reset
2. On the Index Reset page, check the setting for the Deactivate Search Alerts During Reset option. This is checked by default so that search alerts are not fired on every item removal during the reset and every item addition during the full crawl. The alerts can be reactivated after the full crawl completes.
3. Click Reset Now.
4. Click OK.
5. Start a Full Crawl.

Understand FAST for SharePoint 2010

FAST for SharePoint is a separate server product available from Microsoft that can be configured to replace the standard search functionality shipped with SharePoint 2010. FAST for SharePoint offers a wide range of features that extend search capabilities beyond those that come with SharePoint 2010 itself. Among the features that FAST for SharePoint offers are:

Extreme Scale-Out Perhaps the most obvious advantage of FAST is its ability to index more than 100 million items and as much as 1 billion items with the appropriate server architecture.

Thumbnails and Previews FAST will generate thumbnail views of all Word and PowerPoint documents that can be seen directly from the search results page and without opening the files. In addition, users can directly browse the slides in a PowerPoint presentation without opening it.

Visual Best Bets With a Visual Best Bet, a graphic image depicting information about a keyword can be displayed on the search results page to assist users in finding the right result.

Similarity Search The search results can include a Similar Results link which, when clicked, will reexecute the search with a refined filter to retrieve items that are understood to be similar.

User Context from User Profile User contexts are targeted settings for search results that can be linked to users based on information in their user profile and that can be associated with Best Bets, document promotions, and other content prioritizations.

Tunable Relevance Ranking FAST allows the ability to identify specific documents within a site for promotion and to associate these promotions with user contexts.

Custom Property Extractors FAST can make use of add-ins built by developers to identify specific properties in documents to be used in the ranking and sorting of search results.

Inclusion of External Data in Relevance When external data is indexed via the Business Connectivity Services, this data can be used in relevancy rankings of content.

9

Configuring Search Scopes and Search Results

IN THIS CHAPTER, YOU WILL LEARN TO:

▶ **MANAGE SEARCH SCOPES (Pages 284 – 294)**
- Creating Shared Search Scopes (Page 285)
- Creating a Site Collection Search Scope (Page 288)
- Assigning a Search Scope (Page 289)
- Configuring Search Center Tabs for Search Scopes (Page 291)

▶ **CREATE METADATA PROPERTY MAPPINGS (Pages 294 – 297)**
- Viewing Crawled Properties (Page 295)
- Creating a New Managed Property (Page 296)

▶ **CONFIGURE AUTHORITATIVE PAGES (Pages 297 – 299)**

▶ **DEFINE KEYWORDS AND BEST BETS (Pages 299 – 302)**
- Creating a Keyword (Page 299)
- Adding a Best Bet (Page 300)

▶ **REMOVE ITEMS FROM SEARCH RESULTS (Pages 302)**

▶ **CONFIGURE FEDERATED SEARCH (Pages 302 – 309)**
- Creating a Federated Location (Page 303)
- Importing a Federated Location (Page 307)
- Editing, Copying, Deleting, or Exporting a Federated Location (Page 308)
- Configuring a Federated Search Web Part (Page 308)

▶ **VIEW SEARCH REPORTS (Pages 309 – 310)**

A successful corporate search engine requires more than just a complete index of content; it also requires relevant and accurate results. The problem faced in most organizations is that the types of results users need are not easily determined by the search engine itself. Internet search engines can make use of large numbers of search queries across a wide range of content to compile statistics on the most popular results, which can then be ranked more highly. However, in an organizational context, much of the content will contain similar keywords and the most important results will not necessarily be the most popular.

SharePoint 2010 contains an enhanced query engine that provides better relevancy ranking than previous versions. Still, even with the best ranking, if too many results are returned, then the pages or documents that the user is looking for may not appear in the first few pages of the result set. The best experience for users will come by combining optimized relevancy ranking of results returned from a narrow subset of the content, thereby improving the probability of locating the right items. In this chapter, we will explore both ways to narrow the search domain through search scopes and methods for improving the relevancy ranking through authoritative pages and leveraging ranking logic in SharePoint 2010.

Manage Search Scopes

Sometimes when we conduct a search we don't know if the content we're looking for exists on the network and we're just trying to find out what is there. If we get a useful result then we count it as a bonus, but we're not overly disappointed when we don't find anything relevant. However, it is much more frustrating for users when they know that a file or page exists and know that it contains the information they need but they cannot locate it quickly. It is equally frustrating for managers, knowing that users resort to re-creating documents that may already exist somewhere but that can't be located quickly enough.

When users are searching for a known document, they often know some details about the document that could help them find it, such as the author, the department that produced it, an associated metadata value, or the server it should be on. Allowing users to apply these types of criteria in their search can dramatically narrow the range of results that are returned.

A *search scope* is a predefined subset of the index that users can target their search in. Searching within a scope still allows users to apply keywords in their queries, but the keywords are evaluated only within the content covered by the scope.

Creating Shared Search Scopes

Shared search scopes are created by farm administrators and are available to every site collection associated with the search service that the scopes are created in. A shared search scope is not automatically applied and is not automatically available to users. It must be exposed by a site collection administrator via a search site in the site collection. We'll cover configuring the search site later in this chapter in the section "Assigning a Search Scope."

To create a shared search scope, do the following:

1. From SharePoint 2010 Central Administration, under Application Management, click Manage Service Applications.
2. Click the link representing your search application, or click the row that the application is on and click the Manage button on the toolbar.
3. Under Queries and Results, click the Scopes link.
4. The View Scopes page opens. Click New Scope.
5. On the Create Scope page, shown in Figure 9.1, enter the title and description for this scope. You can also specify a search results page, which can be predefined to use only this scope when displaying results. A custom results page can also be created and assigned to the scope later. Click OK.

Figure 9.1: Create Scope page

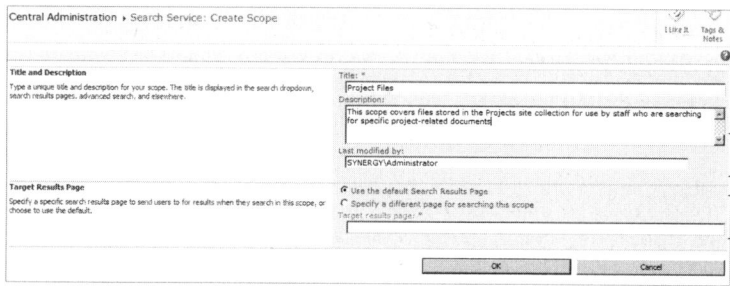

6. The next step is to add filter criteria to narrow the results returned by the scope. On the View Scopes page, click the Add Rules link in the new scope row.

7. On the Add Scope Rule page, select which option you wish to use to filter the content. These rules are described further in the next section, "Understanding Scope Rules." You can add multiple rules to each scope to create highly focused results for users.

8. Select the behavior to apply to this rule. The behavior determines how the rule will be applied in conjunction with other rules:

    - **Include** acts as a logical OR operator and the items covered by this rule will be added to the total result set but can be excluded by other rules.
    - **Require** acts as a logical AND operator and will only allow items in the result set that match this rule.
    - **Exclude** acts as a logical NOT operator and any items that match this rule will not appear in the result set.

9. Click OK.

10. Once the scope has updated, it can be used for searching. Scope updates are covered in the section "Updating Search Scope."

Understanding Scope Rules

Here are the types of scope rules you can create:

Web Address Scope Rule The Web Address scope rule is used to reference any content address and includes SharePoint sites, non-SharePoint websites, file servers, and Exchange public folders. Rules of this type can be used to target searching of a small subsection of the enterprise. For example, a site collection containing project files may be searched quickly for critical project-related materials. By combining several Web Address scope rules, you can bind the results from different locations in the network into one logical location. (See Figure 9.2.)

Figure 9.2: Creating a Web Address scope rule

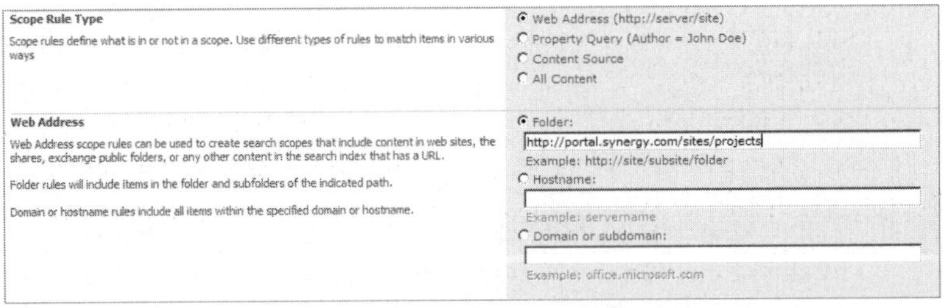

Property Query Scope Rule The Property Query scope rule allows you to restrict the search results to a specific property value. For example, a property query set to FileExtension with a value of xlsx would allow users to search within all Excel files having that extension. Additional rules could be added to cover other file extensions to create a scope that targets all spreadsheet files. (See Figure 9.3.)

Figure 9.3: Creating a Property Query scope rule

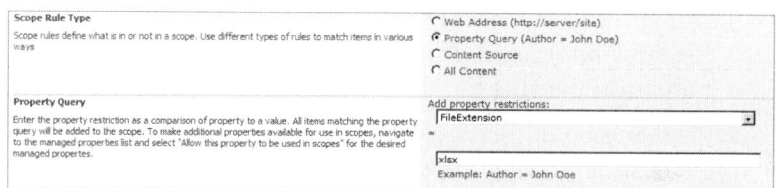

Content Source Scope Rule The Content Source scope rules are a convenient method of exposing a specific content source for searching. For example, a content source may have been created to crawl specific file shares on the company's file servers. Since a large number of older files are stored on these servers, users might be struggling to locate files there. A search scope that targets this content source can give users the immediate benefit of being able to search this legacy content quickly and easily. (See Figure 9.4.)

Figure 9.4: Creating a Content Source scope rule

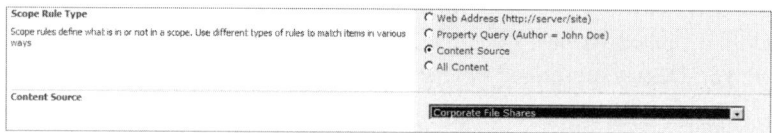

All Content Scope Rule The All Content scope rules have no additional configuration options associated with them and may at first glance appear to be redundant since SharePoint automatically creates a scope for searching all content called "All Sites." However, the All Content scope rule allows you to create a scope that is based on the entire content but that uses Exclude rules to eliminate selective content.

Updating Search Scope

Once you've created a scope and configured it with rules, you need to update it for it to be searchable. Updating a scope is not the same as conducting a content crawl, because it is only calculating what portions of the index will be included within the scope. The index does not need to be rebuilt and therefore the update is relatively fast. By default, search scopes update every 15 minutes, but they can also be updated manually. To force an update, do the following:

1. From within the Search Service Administration site, click the Search Administration link, which will open the main search administration page.

2. In the center of the page, the Scopes Needing Update setting will indicate how many scopes have yet to be updated.

3. Click the Start Update Now link to trigger an update. In a few minutes the update will complete.

Generally, it is advisable to allow SharePoint to update scopes automatically. However, there is an option that disables the automatic update and requires that scopes be updated manually. To change this setting, next to the Scopes Update Schedule setting, click the Automatically Scheduled link and change the value to On Demand Updates Only.

Creating a Site Collection Search Scope

Site collection administrators can create search scopes at the site collection level. These scopes function the same way as shared scopes except that they can only be used within the site collection they are created in. Unlike shared scopes, site collection scope rules can only be created for web addresses, managed properties, and all content. They cannot be created for content sources.

To create a site collection search scope, do the following:

1. Navigate to the home page at the root of a site collection for which you are the administrator.

2. Select Site Actions and click Site Settings.

3. In the Site Collection Administration section, click Search Scopes.

4. On the View Scopes page, click the New Scope link and follow steps 5–10 in the previous section, "Creating Shared Search Scopes."

Assigning a Search Scope

Once search scopes have been created, they need to be assigned, or exposed to the user in a convenient manner. Search scopes can be assigned to the existing drop-down list controls that are built into the SharePoint pages, or they can be connected into the Enterprise Search Site as visible tabs. We'll describe the tabbed approach later in this chapter in the section "Configuring Search Center Tabs for Search Scopes."

Assigning Scope to a Search Drop-down

SharePoint 2010 contains a search scope drop-down list that is connected to the search box visible at the top of most SharePoint site pages, as shown in Figure 9.5.

Figure 9.5: Site collection search drop-down

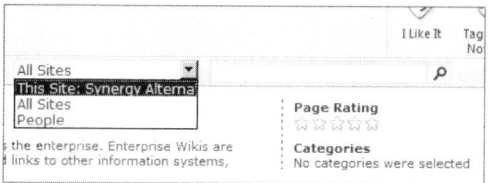

The drop-down list is hidden by default and must be enabled in Site Settings. To configure the search drop-down, do the following:

1. Navigate to the home page at the root of a site collection for which you are the administrator.
2. Select Site Actions, and then click Site Settings.
3. In the Site Collection Administration section, click Search Settings. The Search Settings page appears, partially shown in Figure 9.6.

   Figure 9.6: Site Collection Search Settings page

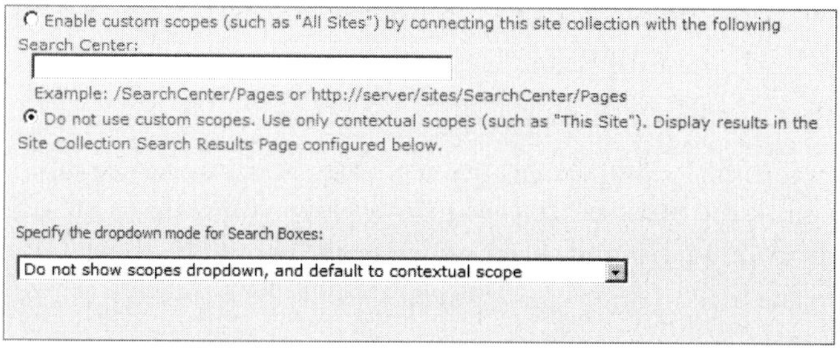

4. Select the option Enable Custom Scopes.

5. In the Search Center box, enter the path to a valid results page in a site based on one of the search site templates (Basic Search Center or Enterprise Search Center).

   - If you have configured the site collection with an Enterprise Search Center, then in the Search Center box, enter the path to the site as follows: **http://sitecollectionurl/searchsite/pages**.

   - If your search site is based on the Basic Search Center, then enter the URL to the search site without /pages at the end.

6. In the menu labeled "Specify the drop-down mode for Search Boxes," select Show Scopes Drop-down.

7. Click OK.

8. Under Site Collection Administration, click Search Scopes. The View Scopes page will open.

9. At the top of the page, click Display Groups.

10. Click the context menu on the Search drop-down and select Edit Display Group. The Edit Scope Display Group page is displayed (partially shown in Figure 9.7).

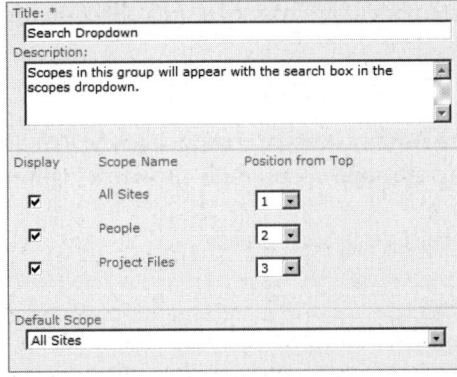

Figure 9.7: Edit Scope Display Group page

11. Check the box next to the custom scope you want to include in the drop-down list and select which scope should be the default value in the list.

12. Click OK.

13. Return to the home page in the site and click the search drop-down to access the scope.

    The scope drop-down list may take a minute or so to show your custom scope. This is normal behavior and only happens at the time of configuration.

Assigning Scope to Advanced Search

You can also configure the Advanced Search page to display custom scopes. This allows users to take advantage of the powerful querying capabilities of the Advanced Search feature in combination with a targeted scope. Configuring this involves editing the Advanced Search page as well. To begin, follow steps 1–9 listed in the previous section, "Assigning Scope to a Search Drop-down," to configure a custom scope for the search drop-down, and then edit the Advanced Search display group. After configuring the scope setting, do the following:

1. Navigate to the search center site in your site collection (typically it is configured with the URL /search or /searchcenter).
2. Click the Advanced link to go to the Advanced Search page.
3. From the Site Actions menu, select Edit Page.
4. On the Web Part Tools Options ribbon tab, click Web Part Properties.
5. In the Properties pane on the right, expand the Scopes section and check the box next to Show The Scope Picker.
6. At the bottom of the Properties pane, click OK.
7. On the Page ribbon tab, click Save And Close or Stop Editing. The custom scopes should appear as a set of check boxes on the page.

Configuring Search Center Tabs for Search Scopes

The Enterprise Search Center site template is specially designed to host custom search scopes by displaying a tab that allows users to select and query a scope. The site template is configured with two tabs by default:

- The All Sites tab and scope includes all content indexed by SharePoint in any content source in the search service.
- The People tab and scope searches only the user profiles.

The SharePoint interface supports creating custom tabs that link to custom search scopes, both those created in Central Administration and those created at the site collection level. Figure 9.8 shows the tabs on a search page with a custom scope tab added for Projects. In this section, we will explain how to configure custom search tabs.

Figure 9.8: Enterprise Search Center with custom tab

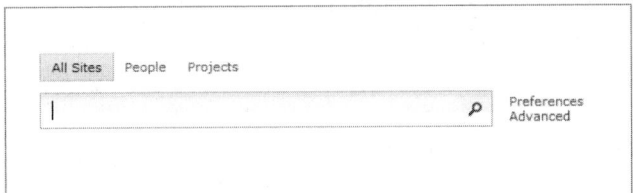

While the Basic Search Center allows searching of all indexed content, it does not support custom scope tabs. The Enterprise Search Center is a publishing site and therefore requires that the SharePoint Server Publishing Infrastructure feature be enabled in the site collection. Configuring a search scope as a tab on the site involves creating both a custom search page and a custom search results page, as described next.

Creating a Search Page with Tabs

The first step in configuring a custom scope tab is to create a custom search page as follows:

1. Navigate to the home page of an Enterprise Search Center site for which you are a site administrator.
2. Select Site Actions, click View All Site Content, and then click the Page library.
3. On the Documents ribbon tab, click the New button.
4. On the Create Page screen, enter a name and URL for the page that relates to the scope that it will be associated with. For example, for the Projects scope a suitable page name would be ProjectsSearch.aspx.
5. In the Page Layout list, select the (Welcome Page) Search box.
6. Click Create.
7. Open the page you just created and, on the Page tab, click the Edit button.

8. Click inside the Search box; then, on the Web Part Tools Options ribbon tab, click Web Part Properties.

9. Expand the Miscellaneous section and locate the Target Search Results Page URL box. Enter a name for the search results page. For example, the results page for the Projects scope might be called ProjectsSearchResults.aspx. Don't worry if the page doesn't exist yet—we'll create the page in the next exercise.

10. Click OK to save the change and close the Web Part Properties pane.

11. With the page still in Edit mode, above the search box, click the Add New Tab link.

12. On the New Item page, in the Tab Name field, enter the display name of the tab (it is best to keep the name short to avoid crowding other tabs). Then enter the name of the search page that you are currently editing—in our example, ProjectsSearch.aspx.

13. Click Save. The new tab will appear on the search page.

14. On the Page ribbon tab, click Save And Close.

Creating a Search Results Page with Tabs

The Enterprise Search Center requires two pages to support user queries:

- The Search page, where users enter their query
- The Search Results page, which executes the search and displays the results

To complete the configuration of the tabbed search scope, you need to create a custom search results page to reference the custom scope:

1. Follow steps 1–4 in the previous section, "Creating a Search Page with Tabs."

2. In the Page Layout list, select (Welcome Page) Search Results.

3. Follow steps 6–8 in the previous section.

4. Expand the Miscellaneous section and locate the Target Search Results Page URL box. Enter a name for the search results page that you just created. This will allow the results page to accept search keywords directly and reload the same page.

5. Click OK to save the change and close the Web Part Properties pane.

6. With the page still in Edit mode, locate the Search Core Results web part and check the box in the upper-right corner of the web part. Then, on the Web Part Tools Options ribbon tab, click Web Part Properties.

7. Expand the Location Properties section and, in the Scope box, enter the name of the custom search scope that you want to use. This should be entered exactly as it appears on the View Scopes page.

8. Click OK to save the change and close the Web Part Properties pane.

9. With the page still in Edit mode, above the search box, click the Add New Tab link.

10. On the New Item page, in the Tab Name field, enter the same display name of the tab that you entered previously on the search page. Then enter the name of the search results page that you are currently editing—in our example, `ProjectsSearchResults.aspx`.

11. Click Save. The new tab will appear on the search page.

12. On the Page ribbon tab, click Save And Close.

Now you can return to the main page of the search site and click the new scope tab to conduct a search. The results page should only display results from the custom scope.

Create Metadata Property Mappings

One of SharePoint's strongest features is the ability to associate metadata (properties) with documents, images, and list items in order to organize the information for a business. Business users use this metadata to sort and filter large numbers of items into more meaningful subsets. Search takes advantage of the same metadata to locate and return relevant results. All metadata attributes found either on a document (as embedded attributes) or associated with an item (as a custom column in the list or library) are indexed by SharePoint. All metadata values are used by SharePoint when it performs a search query. Thus, results will be returned where the keyword was found in a property rather than the text of the document. Many of the properties discovered by SharePoint use names that do not accurately reflect their purpose (e.g., Office:4 is a property that holds the Author value).

To make the crawled properties more usable and to provide a common name for multiple properties, SharePoint ties metadata properties together into *managed properties*, which serve as aliases for the crawled properties. Managed properties can be used explicitly to configure the property-based searching in the search center sites.

To view the managed properties, from within the Search Service Administration site, under Queries And Results, click the Metadata Properties link, which will open the Metadata Property Mappings page, shown in Figure 9.9.

Figure 9.9: Metadata Property Mappings page

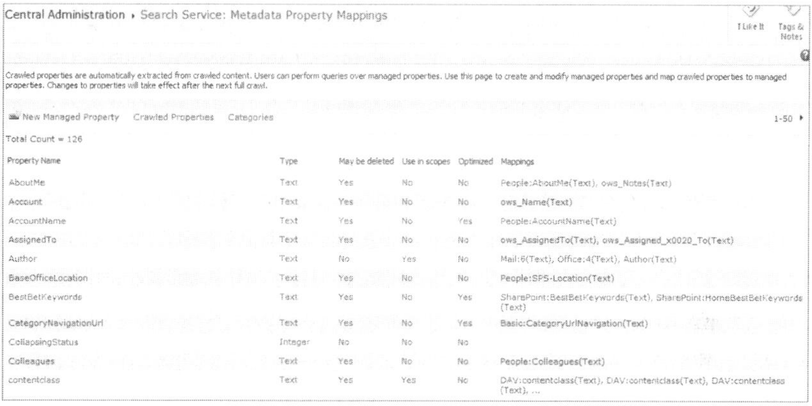
Central Administration › Search Service: Metadata Property Mappings

I Like It | Tags & Notes

Crawled properties are automatically extracted from crawled content. Users can perform queries over managed properties. Use this page to create and modify managed properties and map crawled properties to managed properties. Changes to properties will take effect after the next full crawl.

New Managed Property | Crawled Properties | Categories | 1-50

Total Count = 126

Property Name	Type	May be deleted	Use in scopes	Optimized	Mappings
AboutMe	Text	Yes	No	No	People:AboutMe(Text), ows_Notes(Text)
Account	Text	Yes	No	No	ows_Name(Text)
AccountName	Text	Yes	No	Yes	People:AccountName(Text)
AssignedTo	Text	Yes	No	No	ows_AssignedTo(Text), ows_Assigned_x0020_To(Text)
Author	Text	No	Yes	No	Mail:6(Text), Office:4(Text), Author(Text)
BaseOfficeLocation	Text	Yes	No	No	People:SPS-Location(Text)
BestBetKeywords	Text	Yes	No	Yes	SharePoint:BestBetKeywords(Text), SharePoint:HomeBestBetKeywords (Text)
CategoryNavigationUrl	Text	Yes	No	Yes	Basic:CategoryUrlNavigation(Text)
CollapsingStatus	Integer	No	No	No	
Colleagues	Text	Yes	No	No	People:Colleagues(Text)
contentclass	Text	Yes	Yes	No	DAV:contentclass(Text), DAV:contentclass(Text), DAV:contentclass (Text), ...

Viewing Crawled Properties

SharePoint maintains a catalog of all the metadata properties discovered during indexing. Many of the properties are drawn from Office files and are categorized as such. Others represent SharePoint columns that have been crawled and can be seen as those that have the prefix ows_ and are encoded to replace spaces and other illegal characters. For example, the custom SharePoint column Report Status would be listed under crawled properties as ows_Report_x0020_Status(Text).

This catalog of crawled properties can be viewed by clicking the Crawled Properties link on the Metadata Property Mappings page.

Creating a New Managed Property

Only a few of the crawled properties are mapped onto managed properties that are used by SharePoint. Under most circumstances, the best practice is to not modify any of the existing managed properties installed with SharePoint. Instead, it is often useful to create new managed properties to map onto new crawled properties that correspond to business data that needs to be searched. For example, a document library may have been configured with a column named Report Status that holds values such as Reviewed that users want to search on without getting every document in SharePoint that contains the word. To create a managed property, do the following:

1. From within the Search Service Administration site, under Queries And Results, click the Metadata Properties link, which will open the New Managed Property page. This page with completed fields for a new property is shown partially in Figure 9.10.

Figure 9.10: New Managed Property page

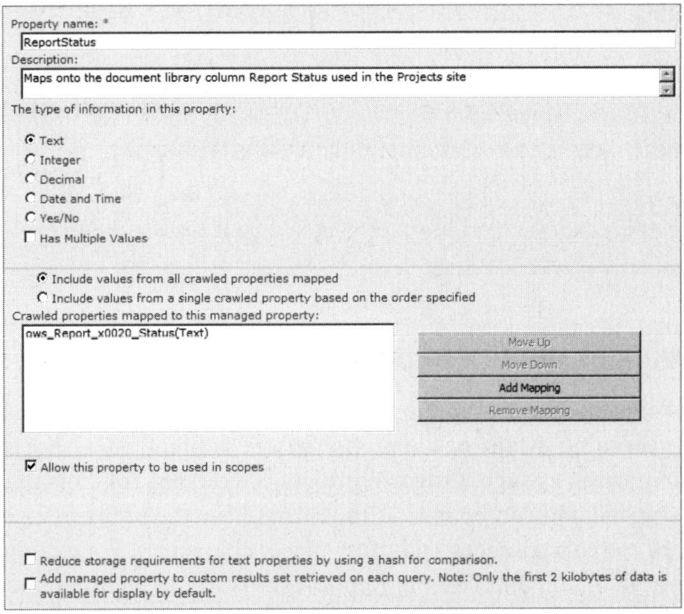

2. In the Property Name field, enter a name for the new property, leaving out spaces between any words. Optionally, enter a description of the property.

3. Select the data type of the property and whether or not it will contain multiple values that need to be split.

4. In the Mappings To Crawled Properties section, click the Add Mapping button.

5. In the Crawled Property Selection dialog box, enter a portion of the column name or property you are mapping onto and click Find or browse the list to find the property. Select the property and click OK.

   If the property you are looking for does not appear, then it may be necessary to conduct a Full Crawl to let SharePoint discover it.

6. If you want to use this property in the rule of a shared scope, select the check box Allow This Property To Be Used In Scopes. (See the section "Understanding Scope Rules" earlier in this chapter for more information.)

7. Optionally, check the boxes labeled "Reduce storage requirements for text properties by using a hash for comparison" or "Add managed property to custom results set retrieved on each query."

8. Click OK.

NOTE To get results from the new property in a custom scope, you will need to perform a Full Crawl to incorporate the new mapping into the index.

Configure Authoritative Pages

The order in which pages are ranked in SharePoint search results is determined by many factors, such as ratings, social tagging, and click-through totals. However, these criteria are not under central control to help determine what rankings a page will have and can make the results unpredictable.

Another factor that SharePoint uses is the distance, in clicks, that a page or document is from the root page in a site. Typically, the root page is the page used as the intranet portal or Internet site home page; however, any page can be designated as the root for index ranking purposes. Multiple pages can be considered authoritative for ranking purposes and all pages will be ranked in descending order based on how far they are from these authoritative pages. Administrators can also designate second-level and third-level authoritative pages as well as nonauthoritative sites, which will be deprecated in the rankings.

Before configuring authoritative pages, it is a good idea to develop a taxonomy diagram of your site that identifies where the most important information is stored from a search point of view. The most important information is not necessarily on the first page that users see when they browse to the root site. In many cases, the "portal" of a SharePoint environment is used for browsing topics for general information. When users are searching, they are often looking for documents or information related to business processes such as projects, proposals, and cases. These types of information would normally not be stored in the root site. If results from the root site show up in every search, more meaningful results might be pushed further down the list.

Once you have determined what the most authoritative site in SharePoint should be, along with the second and third sites, you can configure them by doing the following:

1. From within the Search Service Administration site, under Queries And Results, click the Authoritative Pages link, which will open the Specify Authoritative Pages page shown in Figure 9.11.

Figure 9.11: Specify Authoritative Pages settings

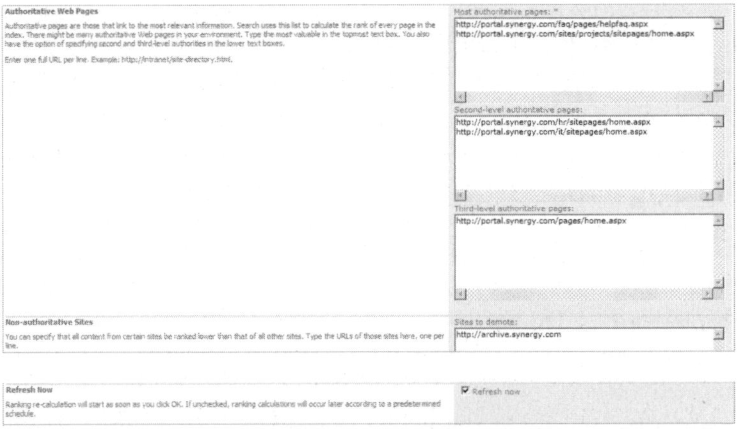

2. In the Most Authoritative Pages box, enter pages, in order of importance, that should be ranked highly in search results. Enter the full URL to each page.

3. In the Second-Level Authoritative Pages and Third-Level Authoritative Pages boxes, enter those pages that would be ranked at a second and third level of priority, respectively.

4. In the Sites To Demote box, enter those sites that are likely to have searched keywords but that aren't relevant to most users. For example, a site that keeps read-only archive copies of documents may not be useful for general purposes.

5. Relevancy ranking will need to be recomputed after changing the authoritative pages, so leave the Refresh Now box checked in order to initiate recalculation.

6. Click OK.

Define Keywords and Best Bets

Keywords are phrases or words that have specific or unique meaning in an organization and may be used frequently in searches by people trying to clarify their meaning. This is often the case with acronyms and industry-specific terms, which can cause confusion for those not familiar with them. Site collection administrators can configure SharePoint with a list of keyword definitions that will be displayed on the search results page. This list can provide a form of glossary for users and a ready reference that is easy for users to consult. In many cases, a keyword is also associated with one or more pages or documents that explain the term or that serve as the best source of information related to that term. These links can be configured as Best Bets by the administrator to be displayed along with the keyword in the search results. Keywords and Best Bets will only be shown when a user searches for the exact term that is configured as the keyword. Keywords can have synonyms so that variations on the terms can be included to increase the likelihood of a match.

Creating a Keyword

To create and manage keywords, you need to have site collection administrator rights to a site. Keywords only apply to searches done within the site collection that the keywords are configured in. Browse to the root of the site, then do the following:

1. From the site collection home page, click Site Actions, and then select Site Settings.

2. Under Site Collection Administration, click Search Keywords. The Manage Keywords page appears.

3. On the Manage Keywords page, click Add Keyword.

4. On the Add Keyword page, shown partially in Figure 9.12, enter a keyword phrase, which is the word or combination of words that users will be searching on. You can also enter synonyms so that several search terms can match the same keyword. Separate the synonyms by semicolons.

Figure 9.12: Adding a keyword

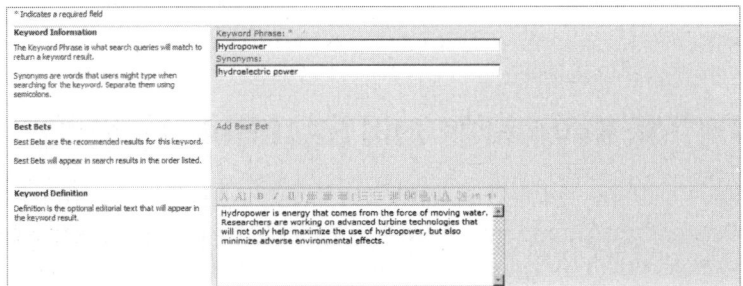

5. In the Keyword Definition box, type a description that will appear on the search results page under the keyword.

6. In the Contact field, enter the username of the person who will be periodically reviewing and updating this keyword.

7. In the Publishing section, enter the start date when this keyword becomes available, and optionally, an end date and a review date. If no end date is provided, then the term will not expire.

8. Click OK.

There is no need to wait for a crawl for the keywords to be applied. They will appear on the search results as soon as the start date is reached and a user searches for a matching term.

Adding a Best Bet

When there is a specific page or document that you would like to direct users to for more information about a keyword, you can add one or more Best Bets to the entry. Best Bets can be links to any location and do not have to appear normally in the search results nor have the keyword in their content. To create a Best Bet, do the following:

1. From the site collection home page, click Site Actions, and then select Site Settings.
2. Under Site Collection Administration, click Search Keywords.
3. On the Manage Keywords page, locate the keyword you want to edit and from the context menu, select Edit.
4. On the Edit Keyword page, click Add Best Bet.
5. In the Add Best Bet dialog box, shown in Figure 9.13, enter the URL, Title, and Description for the Best Bet link.

Figure 9.13: Adding a Best Bet

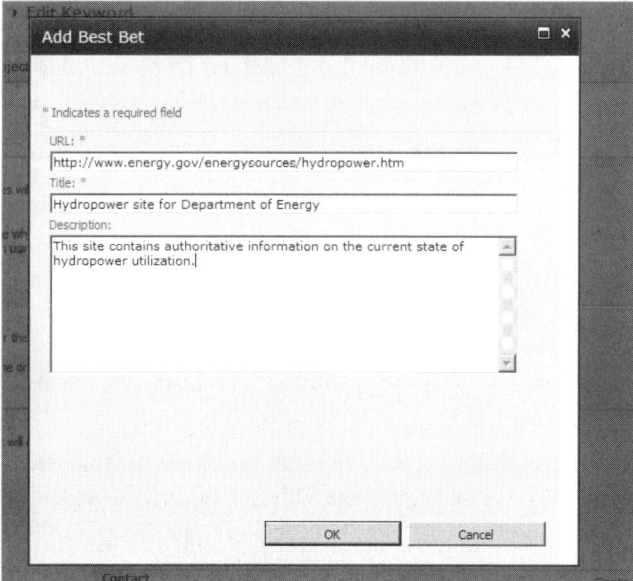

6. Click OK.
7. On the Edit Keyword page, click OK.

The keyword and Best Bets will appear similar to the example shown in Figure 9.14.

Figure 9.14: Keyword and Best Bet results

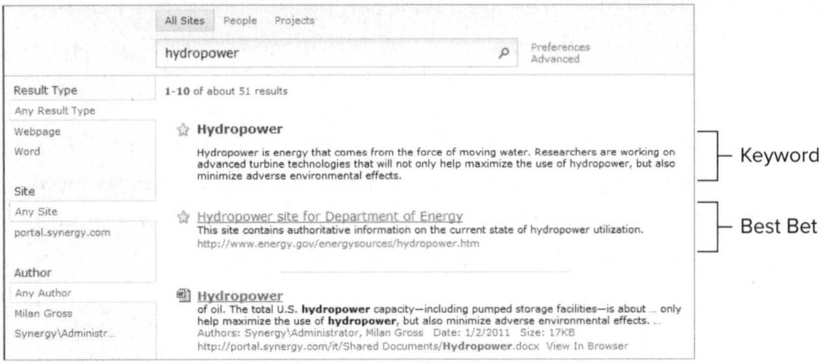

Remove Items from Search Results

There are cases where content has been indexed by SharePoint that should not have been. An example of this would be a when a page describing a corporate merger is inadvertently published internally before it was scheduled for release. Even if the security on the page is modified to remove user access, this will not remove the item immediately from the search results. The Search Result Removal command will immediately hide a page from the search results and will create a crawl rule to block the page from being crawled again. The removal only works on pages, not documents.

To immediately remove a link from the search results, do the following:

1. From within the Search Service Administration site, under Queries And Results, click the Search Result Removal link.
2. In the URLs To Remove box, type the full URLs for the pages that you want to remove. (You cannot include wildcards.)
3. Click OK.

Configure Federated Search

One of the challenges with searching in large organizations is that many times there are multiple SharePoint farms in distributed geographic locations. In previous versions of SharePoint, farm administrators had to configure cross-farm crawls, which were both time-consuming and resource-intensive on the servers. SharePoint 2010 incorporates a feature called Federated Search, which allows a search page to query additional data sources beyond the local SharePoint Search Service. This feature makes use of the open standard OpenSearch 1.1 to query any compliant search server and retrieve results for the same keyword or phrase that has been entered on the search page. This not only eliminates the need for cross-farm crawling but also minimizes the amount of traffic across the WAN because only the query is being sent and a limited number of result links are returned.

To view the existing federated locations installed with SharePoint, from within the Search Service Administration site, under Queries And Results, click the Federated Locations link. The Manage Federated Locations page shown in Figure 9.15 appears.

Figure 9.15: Manage Federated Locations page

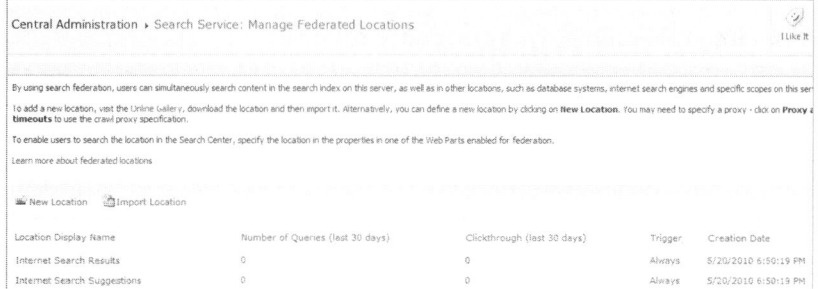

There are two methods for creating federated locations:

- Manually configure the settings that direct SharePoint 2010 to the remote search service (described in the next section).

- Import a configuration file that contains all the federated location details (described in "Importing a Federated Location," later in this chapter).

Creating a Federated Location

To create a new federated location, follow these steps:

1. From the Manage Federated Locations page, click the New Location link. This will open the Add Federated Location page shown partially in Figure 9.16.

Figure 9.16: Add Federated Location page

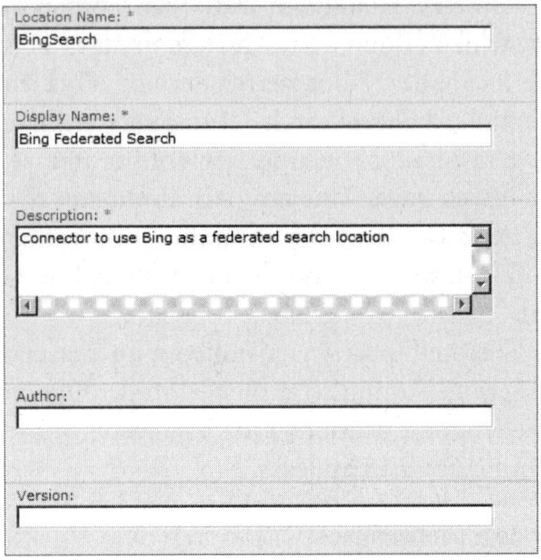

2. Enter the required information as follows:

   - Location Name uniquely identifies this location to SharePoint.
   - Display Name is visible in the administrative interface.
   - Description explains to others what the purpose of this location is.
   - The Author and Version fields are optional and can help administrators manage the search locations.

3. In the Trigger section, shown in Figure 9.17, determine how this location will be executed on the search page.

Figure 9.17: Trigger section, Add Federated Location page

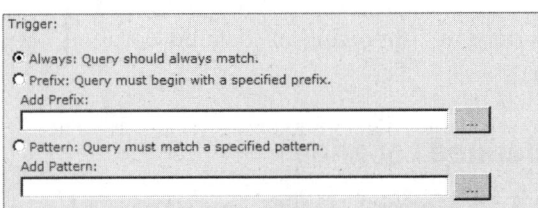

The options are:

   - Always ensures that this location will be queried during every search.

- Prefix allows you to specify a keyword that will trigger this particular location to be called. A search page may be configured to call multiple different locations depending on what prefix is supplied. Note that only the term following the prefix will be submitted to the federated location, which could produce skewed results. For example, if the prefix is "power" and a user enters the term "power solar" in the search box, the local search will be executed using the full phrase but only "solar" will be sent to the remote location for querying.

- Pattern uses a .NET regular expression capture group to store part of the query in a variable. For example, the pattern power(?<type>.*) would match when a user enters "power solar" and would capture the word "solar" in the variable <type> and send it to the search location.

4. Choose the Location Type setting for the search:

    - Search Index On This Server shows results from the SharePoint index managed by this search service. You can filter the search by targeting a custom shared scope or a managed property value.

    - FAST Index shows results from a specific FAST server index.

    - OpenSearch 1.0/1.1 queries any external search engine that complies with the OpenSearch standard. This standard provides a common XML format for search queries and results that are then formatted and displayed by SharePoint.

5. If you chose the OpenSearch option for the Location Type setting, configure the query template for the federated location. The query template is equivalent to the URL template in OpenSearch. It references the location's URL and includes the parameter placeholder for the query terms that will be passed to the location in the query. The template will contain a case-sensitive parameter, {searchTerms}, which will hold the search terms entered by the user. The template can also include other parameters used to filter the query using managed properties. For example, the following is the query template for a Bing search:

    ```
    http://api.bing.com/rss.aspx?source=web&amp;
    query={searchTerms}&amp;web.count={count}&amp;
    web.offset={startIndex}&amp;market={language}&
    amp;FORM=MOO000&amp;version=2.0" indexOffset="0"
    ```

6. In the "More Results" Link Template box, enter a link to the full search results page on the federated location that can be queried directly, along with the replacement parameters. The following example will open the Bing search results page and pass the keyword parameters to it:

   http://www.bing.com/search?q={searchTerms}&FORM=MO0001

7. In the Display Information section, shown partially in Figure 9.18, customize how the federated search results will appear.

   Figure 9.18: Display Information section

   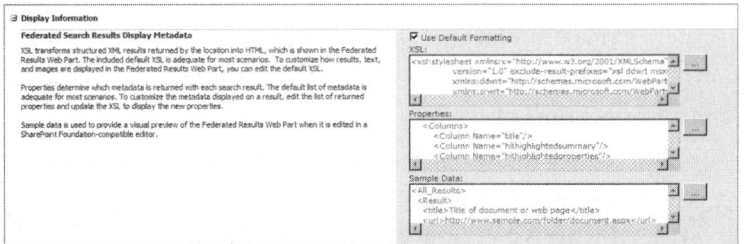

There are three subsections, each for its associated web page:

- Federated Search Results Display Metadata
- Core Search Results Display Metadata
- Top Federated Results Display Metadata

Each section has three boxes for formatting the appearance:

- The XSL box contains a template that transforms SharePoint XML search results into valid HTML.
- The Properties box holds the list of metadata that will be returned from the federated location for use in the XSL transformation.
- The Sample Data box helps designers lay out the appearance of the web part results.

8. In the Restrict Usage section, shown in Figure 9.19, select whether you want to control which sites can use this location. The No Restriction option allows any site to use the location. The Use Restriction option will limit the sites to the list specified in the Allowed Sites field. Separate the URLs entered with a semicolon.

Figure 9.19: Restrict Usage and Specify Credentials sections

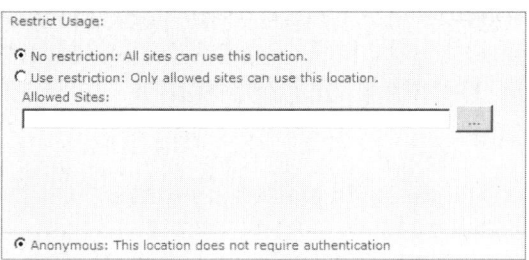

9. If you selected either the FAST Index or OpenSearch options, then select an authentication method in the Specify Credentials section:

   - Anonymous authentication does not require a username and password and works for public Internet search engines that do not authenticate users.

   - Common authentication allows you to provide a single username and password that will be used for all users. This method is useful when the location requires authentication but the users do not have logins to the remote server or they are on an untrusted domain. The disadvantage of this approach is that all users will see the same results with no permissions filtering applied.

   - User authentication allows users to authenticate to the remote server using their own accounts. This works best if Kerberos authentication has been enabled so that user credentials can be passed through.

10. Click OK.

Importing a Federated Location

SharePoint supports importing a predefined search connector file that contains most or all of the appropriate location settings already configured. These files either have the extension .fld (Federated Location Definition file) or .osdx (Windows Search Connector), and you can download samples of both from Microsoft at

http://technet.microsoft.com/en-us/enterprisesearch/ff727944.aspx

To use a location file, open the Manage Federated Locations page and click the Import Location link. On the Import Federated Location page, browse to the file and click OK. You can then edit the definition to customize the settings.

Editing, Copying, Deleting, or Exporting a Federated Location

From the Manage Federated Locations page, click the context menu for any of the existing locations. From here you can edit or delete a location. You can also create a new location by copying an existing one. Doing so duplicates all the settings except the name, which must be unique. The last option is to export the location as an .osdx file for use on another server.

Configuring a Federated Search Web Part

There are three web parts shipped with SharePoint 2010 that support consuming federated locations and displaying the results:

Core Results Web Part This web part is not commonly used to display federated results, but it fully supports locations. The web part Location Properties pane, shown in Figure 9.20, is normally set to the Local Search Results location but can be configured for any federated location. In Figure 9.20 the Bing Federated Search location, which was previously configured, has been selected.

Figure 9.20: Core Results web part Location Properties pane

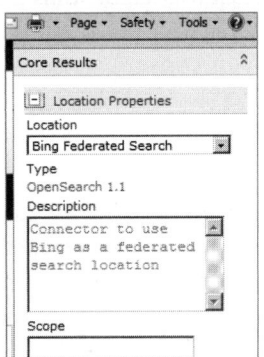

Federated Results Web Part This web part is similar to the Core Results web part but is specifically designed to support passing a search query to a remote location and displaying the results in

a sidebar format on the page. In the web part Properties pane, select the Location property in the same way you did for the Core Results web part. Under Display Properties you can specify the number of results to be displayed on the page (the default is 3). The setting Retrieve Results Asynchronously allows the web part to load the search results after the main page has been loaded. This option is checked by default. A Federated Results web part is automatically added to the standard search results page as the People Matches web part.

Top Federated Results Web Part This web part is almost identical to the Federated Results web part except that it can be configured with multiple federated locations. It will query all of the locations but only loads the first set of results returned.

View Search Reports

SharePoint 2010 provides search and query reports for different views at various levels in the application. These reports help identify trends and possible areas where search can be improved. Table 9.1 summarizes the various reports available to farm administrators and site collection administrators.

Table 9.1: SharePoint search reports by scope

Report	Search Service	Web Application	Site Collection
Number of Queries	X	X	X
Top Queries	X		X
No Result Queries/ Failed Queries	X		X
Best Bet Usage			X
Best Bet Suggestions			X
Best Bet Suggestions Action History			X

To access the reports at the Search Service level, from within the Search Service Administration site, under Queries And Results, click the Web Analytics Reports link, which will open the Search Service

Application Web Analytics Reports – Summary page. From this page you can view several useful reports:

Number Of Queries   Shows the total and average number of queries per day

Top Queries   Shows the most popular queries per day

No Result Queries   Queries for which no results were returned

There is only one set of statistics aggregated at the web application level. The total number of queries can be viewed by navigating to Central Administration, clicking the Monitoring link, and clicking View Web Analytics Reports. This page displays the total number of search queries for each web application.

Most search reports are available at the site collection level and can be viewed by navigating to the root site in a site collection, clicking Site Actions, and then selecting Site Settings. On the Site Settings page, in the Site Actions section, click Site Collection Web Analytics Reports, which opens the Site Collection Web Analytics Reports – Summary page. From this page you can view the following reports in addition to those available at the other levels:

Failed Queries   Queries for which no results were returned

Best Bet Usage   Lists queries that returned Best Bets

Best Bet Suggestions   Suggests terms and phrases that would make good Best Bets

Best Bet Suggestions Action History   Tracks whether Best Bet Suggestions were accepted or rejected

10

Configuring Document Management

IN THIS CHAPTER, YOU WILL LEARN TO:

▸ **CONFIGURE VERSIONING AND APPROVAL** (Pages 312–321)
- Enabling Document Versioning (Page 312)
- Restoring a Document Version (Page 314)
- Requiring Explicit Checkout (Page 315)
- Taking Ownership of Checked-Out Files (Page 317)
- Configuring Draft Item Security (Page 318)
- Enabling and Configuring Content Approval (Page 319)

▸ **CREATE VIEWS** (Pages 321–324)

▸ **CREATE CONTENT TYPES** (Pages 324–326)

▸ **CREATE DOCUMENT SETS** (Pages 327–328)

▸ **CONFIGURE DOCUMENT IDs** (Pages 328–330)

▸ **CONFIGURE THE CONTENT ORGANIZER** (Pages 330–332)
- Configuring Content Organizer Settings (Page 330)
- Creating Content Organizer Rules (Page 331)

Of all SharePoint's capabilities, the one area that is arguably the most sought after is document management. Organizations of all sizes have document management requirements: from a small dental office filing electronic patient letters to a Fortune 500 company organizing, storing, and retrieving its millions upon millions of files. Although file servers are still around, many organizations are migrating to document management systems like SharePoint because of all the benefits they deliver. This chapter covers many of these benefits, including document versioning, approval, content types, views, document sets, unique document IDs, and the Content Organizer.

Configure Versioning and Approval

As documents are created and evolve, they usually go through different stages. Document versioning allows you to store and recall historical versions of a document. SharePoint's versioning system lets you store each and every version from the beginning, or you can choose to store just some of the most recent versions. Or, if you don't need the feature, you can turn off versioning and only the most recent version is stored.

SharePoint also supports document approval. Approval allows you to use a formal document-publishing process. For example, if HR personnel are working on a new employee manual, the document may need to be formally approved by the vice president of HR.

> **NOTE** This chapter will frequently use the term *document*. The term does not refer to just Microsoft Word documents. In the context of SharePoint, a document is any electronic file type that can be stored and managed within a library.

Enabling Document Versioning

Most libraries in SharePoint have versioning turned off by default. For example, if you create a new team site, the Shared Documents library will not have versioning enabled. Conversely, if a Document Center site (a template that comes with SharePoint Server) is created, the Documents library has versioning enabled. These default settings can be adjusted as needed.

When working with versioning, you'll notice that two types of versions are supported:

A Major Version (e.g., 1.0)   A published version of the document that is ready for dissemination

A Minor Version (e.g., 0.1)   A draft that is still going through various edits and not ready to be published yet

Having SharePoint manage both the draft and published versions of files gives you a great deal of flexibility.

Let's say that the HR department is writing an employee manual. This document could easily go through 10 or more draft versions before it is ready to be published. It is best to keep draft versions in SharePoint (and not in, say, My Documents stored locally) for easy access by others who also collaborate on the document. Storing a draft version in SharePoint also helps in restoring the document if contents in a file has been accidentally erased or the file becomes corrupted.

To enable document versioning for a library, follow these steps:

1. Access the library.
2. Just above the ribbon, click the Library tab (underneath Library Tools).
3. Click the Library Settings button in the ribbon.
4. In the General Settings section, click Versioning Settings.
5. As shown in Figure 10.1, select either Create Major Versions or Create Major And Minor (Draft) Versions.

   Figure 10.1: Enabling document versioning

   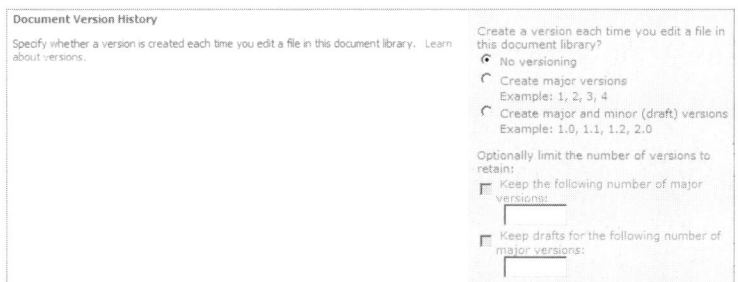

6. Optionally, specify how many previous versions SharePoint should keep by selecting the "Keep the following number of major versions" check box and entering a number. For instance, if the

current version is 3.0 and you enter 2, SharePoint keeps the 1.0 and 2.0 versions. When 4.0 is saved, version 1.0 will be removed.

7. Optionally (if you have enabled both major and minor versions), select the "Keep drafts for the following number of major versions" check box and enter a number.

8. Click OK to save changes.

SharePoint creates a new version automatically in these cases:

- Modifying the metadata for document—for example, changing the title
- Uploading another document with the same filename
- Opening and saving a file
- Explicitly checking out and then checking in the file

Only by explicitly checking out and then checking in a file can a user control whether a newly saved version becomes a major or minor version.

> **NOTE** When storing major and minor versions, SharePoint stores complete copies of the file, and not just the changes from the previous version. So, if just one bullet in a 2 MB PowerPoint file changes, it will store another full copy of the 2 MB file. This becomes a space concern, which is one reason versioning is turned off by default for most libraries. When turning on versioning, remember that there may be a site collection quota that is restricting the amount of space available for storing versions. (See Chapter 3, "Creating and Managing Site Collections.")

Restoring a Document Version

Restoring or viewing a previous document version is easy, assuming versioning has been enabled. For Microsoft Office files, such as an Excel worksheet, you can do so inside the client application in versions 2007 and 2010. You can also accomplish this from the browser by following these steps:

1. Access the document's context menu from one of the library views and select Version History.

2. The document's version history is shown in a pop-up window (see Figure 10.2).

Figure 10.2: Viewing a document's version history

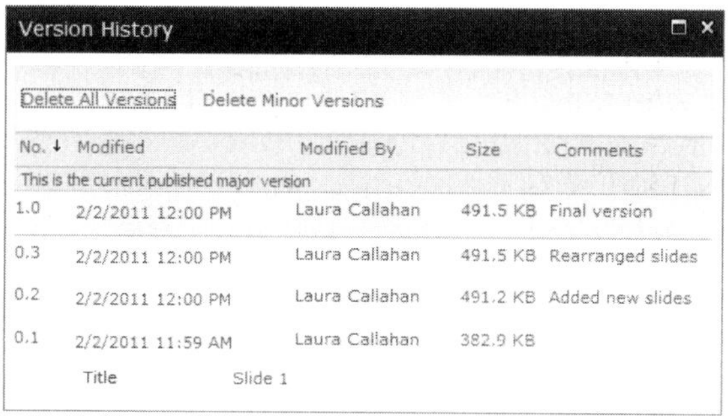

3. To restore an old version, select the document version (e.g., 1.0 or 0.3 from Figure 10.2) and from the context menu, choose Restore. (You can also view the version from this menu.)
4. Confirm the action by clicking OK.

When restoring a previous version, the current version is not replaced. Instead, the version to be restored is copied and inserted as a new version. If draft versions are enabled, the restored copy becomes a draft; otherwise, it becomes the latest major version. In Figure 10.3, version 0.2 from Figure 10.2 has been restored and now also appears as version 1.1.

Figure 10.3: Version history after restoring a prior version

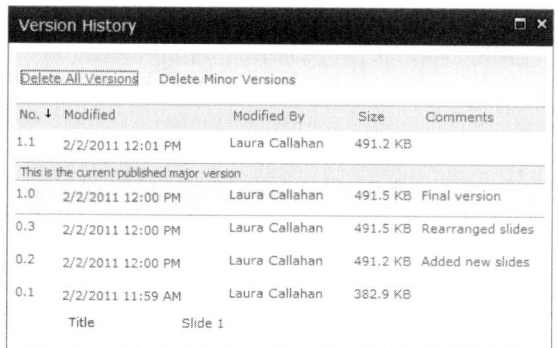

Requiring Explicit Checkout

SharePoint has two types of checkout: implicit and explicit.

Implicit (or short-term) checkout happens automatically when you open and edit a document in a SharePoint-aware application such as

Microsoft Word 2007. When a file is opened for edit, SharePoint internally locks the item as being edited. In most cases, the lock is kept for 60 minutes. Each time the file is saved, the lock's timer is reset back to 60 minutes. If there is no save activity after 60 minutes, the lock is removed. A lock is also removed when the file is closed. If another user tries to edit the file while another user has a short-term checkout, they will see the message shown in Figure 10.4.

Figure 10.4: Message displayed when attempting to edit a locked file.

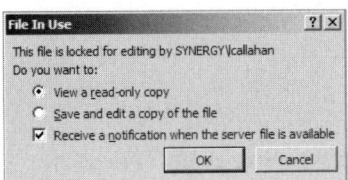

Implicit checkout has some advantages. For example, it is compatible with the co-authoring feature of Office 2010, which allows multiple users to edit the same file at the same time. But it's not a robust checkout mechanism and is prone to errors. One common problem is that two people can unintentionally edit the same file concurrently and whoever saves it last overwrites the other user's changes.

With explicit checkout, a more robust mechanism, the user must specifically check out a document from the browser or a SharePoint-aware application prior to editing. Only one user at a time can explicitly check out a file. A user with full control permissions to the library can require explicit checkouts for all edit operations. This setting will prevent implicit checkouts.

Here is how to require explicit checkouts within a library:

1. Click the Library Settings button in the ribbon.
2. Click Versioning Settings.
3. In the Require Check out area (see Figure 10.5), click Yes to require checkout.

    Figure 10.5: Click Yes to require checkout

    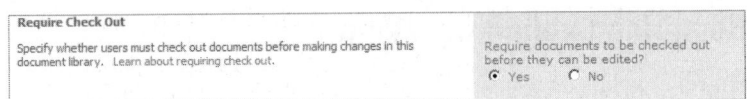

4. Click OK to save.

While requiring explicit checkouts is a useful feature to prevent concurrent editing, there are a few caveats you should be aware of:

- Required checkout also means required check-in. When you add one or more new files to a library, they will remain in a checked-out state until you explicitly check them in.
- The datasheet view becomes read only.
- Requiring checkout disables co-authoring for a library.

Taking Ownership of Checked-Out Files

While requiring checkout is recommended to avoid accidental overwrites by other users, here's a common problem it can cause:

Manager: Be sure to have those new TPS reports uploaded into SharePoint by the end of the day.

Employee: Sure thing, boss. I'm working on them right now.

(As employee is rushing out of the office at 6 p.m., he quickly uploads the files into a document library. The document library has Require Checkout enabled. At 7 p.m., the manager is looking for the files and cannot find them.)

Manager (angrily calling the employee at home): Where are those reports I told you to upload?

Employee: I did upload them right before I left.

Manager: Well, I'm looking right now and I don't see them.

When documents have been uploaded but not checked in, the documents are invisible to other users, including administrators. There are two solutions to this problem:

- The user who uploaded must check in the files.
- An administrator (or anyone with full control on the library) must take ownership of the files and check them in. Any unsaved changes will be lost.

To take ownership of files created by other users:

1. Click the Library Settings button in the ribbon.
2. Click "Manage files which have no checked in version." You are presented with the screen shown in Figure 10.6.

Figure 10.6: Taking ownership of checked-out files

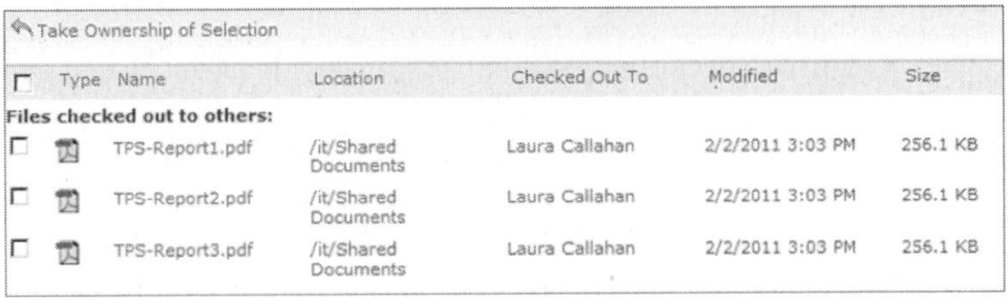

	Type	Name	Location	Checked Out To	Modified	Size
	Files checked out to others:					
☐	📄	TPS-Report1.pdf	/it/Shared Documents	Laura Callahan	2/2/2011 3:03 PM	256.1 KB
☐	📄	TPS-Report2.pdf	/it/Shared Documents	Laura Callahan	2/2/2011 3:03 PM	256.1 KB
☐	📄	TPS-Report3.pdf	/it/Shared Documents	Laura Callahan	2/2/2011 3:03 PM	256.1 KB

3. Select the files you want to take ownership of, and click Take Ownership Of Selection.
4. Confirm the action by clicking OK.
5. Return to the regular view. You should now be able to see the files and check them in as if you had uploaded them.

Configuring Draft Item Security

By default, users who have read permissions to a library are also able to read a document's draft versions. In some cases, this could present a security problem. For example, a link to the current employee manual may be placed on HR's home page in SharePoint. While this document is going through draft edits, you do not want any non-HR personnel to be able to see these unpublished versions. Instead, they should only see the most recent published (i.e., major) version.

To restrict who has access to a document's draft versions:

1. Click the Library Settings button in the ribbon.
2. Click Versioning Settings.
3. In the Draft Item Security section shown in Figure 10.7, adjust the permission as needed. You can restrict visibility of drafts to users with edit permissions or to approvers. (Approving documents is covered in the next section.)

Figure 10.7: Configuring draft item security

Draft Item Security	
Drafts are minor versions or items which have not been approved. Specify which users should be able to view drafts in this document library. Learn about specifying who can view and edit drafts.	Who should see draft items in this document library? ○ Any user who can read items ● Only users who can edit items ○ Only users who can approve items (and the author of the item)

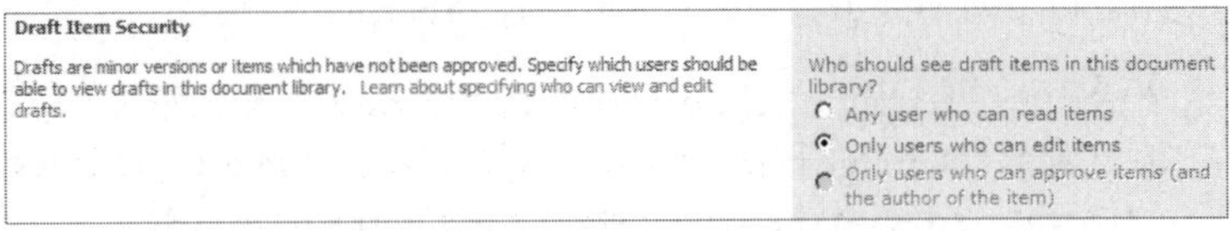

4. Click OK to save.

Enabling and Configuring Content Approval

Content approval means that one or more designated users must explicitly approve a document before it can be published as a major version. Without content approval, the publishing life cycle looks like this:

1. Draft (minor) version
2. Published (major) version

Any user with edit permissions on the file can publish it as a major version. With content approval enabled, the publishing life cycle has a third step:

1. Draft (minor) version
2. Pending (minor version awaiting approval)
3. Approved published (major) version

By default, content approval is turned off.

Enabling Content Approval

To enable content approval on a library, follow these steps:

1. Click the Library Settings button in the ribbon.
2. Click Versioning Settings.
3. In the Content Approval section shown in Figure 10.8, select Yes.

Figure 10.8: Enabling content approval

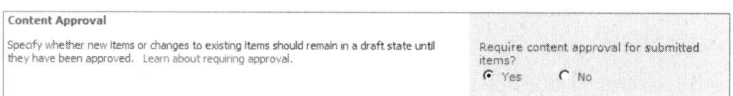

4. Click OK to save.

Configuring Content Approval

The content approval requirement can be handled in one of two ways:

Publish as a Major Version Pending Approval   Any user that has the Approve permission level can approve documents. This is the only supported way in SharePoint Foundation and it also works in SharePoint Server. To submit a document for approval, select

"Publish as a major version" in the context menu for the draft item, or check in the file as a major version. Either way, the file's approval status changes to Pending, and the file is still listed as a draft version.

To approve a document that is pending:

1. Click the Approve/Reject option in the item's context menu.
2. In the pop-up dialog box, choose Approved.
3. Optionally, enter comments.
4. Click OK.

Approve Content Using a Workflow The approval workflow method is supported only in SharePoint Server. This is done by configuring an approval workflow and associating it to the library that has content approval enabled. Users defined in the workflow will have the authority to approve.

> **NOTE** For more information on configuring approval workflows, see the article "Understand Approval Workflows in SharePoint 2010" located at http://office.microsoft.com/en-us/sharepoint-designer-help/understand-approval-workflows-in-sharepoint-2010-HA101857172.aspx.

To create an approval workflow to be used for document approval, follow these steps:

1. Access the library.
2. Just above the ribbon, click the Library tab (underneath Library Tools).
3. In the ribbon, click Workflow Settings ➢ Add A Workflow.
4. In the Add A Workflow dialog box, select the Approval - SharePoint 2010 workflow template.
5. In the Name text box, type a unique name for the workflow.
6. Optionally, adjust the task and history lists to be used for this workflow.
7. In the Start Options section, select "Start this workflow to approve publishing a major version of an item," as shown in Figure 10.9.

Figure 10.9: Starting a content approval workflow

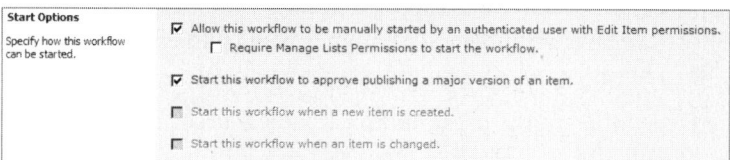

8. Click Next to continue to the next page.

9. Assign people as workflow approvers and specify whether the approval should be serial (each person must approve in a defined order) or parallel (approvers can approve in any order).

10. As needed, configure the remaining options that are supported by the approval workflow.

11. Click Save to associate this approval workflow with the library.

When the next request to publish as a major version occurs, SharePoint automatically starts this workflow. Only upon successful approval does the document become a published major version.

Create Views

A view in SharePoint controls how items in a list or library are displayed. At a basic level, the view sets the columns to be displayed (normally shown from left to right, like columns in a spreadsheet), how the items are sorted, and which items to filter. Views are used to help categorize and locate items within a single library. While creating views is easy, there are many optional settings that you can use.

Any list or library will have at least one view that is marked as the default. You can create new views as well; here are a few practical examples:

- Sales personnel who store their customer proposals in SharePoint can use separate views to manage the documents by region, salesperson, size, or type.

- Accounting staff can use views to manage invoices. Some users use a view to organize invoices by the number of days overdue (30–60, 60–90, etc.), whereas others use a different view to group invoices by customer.

- Magazine publishers can use views to organize pictures based on tags that have been applied to each photo. For example, if an article on environmental cleanup is being published, items in a picture library can be found quickly and perused.

Depending on the list or library template used, different views are automatically created when creating the list or library. The built-in views on a tasks list are a good example. These include All Tasks, My Tasks, Due Today, and Active Tasks, among others. Although this chapter focuses on managing documents in libraries, views on a list or library work the same.

When you're creating a view, two types are supported:

- A personal view can only be used by the person who created it. Any user with Contribute access on the library can create personal views.

- A public view can be used by anyone who has read permissions on the library. Only users with Full Control, Design, and Manage Hierarchy permission levels can create public views.

The configuration options when creating a personal view and a public view are the same.

> **NOTE** SharePoint 2010 views are built using an XSLT List View Web Part, which you can create and edit using SharePoint Designer 2010. The web part gives you more advanced options such as conditional formatting on certain columns. To learn more, see the article "Create a Custom List View Using SharePoint Designer" located at http://office.microsoft.com/en-us/sharepoint-designer-help/create-a-custom-list-view-using-sharepoint-designer-HA010379079.aspx.

Here are the steps to create a new view on a library:

1. Access the library.
2. Just above the ribbon, click the Library tab (underneath Library Tools).
3. Click the Create View button in the ribbon.
4. Choose the view format or select an existing view to start from. The options available vary somewhat depending on the type of view. The Standard format is the most common and is the one used in the following steps.

5. Enter a short but recognizable name for the view. If this is a public view, the name is also used for the new web page that is created.

6. For Audience, specify whether this is a personal or public view.

7. Select the columns that you want to appear in the view. Also, select the position in which you want each column to appear (from right to left).

8. For Sort, specify the column or columns to be used when ordering items in the view. Up to two columns can be used. For example, you can first sort by state, then by city. (Items can also be sorted on-demand from the view by clicking on the column heading.)

9. For Filter, specify a condition to be used to exclude items from the view. For example, you might want to hide documents that were last modified more than 30 days ago.

    For large lists containing more than a thousand items, it is best to use an indexed column when creating a filter. To learn more about creating indexed columns, see the article on The Sanity Point blog titled "Indexing SharePoint List Columns" located at www.thesanitypoint.com/archive/2009/09/20/indexing-sharepoint-list-columns.aspx.

10. For Inline Editing, check whether you want to allow users to edit an item "inline" in addition to editing through the usual pop-up dialog box.

11. For Group By, choose a maximum of two columns to configure grouping and subgrouping. This is a helpful way to collapse a large number of items into manageable groups. For example, you might want to group by document type or by author (Created By column).

12. For Totals, choose the column or columns to display a total value based on an aggregate function (e.g., count, sum, average). Unfortunately, the total is figured for all the items displayed and you cannot subtotal if you are grouping. (But you can create subtotals by customizing the view in SharePoint Designer.)

13. For Style, choose how the items should appear. For example, the Shaded style displays every other item with a shaded background color.

14. For Folders, you can optionally display items without folders, organizing them into a single list of items. Be careful when using this option if you have thousands of items and are not limiting the item count in the next step, as this option can cause performance problems.

15. For Item Count, select the maximum number of items to display in a single page. The default value is 30 items, and additional items are visible by navigating to subsequent pages. Although this value can be increased, proceed with caution as doing so can cause performance problems. Also, SharePoint employs item count throttling on large lists, and by default, users can see a maximum of only 5,000 items. For more information, see Chapter 2, "Creating and Managing Web Applications."

16. For Mobile, adjust the settings for how this view is shown for mobile clients. These settings apply only to public views.

17. Click OK to save the view.

Create Content Types

Content types allow you to package and reuse specific settings within lists and libraries. These settings include metadata columns, workflow, information management policies (e.g., when a document expires), and a document template (e.g., a form). One big advantage is that you can define these settings one time and use them on multiple libraries. If the settings need to change, you can change them on the content type once and immediately propagate the changes to all documents based on this content type. In this way, you can better organize content in a consistent way.

For example, a manufacturing company might want to capture consistent metadata such as Product ID, Revision Number, and Author for all of its product designs. These designs might be stored as different file types in hundreds of team sites. One content type can be created to encapsulate these columns and then be applied to the necessary libraries.

Content types are optional, but using them carefully can save a lot of time. They also facilitate other SharePoint features such as Records Management (covered in Chapter 12, "Configuring Records Management") and the Content Organizer (covered later in this chapter), which depends on content types for automated routing and storage of documents.

A content type can be created within any website in a site collection. The scope or reach of the content type is the site in which it is created and all of its subsites. Thus, if a content type is created in the top-level website, it can be used throughout the site collection.

> **NOTE** Using content type syndication, a feature that is part of the Managed Metadata Service, content types from a designated site collection can be published to other site collections in the farm and other trusted farms. For more information, see Chapter 11, "Configuring the Managed Metadata Service."

After a content type has been created, it must be added to one or more libraries to be used. A library can also have multiple content types associated with it.

Here are the steps to create a content type:

1. Connect to the website where the content type is to be created.
2. Go to Site Actions ➢ Site Settings.
3. Under Galleries, click Site Content Types. The list of built-in content types is displayed, categorized by groups.
4. Click Create. The New Content Type screen is shown in Figure 10.10.

Figure 10.10: Creating a content type

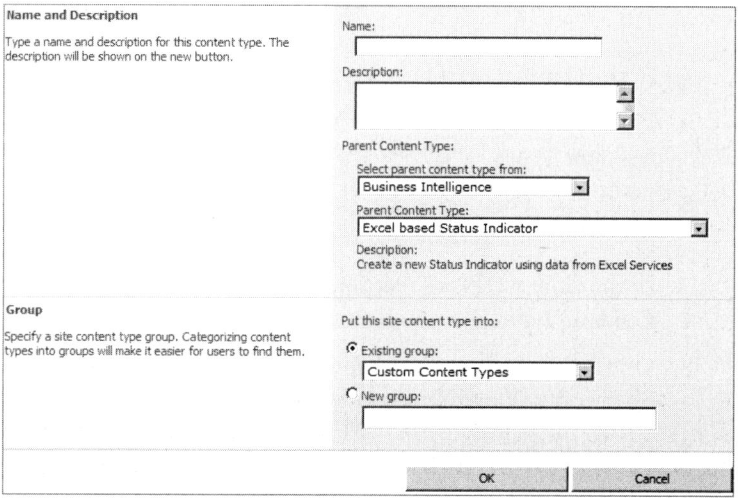

5. For Name, provide an intuitive and friendly name for the content type.

6. Optionally, for Description, describe the content type.

7. For Parent Content Type, choose the underlying content type that is to be used. All content types must derive (or inherit) from an existing built-in or custom content type. For libraries, the most common underlying content type selected is Documents.

8. For Group, specify which existing group this content type belongs to, or create a new group for this content type. Groups are only used to categorize content types and don't affect how the content type is used.

9. Click OK to create the content type.

Once the content type is created, it is ready to be configured. You are automatically taken to a new screen where all the shared settings can be defined. This includes adding columns, associating a workflow, creating information management policies, or providing a document template to be used.

After you create and configure a content type, you need to add it to a library. When the content type is added to a library, all of its settings become available on that library. For example, columns are added and workflow is associated. Here is how to add a content type to an existing library:

1. Access the library.

2. Just above the ribbon, click the Library tab (underneath Library Tools).

3. In the ribbon, click Library Settings.

4. In the General Settings section, click Advanced Settings.

5. For the first question, select Yes to Allow Management Of Content Types.

6. Click OK. This configures the library to allow you to add content types. You are returned to the previous screen.

7. In the Content Types section, click Add From Existing Site Content Types.

8. On the left, select one or more content types to be added to this library. You can filter them by selecting a group.

9. Click the Add button.

10. Click OK to save your changes.

Create Document Sets

One of the problems with associating metadata with documents is that each document maintains its own separate values. For example, if a sales proposal is being assembled and it consists of several files, you have to repeatedly enter the same metadata values for each file. This is where document sets come in handy.

A document set is a collection of files that are managed together as a unit. You fill out metadata once and it applies to the whole set. The files are also versioned as a set. The files participate together in a workflow, and the files can be secured as a set. SharePoint even uses a different interface when you are working with document sets.

Document sets are supported only in SharePoint Server. To use document sets, you must first activate the Document Sets site collection feature. Here are the steps:

1. Go to the top-level website in the site collection.
2. Click Site Actions ➤ Site Settings.
3. In Site Collection Administration, select Site Collection Features.
4. Look for the feature named Document Sets and click the Activate button.

When the feature is activated, a new content type called Document Set is created. This content type can be added directly to a library, but the recommended way is to create a new content type that inherits from the Document Set content type. You then add this new content type to your library. Once that is done, follow these steps to create a new document set in a library:

1. Access the library where a Document Set content type has been added.
2. Just above the ribbon, click the Documents tab (underneath Library Tools).
3. In the ribbon, click New Document (be sure to click the lower half of the button with the down arrow).
4. Select Document Set (or the name of your custom Document Set content type).
5. In the resulting dialog box, provide a name and description.
6. Enter any other metadata as required by the content type.
7. Click OK to create the document set.

Once the document set is created, you are taken to a page designed just for document sets, as shown in Figure 10.11. From here, you can add or remove documents from the set and view/edit the document set's metadata. You can also manage many of this set's properties by using the buttons found in the Manage tab, also shown in Figure 10.11.

Figure 10.11: Managing a newly created document set

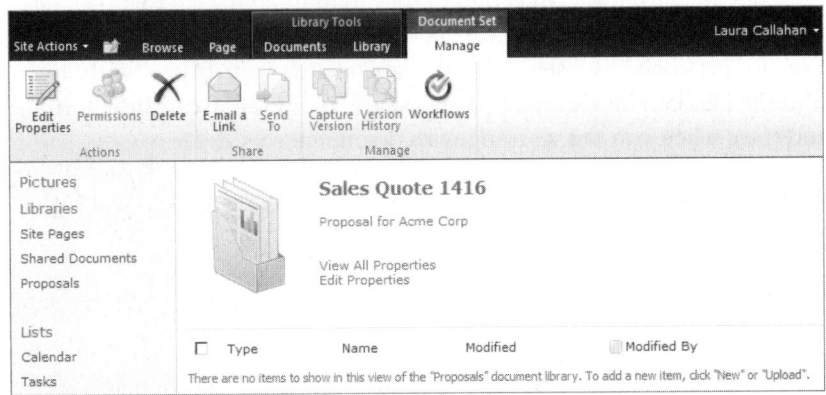

Configure Document IDs

As SharePoint becomes fully adopted as a document management solution, it is common (and recommended) to refrain from attaching files to email messages. Instead, you store files in a suitable library and email a link instead. Great solution! But wait, what happens if the document is renamed? You then have a broken link.

The Document ID feature in SharePoint Server stamps each document in a site collection with a unique document ID. In addition, SharePoint generates a static URL that also links to the document. This static URL still works even if the document is renamed or moved within the same site collection. Instead of emailing the regular URL to the file, you can email the static URL instead.

> **NOTE** For the static URL to work, the document ID must not change. If you copy a document or use the Send To context menu command, a new document ID is created. To preserve the document ID, you can move the document using the Site Content And Structure tool, as discussed in Chapter 3.

To use this Document ID capability, you must first activate the Document ID Service feature for the site collection. Here's how:

1. Go to the top-level website in the site collection.
2. Click Site Actions ➢ Site Settings.
3. In Site Collection Administration, select Site Collection Features.
4. Look for the feature named Document ID Service and click the Activate button.

If there is just one website in this site collection, the Document ID feature should be ready once activated. If there is more than one website, a timer job named Document ID Enable/Disable Job must first run before Document IDs can be generated. A separate timer job named Document ID Assignment Job assigns unique IDs to all existing documents in the site collection. Both of these timer jobs are scheduled to run daily and can also be run manually.

To test whether the Document ID feature is functioning, perform this simple test:

1. Upload a new file into a library.
2. Go to the context menu for the file and select View Properties.
3. Look for a column called Document ID. This column contains the static URL.

By default, the ID will begin with a random prefix like U7DVSDAQ4X7X. If needed, you can adjust the prefix to a more suitable value. Here are the steps:

1. Go to the top-level website in the site collection.
2. Click Site Actions ➢ Site Settings.
3. In Site Collection Administration, select Document ID Settings.
4. For the field labeled "Begin IDs with the following characters," enter a suitable prefix. It must be 4 to 12 characters long and contain only letters and numbers.
5. Optionally, select the check box to reset all Document IDs in this site collection.
6. Click OK to save the settings.

> **NOTE** If a file is moved and a user navigates to the file's static URL, SharePoint issues a search query to find the new location of the file. If an incremental search has not been run since the file was moved, the file will not be found.

Configure the Content Organizer

The Content Organizer is a SharePoint Server feature that facilitates the routing of documents. The goal is to ensure that files are stored consistently in the correct locations, freeing users from having to remember exactly where files should be saved. The Content Organizer works by using a library named "Drop Off Library", which works like a queue. Users upload files into the Drop Off Library. Based on rules that you define, the files are routed and stored in various destination libraries. After a file is uploaded, users are provided with the link to the file in its newly saved location.

The Content Organizer is used on a website-by-website basis and must be enabled by activating a website-scoped feature. Here are the steps to activate it:

1. Navigate to the website where the Content Organizer will be used.
2. Click Site Actions ➤ Site Settings.
3. In the Site Actions category, select Manage Site Features.
4. Look for the feature named Content Organizer and click the Activate button.

When this feature is enabled, a new library named Drop Off Library is created. Two new menu items are also created on the Site Settings menu that you can use to configure the organizer:

Content Organizer Settings Defines how the organizer works overall

Content Organizer Rules Defines the rules that route documents to their correct destination library

Configuring Content Organizer Settings

Here are the steps to configure Content Organizer settings:

1. Click Site Actions ➤ Site Settings.

2. Under Site Administration, click Content Organizer Settings.

3. Check the Redirect Users To The Drop Off Library setting to prevent users from uploading files directly into a library that has an associated Content Organizer rule. When enabled, if a user tries to upload a file directly into a library, the file is redirected to the Drop Off Library and then automatically routed as defined by rules.

4. Check the setting Sending To Another Site to allow the Content Organizer to route files into libraries belonging to different websites in this or other site collections. By default, the organizer allows you to route only into libraries within the same website.

5. For Folder Partitioning, specify whether the Content Organizer should automatically create new folders once a folder has accumulated a certain number of files. This setting ensures that folders do not get too large, which can cause performance problems.

6. For Duplicate Submissions, decide how the Content Organizer should handle files with duplicate filenames. You can either add a new version to the file (this setting requires that versioning be enabled), or have random characters appended to the filename.

7. For Preserving Context, specify whether the original audit log entries should be kept after moving the file to its new location.

8. For Rule Managers, define which users have permissions to create and edit Content Organizer rules (covered in the next section). You can specify whether SharePoint sends an email to these users if no routing rule exists for an uploaded document.

9. Click OK to save the settings.

Creating Content Organizer Rules

Content Organizer rules define where documents are routed when they are uploaded to the Drop Off Library. Each rule determines how documents can be routed to one library. Here are the steps to create a Content Organizer rule:

1. Click Site Actions ➢ Site Settings.

2. Under Site Administration, click Content Organizer Rules.

3. Click Add New Item to create a new rule. A new dialog window appears.

4. For Rule Name, enter a friendly and unique name for this rule.

5. For Rule Status And Priority, define the priority level (from 1 to 9, with 1 being the highest) for this rule. Priority is applied when more than one rule can be applied to an incoming document. The rule with the highest priority is the one selected for routing.

6. For Content Type, define the incoming document's content type. This is the primary criterion that is used in document routing.

7. For Conditions, optionally enter one or more conditions that must be satisfied in addition to the content type for this rule to be applied. The properties that are available in the drop-down come from columns based on the content type selected.

8. For Target Location, select the library and folder to which this rule will route documents. This library must already have the content type that was selected in step 6. By default, you can only choose libraries from this current website.

   To select a library from a different website, there are three additional steps that are needed before being able to select it:

   a. You must activate the Content Organizer feature in the other website.

   b. You must configure Content Organizer rules for the other website.

   c. You must create a new Send To Connection from Central Administration (covered in Chapter 12).

   With this in place, the Content Organizer stores the file in the Drop Off Library of the other website, where the other organizer rules in that website move the file where it should go.

9. Click OK to save the rule.

Once rules are created, they are applied automatically when you upload and check in a file to the Drop Off Library. However, if multiple documents are uploaded at once, a timer job for the web application called Content Organizer Processing will move these items. By default, this job is scheduled to run once a day. If you need these items to move more quickly, you can change the job's schedule as described in Chapter 15, "Managing Auditing, Monitoring, and Analytics."

11
Configuring the Managed Metadata Service

IN THIS CHAPTER, YOU WILL LEARN TO:

▶ **CONFIGURE CONTENT TYPE SYNDICATION (Pages 334–342)**
- Creating the Content Type Syndication Hub (Page 335)
- Configuring the Content Type Hub (Page 338)

▶ **CONFIGURE TERM SETS (Pages 342–350)**
- Using the Term Store Tool (Page 343)
- Creating a Term Set Group (Page 345)
- Creating a Term Set (Page 347)
- Importing and Exporting a Term Set (Page 349)
- Creating and Configuring a Term (Page 349)

▶ **USE TERM SETS (Pages 350–356)**
- Creating a Managed Metadata Column (Page 351)
- Using a Managed Metadata Column (Page 353)
- Configuring Metadata Navigation (Page 354)

▶ **MANAGE ENTERPRISE KEYWORDS (Pages 356–359)**
- Enabling Keyword Tagging (Page 357)
- Viewing Keywords (Page 358)
- Modifying, Deleting, and Moving Keywords (Page 358)
- Blocking Keywords (Page 359)

One of the key features that sets SharePoint document management apart from storing documents on a file server is the ability to attach custom metadata. *Metadata* is the term used for the descriptive attributes or properties of files, separate from the content in the files. Metadata is sometimes embedded in the file format, as in the case with the Author and Keywords properties found on Microsoft Office documents. In some cases (such as PDF files), the file formats allow for custom properties to be created on files.

Prior to SharePoint 2010, however, no method existed to ensure that all the file formats stored by an organization supported the exact same set of properties. This made it difficult to rely on the metadata for document management and searching because you could never be sure that all the files you needed had been assigned the values you were looking for.

SharePoint 2010 introduces Content Type Syndication, which allows a single set of content types to be used throughout all site collections. In addition, the Term Sets feature lets you create centralized lists of values for use in metadata columns. In this chapter, we will look at both of these features and the service that supports them, known as the Managed Metadata Service. We will also explain the Enterprise Keywords feature, which supports free-form tagging of documents with metadata.

Configure Content Type Syndication

Content types are essential to virtually all information stored in SharePoint. SharePoint uses content types to define which columns of information will be tracked for a document, a contact, an appointment, and other items that can be created in SharePoint. Content types are also used to bind workflows, document templates, and expiration policies to items in a consistent manner that can support an organization's compliance requirements. In SharePoint 2010, it is possible to create a single set of content types in a single site collection and then publish those content types to other site collections throughout the SharePoint farm and even to other SharePoint farms. This process, referred to as *content type syndication*, is handled by the Managed Metadata Service, one of the services introduced in Chapter 4, "Creating Service Applications."

To syndicate content types, you designate a source site collection as the *syndication hub*, which publishes the content types, and other site collections become consumers of these content types. Content types in the consumer site collections are largely read-only and cannot be modified. Only content types in the hub site collection can be modified. This allows these centralized content types to serve as a metadata schema for the entire farm.

Creating the Content Type Syndication Hub

The best practices for creating and configuring the content type hub involve the following steps:

1. Create a dedicated web application.
2. Create a dedicated site collection.
3. Enable the required features.
4. Create the content types to be published.

Creating a Dedicated Web Application

Any site collection in SharePoint can be used as the syndication hub, but it is generally a good idea to create a web application and a separate site collection dedicated to use as the syndication hub. There are two reasons for creating a dedicated hub:

- Only site collection administrators can manage all features of the content type hub. By creating a dedicated site collection, which has no other content in it, you can delegate control of this site collection to a content manager or records librarian who is specifically responsible for managing the syndicated content types.

- The Managed Metadata Service does not support changing the choice of site collection for the hub through Central Administration once it has been set. Creating a dedicated web application with a specific URL allows this URL to be permanently reserved for use by the content type hub, freeing it from any dependency on other web applications or site collections.

The following are the specific steps for creating a content type hub web application. For full details, see Chapter 2, "Creating and Managing Web Applications."

1. From SharePoint 2010 Central Administration, under Application Management, click Manage Web Applications.
2. On the Web Applications Management page, from the ribbon, click the New Web Application link.

3. On the New Web Application page, fill in the details based on your organization's authentication and security requirements, keeping in mind a few recommendations:

   Authentication Settings Communication with the hub is handled by the Managed Metadata Service, which can usually take advantage of Windows authentication. So this option will almost always be set to Classic Mode Authentication.

   IIS Web Site Settings The web application can use a different port number than 80 to prevent users from accidentally trying to browse to the URL. The site collection will be secured so that users will generally not have access to it anyway, which means using an alternative port number is not necessary for security purposes. If you intend to share this Managed Metadata Service with other SharePoint farms in the organization, then it is a good idea to create a unique hostname such as `metadatahub.synergy.com` for the hub site collection.

   Application Pool Settings This web application will consume relatively few resources so it should not require its own application pool and can share one of the existing application pools used for SharePoint sites.

4. Click OK.

Creating a Dedicated Site Collection

Once the web application has been created, the next step is to create a site collection at the root of the web application. This site collection can be based on any site template, but since it is not intended to host any content itself, a simple site template such as the Team Site is commonly used. For full details on creating a site collection, see Chapter 3.

1. From SharePoint 2010 Central Administration, under Application Management, click Create Site Collections.

2. On the Create Site Collection page, enter a name and description. Leave the URL at the default setting of the root site, "/".

3. Select a site template. Choose Team Site if you do not intend to use this site collection for any other specific purpose. Otherwise, select a template that fits your needs. As a best practice, it is not a good idea to use the Blank Site template because it does not have the Taxonomy Feature enabled on it. We'll cover that topic later in this chapter in the "Use Term Sets" section.

4. Enter the username of the Primary Site Collection Administrator, who should be a person responsible for the management and maintenance of the content types. This person may be a records librarian or someone in IT who has assumed this responsibility. Enter the username of a Secondary Site Collection Administrator, who should normally be an IT administrator acting as a backup to the Primary Site Collection Administrator.

5. Click OK.

Enabling Required Features

In order for a site collection to function as the content type hub, some specific features must be enabled in the site collection. The most important of these is the Content Type Syndication Hub feature, which enables a site to become a hub site. This is a required feature.

To activate the Content Type Syndication Hub feature:

1. Open the hub site collection you created earlier.
2. From the Site Actions menu, select Site Settings.
3. In the Site Collection Administration section, click Site Collection Features.
4. Next to the Content Type Syndication Hub Feature, click Activate.

> **NOTE** Another feature that you may need to activate is the Document ID Service. If the sites that will be consuming content types from the hub have the Document ID Service enabled but the hub site does not, then content types will not propagate correctly. This is because the Document ID Service adds a new column to every content type in the site and manages the values in the column. To correct this issue, on the Site Collection Features page mentioned in the previous steps, click Activate next to the Document ID Service.

Planning and Creating Content Types

The final step in preparing the content type hub is to plan and create the content types that you will publish to the rest of the farm. It is important to carefully plan which content types will be created in the hub. They will act as the central templates for all metadata use in the organization and they should be designed to change very little, if at all.

Creating and configuring content types are covered in detail in Chapter 10, "Configuring Document Management," so we won't go through the steps here.

Configuring the Content Type Hub

Once the content type hub has been created, it can be configured in the Managed Metadata Service and the content types published. Each Managed Metadata Service created in SharePoint can support one content type hub. If you want to have multiple hubs in your organization, you can create more than one Managed Metadata Service to support them. You will then need to ensure that you associate each Managed Metadata Service with one or more of the web applications that hold user content. For more details on service applications, see Chapter 4.

1. Set the Content Hub Type property for the Managed Metadata Service application.
2. Configure the service proxy to syndicate published content types back to associated web applications.
3. Choose which content types will be shared with other site collections and publish them.

Configuring the Managed Metadata Service

The first configuration step is to set the Content Hub Type property. The Content Type Hub property is used by the Managed Metadata Service to configure the connection to the appropriate site collection from which you want to retrieve content types for publication. Configuring this setting alone does not automatically trigger the propagation of content types. Before that can happen, the content types themselves must be designated for publication. However, this setting is required for the SharePoint timer job to identify which site collection to reference for content types. To set the Content Type Hub property:

1. From SharePoint 2010 Central Administration, under Application Management, click Manage Service Applications.
2. On the Manage Service Applications page, click the row for the Managed Metadata Service application; then from the ribbon, click the Properties button, as shown in Figure 11.1.

Figure 11.1: Managed Metadata Service Properties button

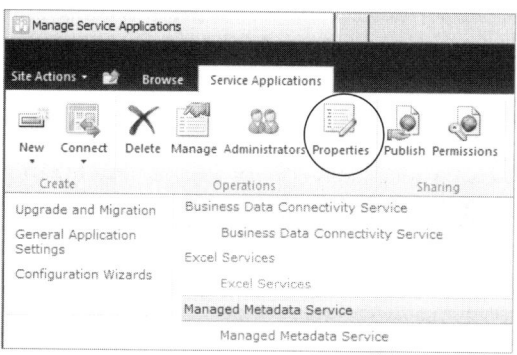

3. At the bottom of the dialog box, in the Content Type Hub box, enter the URL to the content type hub site collection that you created in the previous section, as shown in Figure 11.2. Then click OK.

Figure 11.2: Content Type Hub URL

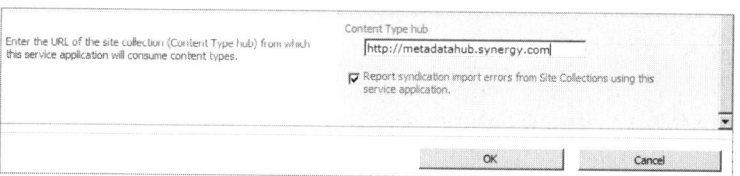

NOTE Be very careful when you enter this value. Once you click OK, the field becomes read-only in the properties page and can only be changed through an Stsadm or PowerShell command-line operation.

Each Managed Metadata Service is responsible not only for publishing content types but also for subscribing to published content types. The setting for syndicating the published content types back to all the web applications associated with the Managed Metadata Service is defined under the service proxy. If you don't configure this setting, then the content types will not appear in all your user site collections. To configure the proxy:

1. On the Manage Service Applications page, click the second row shown for the Managed Metadata Service application—the one for which the Type column reads Managed Metadata Service Connection. Then from the ribbon, click the Properties button.

2. On the Edit Managed Metadata Service Connection page, shown in Figure 11.3, check the box next to "Consumes content types from the Content Type Gallery at <URL>."

Figure 11.3: Content type consumer setting

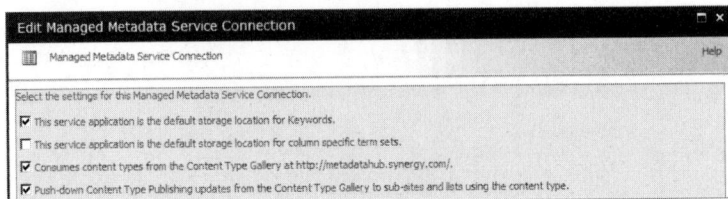

3. Also on this page, it is a good idea to check the box "Push-down Content Type Publishing updates from the Content Type Gallery to sub-sites and lists using the content type." Enabling this option allows changes to existing content types to be automatically copied down to any subsites in a site collection and to update the content types anywhere they are being used.

4. Click OK.

Publishing, Republishing, and Unpublishing Content Types

The final step in publishing content types from the hub is to choose which content types will be shared with other site collections and to publish them. Content types can also be unpublished if necessary to remove them from syndication.

To publish, unpublish, or republish content types:

1. Open the hub site collection.
2. From the Site Actions menu, select Site Settings.
3. Under the Galleries section, click Site Content Types.
4. On the Site Content Types page, click the content type you want to publish.
5. On the Content Type Page, click Manage Publishing For This Content Type.
6. On the Content Type Publishing page, click one of the following:

   Publish If this is the first time that the content type is being published, then Publish is the only option available. This option will propagate this content type to all site collections in all web applications that are associated with the Managed Metadata Service.

Unpublish Once a content type has been published, this option becomes available and will stop the publishing of a content type. Any content types in the subscribing site collections will be converted into local content types disconnected from the hub. If this content type is published again in the future, it will overwrite the local version of the content type.

Republish Any time that changes are made to the content type, use this option to propagate those changes out to the subscribing site collections.

7. Click OK.

Managing Publishing in Subscriber Sites

The subscriber sites that are consuming content types published by the hub can monitor and troubleshoot the publishing process. Monitoring is useful for site collection administrators who are responsible for site collections that are consuming content types but who have no permissions to manage the hub itself.

To configure these settings:

1. Open the subscriber site collection.
2. From the Site Actions menu, select Site Settings.
3. Under the Site Collection Administration section, click Content Type Publishing. The Content Type Publishing Hubs page appears (see Figure 11.4).

Figure 11.4: Content Type Publishing Hubs settings

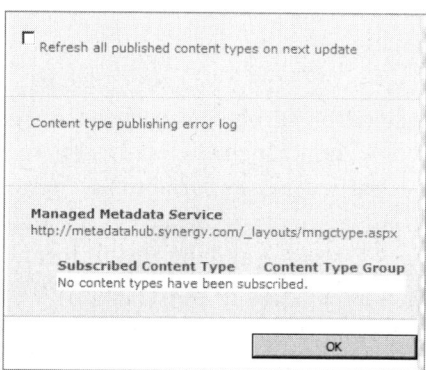

4. Perform the following monitoring tasks as needed:
   - Force the content types from the hub to overwrite those in the current site collection by checking the box next to "Refresh all published content types on next update."

     In most cases, when a content type is published, the subscribing site collections receive the updates and display any changes. But sometimes the content types in the subscribing site collection become unsynchronized with the content type hub and show a different structure.

   - View the Content Type Publishing Error Log by clicking its link.

     This log is a list in the site collection that tracks errors generated during the publishing of content types to this site.

   - View the URL to the hub site collection configured in the Managed Metadata Service that this site is subscribed to. This section also lists any content types that have been published to this site collection.

You can also view error logs from within the hub site collection:

1. Open the hub site collection.
2. From the Site Actions menu, select Site Settings.
3. In the Site Collection Administration section, click Content Type Service Application Error Log.

The service log indicates the item that failed to publish, the date and time of the failure, and the message explaining the cause.

Configure Term Sets

One of the core functions of any effective content management system is to provide a centralized list of values that can be used as the source for metadata properties. This is particularly important in scenarios where the system is used for compliance purposes such as meeting the requirements of the Sarbanes-Oxley act and the Health Insurance Portability and Accountability Act (HIPAA). In SharePoint 2010, the Managed Metadata Service introduces the term set, which is a managed list of values stored in a central location in the farm, and which can be used to create columns that use the same sets of values.

The term set supports a hierarchical model of related terms—terms can have child terms and grandchild terms, creating a layered taxonomy suitable for structured classification. An example of a term set is shown in Figure 11.5. Terms can be added to and removed from the list, and these changes will be propagated out to all columns that consume the term set. Terms can also be locked so that they appear in the list but cannot be selected by users as values in the column. This approach is appropriate when a term represents a general class of values and not a value itself.

Figure 11.5: Hierarchical term set

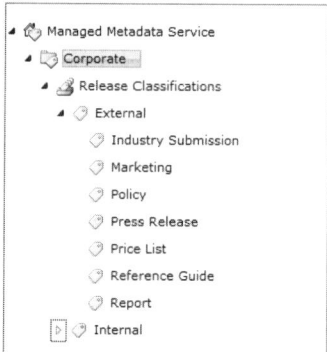

Term sets are designed to be managed by nontechnical users. While they are hosted in a shared service administered through Central Administration, control of the entire Managed Metadata Service or groups of term sets can be assigned to any site administrator. With this capability for delegation, an organization can delegate to business users the responsibility for managing term set values and maintaining them on a daily basis. This flexible model can be responsive to the way in which business needs change over time, dictating new uses for metadata.

Using the Term Store Tool

To create a term set, you can access the Managed Metadata Service either from Central Administration or from the Site Settings page of any site.

Chapter 11 ▶ Configuring the Managed Metadata Service

To access the term store tool from Central Administration:

1. From SharePoint 2010 Central Administration, under Application Management, click Manage Service Applications.
2. On the Manage Service Applications page, click the row for the Managed Metadata Service application, then from the ribbon, click the Manage button.
3. The Term Store Management Tool page opens, shown in Figure 11.6.

Figure 11.6: Term Store Management Tool page

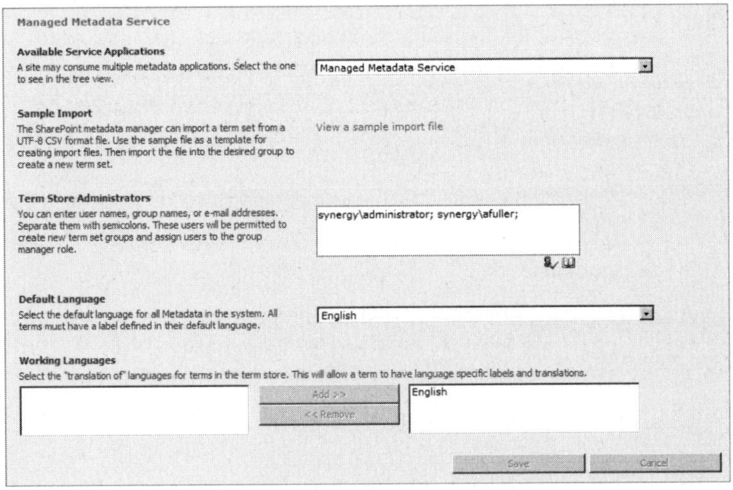

To access the term store tool from Site Settings:

1. In any site, from the Site Actions menu, select Site Settings.
2. Under Site Administration, click Term Store Management
3. The Term Store Management Tool page opens.

The Term Store Management Tool page allows for the centralized administration of all term sets. You can perform the following tasks:

- Select from the Available Service Applications drop-down to choose which Managed Metadata Service to administer.

While most organizations will only need one Managed Metadata Service, it is possible to host multiple services and to segregate the term sets into different services in order that different divisions or departments in the organization have access to different groups of terms.

- Create new term set groups and modify the list of term store administrators. In the Term Store Administrators box, enter the Active Directory user or group accounts for those who will be managing this term store.
- Manage the languages used by term sets.

  SharePoint 2010 supports multiple languages in term sets. A term represents the meaning of the information being stored and can be associated with multiple labels in different languages (e.g., "house," "casa," "maison"). If you have configured multiple languages on the server, you can use the Default Language setting to define which language is considered mandatory. Every term created must have an entry in the default language. If no label is available in an alternate language, the default label is used. If multiple language packs have been installed on the server, the languages appear on the left of the Working Languages section. To make a language available for labeling on a term, select the language and click Add to add it to the list on the right.

Creating a Term Set Group

Within the Managed Metadata Service, all term sets are organized into term set groups. Some organizations may only need one group for their term sets; others will find it convenient to organize term sets into separate groups. A term set group acts as a security boundary and allows for the administration of all term sets within the group to be delegated to one or more users. A term set group can hold multiple term sets. To create a term set group, do the following:

1. From the Term Store Management Tool page, click the drop-down context menu on Managed Metadata Service on the left, shown in Figure 11.7, and select New Group. Type a name for the group in the text box.

Figure 11.7: Creating a new term set group

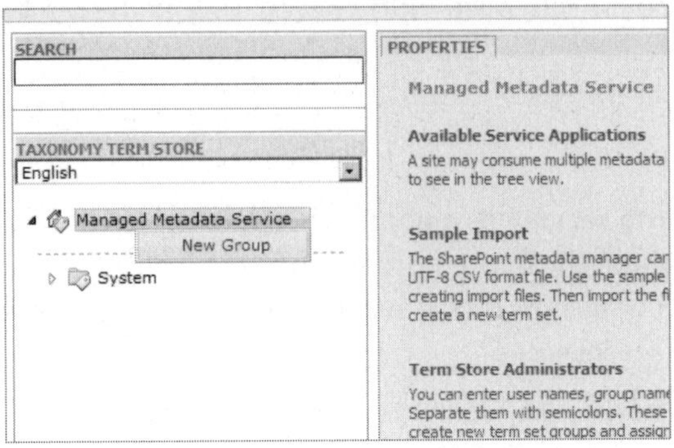

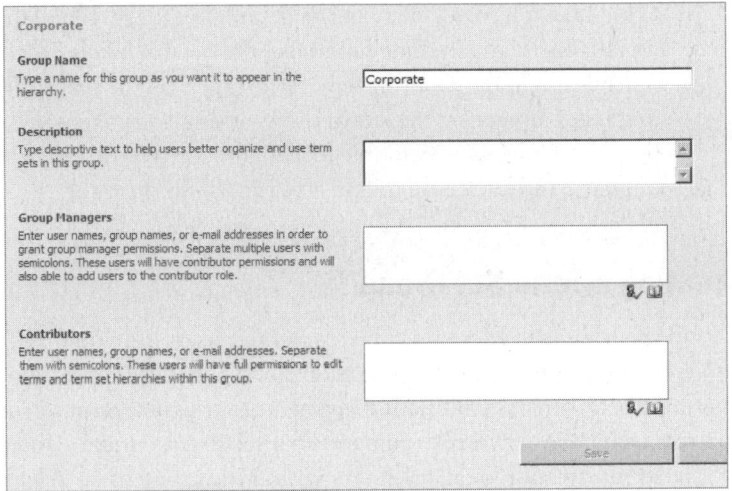

2. In the Properties area, shown in Figure 11.8, you can enter an optional description to document the purpose of the group.

Figure 11.8: Term set group properties

3. In the Group Managers field, enter the Active Directory users or groups who will administer this term set group.

   Group managers can add, edit, and delete term sets and also change the Term Store Contributors list. Delegating control of the group to others is particularly useful when the term store is used for mission-critical purposes that require a highly trained set of users who are responsible for all the terms in the group.

4. Enter the Active Directory users or groups who will be designated as Term Store Contributors.

Contributors have the right to add, edit, and delete term sets. Granting this right is beneficial when terms have highly specific meanings and uses that would not necessarily be familiar to a SharePoint administrator. Delegating control to one or more users who are familiar with the terms minimizes the chance of error and misrepresenting the values.

Creating a Term Set

Each term set can have multiple child terms in a hierarchical structure. Term sets can be created either manually or by importing a term set stored in a .csv file. The manual approach may be preferred in smaller-scale environments with simple needs. The import method is recommended for environments with larger term set needs.

To create a term set manually:

1. In the Term Store Management Tool page, locate the term store group in which you want to create the term set and click the context menu on the group; then select New Term Set from the menu, as shown in Figure 11.9, and enter a name for the term set.

Figure 11.9: Creating a new term set

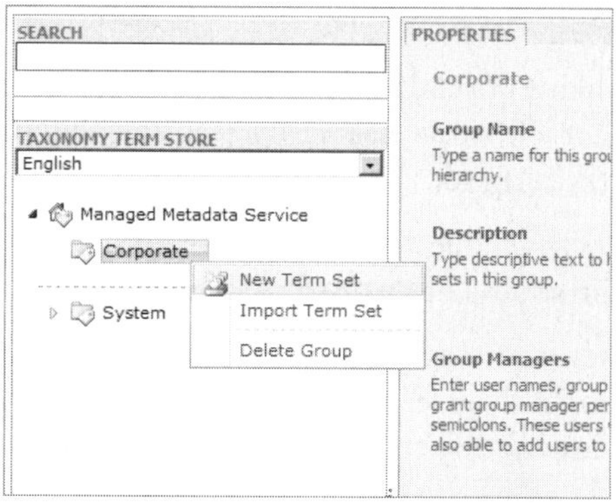

2. In the Properties area for the term set, shown in Figure 11.10, specify the following:

Figure 11.10: Term set properties

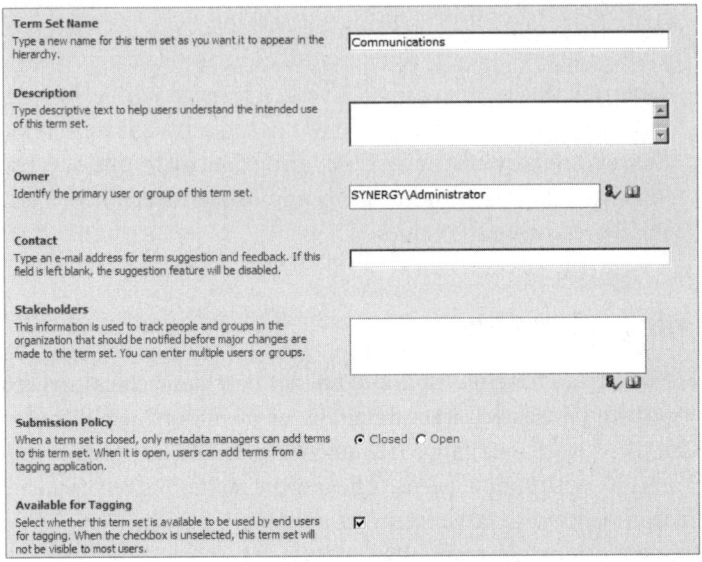

- The Description field should be populated with information about the purpose of the term set and where it is expected to be used.
- The Owner field is mandatory and it specifies the person or group who controls the information related to the term set. The Owner is not granted any permissions on the term set. The field is used to document the person who is the subject matter authority on the terms.
- The Contact field is optional and can be populated with an email address that will allow users to provide feedback or suggestions on the term set.
- The Stakeholders field contains users and groups in the organization who should be notified of changes to the term set.
- Submission Policy is an important setting. By default, term sets are closed and only group managers, contributors, and administrators can modify the terms. If you want all users to be able to add to the term set or change terms within it, click Open. (Later in this chapter in the "Manage Enterprise Keywords" section, we will discuss keywords, which are a specific type of term set that is open.)
- Uncheck Available For Tagging to prevent this term set from being accessed by users.

Importing and Exporting a Term Set

Importing a term set allows for much easier population and administration of term sets during the initial design and testing phases of a project. Microsoft provides a sample of the CSV file format for building a term set that can be imported into SharePoint. To view the sample file, from the Term Store Management Tool page, click the link View A Sample Import File. Doing so allows you to open or save the `ImportTermSet.csv` file. This file contains a sample term set that demonstrates how to populate the columns with hierarchical terms. Once you have completed a new term set file, you can import it by clicking the context menu of any term set group and selecting Import Term Set from the menu.

One function that is missing from SharePoint 2010 is the ability to export content from the term store. However, developers can write code to export terms, and there are several free utilities for exporting term sets posted on the CodePlex site (www.codeplex.com).

Creating and Configuring a Term

Individual terms represent the values that will be selected by users when referencing the term set in metadata.

To create a term manually:

1. Right-click the term set and select Create Term from the context menu; then type the name of the term.

2. On the term's properties page, shown in Figure 11.11, specify the following settings:

    Figure 11.11: Term's properties

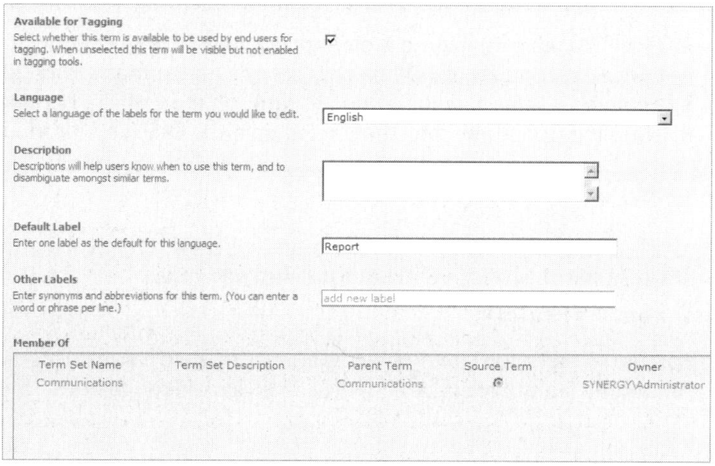

- Uncheck the Available For Tagging option to prevent users from selecting an option that exists only in the term set for hierarchical classification purposes. For example, in the sample Release Classifications term set (Figure 11.5 earlier in this chapter), the term External exists only to separate the internal release terms from the external release terms.
- Enter text in the Description field that will help users distinguish between similar terms.
- The remaining settings on the term's properties page appear if the server is configured with additional language service packs. You can select a language from the Language drop-down, add or change the default label, and enter other labels associated with the term in that language.

Use Term Sets

Term sets are used primarily to populate the values in Managed Metadata columns in lists, libraries, and content types. The Managed Metadata column is new to SharePoint 2010 and is part of the feature set provided by the Managed Metadata Service. A Managed Metadata column provides users with choices derived from a single term set and supports multiselect values and user-defined values. The Managed Metadata column provides an alternative to the Choice column and the Lookup column by allowing users to pick values from a set of options. But, in this case, the values are selected from a term set that is managed independently from any of the columns.

NOTE Because Managed Metadata is a new type of column, it will not be recognized by Office applications earlier than Office 2010. The column values can still be edited through the website but not through the Document Information Panel in the Office application.

Troubleshoot Managed Metadata: Activate the Taxonomy Feature

For you to make full use of the Managed Metadata column, the Taxonomy feature must be activated. This is a hidden feature—there is no option to activate it manually through the Site Settings page. It is automatically activated through most site templates, with the exception of the Blank Site template.

If you encounter an error when trying to add a Managed Metadata column to a site collection, the fix may be to activate this feature through the command line. To activate the feature, do the following:

1. From the Start menu on the SharePoint server, select All Programs ➢ Microsoft SharePoint 2010 Products ➢ SharePoint 2010 Management Shell.
2. Enter the following command at the command prompt, replacing *sitecollectionurl* with the URL of the site collection where you want the feature activated:
   Enable-SPFeature -Identity
   73EF14B1-13A9-416b-A9B5-ECECA2B0604C -Url
   http://*sitecollectionurl*

Creating a Managed Metadata Column

To create a Managed Metadata column, follow these steps:

1. In any site, from the Site Actions menu, select Site Settings.
2. Under Galleries, click Site Columns.
3. On the Site Columns page, click Create.
4. On the Create Column page, enter a name for the column, and then select Managed Metadata as the type.
5. Select a group to save the column under and configure additional column settings as required. These settings operate the same as they do under the Choice column type.
6. In the Multiple Value Field section, check Allow Multiple Values if you want to allow users to enter more than one value in the property when they edit.
7. The Display Format area determines how hierarchical values are displayed. The default option, Display Term Label In The Field, displays only the value selected in the text field. If you want to allow

users to see the hierarchical path of parent terms to the selected value, select Display The Entire Path To The Term In The Field.

8. Determine how to populate values for this column as follows:

- To have values populated from an existing term set, select Use A Managed Term Set, as shown in Figure 11.12. Then select the term set to use as the source of values. To find a term set, you can enter a term in the search box and click the find icon. Note that the find function searches only terms, not the names of the term set group or term sets themselves.

Figure 11.12: Setting up a managed term set

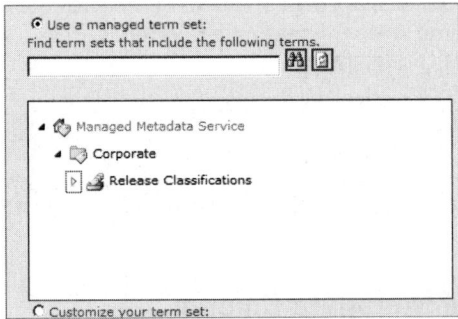

- To populate values manually, select Customize Your Term Set, as shown in Figure 11.13, and then enter a description and add terms.

Figure 11.13: Click the Customize Your Term Set radio button.

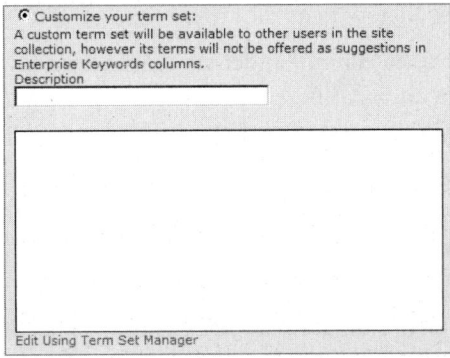

9. If the term set was configured as an open term set and you want to allow users to enter values that are not in the term set, then under the Allow Fill-In Choices setting, you can select the Yes option.
10. In the Default Value setting, provide a default value for the column. If you don't, the column will be blank.
11. Click OK.

Using a Managed Metadata Column

The Managed Metadata column is designed to work with large value sets and can be used in lists, libraries, and content types throughout SharePoint 2010. To use a Managed Metadata column in a content type, do the following:

1. Open the root site in a site collection.
2. From the Site Actions menu, select Site Settings.
3. Under the Galleries section, click Site Content Types.
4. On the Site Content Types page, click the content type you want to modify.
5. Under Columns, click Add From Existing Site Columns.
6. Locate the Managed Metadata column in the list and click Add. You will see a message warning you that this column cannot be used in older applications. Click OK to dismiss the message.
7. Click OK to add the column.

> **NOTE** If this content type is in a syndicated hub, then you will need to republish the content type to propagate the new column to all subscribing site collections.

Once the column has been added and the content type associated with a list or library, then users can edit the properties of the document or item and fill in the value of the Managed Metadata column. To do so:

1. From the item's context menu, choose the Edit Properties command.
2. On the Edit Properties page, type the value that you want to select from the term set or click the browse button on the right side of the Managed Metadata column text box and select the value from the term set, as shown in Figure 11.14.

Figure 11.14: Adding metadata to a document

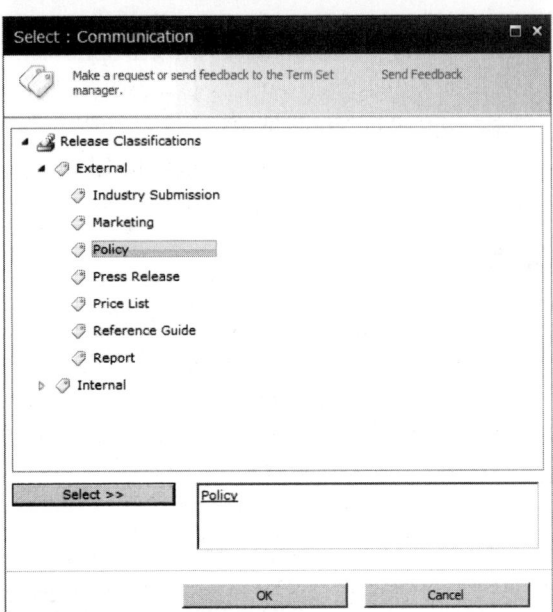

Configuring Metadata Navigation

The Managed Metadata column and its structured set of terms allow you to use the Metadata Navigation feature to easily locate documents and items. Metadata Navigation provides a list of values that users can click on to quickly filter the contents of a list or library. Metadata Navigation supports both a list of fixed values drawn from a term set and a key filter option, which allows users to easily filter on nonmanaged columns.

To configure Metadata Navigation, you first must ensure that the appropriate site feature has been enabled. The Metadata Navigation and Filtering feature is enabled automatically in most cases. To check this feature, browse to the Site Settings page in a site and click Manage Site Features. If the Metadata Navigation and Filtering feature is not enabled, click Activate to enable it.

By default, the Metadata Navigation and Filtering feature also generates indices automatically for all columns that it manages. These indices are separate from the indexing conducted by the search crawler and are created to allow SharePoint to quickly generate filtered views. SharePoint analyzes the query that will be required to retrieve content filtered on each column and determines whether an artificial index would improve the query time and then creates the index for the appropriate column. Indexes can also be created manually, but we recommend that you let SharePoint create them in most cases.

To configure Metadata Navigation on a list or library, follow these steps:

1. Browse to the list or library and, on the ribbon, click the List or Library tab, and then click the List Settings or Library Settings button.

2. Under General Settings, click Metadata Navigation Settings.

3. In the Configure Navigation Hierarchies section, shown in Figure 11.15, select the columns that will be enabled for one-click navigation. (To do so, select the column on the left and click Add to move it to the list of navigation columns.) Note that only columns based on fixed lists of values are available in this section.

Figure 11.15: Configuring Metadata Navigation settings

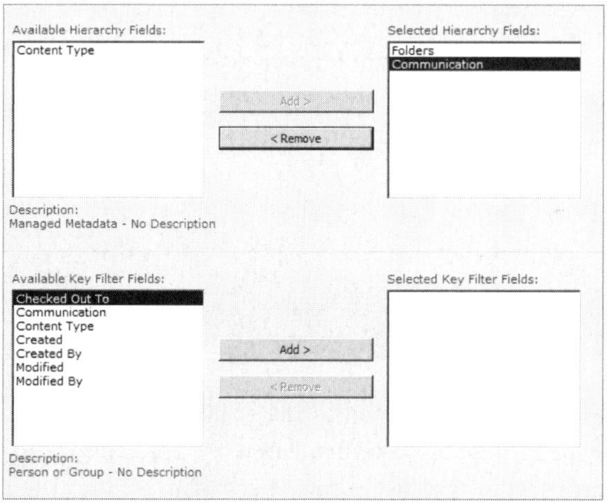

4. In the Configure Key Filters section, add to the Selected Key Filter Fields those columns that you want users to be able to navigate with but that aren't supported under the Navigation Hierarchies section. (To do so, select an item in Available Key Filter Fields and click Add.)

5. In the Configure Automatic Column Indexing For This List section, you can disable the automatic index creation if you

have alternative optimization planned. However, we generally recommend that you allow SharePoint to build the indices.

6. Click OK.

With Metadata Navigation configured, the user will see a new set of controls on the left side of the list or library page, as shown in Figure 11.16. Clicking on a metadata value will filter the list, as will entering a key value in the Key Filters section and clicking Apply.

Figure 11.16: Metadata Navigation controls

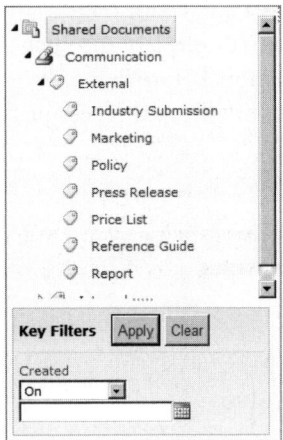

Manage Enterprise Keywords

Enterprise keywords are user-defined terms and phrases that can be entered as metadata values for columns. Keywords are similar to the term values in term sets in that users can select from an existing set of values. The difference is that users can enter their own keywords, which are automatically added to the list of terms available to other users. Keywords are stored in the Managed Metadata Service term store under a term set group called System and a term set called Keywords. Because of their free-form flexibility, keywords can be used to build a folksonomy out of terms entered by users. This is often described as *tagging* content because it is used by people to quickly find things that they are interested in later rather than as part of a structured data management plan. This may be sufficient to develop a metadata set that serves to classify content by itself. Alternatively, term store administrators can move terms from the Keywords term set into a closed and managed term set, which converts the terms from an informal folksonomy to a formal taxonomy.

Enabling Keyword Tagging

Keywords provide two levels of benefit for users. When keywords are enabled by themselves, users can easily assign metadata values without having to wait for them to be prepopulated into a term set. In addition, keywords can be synchronized with a user profile so that when users navigate to the Tags And Notes tab in their profile, they'll see a list of all the keywords they've used and they can filter a list of all the content they've tagged.

To enable users to tag content with keywords:

1. Browse to the list or library and, on the ribbon, click the List or Library tab, then click the List Settings or Library Settings button.

2. Under Permissions And Management, click Enterprise Metadata and Keywords Settings.

3. To allow users to enter values in the Keywords field, under Enterprise Keywords, as shown in Figure 11.17, check the box "Add an Enterprise Keywords column to this list and enable Keyword synchronization."

Figure 11.17: Enterprise Metadata and Keyword Settings

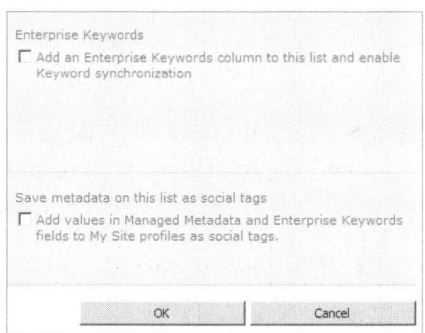

4. To allow users to see the keywords they've entered as a tag cloud in their user profile, under Save Metadata On This List As Social

Tags, check the box "Add values in Managed Metadata and Enterprise Keywords fields to My Site profiles as social tags."

5. Click OK.

Site administrators can show a tag cloud of keywords that have been entered in that site by adding the Tag Cloud web part to a page. The web part will display all the keywords that users have entered in that site, and when a keyword is clicked, it will take users to a page displaying all the content tagged with that keyword.

Viewing Keywords

Keywords are stored in the Managed Metadata Service as a term set. To view the keywords that users have entered, do the following:

1. From SharePoint 2010 Central Administration, under Application Management, click Manage Service Applications.

2. On the Manage Service Applications page, click the row for the Managed Metadata Service application; then from the ribbon, click the Manage button.

3. The Term Store Management Tool page opens.

4. Under the Taxonomy Term Store, expand the System term set group and then expand the Keywords term set. This set will contain the list of all the keywords that users have entered.

Modifying, Deleting, and Moving Keywords

From the Term Store Management Tool page, a keyword can be edited, moved, or deleted. Editing a keyword has the following effects:

- The new value will become available for other users to see.
- The value that is stored in the Keywords field will not change. Existing keywords that have already been saved with that value will not be altered.

To completely change a keyword value, it is necessary to delete it. To delete a keyword, click the context menu on the keyword and select Delete Keyword from the menu. Deleting a keyword has the following effects:

- The keyword is no longer available for any user to select.
- Users may still enter the value as a new keyword.

- Columns that still hold the old value of the keyword will not be affected.
- The keyword no longer will appear in the tag cloud on the site or in the user profiles.

Keywords can be moved to other term sets. To move a keyword, click the context menu on the keyword and select Move Keyword from the menu; then select the destination term set to move it to.

Blocking Keywords

Blocking a keyword stops it from being used and also prevents it from being reentered as a new keyword. To block a keyword, click on the keyword in the Term Store Management Tool and then uncheck the Available For Tagging option on the term's properties page.

Making a term no longer available for tagging blocks it from view in the Tag Cloud web part and in user profiles, and prevents users from entering it or selecting it in the Enterprise Keywords field.

12

Configuring Records Management

IN THIS CHAPTER, YOU WILL LEARN TO:

▶ **UNDERSTAND RECORDS MANAGEMENT IN SHAREPOINT** (Pages 362–363)

▶ **CONFIGURE IN-PLACE RECORDS MANAGEMENT** (Pages 363–372)
- Activating the In-Place Records Management Feature (Page 364)
- Configuring Record Declaration Settings (Page 364)
- Configuring Lists and Libraries for Records Management (Page 365)
- Declaring and Undeclaring Records Manually (Page 367)
- Declaring Records Through Workflow (Page 369)
- Declaring Records Through a Retention Policy (Page 371)

▶ **CONFIGURE A RECORDS CENTER** (Pages 372–381)
- Creating a Records Center Site (Page 373)
- Creating Libraries in a Records Center (Page 374)
- Configuring Organizer Rules for Submitted Records (Page 375)
- Creating Custom Send To Connections (Page 377)
- Submitting Records (Page 379)

▶ **CONFIGURE INFORMATION MANAGEMENT POLICIES** (Pages 381–388)
- Creating an Information Management Policy (Page 382)
- Creating a Site Collection Policy (Page 387)

▶ **CONFIGURE EDISCOVERY AND HOLDS** (Pages 388–390)
- Creating a Hold Definition (Page 389)
- Searching for Items to Hold (Page 389)
- Holding and Releasing Individual Items (Page 390)

In this chapter, we look at how SharePoint 2010 can provide the sophisticated records management services required for electronic document and records management systems (EDRMSs). As a combined suite of software services, SharePoint 2010 is not designed specifically as an EDRMS, but it does provide most of the functionality that an organization would typically require. SharePoint 2010 provides a much more scalable storage system than previous versions of the product, and is able to store and manage up to one million items in a folder, tens of millions of items in a single library, and potentially hundreds of millions of items in a large archive.

Understand Records Management in SharePoint

Records management involves tracking and organizing the critical files and information generated by an organization throughout the life of the items, from the time they are created to the time they are purged. Not all files are considered records. A record is a piece of information that is required to be held as evidence for a legal, regulatory, or essential business need. Some examples of records are as follows:

- Signed contracts are legal documents that are usually treated as records.
- Documents reviewed, approved, and signed by a specific person may be essential to keep.
- A calendar appointment or a task might be needed to prove that an organization was meeting a regulatory demand.

While much of records management focuses on retaining information to ensure it is not deleted inadvertently (or on purpose to dispose of evidence), an equally important function of records management is to ensure that records are reviewed and deleted when they are no longer needed. In some scenarios, companies are legally required to dispose of information that they no longer have a right to hold after a period of time, and they can be penalized for keeping the information. In other cases the penalty for keeping records too long may be more subtle: Information held longer than legally required might be used against a company in legal proceedings.

Where does SharePoint come in? In a *Wise Technology Management* study published in 2010, researchers analyzed SharePoint 2010 against the Australian records management standards as embodied in the International Council on Archives' *Principles and Functional Requirements for Records in Electronic Office Environments – Module 2*. They found that SharePoint 2010 could meet 88 percent of the functional requirements of records management through built-in functionality and careful configuration. The remaining 12 percent of functional requirements could be met through custom software or third-party software. While this whitepaper was only intended to measure SharePoint 2010 against a single set of standards, the findings give a general idea of the level of compliance most organizations can expect to achieve with SharePoint 2010.

Configure In-Place Records Management

To achieve the goal of preserving information as a record (which includes preventing unauthorized changes to the information), SharePoint 2010 offers two primary mechanisms:

In-Place Records Management In this approach, information is kept in the location it was last edited but is locked to prevent further editing. In-place records management is designed for scenarios in which a document or list item is finalized and ready for preservation, and the document must remain in its original context. For example, when a project is completed and the final report is sent to the customer and approved by them, the project is brought to an official close. There may be a number of documents associated with the project (e.g., working files, diagrams, or unused material), but only a few, such as the final report, are critical from a legal point of view. The project manager might decide to keep the entire site, including the final report, in place for future reference. SharePoint 2010 does not support declaring an entire site or library as a record; only documents and list items can be declared. But if the final report is declared a record, this will prevent both the document and the library it is in from being deleted.

Records Center The Records Center site template allows you to create a separate site collection that acts as a records repository. This approach is discussed later in the chapter in the section "Configure a Records Center."

Activating the In-Place Records Management Feature

In-place records management is configured through a site collection feature and is not enabled by default. Once it is enabled, records will be supported in all lists and libraries in the site collection. To enable in-place records management:

1. Open the site collection you want to configure.
2. From the Site Actions menu, select Site Settings.
3. Under the Site Collection Administration section, click Site Collection Features.
4. Next to In Place Records Management Feature, click Activate.

Configuring Record Declaration Settings

Once in-place records management has been enabled, a new command becomes available on the Site Settings page that allows you to configure the record declaration settings. To configure these settings, follow these steps:

1. Open the site collection you want to configure; then, from the Site Actions menu, select Site Settings. Under the Site Collection Administration section, click Record Declaration Settings. The Record Declaration Settings page opens, as shown in Figure 12.1.

Figure 12.1: Recording Declaration Settings page

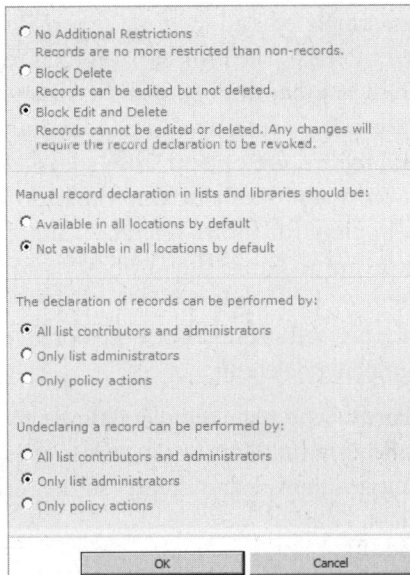

2. Define what type of controls will be applied to items declared as records:

   - Block Edit And Delete is the default setting and makes the record read-only.

   - No Restrictions does not control access to the record but marks it for future action via workflow or policy.

   - Block Delete allows users to edit the item but blocks them from moving or deleting it. This is similar to removing the delete permission, but it is much easier to administer.

3. Define whether users will be able to manually declare records by default:

   - Not Available In All Locations By Default prevents users from manually declaring records. This is the default setting.

   - Available In All Locations By Default allows users to declare records manually. This setting is rarely used because the best records management strategies usually rely on workflows, policies, or custom code to avoid problems with user error. However, in situations where only a few documents need to become records and the people editing them are the best authorities to make the decision, then this setting may be appropriate.

4. Determine who is allowed to declare records and undeclare records.

   By default, all list contributors and administrators can declare records. You can limit this to only list administrators or only policy actions.

   By default, only list administrators can "undeclare" a record. You can change this setting to All List Contributors And Administrators or Only Policy Actions.

NOTE The term *list administrator* is not a formal security role in SharePoint but refers to any user who is assigned the Manage Lists granular permission. All users with the Full Control permission level are granted this right by default.

Configuring Lists and Libraries for Records Management

By default, lists and libraries are configured to inherit the records declaration settings defined at the site collection level, but these settings can be overridden through list settings.

To configure records declaration settings on a list or library, follow these steps:

1. Browse to the list or library and, on the ribbon, click the List or Library tab; then click the List Settings or Library Settings button.

2. Under Permissions And Management, click Record Declaration Settings. The list or library Record Declaration Settings page displays, as shown in Figure 12.2.

Figure 12.2: Recording declaration settings for a list or library

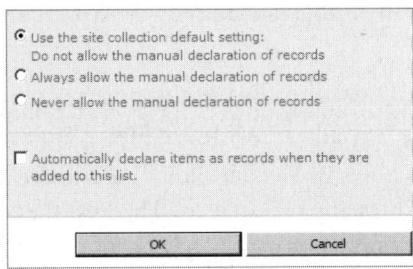

3. Specify whether to allow records to be declared manually.

   The default option is Use The Site Collection Default Setting. You can override that setting, but do so with caution because these settings also affect the ability to undeclare items as records. Choosing Never Allow The Manual Declaration Of Records will also prevent administrators from undeclaring items as records.

4. Decide whether to automatically declare items as records when they are added to this list by checking or unchecking the appropriate check box. Use this setting when it is necessary to ensure that all items are considered to be read-only once they are created or uploaded.

Declaring an item as a record will also prevent the list or library from being deleted (but not the site or site collection). You will notice that the link to delete the list or library disappears from the settings page. In order for you to be able to delete a list or library, all the items in it must first be undeclared as records. However, even when this is done, the link to delete the list or library may not appear right away. This is because SharePoint uses a scheduled timer job to periodically survey all lists and libraries to look for declared records or holds that should prevent the list or library from being deleted. To force SharePoint to review the list or library immediately, open SharePoint 2010 Central Administration and click Monitoring. Then click Review Job Definitions, select Hold Processing And Reporting for the web application that the list or library is in, and click Run Now.

Declaring and Undeclaring Records Manually

Declaring records manually is the simplest approach. It allows users to declare records based on an individual judgment and to force a record when an item did not meet the criteria for a policy or workflow. To declare a record manually:

1. Open the list or library and locate the document or item that should be declared. Then use one of these two techniques:

    - Click the check box next to the item to select it, and then from the Documents tab on the ribbon, click the Declare Record button, as shown in Figure 12.3. Click OK in the confirmation dialog box.

    Figure 12.3: Declaring a record

    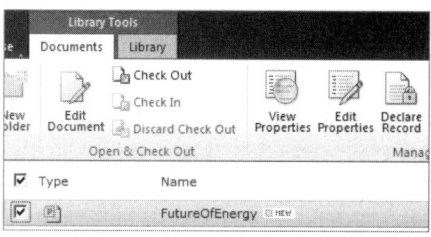

    - Click the drop-down context menu on the item and click Compliance Details. In the Compliance Details dialog box, shown in Figure 12.4, click the Declare as a record link. Click OK in the confirmation dialog box.

Figure 12.4: Specifying compliance details

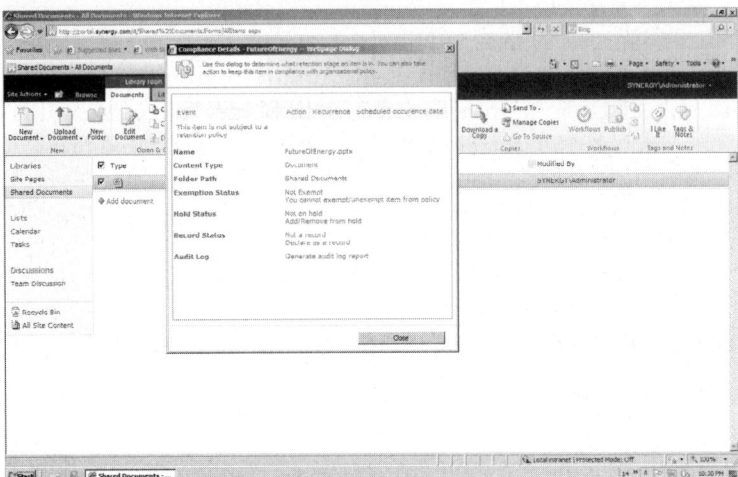

2. Once the record has been declared, refresh the view of the list and you will see that in libraries the file icon will now display a gold lock in the image, as shown in Figure 12.5.

Figure 12.5: Icon indicating record file

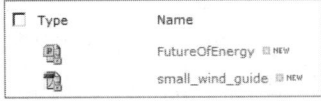

Undeclaring records manually can be done only if manual declaration has been enabled on the list or library. (By default, only list administrators have the right to undeclare records.) To undeclare a record:

1. Open the list or library and locate the document or item that should be undeclared.

2. Click the drop-down context menu on the item and click the Compliance Details link. In the Compliance Details dialog box, click the Undeclare Record link. Click OK in the confirmation dialog box.

Declaring Records Through Workflow

SharePoint 2010 includes native support for workflows that can declare records. However, SharePoint does not include a workflow template with the capability to declare a record built into it. So any approach to using workflows to declare records will require that a custom workflow be built. Fortunately, Microsoft provides a product called SharePoint Designer 2010, which is free to download from the Microsoft website. This product is, among other things, a workflow development tool that can be used to build custom workflows which can declare records. There are other tools available from software vendors that also include the ability to declare records, but we will only be using SharePoint Designer in our example.

The advantage of using a workflow to manage record declaration is that organizations can configure multiple conditions and steps involved in the process that result in an item being declared a record. For simplicity's sake, the steps that follow assume that a library has the Versioning and Require Approval options configured. You will create a list workflow to declare a record when a document has been approved:

1. Open the site you want to configure.
2. From the Site Actions menu, select Edit In SharePoint Designer.
3. Inside SharePoint Designer, from the Site tab, click the List Workflow menu and select the list or library on which you wish to configure the workflow, as shown in Figure 12.6.

Figure 12.6: List Workflow menu

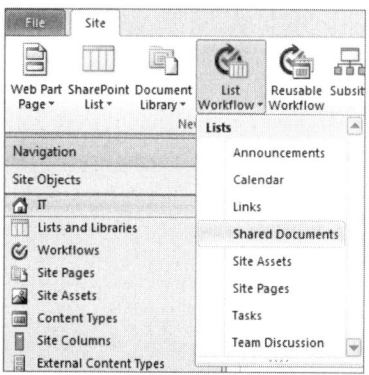

4. In the Create List Workflow dialog box, enter a name and a description for the workflow, and then click OK.

5. From the Workflow tab, click the Condition menu and select the item labeled "If current item field equals value," as shown in Figure 12.7.

Figure 12.7: Condition menu

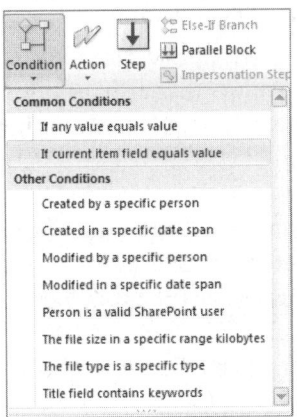

6. On the condition row, click the Field link and select Approval Status from the drop-down list, then click the Value link and select 0;#Approved from the drop-down list. The result is shown in Figure 12.8.

Figure 12.8: Condition Editor

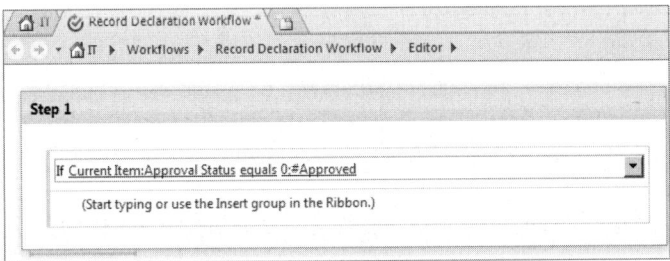

7. From the Workflow tab, click the Action menu and, under the List Actions category, select Declare Record, as shown in Figure 12.9.

Figure 12.9: Action Editor

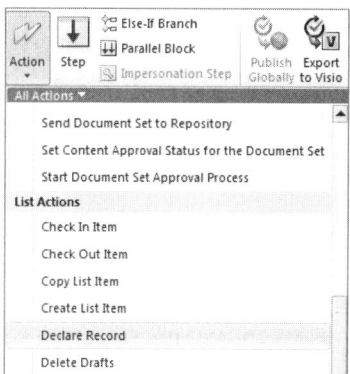

8. From the Workflow tab, click the Workflow Settings button
9. On the Workflow Settings page, check the box labeled "Start workflow automatically when an item is changed," as shown in Figure 12.10.

Figure 12.10: Start Options

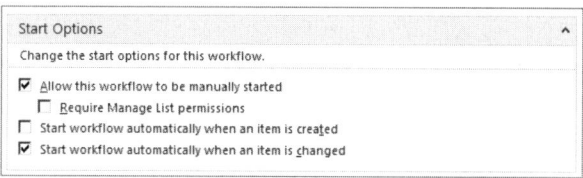

10. From the Workflow tab, click the Save button, and then click the Publish button.

When a document in the library is checked in as a major version and then approved, the workflow automatically declares it as a record.

Declaring Records Through a Retention Policy

A retention policy is a built-in function of SharePoint and requires only configuration to use. A retention policy is a procedure defined in SharePoint by a list or site administrator to perform some action on an item after a number days, months, or years. One of the actions that can be performed is to declare the item as a record. While the retention policy does not support the sophisticated conditional criteria of a workflow, it can include multiple retention stages of which declaring as a record is only one. For more details on policies, see the section "Configure Information Management Policies" later in this chapter.

Configure a Records Center

The alternative model to in-place records management in SharePoint 2010 is to send a copy of each item to a separate site collection built on the Records Center site template that acts as a records repository. A Records Center is used when a specific version of a document must be archived for compliance purposes while the document continues to be edited in its original location as it continues to evolve into new versions. For example, a Human Resources policy might cover the personal use of company-issued cell phones. When a new version of the policy is drafted and approved by management, that version must be archived so that it can be retrieved if a question arises about which version of the policy was applied on a given date. Meanwhile, the policy document will continue to be revised to meet changing business requirements.

While SharePoint 2010 does include a built-in versioning feature that allows users to review and retrieve older versions of the same document, this feature does not meet records compliance requirements for several reasons:

- Older versions of a document can be deleted even when the document is declared as a record.
- SharePoint does not have the ability to execute separate information management policies, such as an expiration policy, on older versions of a document; it can only do it to the entire document.
- SharePoint Search only indexes the last version of a document, so any content in older versions of the same document would not appear in the search.

However, by saving a copy of the document in a separate location, SharePoint can apply policies to and index the document separately from any other versions of it.

One purpose of a Records Center is to serve as a storage location that users can place documents into but for which they do not have edit rights or even, in many cases, read rights. SharePoint 2010 provides this functionality through the Records Center site template and custom Send To links, which allow users to route documents to it.

The following steps are required to create and use a Records Center:

1. Create a separate web application.
2. Create the Records Center site collection.
3. Create libraries in the Records Center.
4. Configure Content Organizer rules to route documents to specific libraries.
5. Create custom Send To connections.
6. Submit documents to the Records Center.

This section describes these tasks in detail.

Creating a Records Center Site

The Records Center is intended to be a secure and relatively isolated site for records to reside under the control of a few select individuals. Usually, the management of the Records Center is delegated to dedicated records managers in the organization, and most users will have either no access to the site or read-only access. For this reason, we recommend that you create the site in its own web application. This approach offers several benefits:

- The new web application will have its own content database, thereby separating the storage of the records from that of other site collections.

- As a separate web application, it will also allow farm administrators the ability to use the web application User Policies security feature (see Chapter 14, "Managing Security," for more details) to easily grant access to the site to auditors and others who need to reference the archived documents.

To begin, create a new web application from within SharePoint 2010 Central Administration. For the steps to create a new web application, see Chapter 2, "Creating and Managing Web Applications." The web application can either use a fully qualified URL, such as `repository.synergy.com`, or a unique port number on an existing URL. In most cases, the Records Center is visited directly by very few users so the reference URL is not as vital as with other web applications. Likewise, because the Records Center will probably be queried infrequently, it is acceptable for it to share the same application pool as an existing web application.

Once the web application is created, create a new site collection at the root of the web application. It is possible to create and use additional site collections for records management for additional segregation of content for security and administration purposes.

To create the Records Center site, perform the following steps:

1. From SharePoint 2010 Central Administration, under Application Management, click Create Site Collections.

2. From the Web Application drop-down menu, select the Records Center web application you created earlier.

3. In the Title box, enter a title that will appear to users (such as **Repository**), and in the Description box, enter the purpose of this site.

4. In the Web Site Address drop-down list, select the URL root (/).

5. In the Template Selection section, click the Enterprise tab, and then select Records Center.

6. In the Primary Site Collection Administrator box, enter the username for the user who will be the site collection administrator; use the pattern *domain\username*.

7. Click OK.

Creating Libraries in a Records Center

The Records Center site template includes several libraries, two of which are specifically oriented toward the records management functions of the Records Center:

- The Drop Off Library is created as part of the Content Organizer functionality when that feature is activated.

- The Record Library is a standard library with Major versioning enabled and is configured to automatically declare documents as records when they are uploaded.

To take full advantage of the record routing options in the Content Organizer (discussed in the next step), you may want to create additional libraries in the site. Each library can be configured with different content types, columns, folder structures, policies, and workflows to govern the treatment of the documents stored in them. The actual number and use of libraries will depend on your records management plan. A key factor in setting up the libraries is to ensure that the correct metadata is captured with documents to ensure that they can be retrieved efficiently at a future point during an audit or eDiscovery. If you have implemented a content type syndication hub (as discussed in Chapter 11, "Configuring the Managed Metadata Service"), then the same content types can be applied in the Records Center as are used elsewhere in the farm. By assigning the appropriate content type or types to each library and routing the documents to the correct library, you make it possible to capture the metadata you need.

To create additional libraries in the Records Center:

1. From the Site Actions menu, select More Options.
2. Select the Document Library template and provide a name for the library.
3. Click Create.
4. Once a library is created, edit the library settings to configure it with one or more existing content types or specific columns as needed. For more details on columns and content types, see Chapter 10, "Configuring Document Management."

Configuring Organizer Rules for Submitted Records

The Records Center leverages the Content Organizer functionality to route documents to a specific library or folder based on criteria specified in rules. When a document is uploaded to a library or submitted using a Send To connection, the Content Organizer determines where the document should be stored and moves it to that location. See Chapter 10 for full details on the Content Organizer.

To configure a Content Organizer rule:

1. From the Site Actions menu, select Site Settings.
2. Under the Site Administration section, click Content Organizer Rules.

3. Click Add New Item. The Edit Rule dialog appears, as shown in Figure 12.11.

Figure 12.11: Edit Rule dialog

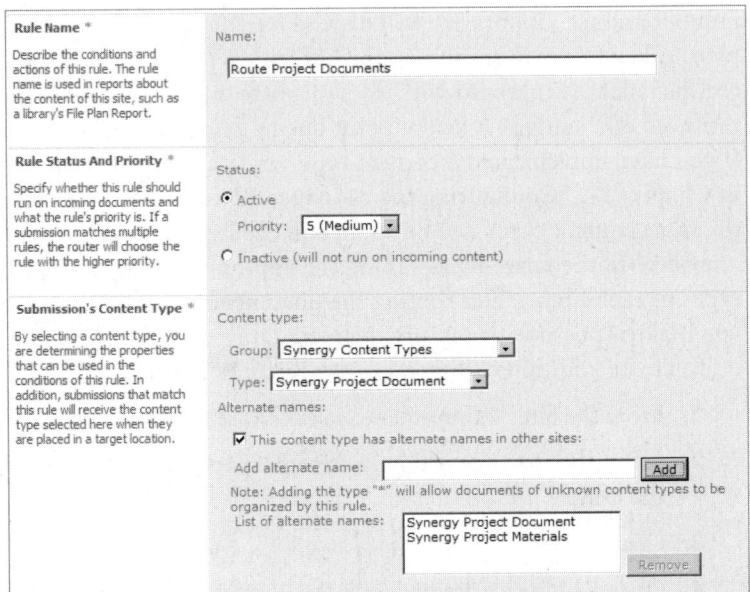

4. In the Rule Name text box, enter a unique name for this rule.

5. In the Rule Status And Priority section, leave Status set to the default of 5 unless you plan to create multiple rules for this type of document. The rule with the highest priority will be applied for routing.

6. In the Submission's Content Type section, from the drop-down lists, select the content type that this rule will match against. This is the principal value used to route documents. If multiple content types should be routed in the same way, add them in the Alternate Names section.

7. Use the Conditions section (shown in Figure 12.12) to add further selection criteria. You can select from any of the columns contained in the content type chosen in step 6.

Figure 12.12: Specifying conditions and target location

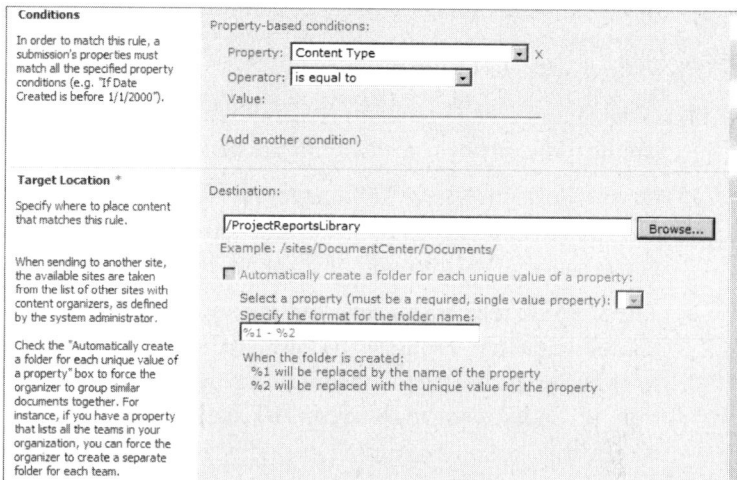

8. Select a destination document library in the Target Location section. Optionally, you can specify a folder within the library where the document will be placed. The folder must be configured with the content type selected in step 6.
9. Click OK.

Creating Custom Send To Connections

Documents may be uploaded directly to the Records Center if users are granted permissions to do so. However, it may be inappropriate to grant multiple staff members edit access to the Records Center, either for confidentiality reasons or to minimize the risk of accidental overwrite or deletion of content. SharePoint 2010 provides Send To connections, a means for users to submit documents to the Records Center even if they do not have permissions to access the site. A Send To connection does the following:

- Calls a built-in web service in SharePoint that handles the copying or moving of the documents.
- Supports the option to move a document into the Records Center and to leave a link to the new location in its place.
- Transfers the metadata values configured on the original document to the file into the Records Center. (However, the metadata

will only be applied if the columns in the destination library match those of the metadata on the document being transferred.)

To create a Send To command:

1. From SharePoint 2010 Central Administration, under General Application Settings, click Configure Send To Connections.

2. On the Configure Send To Connections page, select the web application that content will be sent from. This is the web application where the send to links will be displayed for the users to use.

3. The Site Subscription Settings section applies in situations where SharePoint Multi-Tenancy has been configured. Use this section to enable sites to send to locations outside the current subscription. If you have not enabled Multi-Tenancy, then this setting has no effect.

    For more information on Multi-tenancy, see the white paper "SharePoint 2010 for Hosters" available at http://technet.microsoft.com/en-us/library/ff652528.aspx.

4. In the Connection Settings section, shown in Figure 12.13, enter a display name for the connection that users will see in their sites.

Figure 12.13: Specifying connection settings

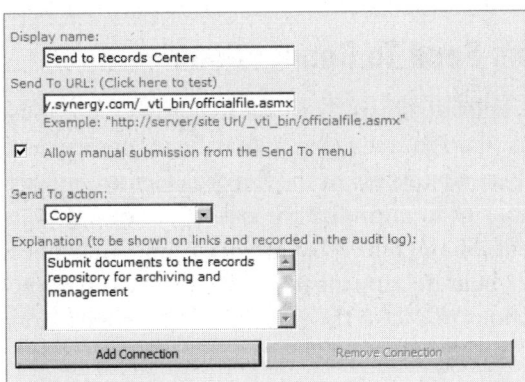

5. In the Send To URL text box, enter the full URL to the Records Center site without including any folder or page portion of the URL. Append to the URL *_vti_bin/officialfile.asmx*, which is the reference to the XML web service that will be called to transfer the file.

6. If you want to allow users to send documents to the Records Center themselves, make sure the box labeled "Allow manual submission from the Send To menu" is checked. If not, documents must be submitted to the connection through a workflow or custom code.

7. In the Send To Action drop-down list, select how SharePoint should process the document:

- Copy leaves the document in the original location and places a copy in the Records Center.

- Move copies the document to the Records Center and then deletes the original.

- Move And Leave A Link copies the document, then deletes the original and creates a link object that directs users to the new location for the document in the Records Center.

8. In the Explanation text box, enter a description of this connection.

9. Click Add Connection.

Submitting Records

The Records Center is designed to allow submission of records in several ways: manually, through a Send To connection, through a workflow, or through a retention policy.

NOTE If the document is routed to a library with required columns configured and some metadata is missing, the document will be placed into the Drop Off Library and its status will be set to Pending Submission. To complete the process, a user must log into the Records Center and manually edit the document properties to supply the missing metadata. Once that is done and the document is checked in, the Content Organizer will automatically route the document to its final destination.

Submitting Through Manual Upload

One method is to upload a document directly to the site. This method may be best suited for smaller numbers of documents that are being produced outside of SharePoint. Users do not have to know which library to upload the document to. They can click the Submit A Record button, shown on the home page of the Records Center site, which will upload the document to the Drop Off Library and trigger the Content Organizer to route it to the correct library.

One drawback to this method is that users require Add and Edit permissions on the site. Another drawback is that, because the document is being uploaded from outside of SharePoint, the Content Organizer rules cannot route it based on its content type. The routing will be based on the metadata submitted with the document.

Submitting Through a Send To Connection

Another method is to use the Send To connection (configured in the previous section). Any user with Read permissions can submit the document by selecting Send To from the context menu and then selecting the link for the destination Records Center, as shown in Figure 12.14.

Figure 12.14: Submitting a document using a Send To connection

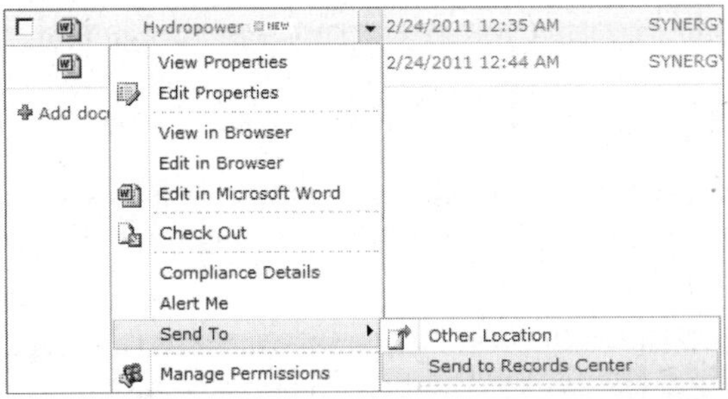

The `officialfile.asmx` web service is invoked and the document, along with all of its metadata, is submitted to the Records Center and routed based on the Content Organizer rules.

Submitting Through a Workflow

In many cases it is preferable for the submission of content to the Records Center to be automated through a workflow. SharePoint Designer 2010 includes a workflow action that will do this. While you may also want to expose a Send To connection to allow manual submission, this is not necessary as the workflow action supports directly addressing the Records Center. To configure the workflow, follow steps 1–6 in the section "Declaring Records Through Workflow," earlier in this chapter. Then do the following:

1. From the Action menu, under the Core Actions category, select Send Document To Repository.
2. Click This Action and choose a behavior: Copy, Move, or Move And Leave a Link.
3. Click the This Destination Router link and enter the full URL to the Records Center, including the suffix of _vti_bin/officialfile.asmx, in the same manner as configuring a Send To connection.
4. Click This Explanation and enter a reason for the submission. Then follow the remainder of the steps in the "Declaring Records Through Workflow" section. The results of this configuration are shown in Figure 12.15.

Figure 12.15: Configuring document submission through a workflow

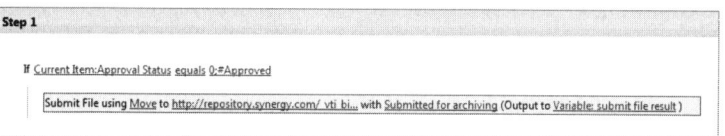

Submitting Through a Retention Policy

The final method that can be configured to submit a document is to configure an information management policy. One of the actions that is supported by the retention policy (discussed in more detail in the next section) is Transfer To Another Location. You do so by referencing an existing Send To connection. Information Management Policies are discussed further in the next section.

Configure Information Management Policies

Information management policies are sets of rules designed to affect documents and items based on their content type. Policies can be applied directly to site content types, thereby applying wherever the content type is used, or they can be applied to specific lists or libraries. There are four types of information management policies in SharePoint

2010: retention policies, auditing policies, barcodes, and labels. Together, these policies allow records managers to apply consistent behavioral rules to content to meet compliance requirements.

Creating an Information Management Policy

Sometimes an information management policy is being implemented to conform to compliance requirements. Such a policy must be applied consistently to all content in a site or site collection. In this case, it is best to apply a policy directly to a content type. Then when the content type is assigned, the policies apply to that content automatically.

In some cases, a policy requirement should apply only to a single list or library, or a user does not have permissions to configure a policy on a content type. In these situations, an information management policy can be configured in the list or library. The policy is still applied per content type, but the scope is limited to the specific list or library.

SharePoint 2010 also provides the ability to create a site collection policy. This is a form of policy template that can be applied to either a content type or a list or library. Site collection policies allow content managers to create predefined policies at the site collection level. These policies can then be applied by users at a lower level in the site without the users' needing to understand policy creation details. Later in this chapter, in the section "Creating a Site Collection Policy," we will look at creating policy templates. Now let's discuss creating each of the types of policies.

To create an information management policy on a content type:

1. Open the site you want to configure.
2. From the Site Actions menu, select Site Settings.
3. In the Galleries section, click Site Content Types.
4. Click the link for the content type you want to configure.
5. In the Settings section, click Information Management Policy Settings.
6. In the Name and Administrative Description boxes, enter a unique name and a description that is meaningful to others who will be editing this policy.

7. In the Policy Statement box, enter text that will help users understand how this policy operates.
8. Check the box next to the policy actions that you want to enable for this policy and configure the settings by referencing one of the sections that follow: Creating a Retention Policy; Creating an Auditing Policy; Creating a Barcodes Policy; Creating a Label Policy.
9. Click OK.

Creating a Retention Policy

The retention policy is a core element in any records management plan that must track and dispose of content in a consistent manner. The policy specifies an expiration time for a document or item. The expiration time is measured in days, months, or years from a date set on the document or item. The date is typically drawn from one of the metadata columns available. The created date or modified date is commonly used, but a custom date column can be used as well. When the expiration date is reached, the policy dictates what action will be taken on the item (e.g., deleting or archiving).

To configure a retention policy:

1. From the Edit Policy page, check the box next to Enable Retention to display the options shown in Figure 12.16.

Figure 12.16: Retention policy options

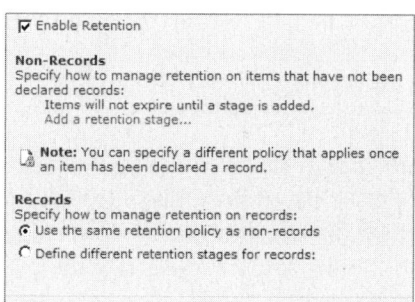

2. Under the Non-Records section, click the link Add A Retention Stage. The Stage Properties page opens, as shown in Figure 12.17.

Figure 12.17: Stage Properties page

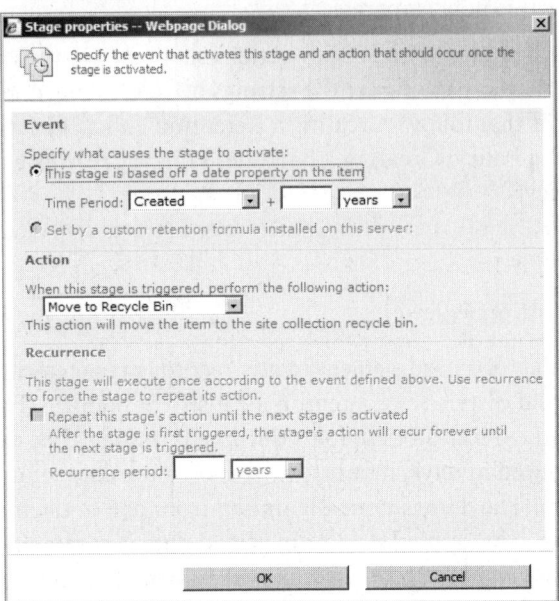

3. In the Event section, choose the field that will be used to provide the start date of the retention period calculation. The drop-down list will show only Date and Time columns. Then enter the interval number and select the interval increment (Days, Months, or Years).

4. In the Action section, select which operation this stage of the policy will perform.

5. Click OK.

Note that applying a retention policy on a content type can be overridden if the Library And Folder Based Retention site collection feature is enabled. This feature allows list administrators to create retention schedules at the list or library level that override the content type policies.

Creating an Auditing Policy

An auditing policy is a means for content managers to implement tracking and reporting of actions on documents for compliance purposes.

Auditing in SharePoint monitors and records specific actions taken by individuals so that these actions can be retrieved and analyzed later. The purpose of enabling auditing through a policy is to capture only the details that are specifically required to limit the amount of data that is stored and reported. Auditing and audit reports are covered in further detail in Chapter 15, "Managing Security."

To configure an auditing policy:

1. From the Edit Policy page, check the box next to Enable Auditing to display the options shown in Figure 12.18.

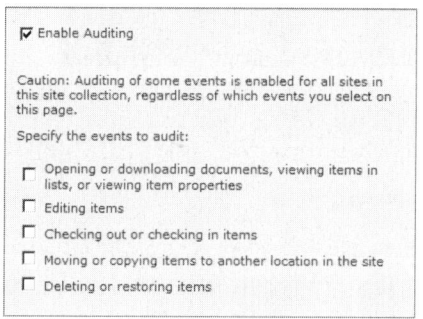

Figure 12.18: Auditing policy options

2. Select the appropriate actions to audit.
3. Click OK.

Creating a Barcodes Policy

A barcodes policy enables SharePoint 2010 to generate a random and unique barcode image for each document that the policy is applied to. This barcode can be printed onto a label or inserted into an Office 2007 or Office 2010 document to be printed out along with the document for tracking purposes. The built-in barcode provider generates barcodes using the Code 39 standard (ANSI/AIM BC1-1995, Code 39). SharePoint also supports custom barcode generators created through the policies object model.

To configure a barcodes policy:

1. From the Edit Policy page, check the box next to Enable Barcodes.
2. If you wish, check the option labeled "Prompt users to insert a barcode before saving or printing." This reminds users working in

Office 2007 or Office 2010 to insert a barcode into the document before saving or printing.

3. Click OK.

Once the barcodes policy is enabled, you will need to edit the properties of a document to trigger SharePoint to generate the barcode. Then, from the document context menu in the library, select View Properties to see the generated barcode, as shown in Figure 12.19.

Figure 12.19: Document properties showing SharePoint 2010 barcode

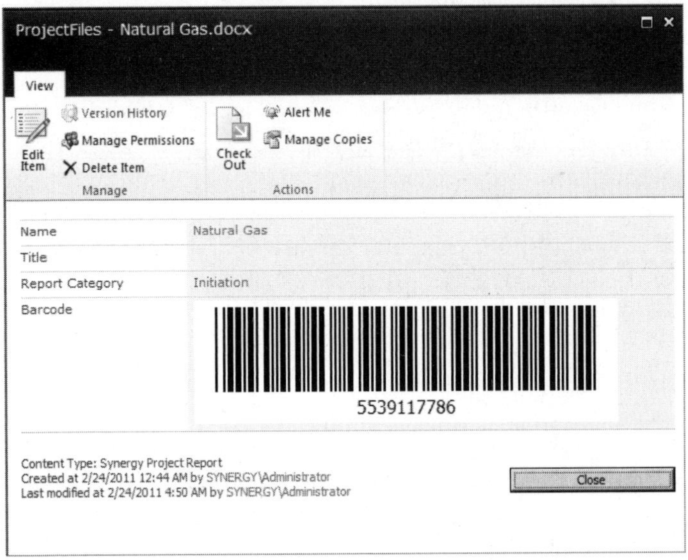

Creating a Labels Policy

Labels are used to create formatted messages that can include metadata values and can be inserted into an Office 2007 or Office 2010 document. Labels are typically used to create preformatted text that is inserted onto the first page of a document as part of the cover sheet or into the footer. Labels do not dynamically update unless the file is opened and edited or printed.

To configure a labels policy:

1. From the Edit Policy page, check the box next to Enable Labels to display the options shown in Figure 12.20.

Figure 12.20: Labels policy options

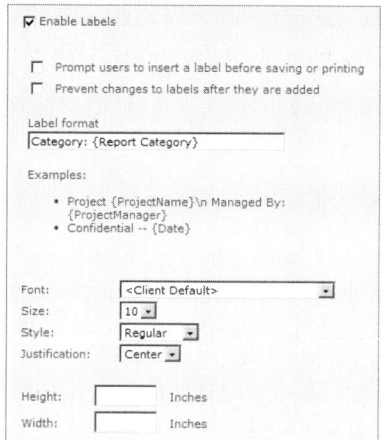

2. If you wish, check the option labeled "Prompt users to insert a label before saving or printing" to remind users who are working in either Office 2007 or Office 2010 to insert a label into the document before saving or printing.

3. In the Label Format field, enter text and incorporate values from columns in the content type by placing the column name between braces, as shown in Figure 12.20.

4. Select font formatting and sizing options and click the Refresh button (not shown in the figure) to show a preview of the label output.

5. Click OK.

Creating a Site Collection Policy

Policies that are created on content types are reusable wherever the content type is used. It is also possible to apply policies directly to lists and libraries; however, doing so makes it difficult to apply the same policies on multiple lists or libraries. SharePoint 2010 supports site collection policies, which act as policy templates that can be applied to lists and libraries throughout the site collection.

To create a site collection policy:

1. Open the site collection you want to configure.
2. From the Site Actions menu, select Site Settings.
3. In the Site Collection Administration section, click Site Collection Policies.

4. On the Policies page, click Create.
5. Configure the policies using the same options as described in the "Creating an Information Management Policy" section earlier for a policy on a content type.
6. Click OK.

Exporting and Importing a Site Collection Policy

Once created, a site collection policy can be exported and reused in another site collection. To export the policy, from the Policies page, click the policy link and, at the bottom of the Policies page, click Export to save the policy as an XML file to a local drive.

To import a policy, from the Policies page, click Import and browse to a policy XML file to upload and import it.

Applying a Site Collection Policy

To apply a site collection policy, open a list or library that you want to apply the policy to; then open the list or library settings page and click the Information Management Policies link. Click the content type that the policy should be applied to, and then click the Use A Site Collection Policy option. Select the policy you want to apply, as shown in Figure 12.21, and click OK.

Figure 12.21: Applying a site collection policy

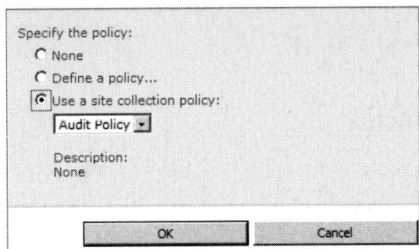

Configure eDiscovery and Holds

When a compliance review or a legal case requires that specific documents be retrieved from an EDRMS, this is referred to as an *eDiscovery*. An eDiscovery involves finding and securing documents that are required to be held in a read-only state for the duration of the review or case that requires them. Since there may be several eDiscovery efforts ongoing at any given time, EDRMSs use a method called a *hold* to lock the documents. Unlike other forms of protection, such as permissions or record declaration, multiple holds can be placed on the same document successively. As long as at least one hold applies to a document, it cannot be edited or deleted and any retention policies that might affect it are deferred. Once all holds have been removed from a document, policies will once again take effect. To make use of these functions in SharePoint 2010, you must enable the hold and eDiscovery site feature.

Creating a Hold Definition

Before placing any items on hold, it is necessary to create a hold definition in the site where the documents reside. Once the hold and eDiscovery feature is activated, a new section of commands called Hold And eDiscovery appears on the Site Settings page. To create a hold, click the Holds link and then click Add New Item. Enter a title, a description, and the person who is managing the hold; then click OK.

Searching for Items to Hold

To populate a hold with a large number of items, the easiest method is to conduct a search for content:

1. On the Site Settings page, in the Hold And eDiscovery section, click Discover And Hold Content, which opens the Search And Add To Hold page shown in Figure 12.22.

Figure 12.22: Searching and adding documents to hold

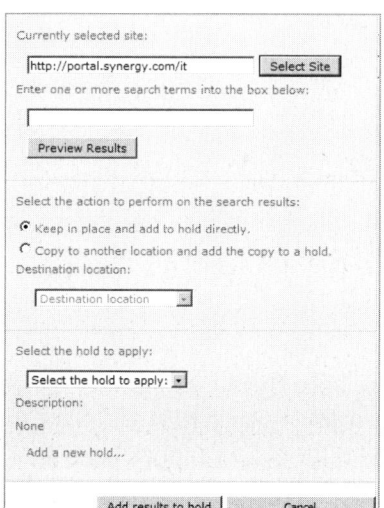

2. In the Search Criteria section, select the site you want to search and then enter a keyword or phrase to search for and click Preview Results. This will open a search results page showing the range of content that is covered by the search term entered. Refine the keywords to capture the relevant content for the discovery.

3. In the Local Hold Or Export section, select whether you want to keep the content in its existing location and place a lock on it, or copy the content to another location and place a lock on the copy. The locations available will be any Send To connections configured for the current web application.

4. In the Relevant Hold section, select the hold you want to apply to the content and click the Add Results To Hold button.

Holding and Releasing Individual Items

In many cases, the eDiscovery approach we just described will not capture every relevant document. To add a specific document to a hold, locate the document in the library and click the context menu, then select Compliance Details. On the Compliance Details page (shown in Figure 12.4, earlier in this chapter), click the Add/Remove from hold link. In the Add Or Remove From Hold section, shown in Figure 12.23, click the option Add To A Hold and select the hold you want to place on the document. Then click Save.

Figure 12.23: Adding or removing documents from a hold

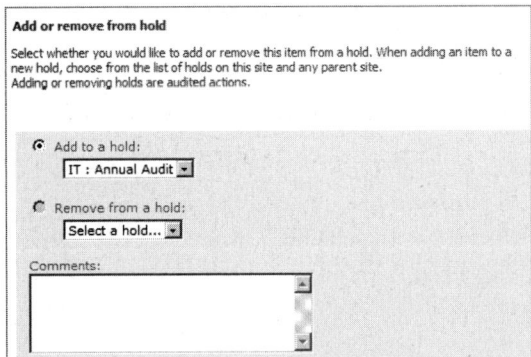

To remove an item from a hold, open the same page and click the option Remove From A Hold; then select which hold you want to remove and click Save.

13

Configuring Web Content Management and Publishing

IN THIS CHAPTER, YOU WILL LEARN TO:

▶ **CONFIGURE PUBLISHING FEATURES** (Pages 392 – 403)
- Activating the Site Collection Publishing Infrastructure Feature (Page 393)
- Activating the SharePoint Server Publishing Feature (Page 394)
- Creating a Publishing Page (Page 394)
- Selecting a Page Layout (Page 367)
- Understanding Page Properties (Page 399)
- Creating Reusable Content (Page 401)

▶ **CONFIGURE SHAREPOINT 2010 CACHING** (Pages 403 – 413)
- Configuring Publishing Cache Profiles (Page 403)
- Configuring the Output Cache (Page 407)
- Configuring the Object Cache (Page 409)
- Configuring the BLOB Cache (Page 411)

▶ **CONFIGURE CONTENT DEPLOYMENT** (Pages 413 – 420)
- Configuring Content Deployment Paths (Page 415)
- Configuring Content Deployment Jobs (Page 418)

Web content management is one of the cornerstones of SharePoint 2010 and is a feature set that distinguishes SharePoint from most other collaboration systems. Web content management systems are designed to allow users with little or no knowledge of web development to create and administer websites and web pages. While all SharePoint 2010 sites are designed to be user friendly and easy for users to manage, web content management sites make use of functionality included in the Publishing features (available in SharePoint Server 2010 Standard and Enterprise editions), which allow for greater flexibility and control over the drafting and presentation of content pages. This functionality is not available in the SharePoint Foundation 2010 product.

In this chapter we'll explore the Publishing features and how they transform the capabilities of a SharePoint site to support web content management. We'll also look at the templates and tools, such as page layouts and reusable content, which the Publishing features make available. You'll learn how to configure the caching options in publishing sites to improve the performance and reduce the load time of content pages. Finally, we'll discuss the content deployment functionality, which allows administrators to replicate entire sites and site collections of content from one SharePoint farm to another to create production sites that are separate from staging sites.

Configure Publishing Features

In SharePoint 2010 Standard Edition or higher, all sites have the ability to support web content management functionality. However, not every site needs the functionality or would benefit from it. An intranet portal, for example, would likely need web content management tools, but a collaboration site, such as a project team site, would not.

In the portal, the presentation of information is usually as important as the content itself and a great deal of attention needs to be given to the drafting, editing, approval, and release of content pages. These tasks often require a dedicated web content manager and someone who will have time to master the tools and techniques involved. In a team site, by contrast, the focus is typically on sharing documents and information with a minimum of administrative overhead and with more emphasis on the approval of documents than on the pages used to navigate to them.

To support these different requirements, Microsoft has implemented the web content management functionality in a set of features that are disabled by default in most sites but that can be enabled if needed. These include the SharePoint Server Publishing Infrastructure feature, which can be enabled at the site collection level, and the SharePoint Server Publishing feature, which can be enabled at the site or subsite level.

Activating the Site Collection Publishing Infrastructure Feature

Two site templates built into SharePoint 2010 have the Publishing features automatically activated. Both of these templates create site collections that are fully functional web content management sites:

Publishing Portal This site collection template is used when creating a formal intranet or internet site where the content will generally be contributed by a limited set of authors and organized by a content manager.

Enterprise Wiki This site collection template is used to create a site where a collaborative approach is used that relies on many authors and features a less structured environment than the Publishing Portal provides.

Some other site templates can be used to create subsites only within site collections that have the Publishing features enabled. These are the Enterprise Wiki site template and the Enterprise Search Center site template.

While it is common to create a new web content management site by using one of the publishing site templates, it is also possible to turn any site into a web content management site by activating specific SharePoint features.

SharePoint Server Publishing Infrastructure Feature This site collection feature creates the supporting libraries, lists, and command links that allow publishing capabilities in a site collection.

SharePoint Server Publishing Feature This site feature creates a library named Pages in the site that allows the creation of pages that use the full web content management options of SharePoint.

To activate the Publishing Infrastructure feature in a site collection:

1. Open the root site in a site collection.
2. From the Site Actions menu, select Site Settings.

3. In the Site Collection Administration section, click Site Collection Features.

4. Next to the SharePoint Server Publishing Infrastructure feature, click Activate, as shown in Figure 13.1.

Figure 13.1: Activating the SharePoint Server Publishing Infrastructure feature

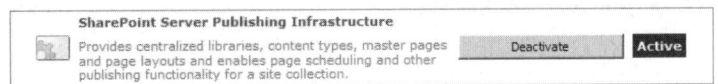

Activating the SharePoint Server Publishing Feature

To activate the SharePoint Server Publishing feature in a site:

1. Open the root site in a site collection.

2. From the Site Actions menu, select Site Settings.

3. In the Site Actions section, click Manage Site Features.

4. Next to the SharePoint Server Publishing feature, click Activate, as shown in Figure 13.2.

Figure 13.2: Activating the SharePoint Server Publishing feature

Creating a Publishing Page

Publishing pages are designed to allow users to edit content without needing to know much about HTML or how web technology works. One of the unique aspects of a publishing site is that it contains a Pages library where all new pages are automatically placed when they are created. Nonpublishing sites have a SitePages library that serves the same purpose.

SharePoint 2010 includes several forms of publishing pages, associated with different content types. All of the pages contain predefined editable regions. In this section we will look at the publishing page known as the Wiki page, one of the most common publishing page types.

Creating a Wiki Page

Wiki pages are a form of SharePoint publishing page designed explicitly for open and relatively free-form communication. As with other pages, anyone with edit permissions can overwrite and change the content and add their own thoughts. Wiki pages automatically save previous versions of the page and make it easy for them to be recovered and restored. The idea behind Wiki pages is to remove the fear people may have of "losing" information by changing live content, and to encourage users to put their thoughts on the page so that ideas are captured and shared. To this end, the Wiki page in SharePoint 2010 supports a new content editing field that accepts virtually any form of content that SharePoint 2010 supports. Figure 13.3 shows a Wiki page with several kinds of content.

Figure 13.3: Wiki page

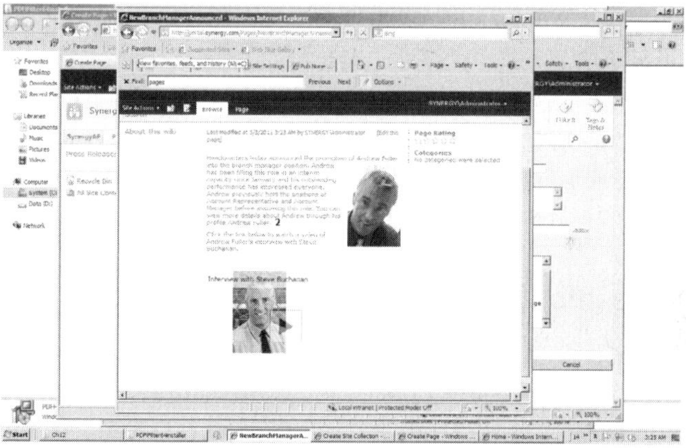

On this page you see the following elements:

- Editable text content
- HTML—a hyperlink
- Embedded web part—the Media Web Part connected to a video stored in SharePoint
- Embedded picture with text wrapping around it
- Edit This Page link—clicking this link places the page in Edit Mode to provide an intuitive means of participating in collaboration

To create a Wiki page:

1. Inside a publishing site, from the Site Actions menu, select New Page.
2. In the New Page dialog box, enter the name for the page. The page name becomes part of the URL. It can contain any characters except for characters that are illegal in URLs:

    # % & * : < > ? \ / { } ~ |

3. Click Create.

The new page will appear in Edit mode. The SharePoint 2010 ribbon is a new feature of all pages and provides extensive editing tools (see Figure 13.4).

Figure 13.4: Wiki page Edit ribbon

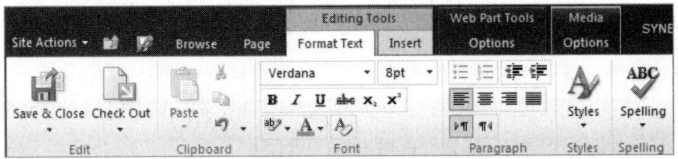

The Wiki page includes both a Ratings field and a Categories field on every page, which are visible in Figure 13.3, earlier in this section.

Using Ratings Information on a Wiki Page

The Ratings field is an available option for most lists and libraries in SharePoint. It can be enabled under the list or library settings. Usually the Ratings column appears only in the list or library view. In the case of the Wiki page, the Ratings column is included by default in the layout of the page itself.

Clicking on one of the five stars in the Ratings column will cast the user's "vote" for the rating of this content. All ratings are aggregated and processed by two timer jobs executing on an hourly basis. You can force ratings to be recalculated manually by running these two jobs:

User Profile Service – Social Data Maintenance Job Aggregates the ratings and resets the social data change log

User Profile Service – Social Rating Synchronization Job Synchronizes the ratings values between the social database and content database

Using a Term Set on a Wiki Page

Categories on Wiki pages make use of the term store, discussed in Chapter 11, "Configuring the Managed Metadata Service." To make a set of category values available to users, you need to configure a term set and assign it to the Wiki Categories site column as follows:

1. Open the root site in a site collection.
2. From the Site Actions menu, select Site Settings.
3. Under the Site Administration, click Term Store Management. Choose an appropriate term set or create one following the steps provided in Chapter 11.
4. Return to the Site Settings page and, under Galleries, click Site Columns.
5. On the Site Columns page, in the Custom Columns section, click Wiki Categories.
6. In the Term Set Settings box, select the term set that will provide values for the Wiki Categories column.
7. Click OK.

Selecting a Page Layout

A valuable feature of pages in a publishing site is the ability to change the way a page is organized without re-creating it. This is done by changing the page's Layout setting. A page layout is a template for the arrangement of the fields or columns on a page. It is easy to change a page layout because behind the scenes the information on publishing pages has no discrete arrangement in itself, but instead is simply a set of metadata that is stored in a SharePoint content database under the page name. The page layout is the "framework" that the metadata hangs on when the page is rendered. By switching to a different layout, the arrangement of the information can be changed without editing the content itself.

To change a page's layout:

1. Open the page and select Site Actions and then Edit Page to place the page in Edit mode.
2. From the Page ribbon tab, click the Page Layout drop-down menu, as shown for a Wiki page in Figure 13.5.

Figure 13.5: Wiki page layouts

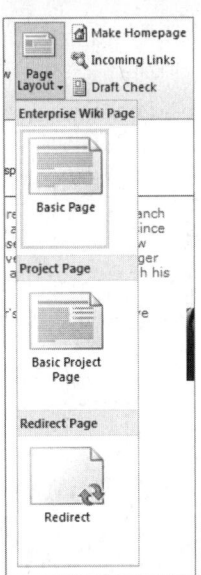

3. Select the desired layout.

Some standard layouts are as follows:

Basic Page   The standard page based on the Enterprise Wiki content type

Project Page   Adds Web Page, Contact, and Status columns to the page for project tracking

Redirect Page   Designed to automatically redirect viewers to a different page after 5 seconds

Page layouts are based on content types, so selecting a page layout conveniently assigns the content type and the page layout to the page at the same time.

The Publishing Portal creates a Pages library, which has many more content types and layouts associated with it. These include two additional content types:

Article Page   These layouts do not have any web part zones on them and therefore contain only metadata. They are ideal for Internet-facing sites.

Welcome Page These layouts have web part zones, making them effective for intranet-facing sites where list and library data are more likely to be displayed.

Clicking the Layouts drop-down from a page created in a Publishing Portal displays a list that includes the same layouts as the Wiki site along with many others, such as the Article layouts, as shown in Figure 13.6. These provide convenient arrangements of content that include fields for Page Image, Image Caption, Byline, and Article Date.

Figure 13.6: Publishing Portal page layouts

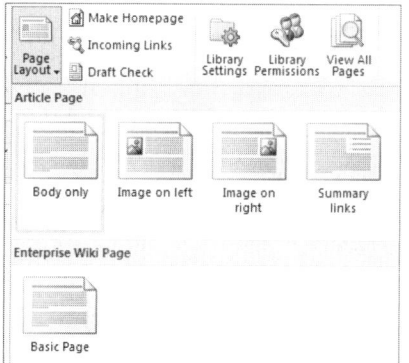

Understanding Page Properties

With the page open in Edit mode, from the Page ribbon tab select Edit Properties. One of the first things that you'll notice is that many of the properties shown on this page are the same ones that are edited when the page is open in Edit mode. All the content of a publishing page can be edited from the properties page and the Edit mode of the page itself. The properties of the page are derived, in part, from the columns of the content type the page is based on. Therefore, no single set of properties exists that applies to all pages. However, all pages will have a common set of properties derived from the base page content type from which they all inherit and which are shown in Figure 13.7. These common properties are used primarily for administrative purposes by content editors or managers who want to understand what the purpose of the page is and who the primary contact person is for the page. They are not displayed to readers of the page.

Figure 13.7: Page properties

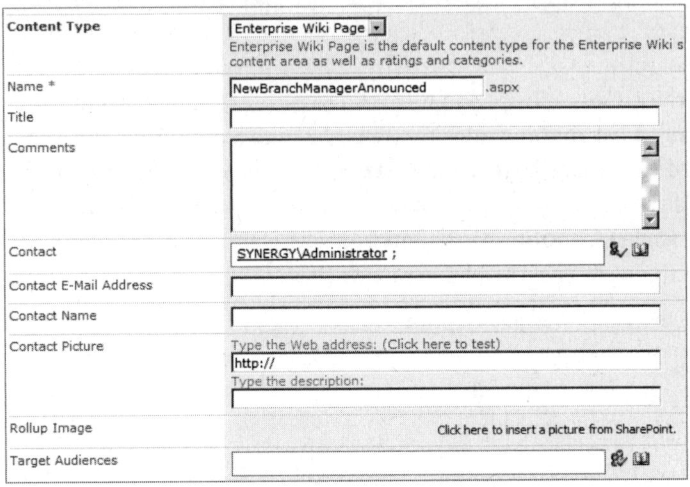

One of the properties found on the properties page that is not displayed in the Edit mode is Scheduling, shown in Figure 13.8.

Figure 13.8: Scheduling settings

Content scheduling allows pages to be made visible and invisible at specific dates and times. Scheduling is supported only when Content Approval has been enabled on the library and versioning has been set to both Major and Minor versions. The goal of scheduling is to provide a process whereby a page can be created by a content editor (someone with Contributor rights), published to the site, and scheduled to be available at some point in the future or scheduled to expire at some point in the future. A timer job monitors the schedule and publishes the page at the correct time.

Creating Reusable Content

Often, a content editor is faced with the challenge of needing to include the same text on many different pages, such as a legal disclaimer at the bottom of an article. While the use of copy-and-paste may allow the content to be reproduced, it isn't always accurate and some content, such as HTML with embedded formatting, is difficult to copy this way. A Publishing site collection contains a Reusable Content list, which allows content editors to store prewritten content that can inserted into any publishing page, as shown in Figure 13.9.

Figure 13.9: Reusable Content list

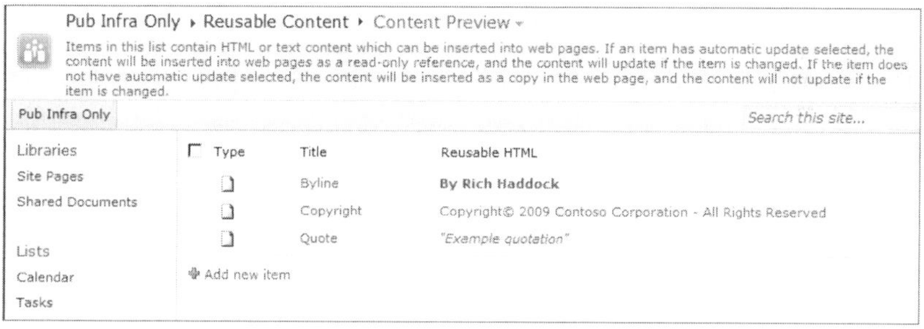

There are two forms of reusable content:

Reusable HTML   This type allows editors to capture and store any valid HTML tags and text. Reusable HTML is useful for storing formatted text, hyperlinks, and images. Code such as JavaScript cannot be included because it is not allowed inside publishing page content.

Reusable Text   Reusable Text content is useful when you want text to take on the font and style of the paragraph it is in.

To create a reusable content item:

1. Open the root site in a site collection.
2. From the Site Actions menu, select View All Site Content.
3. Under Lists, click Reusable Content.
4. From the Items tab, click either Reusable HTML or Reusable Text. The Reusable Content page is displayed, as shown in Figure 13.10.

Figure 13.10: Reusable Content page

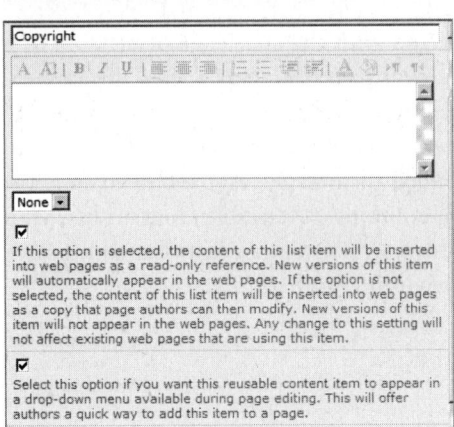

5. Enter a name in the Title field. In the Comments field, enter a description for the item.

6. Select a Content Category, which can help in sorting multiple items in a list.

7. Choose whether to enable the Automatic Update option. When you enable this option, SharePoint automatically pushes any changes to the content item out to all the pages where the item is being used. For instance, this would allow a change to the copyright notice to be propagated throughout the site without requiring the pages in the site to be edited again.

8. Choose whether to enable the Show In Drop-Down Menu option. This allows the item to be displayed in the SharePoint edit ribbon when the page is being edited, as shown in Figure 13.11.

Figure 13.11: Reusable Content drop-down menu

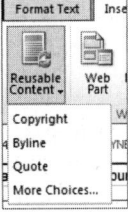

9. In the Reusable HTML or Reusable Text field, enter the content that will be displayed inside the web page.
10. Click Save.

To use a reusable content item:

1. Open the publishing page in Edit mode.
2. Click inside the page content area of the page.
3. From the Editing Tools ribbon, click the Insert tab, and then click the Reusable Content drop-down menu, as shown in Figure 13.11. Either select one of the items displayed in the menu or select More Choices to see all the reusable content available.

Configure SharePoint 2010 Caching

Publishing sites are typically accessed far more frequently by viewers than by editors. One quality that helps contribute to the acceptability and success of a publishing site is the speed with which it loads and can be viewed. Publishing sites also tend to host more pictures and media content than collaboration sites do, which can slow down the load time and responsiveness of the site. For this reason, a publishing site in SharePoint supports sophisticated cache management settings to allow administrators to optimize the site for better performance.

Configuring Publishing Cache Profiles

Cache profiles are sets of options that are applied in the configuration of the site collection output cache. A cache profile describes the type of caching behavior that SharePoint should use to treat the content that users are viewing in a site depending on whether they are accessing the site anonymously or as an authenticated user. In order for cache profiles to apply, the site collection output cache must be enabled.

Four cache profiles are available in a SharePoint site collection by default. Each consists of a collection of settings that have been selected to improve performance for a typical network scenario.

Disabled This profile does not have any caching settings configured, so it can be assigned to the site collection output cache when caching is not desired over a specific connection type.

Public Internet (Purely Anonymous)   This profile is optimized for connections that will be read-only and where users will have limited access to lists and libraries. This profile provides the highest caching performance but is only for anonymous access.

Extranet (Published Site)   This profile is designed for scenarios where users are connecting to a site as authenticated users and are consuming content that changes infrequently. This scenario is common with an extranet or intranet portal. This profile provides the best caching performance for authenticated users.

Intranet (Collaboration Site)   This profile is used for sites where authenticated users are consuming content that changes frequently and where it is important that they view the latest page versions every time they refresh. This setting is appropriate for a very dynamic intranet portal or a team site.

While you can edit any of the existing profiles, it is a best practice to create a new profile for any custom combinations of cache settings that you wish to use.

To create a cache profile:

1. Open the root site in a site collection.
2. From the Site Actions menu, select Site Settings.
3. In the Site Collection Administration section, click Site Collection Cache Profiles.
4. On the Cache Profiles page, shown in Figure 13.12, click Add New Item.

   Figure 13.12: Cache Profiles page

   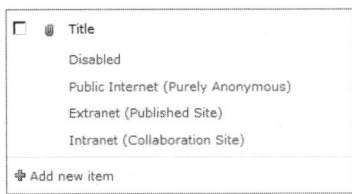

5. In the Cache Profiles – New Item page, shown in Figure 13.13, enter information in the Title, Display Name, and Display Description sections. The latter two fields are displayed to site owners and page layout owners if they are allowed to override

the output cache settings at the site collection level. Entering information in these fields is optional.

Figure 13.13: New Cache Profile settings

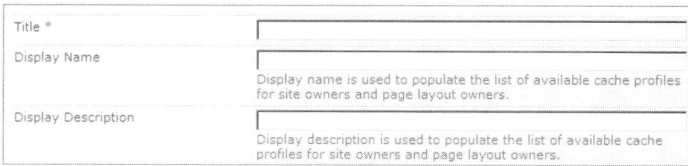

6. Choose whether to enable Perform ACL Check, shown in Figure 13.14. This setting is typically unchecked when it can be assumed that most users will have the same level of permissions on the site.

Figure 13.14: More New Cache Profile settings

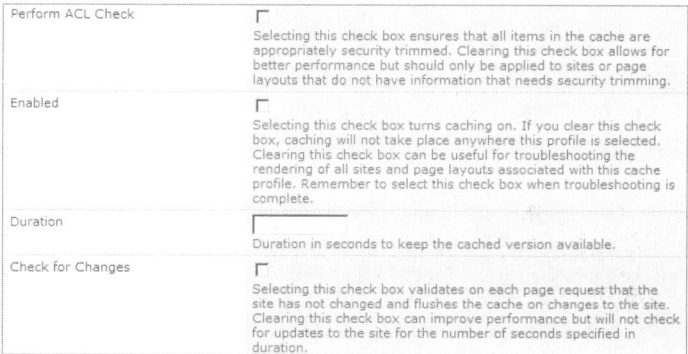

7. Make sure that the Enabled check box is selected to activate caching in this profile. This would normally only be unchecked in the Disabled profile.

8. Enter a value in the Duration box. This is the number of seconds that items will remain in cache before being reloaded from the database. The default value is 180 seconds, or 3 minutes.

9. Choose whether to enable the Check For Changes option. This option is typically enabled only when content on a site changes frequently and users want to see the latest updates at all times.

10. If desired, enter information in one or more of the Vary By fields, shown in Figure 13.15:

Figure 13.15: Vary By settings

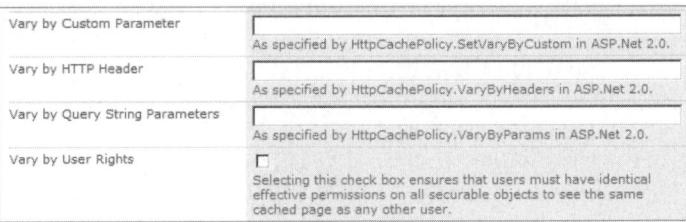

Vary By Custom Parameter   This field allows administrators to configure SharePoint to take advantage of any value that is passed to SharePoint by the client. For example, the Public Internet (Purely Anonymous) profile has the value of Browser in this setting to ensure that different browser versions receive different cached output. This matters if you are using browser-specific versions of CSSs and JavaScripts.

Vary By HTTP Header   This field accepts a value matching a standard HTTP request header passed to SharePoint by the browser. For example, if your site has pages in different languages and you enter **Accept-Language**, the browser receives the language that the user's browser is configured for, such as "de-lu" or "en-us." All the requests that have the same header will receive the same set of cached output.

Vary By Query String Parameters   This field allows SharePoint to use a parameter that is submitted after a question mark (?) in the request URL. For example, if your site has different results for different locations, the parameter CustomerCity might be used as a query string parameter in a custom list filter on a page. This would allow the results for "New York" to be cached separately from the results for "Los Angeles."

Vary By User Rights   This field allows SharePoint to cache separate content for each distinct set of permissions so that users only see cached content that they have the right to see.

11. Choose an item in the Cacheability drop-down, shown in Figure 13.16, to control where the cached content will be stored.

Figure 13.16: Cacheability settings

Cacheability	
	As specified by HttpCacheability in ASP.Net 2.0.
Safe for Authenticated Use	☐
	This check box should be selected for only those policies that you want to allow to be applied to authenticated scenarios by administrators and page layout designers.
Allow writers to view cached content	☐
	Selecting this check box bypasses the normal behavior of not allowing people with edit permissions to have their pages cached. This check box should be selected only in scenarios in which you know that the page will be published, but will not have any content that might be checked out or in draft.

The options are as follows:

NoCache   Forces each request to get fresh content from the server. This setting is used when the content caching is not the primary focus of the cache profile.

Private   Caches content only on the client. This effectively means that the first request from any user will cause a full download of content. After that, a refresh of the page may use the existing cache to display it.

Server   Caches content only on the server. No content is cached on the client. This setting is equivalent to the ServerAndNoCache setting.

Public   Allows content to be cached by both clients and proxy servers.

ServerAndPrivate   Specifies that content can be cached on both the SharePoint server and on the client but not on proxy servers. Proxy servers will respect the Cacheability setting and only cache content when allowed to by SharePoint.

12. Choose options for the Safe For Authenticated Use and Allow Writers To View Cached Content settings, as shown in Figure 13.16.
13. Click Save.

Configuring the Output Cache

The page output cache controls the caching settings that are applied to pages in a site collection. The output cache is disabled by default. It can improve overall performance, but some pages that users see might not show all the latest updates to the site. In addition to the site collection settings, page output caching can be configured at the subsite and page layout levels. When a page executes, all of the controls on the page render their output from the SharePoint content database into the HTML that makes up the page. For example, the navigation menus on a SharePoint page do not exist as static HTML; however, each time the page is refreshed, the menus are constructed by an ASP.NET control that reads the current navigation structure from the database and creates the appropriate HTML to display tabs and menus. When output caching is turned on, that control does not need to execute again the next time the page is requested and the fully rendered navigation menus can be loaded from cache, a process that is much faster than regenerating the menus from the control.

You should keep a number of considerations in mind when deciding to enable output caching. The primary benefit is that rendering a page with cached content will take less time and therefore the page can be delivered to the user's browser more quickly. Not only will this increase the responsiveness of the server as far as users are concerned, but it can also reduce the overall load on the server and free up processing time for other tasks. This same benefit applies to the SQL server as well because cached items do not require queries to the database to retrieve content. However, the price that is paid for this will be in the form of additional memory consumed by the SharePoint server to store the cached versions of the pages. Also, if the cache is stored on the SharePoint server and there are multiple load-balanced front-end servers, each server could, temporarily, end up displaying a different version of the cached page.

To configure the page output cache:

1. Open the root site in a site collection.
2. From the Site Actions menu, select Site Settings.
3. In the Site Collection Administration section, click Site Collection Output Cache.
4. To enable output caching, click the Enable Output Cache check box, shown in Figure 13.17.

Figure 13.17: Output cache settings

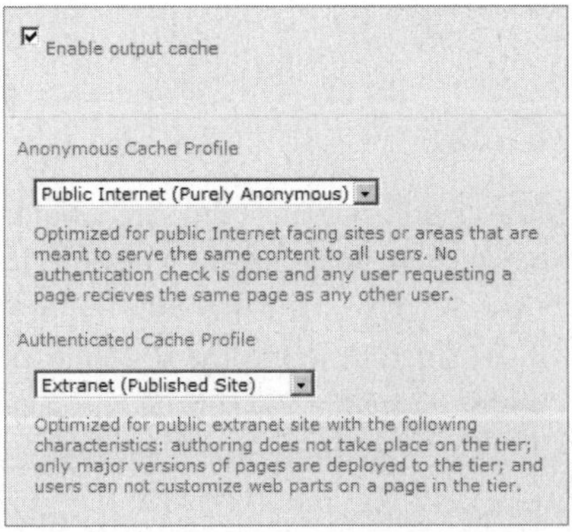

5. Choose which cache profiles will be applied to users depending on their authentication to the site collection. A web application can support multiple authentication methods. For example, visitors can initially connect to the site as anonymous users and then click a Log In link and be authenticated. In this scenario, the caching profile applied to the user would change.

   The Anonymous Cache Profile drop-down controls which cache profile will be applied to anonymous users.

   The Authenticated Cache Profile drop-down controls which cache profile will be applied to authenticated users.

6. In the Page Output Cache Policy section, shown in Figure 13.18, choose whether to allow subsites that are publishing sites to apply policy settings that are different from the site collection settings and whether to allow page layouts to apply specific cache profiles by checking the appropriate boxes.

Figure 13.18: Page Output Cache Policy

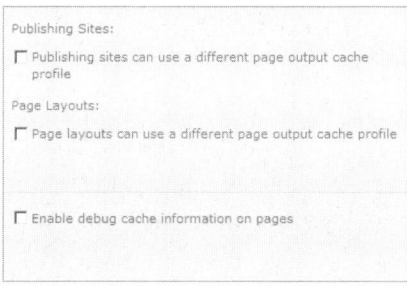

7. In the Enable debug cache information on pages section, choose whether to enable information such as the date and time that the page contents were last rendered.
8. Click OK.

Configuring the Object Cache

The object cache operates separately from the page output cache. The object cache is designed to reduce the traffic between the SharePoint server and the SQL server by capturing in memory, data objects such as lists and libraries, site settings, and page layouts.

To configure the site collection object cache:

1. Open the root site in a site collection.
2. From the Site Actions menu, select Site Settings.
3. In the Site Collection Administration section, click Site Collection Object Cache.
4. In the Object Cache Size section, shown in Figure 13.19, enter the number of megabytes of memory that the object cache will be allowed to use. The amount should be set high enough to ensure that the most commonly used objects will be frequently found in cache. If your system has more than 8 GB of RAM, then it may make sense to increase the object cache size based on the measured performance of the server.

Figure 13.19: Object Cache page

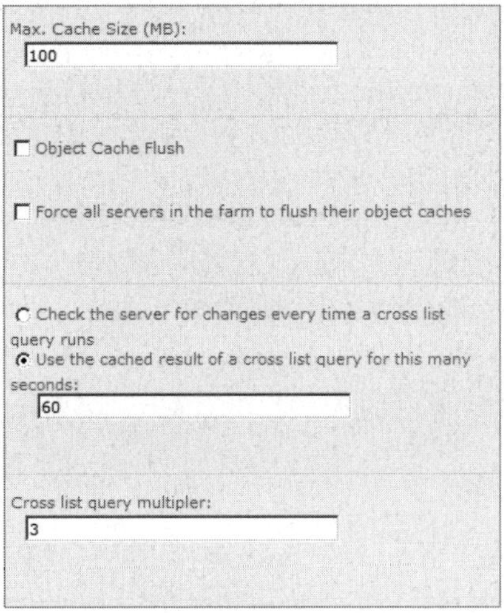

5. Do not make any changes to the Object Cache Reset section at this time. These options are covered later in this section.
6. The Cross List Query Cache Changes section relates to web parts such as the Content Query web part that aggregate content from multiple lists and sites into one view. This operation can be very processor intensive if the query must iterate through many lists. To ensure that the full query is run every time and to display the most accurate results, check the option labeled "Check the server for changes every time a cross list query runs." In cases where the

list content is not likely to change as often, check the box labeled "Use the cached result of a cross list query for this many seconds" and enter the number of seconds to cache the data for. The default value is 60.

7. Use the Cross List Query Results Multiplier value to control the number of results that SharePoint must query to get a valid data set when security trimming is applied. The number represents the multiplier factor of results retrieved above those that will be shown to the user. Larger numbers will return better results if many lists and sites have unique security permissions applied. The default is 3 and valid numbers are 1 to 10.

8. Click OK.

The object cache may need to be cleared at times to ensure that a user is looking at the live data rather than cached data or for testing and troubleshooting purposes. To clear the object cache, do the following:

1. From the Site Actions menu, select Site Settings.

2. In the Site Collection Administration section, click Site Collection Object Cache.

3. In the Object Cache Reset section, check the Object Cache Flush check box to flush the cache for the server that you are currently connected to without affecting other servers in the farm. To clear the cache for all SharePoint servers, check the box labeled "Force all servers in the farm to flush their object caches." These settings will take effect as soon as you click OK.

4. Click OK.

Configuring the BLOB Cache

The term *BLOB* stands for Binary Large Object and refers to any file that is stored as a single object and not converted to text. In most cases, BLOB files are images, audio files, or video files, but a BLOB could also be a document or a spreadsheet. When these types of files are uploaded into a SharePoint site as images on a page, they are stored inside the SQL server content database in BLOB data fields. Because these files tend to be larger in size than the text on the page, retrieving them from the database every time the page loads represents a potential bottleneck in SharePoint performance. The BLOB cache setting can be used by SharePoint to store copies of these files on the file system of the SharePoint web front-end server and to retrieve them from there whenever they are requested as part of a page. A file retrieved in this way can load much faster than when retrieved from the database. While it is possible to enable the BLOB cache for all types of files, this cache is rarely used for documents in collaboration sites because it is important that the latest version of the document always be retrieved from the database. Therefore, BLOB caching is most often used for anonymous websites or sites where most of the users will have read-only permissions.

> **NOTE** BLOB caching is not enabled by default and must be manually configured.

To configure the BLOB cache:

1. Log onto the SharePoint server as a member of the Administrators group.
2. From the Administrative Tools menu, open Internet Information Services (IIS) Manager.
3. On the left side of IIS Manager, expand the server object, then the Sites container, and then expand the web application that you want to configure.
4. Right-click the web application and click Explore to open the file system directory for the web application.
5. Right-click the web.config file and open it with Notepad.
6. In the web.config file, locate the following line:

    ```
    <BlobCache location="C:\BlobCache\14"
    path="\.(gif|jpg|jpeg|jpe|jfif|bmp|dib|tif|tiff|
    ico|png|wdp|hdp|css|js|asf|avi|flv|m4v|mov|mp3|
    mp4|mpeg|mpg|rm|rmvb|wma|wmv)$" maxSize="10"
    enabled="false" />
    ```

    There are several parts to the BlobCache tag that may be modified:

    - location indicates the file system directory on the SharePoint server where the cached files will be stored. This should be set to a folder on a drive that has free space equal at least to the value of the maxSize setting (in GB).
    - path lists all the file extensions that will be cached by the server. The default list can be added to or extensions removed

by editing the line. Ensure that there is a vertical pipe character in between each file type.

- `maxSize` sets the value in gigabytes (GB) of the amount of disk space that the BLOB cache will use. When it exceeds this limit, SharePoint will delete older items in the cache to make room for newer items.
- `enabled` allows SharePoint to use the BLOB cache for this web application when set to `"true"`.

7. Save and close the file.

Configure Content Deployment

SharePoint 2010 Content Deployment enables administrators to copy, or propagate, the contents of an entire source site collection into a destination site collection. The first time a deployment is performed, all objects and contents are copied. In subsequent deployments, only the changes are deployed, making it fast and efficient. Content deployment allows organizations to host an editable "staging" site collection, accessible only to content managers, that is separate from the read-only "production" site collection that most users connect to. The source and destination site collections can be in different farms and even in different domains, allowing for propagation of content from a development or testing environment to a live network environment.

A common content deployment scenario involves an Internet-facing farm that hosts an anonymous site collection on a publicly accessible URL. This farm receives content deployed from a separate, intranet farm that is secured behind a firewall. All content is created and updated on the intranet farm and periodically synchronized to the Internet farm. If the Internet farm fails or is hacked, it is a relatively simple matter to rebuild the SharePoint server and deploy a fresh copy of the content.

In addition to deploying entire site collections, it is also possible to deploy individual subsites and even single pages.

The destination site collection must be created as an empty site collection—that is, a site collection with no site template applied. This is different from the Blank Site template, which is simply a site with no default objects. You can create an empty site collection from within Central Administration by selecting the <Select template later...> template choice on the Custom tab of the Create Site Collection page. Once the deployment has been established, content deployment is always a one-way replication from the source to the destination site collection. Because the replication of changes between the site collections depends on the tracking of specific object and version numbers, making changes to the destination site collection can break the deployment synchronization. Content deployment only copies objects stored in the SharePoint content databases, which includes lists, libraries, pages, images, and so forth. It does not copy any objects or files stored on the file system of the servers, which includes code assemblies and site definitions, as well as features. When items are deployed, the most recent Major and Minor versions are deployed to the destination site.

When setting up the servers that will participate in content deployment, ensure that both the source and the servers in both farms have exactly the same service packs and updates installed on them. While any server in a SharePoint farm can be designated as an export server or an import server, these servers must have the Central Administration Web Application deployed to them in order to process connections. To begin the process of content deployment, both the source and destination farms need to be configured with appropriate settings.

To configure content deployment settings:

1. From SharePoint 2010 Central Administration, click General Application Settings.
2. Under Content Deployment, click Configure Content Deployment.
3. At the top of the Content Deployment Settings page, shown in Figure 13.20, choose Accept Incoming Content Deployment Jobs if you want to allow deployment to this farm. If this server will only be a destination server, then choose Reject Incoming Content Deployment Jobs, which is the default.

Figure 13.20: Accept Content Deployment Jobs settings

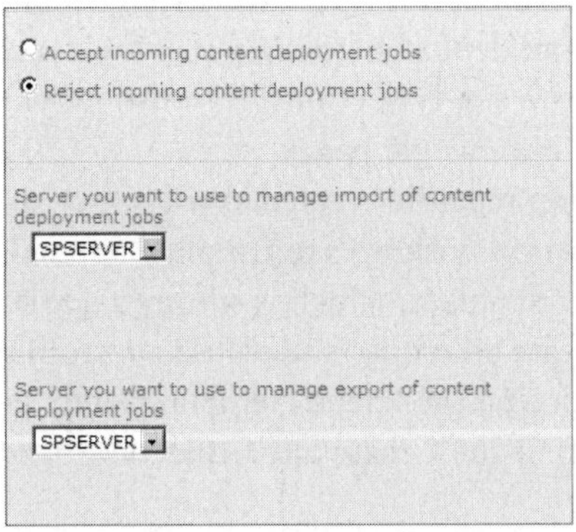

4. Depending on whether this server will be receiving or deploying content, select an import server or export server. This server must be running Central Administration.

5. Under the Connection Security section, shown in Figure 13.21, the Require Encryption (Recommended) setting is selected by default. This setting requires that Central Administration be configured with an SSL certificate and is recommended when the deployment will make use of the Internet for transferring content. If the deployment will be over a secure network or on the intranet, then encryption may not be required. To disable this option, select Do Not Require Encryption.

Figure 13.21: More Content Deployment settings

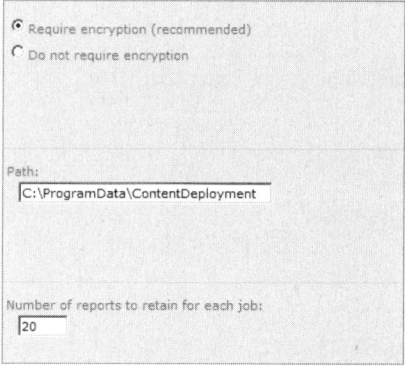

6. Under the Temporary Files section, in the Path box, enter the directory path that will hold the temporary files that contain the compressed content that will be transferred either into or out of this server.

7. In the Reporting section, enter the number of reports that SharePoint will keep for each deployment job. The default value is 20. When this number is reached, the oldest reports will be deleted to make room for newer ones.

8. Click OK.

Configuring Content Deployment Paths

A content deployment path specifies the location of both the source and the destination site collections in a deployment configuration. There may be multiple paths configured that replicate different source site collections to different destinations. The path identifies the authentication method that will be used for connecting to the destination server and the security and identity attributes to deploy.

To configure a content deployment path:

1. From SharePoint 2010 Central Administration, click General Application Settings.

2. Under Content Deployment, click Configure Content Deployment Paths And Jobs.

3. On the Manage Content Deployment Paths And Jobs page, click New Path.

4. On the Create Content Deployment Path page, shown in Figure 13.22, enter a name and description for this path.

Figure 13.22: Create Content Deployment Path page, name and source settings

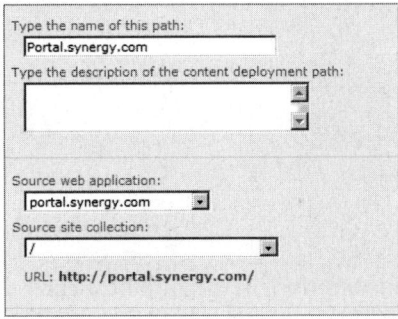

5. In the Source Web Application drop-down list, select the web application that contains the site collection you want to deploy.

6. In the Source Site Collection drop-down list, select the source site collection.

7. In the Destination Central Administration Web Application section, shown in Figure 13.23, enter the URL of the destination Central Administration server. This is required for the source Central Administration server to establish a connection and retrieve a list of available site collections.

Figure 13.23: Specifying the destination Central Administration server

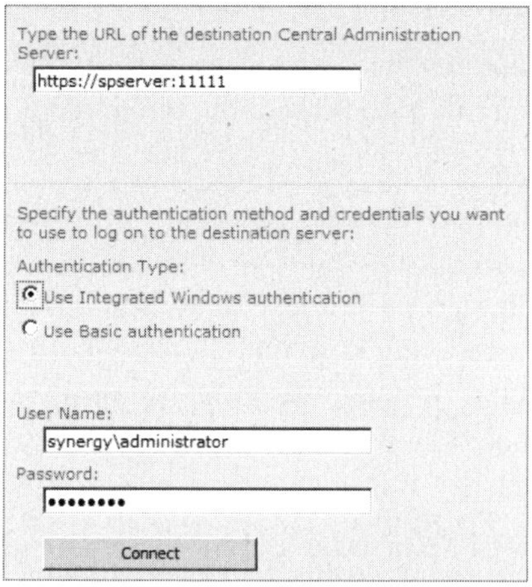

8. In the Authentication Information section, choose the authentication method you want to use. Integrated Windows is the default and most common option. Basic authentication is required if you are establishing a connection through a firewall or proxy server that blocks Windows authentication.

9. Enter the User Name and Password of an account with permissions in the destination Central Administration site, and then click Connect.

    If the authentication is successful, the message Connection Succeeded will appear and the Destination Web Application and Destination Site Collection drop-down lists will be populated.

10. In the Destination Web Application drop-down list, shown in Figure 13.24, select the destination web application.

    Figure 13.24: Destination Web Application and Destination Site Collection drop-down lists

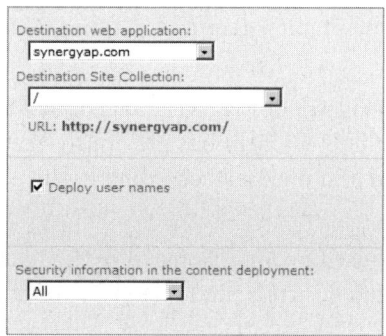

11. In the Destination Site Collection drop-down list, select the destination site collection.

12. Select the Deploy User Names check box to include usernames assigned to content when this path is used for content deployment jobs.

13. In the drop-down list labeled "Security information in the content deployment," you can select what type of security information will be copied along with the content. If the content is being deployed to a server in a different domain that is not trusted by the source server's domain, then any users and groups that are transferred will be unrecognized by the destination domain. The options are as follows:

    All The default option; includes all of the security information that is associated with the content.

    Role Definitions Only Deploys only permission levels, not users and groups.

    None Deploys no security information.

14. Click OK.

Configuring Content Deployment Jobs

A content deployment job defines a schedule for deploying the content from a specific path and determines whether to deploy the entire path content or specific sites within it, the frequency of deployment, and the notifications that will be sent on completion. There are three types of deployment jobs:

Full This deployment type copies all of the content from the source to the destination site collection and overwrites the previously deployed content. Because this job type does not check for changes, it may not delete content from the destination site that was deleted from the source site. This type of job is required in order to deploy new columns and views.

Incremental This type propagates only new, changed, or deleted content. It requires that a full deployment has previously been completed. All content is tracked and updated according to the internal GUID of the object.

Quick Deploy This type is used by SharePoint to deploy individual web pages in between scheduled incremental jobs. Whenever you create a new full or incremental job, a Quick Deploy job is automatically created and scheduled to run every 15 minutes. When a content editor or content manager designates a page for quick deployment, it will be automatically included in the next Quick Deploy execution. Members of the Quick Deploy users group have permissions to flag a web page for quick deployment.

To configure a deployment job:

1. From SharePoint 2010 Central Administration, click General Application Settings.
2. Under Content Deployment, click Configure Content Deployment Paths And Jobs.
3. On the Manage Content Deployment Paths And Jobs page, click New Job.
4. On the Create Content Deployment Job page, shown in Figure 13.25, enter a name and description for this job.

Figure 13.25: Setting the path and scope for a content deployment job

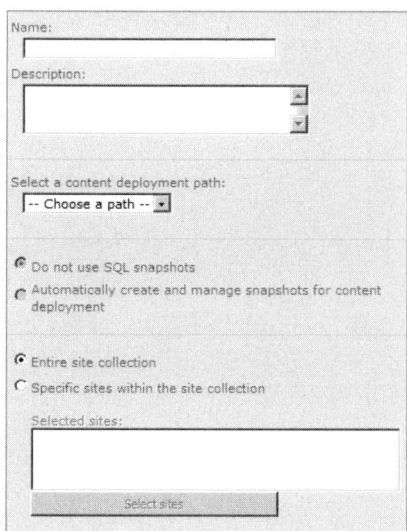

5. In the Select A Content Deployment Path drop-down list, select the path for this job.
6. The SQL Snapshots setting takes advantage of the new Snapshot feature of SQL Server 2008 and 2008 R2. When this option is enabled, a temporary copy of the source content database is created and used by SharePoint during the export phase. This

ensures that deployment will not affect, or be affected by, any users currently editing content. To enable this feature, select the option Automatically Create And Manage Snapshots For Content Deployment.

7. In the Scope section, configure the job to deploy either the entire site collection (the default) or to deploy specific sites within the site collection. To specify sites, select the option Specific Sites Within The Site Collection and click the Select Sites button to choose the sites you want to include.

8. In the Frequency section, shown in Figure 13.26, check the box labeled "Run this job on the following schedule," and choose a schedule.

Figure 13.26: Job Frequency options

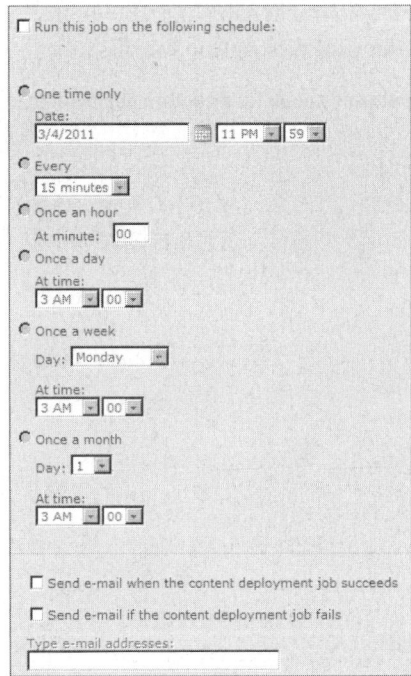

9. Choose the notification emails you want generated. Email can be generated when the content deployment job succeeds and if the content deployment job fails. Then enter an email address for the notification to go to.

10. Click OK.

PART III
Managing SharePoint 2010

IN THIS PART

CHAPTER 14: Managing Security 423

CHAPTER 15: Managing Auditing, Monitoring, and Analytics 449

CHAPTER 16: Managing Backup and Restore 473

14
Managing Security

IN THIS CHAPTER, YOU WILL LEARN TO:

▶ **CONFIGURE FARM-LEVEL SECURITY (Pages 424 – 430)**
- Configuring Farm Administrators (Page 424)
- Configuring Managed Accounts (Page 426)
- Configuring Service Accounts (Page 430)

▶ **CONFIGURE WEB APPLICATION SECURITY (Pages 430 – 436)**
- Configuring Web Application Policies (Page 431)
- Configuring Permission Policy Levels (Page 433)
- Managing Anonymous Access (Page 434)
- Configuring Antivirus Settings (Page 435)

▶ **CONFIGURE SITE COLLECTION SECURITY (Pages 436 – 447)**
- Adding or Removing Site Collection Administrators (Page 437)
- Creating Permission Levels (Page 438)
- Managing SharePoint Groups (Page 440)
- Managing Permission Inheritance (Page 442)
- Managing Permissions (Page 444)

In most organizations, security is an important part of protecting SharePoint content. For others such as governments, security may be mandated by regulation. In this chapter, we will look at how to secure SharePoint and its content from the top of the farm to a single item, and all levels in between.

Configure Farm-Level Security

Farm-level security covers broad-stroke security adjustments to the farm and service applications. This section first introduces how to delegate administrative duties to other farm administrators. We then introduce managed accounts and provide the steps for creating, editing, and deleting these accounts. Lastly, you'll see how you can assign managed accounts to SharePoint components.

> **NOTE** A strong security posture also includes securing the server along with the ports and protocols used. An excellent starting resource is the article "Plan Security Hardening (SharePoint Server 2010)" on TechNet at http://technet.microsoft.com/en-us/library/cc262849.aspx.

Configuring Farm Administrators

Farm administrators are responsible for keeping the farm and its web applications and site collections functional. It is a highly privileged role that must be granted carefully. By and large, a farm administrator's power extends to most administrative duties in Central Administration. However, there are limits to what a farm administrator can do if they are not also a local Windows administrator on the server where the Central Administration web application is being run. Specifically, a farm administrator who is not a local administrator cannot perform these actions:

- Start and stop SharePoint services
- Configure incoming email
- Create, delete, or extend a web application
- Change authentication settings for a web application
- Back up or restore a farm

Additionally, a farm administrator does not implicitly have access to all site collections, but a farm administrator can obtain access by making themselves a site collection administrator.

This section describes how to add and remove farm administrators, and how to grant PowerShell access to farm administrators.

Adding or Removing a Farm Administrator

SharePoint allows multiple farm administrators, and membership can be granted to a user or AD security group. To grant farm administrator privileges using Central Administration:

1. Click Security and then select Manage The Farm Administrators Group.

2. In the list of current farm administrators, click New ➢ Add Users.

3. In the Grant Permissions dialog box, enter the name of one or more users or AD security groups. You can add multiple users and/or groups by separating them with a semicolon.

4. Click OK to save your changes.

Removing a user from the farm administrators group can be done from the same screen. Here's how:

1. Click Security and then select Manage The Farm Administrators Group.

2. In the list of current farm administrators, select the group or user you want to remove.

3. Click Actions ➢ Remove Users from Group.

> **NOTE** SharePoint allows you to delegate access so that users can only administer service applications from inside Central Administration. How to do this is covered in Chapter 4, "Creating Service Applications."

Granting PowerShell Access to Farm Administrators

While Central Administration is commonly used for many day-to-day operations, PowerShell is an incredibly powerful way to administer and automate SharePoint functions from a command-line interface. For reasons having to do with database authentication and OS permissions, a farm administrator does not automatically have permissions to run PowerShell cmdlets.

To grant permissions for others to run PowerShell cmdlets, use the Add-SPShellAdmin cmdlet. This command grants necessary permissions on SharePoint servers, the configuration database, and optionally, a SharePoint content database. Here is the basic syntax for the command:

```
Add-SPShellAdmin <Domain\UserName> [-database ↵
<SPDatabasePipeBind>]
```

If you run the command without specifying a database, the user is only granted access to the farm—specifically, the configuration database and the Central Administration content database—but not any other content databases. To be able to run cmdlets within a content database (for example, to use Get-SPWeb to work with a website), the user must be granted access to the content database by using the -database switch. The following grants a user shell access to one content database:

```
$db = Get-SPContentDatabase SP_Portal_Content
Add-SPShellAdmin -username synergy\afuller -database $db
```

To grant a user shell access to all content databases, you can use a script such as this one:

```
ForEach ($db in (Get-SPContentDatabase)) ↵
{Add-SPShellAdmin -username synergy\afuller -database $db}
```

To revoke PowerShell access, use the Remove-SPShellAdmin cmdlet.

> **NOTE** To grant PowerShell access using the Add-SPShellAdmin cmdlet, you must be a farm administrator, a local administrator on the server where the command is run, a securityadmin on the database server(s) you are granting permission to, *and* a database owner (dbo) on the database(s).

Configuring Managed Accounts

Managed accounts are AD accounts that SharePoint uses for the farm account, service applications, and application pools. SharePoint securely stores the password for each managed account and can regularly change the password if needed. The benefits that managed accounts offer include the following:

- A farm administrator does not need to know an account's password when provisioning services.
- SharePoint can be set up to automatically change an account's password on a recurring schedule.
- An account's password can be set to automatically change if it will expire prior to the next scheduled password change.
- Email notification is sent when an account's password will be changed.

NOTE Not every SharePoint function uses managed accounts. For example, the Default Content Access Account, which is used to crawl content for the Search Service Application, is a regular, unmanaged account.

When you create a new web application, you must define which managed account you will use for the application pool. The same is true when creating most service applications. Thus, it's best to have your managed accounts ready to go prior to provisioning web or service applications.

Creating a New Managed Account

Managed accounts can be created with Central Administration or PowerShell. Before creating a managed account, be sure that the account has been created in AD, either in the same domain in which SharePoint is installed or in a trusted domain. You must also know the account's current password.

To create a new managed account with Central Administration, follow these steps:

1. Click Security and then select Configure Managed Accounts.
2. In the new page, the list of existing managed accounts is displayed. Click the Register Managed Account link to create a new one.
3. For Service Account Credentials, shown in Figure 14.1, enter the account's AD username. It is best to use the *domain\username* format.

Figure 14.1: Creating a managed account

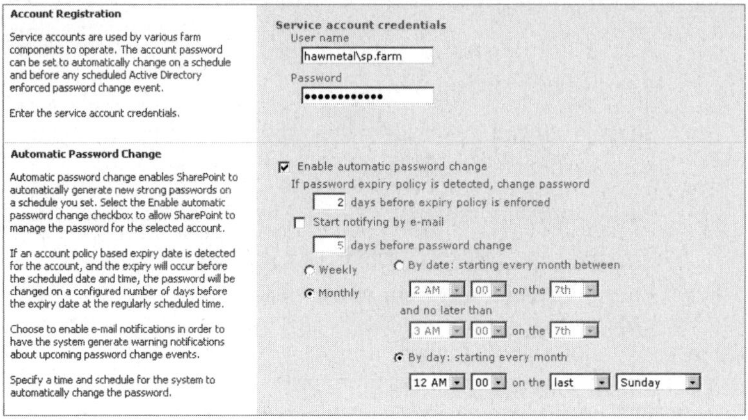

4. Specify the account's password.

5. If you want SharePoint to automatically change this account's password on a regular schedule (weekly or monthly), check the Enable Automatic Password Change check box.

6. Specify when to change the password relative to the expiry policy. The default is 2 days. This is applied only if the password is set to expire in AD (as defined by group policy) before SharePoint's next scheduled password change date.

7. If you want SharePoint to send an email notification before the password is scheduled to change, check the Start Notifying By E-mail check box and specify the number of days before the password change you want to be notified.

8. Specify the schedule for the password change. You can change the password weekly or monthly and specify a time range. You should set changes to occur during scheduled downtime or during light usage, because the password changes will cause momentary service interruptions as application pools are restarted.

9. Click OK to save the new managed account. After the account is saved, you are returned to the list of managed accounts. The date and time for the next password change is shown if you enabled Automatic Password Change.

To create a managed account using PowerShell, use the New-SPManagedAccount cmdlet.

SharePoint sends password change notifications to a single email address. We suggest that you make this an actively monitored account. Here is how you can use Central Administration to set this email address:

1. Click Security and then select Configure Password Change Settings.

2. In the Notification E-Mail Address text box, enter the email address. If you want the notification to go to multiple users, be sure this is a distribution list or group email address.

3. Click OK to save your changes.

Editing a Managed Account

To edit an existing managed account using Central Administration, follow these steps:

1. Click Security and then select Configure Managed Accounts.

2. The list of existing managed accounts is displayed. Click the edit icon for the managed account.

3. Make changes to the account. For details about the settings you can make, see the previous section, "Creating a New Managed Account."

4. Click OK to save your changes.

To edit a managed account using PowerShell, use the Set-SPManagedAccount cmdlet.

Removing a Managed Account

Before removing a managed account, you should first make sure this managed account is not associated with any SharePoint services or application pools. To determine if it is in use, edit the managed account and look at the Account Information section to see what farm components are using this account.

Once you've confirmed the account is not in use, here is how you can use Central Administration to remove the account.

1. Click Security and then select Configure Managed Accounts.

2. Click the delete icon for the managed account you want to remove.

3. In the Remove Managed Account page, confirm the correct account is selected and click OK.

To remove a managed account using PowerShell, use the `Remove-SPManagedAccount` cmdlet.

To learn more about managed accounts and their passwords, see the article "Updating Passwords on SharePoint 2010" located here:

http://blogs.technet.com/b/seanearp/archive/2011/01/25/updating-passwords-on-sharepoint-2010.aspx

Configuring Service Accounts

From time to time, you may need to make an account change to one of your SharePoint services or application pools after it has been created. For example, you might need to change the application pool account for one of your web applications. This can be easily done in SharePoint from a single screen, and this change is automatically propagated to all WFE and application servers in your farm.

Here's how you can make this type of change:

1. Click Security and then select Configure Service Accounts.
2. In the drop-down list, select the SharePoint component that you want to change.
3. Select the managed account that you want this component to use.
4. Click OK to save your changes.

These changes are immediately propagated to farm servers and may cause a short period of downtime, depending on the component that was changed. Therefore, it is best to adjust this during scheduled downtime or during light usage.

Configure Web Application Security

Web application security settings apply to the whole web application and can override permissions within the web application's site collections. In this section, we'll look at controlling what permissions can be assigned, adjusting a web application policy, configuring anonymous access, and configuring antivirus settings.

Before we start, let's define two important terms that are used when managing SharePoint permissions:

Base Permission A *base permission* is a very small unit of access, such as Override Check Out. SharePoint has 33 different built-in base permissions that are organized into three categories: List Permissions, Site Permissions, and Personal Permissions. Since these are so fine-grained, you cannot grant base permissions directly to a user or group. You also cannot create new base permissions. In fact, you only work with base permissions when constructing permission levels.

Permission Level A *permission level*, sometimes called a *role*, is a collection of base permissions. Examples of built-in permission levels include Full Control, Contribute, and Read. When assigning access to users, you do so by granting permission levels. SharePoint lets you create custom permission levels.

Configuring Web Application Policies

A web application policy is a set of permission levels that either grant or deny permissions to a set of users. Permissions defined at the web application level cascade across all site collections in the web application. By default, a web application has these four permission policy levels defined:

- Full Control
- Full Read
- Deny Write
- Deny All

Granting a permission level supplements any existing permissions. For example, if a user has Contribute (read/write) access to some websites and no access to others, granting the Full Read permission gives the user read access to all websites in all site collections. The user also retains Contribute access where it was granted.

Denying a permission level revokes existing permissions. For example, applying Deny All to a user prevents any and all access to a web application and all its site collections, even if the user had permissions on those sites previously.

Permissions granted at the web application level are not visible within site collections and thus are hidden from site collection administrators.

A practical example on where this is useful is in auditing. Granting Full Read permissions to auditors ensures they can access all content in the web application without site collection administrators being involved.

> **NOTE** Adjusting the web application policy is the only way to deny some form of access across SharePoint. SharePoint does not support the ability to deny within a single site collection.

To access the user policy for a web application using Central Administration:

1. Click Application Management, and then select Manage Web Applications.

2. Highlight the web application and click the User Policy button in the ribbon.

3. The current user policy for the web application is displayed as shown in Figure 14.2. If you have configured a Search service application, you'll notice that SharePoint uses the user policy to grant full read access to your search crawling accounts.

Figure 14.2: Policy for web application

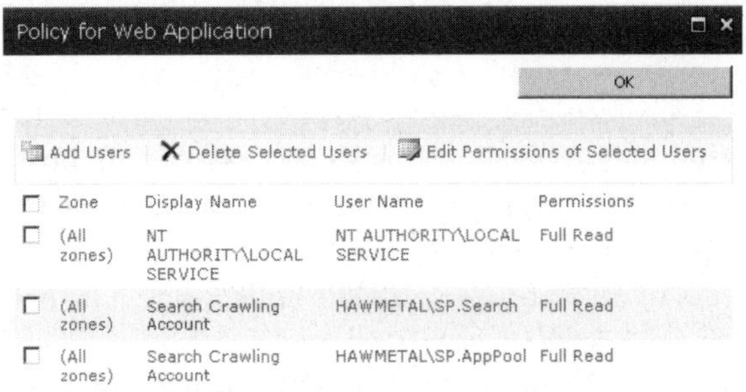

	Zone	Display Name	User Name	Permissions
☐	(All zones)	NT AUTHORITY\LOCAL SERVICE	NT AUTHORITY\LOCAL SERVICE	Full Read
☐	(All zones)	Search Crawling Account	HAWMETAL\SP.Search	Full Read
☐	(All zones)	Search Crawling Account	HAWMETAL\SP.AppPool	Full Read

Once you are viewing the user policy, you can do the following tasks:

- To remove a defined policy, select the policy and click the Delete Selected Users link. Confirm the action when prompted.

- To add a new policy, click the Add Users link. Then perform the following steps:
  1. Select All Zones or a single zone for the web application and click Next. When applying a user policy, you can limit it to a single zone, such as Internet. To learn more about zones, see Chapter 2, "Creating and Managing Web Applications."
  2. Choose the users or groups from AD or from your designated authentication provider. Multiple users or groups can be selected.
  3. Check the permission policy levels that you want to apply. If custom permission policy levels (covered in the next section) exist, they can also be selected.
  4. Optionally, select the Account Operates As System check box. This means that if a user creates or modifies an item in this web application, the Created By and Modified By entries will not show the user's name but instead contain System Account.
  5. Click Finish to save the users or groups added.
- To edit one or more existing policies, check the policy entries and click the Edit Permissions Of Selected Users link. In the Edit Users dialog box, adjust the permissions as needed and click Save when finished.

WARNING Adjusting permissions at the web application level is very powerful and should be used with caution. Any changes made here immediately affect the user interface within site collections, and this may cause confusion or frustration among users. We advise you test any changes you wish to make in a test environment or on a test web application to be sure the behavior is what you expect.

Configuring Permission Policy Levels

A SharePoint permission policy level is a custom set of grant or deny base permissions that can be applied when configuring the web application policy. As covered in the previous section, a web application has four built-in permission policy levels by default, and SharePoint allows you to add custom ones. For example, you might want to create a custom permission policy level that prevents users from just deleting items.

To create a new permission policy level using Central Administration:

1. Click Application Management, and then select Manage Web Applications.
2. Highlight the web application and click the Permission Policy button in the ribbon.
3. The current permission policy levels are displayed. Click Add Permission Policy Level to create a new one.
4. In the Add Permission Policy Level dialog box, enter the name and optional description for this policy.
5. Optionally, specify if this policy level grants Site Collection Administrator or Site Collection Auditor (full read) rights.
6. As appropriate, check the Grant or Deny permission boxes.
7. Click Save to save the new permission policy level.

Managing Anonymous Access

Anonymous access allows nonauthenticated (that is, guest) users to access a SharePoint web application. Anonymous access is commonly used for Internet-based websites but can also be used in an intranet. Anonymous access can be turned on when creating the web application or enabled at a later time on a single web application zone. Anonymous access can be enabled whether you are using Claims or Classic authentication.

> **NOTE** SharePoint allows you to have anonymous access in addition to authenticated access, and using both together has its advantages. Take, for example, an extranet that is public facing. Anonymous guests can use the website to get limited read access to some content. By logging in (do so by clicking the Sign In button, located by default in the upper-right corner), you become an authenticated user and then receive access to private areas.

Anonymous access is controlled at the zone level for a web application. To enable anonymous access for a particular zone, follow these steps using Central Administration:

1. Click Application Management, and then select Manage Web Applications.
2. Highlight the web application and click the Authentication Providers button in the ribbon.
3. In the Authentication Providers dialog box, select the zone on which you want to allow anonymous access.
4. In the Edit Authentication dialog box, enable the check box labeled Enable Anonymous Access.
5. Click Save. These changes are propagated to each WFE server.

By default, anonymous users have no access to site collections until it is granted. Therefore, once anonymous access has been enabled, you must set what permissions anonymous users have. This is usually done within each site collection, as covered in the "Managing Permissions" section later in this chapter. However, as a web application administrator, you can place some restrictions on what level of access anonymous users can receive. This is done through the Anonymous Policy. Through this policy, you can either deny write access or deny all access to anonymous users. As with other web application policies, these settings take precedence over what has been defined within each site collection.

To set the Anonymous Policy, follow these steps using Central Administration:

1. Click Application Management, and then select Manage Web Applications.
2. Highlight the web application and click the Anonymous Policy button in the ribbon.
3. Select either All Zones or a specific zone.
4. Select the anonymous policy to apply. Your three choices are None, Deny Write, and Deny All.
5. Click Save to save your changes.

Configuring Antivirus Settings

SharePoint does not have built-in virus-scanning software. However, SharePoint can integrate with third-party products that are compatible with the Virus Scanning application programming interface (VS API). After a compatible third-party product is installed, SharePoint can automatically call into the product's virus-scanning engine when users upload or download documents. This ensures SharePoint's documents remain virus free.

When installing an antivirus product, be sure to install it on each WFE server in your farm.

Using Central Administration, you can configure when a document scan is done, and whether or not SharePoint should attempt to have an infected document cleaned. Any settings you adjust apply to the whole farm. Here's how you can adjust the antivirus settings:

1. Click Security, and then select Manage Antivirus Settings.

2. To tell SharePoint to scan each uploaded file, select Scan Documents On Upload.

3. To tell SharePoint to scan each file downloaded, select Scan Documents On Download.

4. If necessary, enable Allow Users To Download Infected Documents. This is not usually advised but may be needed if you regularly get false positives from your antivirus engine. (A false positive occurs when an antivirus engine flags a clean file as infected.)

5. If desired, enable Attempt To Clean Infected Documents.

6. Optionally, adjust the Antivirus Time Out value. The default value is 300 seconds and should only be decreased if you are experiencing performance problems or as recommended by the antivirus product.

7. Optionally, adjust the Antivirus Threads setting. The default value is 5 threads and should only be adjusted as recommended by the antivirus product.

8. Click OK to save your changes.

Configure Site Collection Security

While permissions can be granted to multiple site collections through the web application policy as covered in previous sections, this is only used for special cases. Users are authenticated at the web application level, and authorization is usually done at a site collection level. In other words, for regular, day-to-day permission management, permissions are assigned via individual site collections.

By default, permissions are inherited or cascade down to all websites, lists, and libraries in the site collection hierarchy. Thus, permissions granted to the top-level website also apply to a document buried deep within a site collection. As you will learn in successive sections, this inheritance can be broken.

Adding or Removing Site Collection Administrators

A site collection administrator has full control permissions over a site collection. The purpose of this role is to delegate the day-to-day management of a site collection to others in the organization, usually non-IT personnel. This concept is covered more thoroughly in Chapter 3, "Creating and Managing Site Collections." This section describes how to add and remove site collection administrators to and from site collections.

There are three ways site collection administration rights can be assigned or removed:

- Through the web application policy, as covered in the previous section. Keep in mind, this sets site collection administration permissions to all site collections in the web application.

- By changing the site collection administrators in Central Administration. This approach allows you to define a maximum of two site collection administrators for a single site collection.

- Through the Site Settings page for the top-level website within the site collection. This allows you to grant as many site collection administrators as needed.

> **NOTE** A site collection administrator's permissions in a site collection can only be revoked by using a web application policy. Assuming this type of policy is not in force, a site collection administrator always has full control access to all websites, lists, and libraries in the site collection, even if not specifically granted.

To change, add, or remove site collection administrators using Central Administration, follow these steps:

1. Click Application Management, and then select Change Site Collection Administrators.

2. In the Site Collection box shown in Figure 14.3, change the selected site collection if needed. When changing this, you must first select the web application and then the site collection.

Figure 14.3: Managing site collection administrators

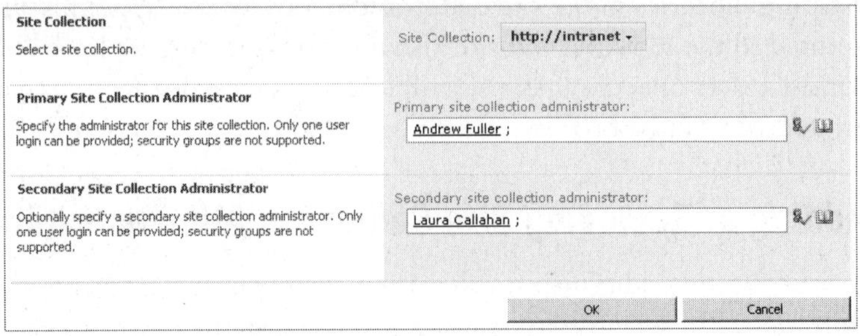

3. The primary and secondary site collection administrators are shown. Accounts specified here must be individual users, not security groups. If two administrators are already assigned, you must remove one of them before you can assign another, or grant access one of the other two ways. As a general rule, it's best to have two site collection administrators for each site collection.

4. Click OK to save your changes.

Site collection administrators can also be granted from within the site collection. To use this option, you must already have access to the site collection as a site collection administrator. So, for example, if a farm administrator does not have access to a site collection and must grant themselves access, this approach cannot be used.

To manage site collection administrators from within the site collection, follow these steps:

1. Access the site collection and connect to the top-level website.

2. Select Site Actions ➢ Site Settings.

3. In the Users And Permissions category, select Site Collection Administrators.

4. Add, change, or remove site collection administrators as needed. As before, only individual users can be specified. More than two administrators can be assigned.

5. Click OK to save changes.

Creating Permission Levels

When assigning permissions to users or groups, you do so by granting permission levels. Each site collection has its own built-in set of permission levels such as Full Control, Design, Contribute, and Read, and you can create custom ones. Recall from the definition in the "Configure Web Application Security" section that a permission level is a collection of base permissions. While you do not grant base permissions directly, you can indirectly do so by creating a custom permission level that includes the base permissions.

A practical example is that you want users to be able to view, create, and edit content but not delete. In other words, you want them to have all of the Contribute base permissions except delete. You can do so by creating a custom permission level and removing the Delete Items base permission. As with all aspects of permission assignments, we advise you to follow the principle of least privilege where possible. This means that you should only grant permissions that are necessary to get the job done.

> **NOTE** SharePoint does allow you to modify the built-in permission levels, but this usually causes confusion and is not recommended.

Here is how you can create a custom permission level.

1. Access the site collection and connect to the top-level website.
2. Select Site Actions ➢ Site Permissions.
3. In the ribbon, select Permission Levels
4. The current permission levels for this site collection are shown. You can either copy an existing permission level and modify it or create a new one from scratch.

   - To copy and modify an existing permission level, click the permission level and then click the Copy Permission Level button.
   - To create a new permission level from scratch, click the Add A Permission Level link.

5. Provide the name and description for the permission level.
6. In the list of base permissions, check those that you want to include in this permission level. Keep in mind that some base permissions are mutually inclusive, so that if you include one permission, it may automatically include others.
7. Click Create to save the new permission level.

Managing SharePoint Groups

A group organizes users to simplify permission assignments. For example, if you have 10 users who all need the same access to a website, it is easier to place the users in a group and give the group permission than to give permissions to each user individually.

When granting permissions, SharePoint supports two different types of groups: SharePoint groups and external groups from your authentication provider, such as AD security groups. SharePoint groups are specific to a site collection and are stored in the top-level website. SharePoint groups cannot be nested, so you cannot place one SharePoint group within another. However, external groups can be placed within SharePoint groups.

Default SharePoint Groups

When creating a site collection, default SharePoint groups are created, which vary depending on the site template selected. The most common ones, however, are shown in Table 14.1.

Table 14.1: Default SharePoint groups and their permissions

SharePoint Group Name	Default Permissions
Visitors	Read
Members	Contribute
Owners	Full Control

Creating a New SharePoint Group

New SharePoint groups can also be created to suit your needs. Here are the steps to create a new group:

1. Click Site Actions ➤ Site Permissions.
2. In the ribbon, click Create Group.
3. The Create Group page is displayed. Enter a meaningful name for the group. The name will be seen when granting permissions.
4. In the About Me section, optionally, provide a description.
5. Specify the owner of the group. This field defaults to the website owner. The owner is able to manage group membership.
6. Define who can view the membership of the group—everyone or just group members.

7. Define who can edit the membership of the group—the Group Owner only, or Group Members. (No matter what setting you use here, any user with Full Control access to the top-level website, including site collection administrators, can also manage group membership.)

8. Decide whether users can request to be added or removed from the group.

9. Decide whether membership requests are automatically accepted. For security reasons, this should be used cautiously.

10. If you are allowing requests to join/leave the group, enter an email address where requests should be sent. This is usually the address of the group owner.

11. Optionally, grant the permission levels shown for the current website. These permissions can also be granted after the group is created.

12. Click Create to create the group.

NOTE Regardless of which website you're working with when you create a SharePoint group, the group is stored in the top-level website and applies to the whole site collection.

Adding Users and Groups to SharePoint Groups

Users and external groups from your authentication provider (for example, AD), can be added to SharePoint groups. Users and groups you add receive the same permissions as other members of the SharePoint group. Here are the steps:

1. Click Site Actions ➤ Site Settings.

2. In the Users And Permissions category, click People And Groups.

3. In the left navigation area, select the SharePoint group. If the group is not listed, click the More link and then select the group.

4. Click New ➤ Add Users.

5. In the Grant Permissions dialog box, specify the users and/or external groups that you want to add. These groups can only be groups from your authentication provider, not SharePoint groups.

6. Optionally, send a welcome email to these users.

7. Click OK to save changes.

Users can also be added to groups when granting permissions. This is described in the "Managing Permissions" section later in this chapter.

Managing Permission Inheritance

By default, when a site collection is built with subsites, lists, libraries, folders, and items, a single set of permissions is shared throughout. These permissions are set in the top-level website, and they are inherited by all content that falls underneath this top-level website. This concept is called *permission inheritance*. For example, a user who has Read permissions to the top-level website will also have Read permissions to document libraries throughout the site collection.

While this inheritance is convenient because it's easy to manage, there will be situations where some content must be secured separately. This requires breaking inheritance. When you break inheritance, you create a new set of permissions which apply to the level where you set them and also to all levels underneath that one.

SharePoint allows you to break inheritance at four different levels: websites, lists/libraries, folders, and individual items. See Figure 14.4 for an example on how this works:

Figure 14.4: Permission inheritance

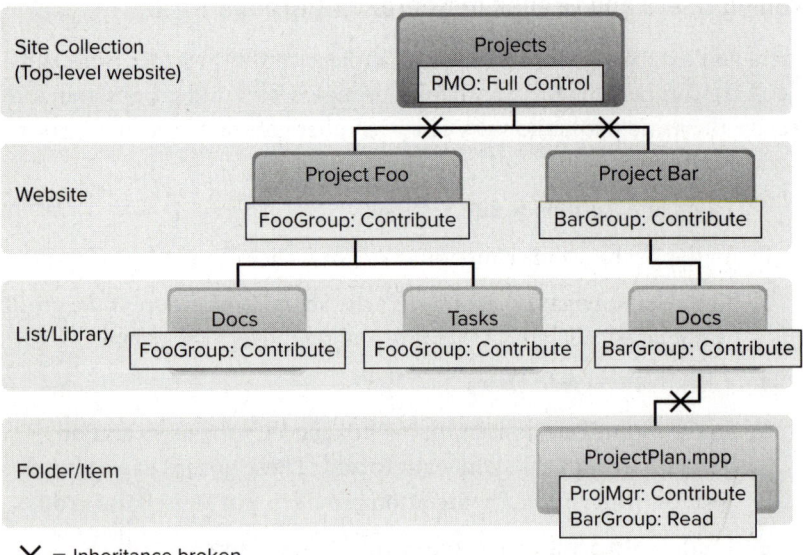

While breaking inheritance gives you needed flexibility, you don't want to break permissions more than necessary. There are two primary reasons for this:

- Breaking permission inheritance extensively adds complexity and requires more time to manage permissions and troubleshoot permissions-related problems.

- Breaking inheritance affects SharePoint's performance. To maintain peak performance, avoid breaking permissions more than 1,000 times within a single level (items in a folder, folders in a library, or same-level subsites). For example, it would be a poor design choice to store thousands of uniquely secured task items in a tasks list.

TIP For more guidance on the performance implications when you break inheritance, see the whitepaper "Best Practices for Using Fine-Grained Permissions," which you can download from www.microsoft.com/downloads/en/details.aspx?FamilyID=8176a682-45e9-4d28-b161-5aac4056ed53.

Breaking permissions is done exactly the same way for the different objects (websites, lists/libraries, folders, items) once you are on the permissions page for the object. Here is how to get to the permissions page for each type of object:

- Website permissions: select Site Actions ➢ Site Permissions.
- List or library permissions:
  1. Connect to the list or library.
  2. Above the ribbon, click the List (or Library) tab.
  3. In the ribbon, click List (or Library) Permissions.
- Folder, list item, or document permissions:
  1. In the list or library view, hover over the folder or item and click the down arrow that appears.
  2. In the context menu, select Manage Permissions.

Once you are on the permissions page for the object, follow these steps to break inheritance for it:

1. In the ribbon, select Stop Inheriting Permissions.

2. SharePoint notifies you that you are about to create unique permissions. Click OK to confirm. SharePoint copies the permissions that are granted to the parent and assigns them to the current object. At this point, you can add and remove permissions as needed.

SharePoint also allows you to reestablish permission inheritance after it has been broken. The steps are the same whether it is a website, list, library, folder, or item object. Here's what you do:

1. Access the permissions page for the object, as described in the previous steps.
2. In the ribbon, click Inherit Permissions.
3. SharePoint notifies you that you are changing to inherited permissions. Any custom permissions that you assigned to this object will be lost. Click OK to confirm.

Managing Permissions

Managing permissions involves granting and removing permissions on a securable SharePoint object (website, list, library, folder or item) to a user or group (called a *principal*). Permissions can only be set on the top-level website or an object where permission inheritance has been broken. There are three primary ways that permissions can be granted within a site collection:

- Granting permissions directly to a SharePoint group. We recommend this approach if the SharePoint group already contains appropriate members or membership can be easily changed.
- Granting permissions directly to an external group (for example, an AD global group). We recommend this approach if the group has appropriate members or it will be used across multiple site collections. This is also the best choice from a performance standpoint if you have many users.
- Granting permissions directly to one or more users. We recommend this approach only in special, one-off situations.

The steps are the same, regardless of the object type, once you are on the permissions page for the object. Here are the steps to grant permissions to users:

1. Access the permissions page for the object (as described in the previous section). The current permissions for the object are listed.

2. To grant new permissions, click the Grant Permissions button in the ribbon.

3. The Grant Permissions dialog box appears. For Select Users, enter the users and/or groups (you can select both SharePoint and external groups) that you want to grant permissions to.

4. For Grant Permissions, either add users to an existing SharePoint group or grant permissions directly:

    - If you will just be adding users to a SharePoint group, select the SharePoint group and make sure no SharePoint groups are listed in the Select Users section.

    - To Grant Users Permissions Directly, click that radio button. The list of permission levels for the site collection will appear. Check the permission levels you with to grant.

5. Optionally, send a welcome email to these new users.

6. Click OK to save changes.

To remove permissions from users or groups:

1. Access the permissions page for the object (as described in the previous section).

2. Select the principals that you want to revoke access from.

3. In the ribbon, click Remove User Permissions.

4. Confirm the action when prompted.

You can also edit existing permissions that have been granted. Here are the steps:

1. Access the permissions page for the object (as described in the previous section).

2. Select the principals that you want to edit.

3. In the ribbon, click Edit User Permissions.

4. In the dialog box, check the new permission levels you want to grant. All existing permissions are removed and these new permission levels are granted.

5. Click OK to save your changes.

Granting Anonymous Access

If the web application is configured to allow anonymous access, you can adjust what permissions should be granted to anonymous users. Granting anonymous access should be used with caution as it allows *any* user (even Internet users if the web application is accessible) some degree of access to content within the site collection.

Here is how you can grant anonymous access:

1. Access the permissions page for the object (as described in the "Managing Permission Inheritance" section).

2. In the ribbon, click the Anonymous Access button. If this button is unavailable, the web application is not configured to allow anonymous access.

3. Choose what permissions to grant to anonymous users:

    - If you are adjusting a website's permissions, your choices are either Entire Web Site, Lists And Libraries, or Nothing. If you select Entire Web Site, anonymous users will have read access to all content in this website and subsites that inherit permissions. If you select Lists and Libraries, anonymous users have no access to the website and can only directly access lists or libraries where inheritance is broken and anonymous permissions have been granted. If you select Nothing, anonymous users have no access to any content in this website.

    - If you are adjusting a list's permissions, your choices are Add Items, Edit Items, Delete Items, and View Items.

    - If you are adjusting a library's permissions, you can only grant View Items.

4. Click OK to save.

Checking User Permissions

When troubleshooting permission problems or trying to validate access, SharePoint has a very useful Check Permissions report that displays the permissions granted to a user or group. Here is how you can run this report:

1. Access the permissions page for the object (as described in the "Managing Permission Inheritance" section).

Configure Site Collection Security   **447**

2. In the ribbon, click the Check Permissions button.
3. In the dialog box, enter a user or group.
4. Click the Check Now button. The permissions are immediately displayed, as shown in Figure 14.5.

Figure 14.5: Check Permissions report

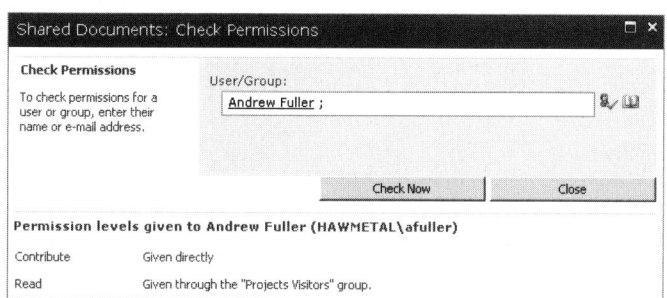

15

Managing Auditing, Monitoring, and Analytics

IN THIS CHAPTER, YOU WILL LEARN TO:

▶ **MANAGE AUDITING AND AUDIT REPORTS** (Pages 450 – 457)
- Configuring Site Collection Auditing (Page 451)
- Managing Audit Log Growth and Size (Page 453)
- Viewing Audit Reports (Page 454)

▶ **CONFIGURE WEB ANALYTICS REPORTING** (Pages 457 – 463)
- Configuring Web Analytics (Page 457)
- Viewing Analytics Reports (Page 459)

▶ **USE THE HEALTH ANALYZER** (Pages 463 – 466)
- Reviewing Problems and Solutions (Page 464)
- Reviewing Rule Definitions (Page 466)

▶ **CONFIGURE DIAGNOSTIC LOGGING** (Pages 466 – 470)
- Working with the Event Log (Page 467)
- Working with the Trace Log (Page 468)
- Configuring Diagnostic Logging Settings (Page 469)

▶ **MANAGE TIMER JOBS** (Pages 470 – 472)
- Viewing Timer Jobs (Page 471)
- Running a Timer Job (Page 472)
- Managing Timer Job Schedules (Page 472)

In any system that stores important and sometimes sensitive information, it is necessary to be able to track activity and report on user actions. This information may be required to identify a violation or simply to validate that documents meet a compliance requirement. In this chapter, we'll explain how SharePoint 2010 auditing meets this need.

Another key aspect of running any web system is to understand the number of people who are using it and what they are using it for. These reports can be used to identify patterns of high and low usage and growth trends in the system. We'll examine the usage analysis reporting features of SharePoint 2010 that provide this information.

An important part of maintaining a successful SharePoint server farm is to identify problems and issues before they occur. We will introduce you to a sophisticated health monitoring system in SharePoint 2010 that provides rule-based analysis of potential problems. When problems do occur, it is essential to be able to quickly obtain detailed information about them. In this chapter, we will explore how to use the diagnostic logging feature of SharePoint 2010 to identify problems and track them to their source.

All of the monitoring features in this chapter, and many of the features described throughout this book, depend on scheduled timer jobs to gather and process data. We'll look at how to manage the frequency of these timer jobs and how to execute them manually when needed.

Manage Auditing and Audit Reports

The ability to record and report the actions that users take in SharePoint is vital for establishing a strong monitoring plan for SharePoint. As an example of where this applies, consider that if the item is deleted and then purged by SharePoint after 30 days (which is the default) there would be no record of who had deleted the item once it is no longer in the recycle bin. Another example is monitoring who has viewed or opened a file but not modified it. In situations where it must be established whether a person had gained access to certain information, this record becomes invaluable. The SharePoint 2010 auditing feature allows administrators to capture user actions on sites, including the lists, libraries, and pages in the site. You can also generate reports on this information filtered by the type of action, the date range in which it occurred, and the user who performed it.

In Chapter 12, "Configuring Records Management," we looked at one way of configuring auditing on content through setting up information management policies. That method is designed to allow record managers to define auditing on specific libraries and content types when they have either list management or site ownership permissions. From the point of view of establishing comprehensive auditing coverage, SharePoint also allows site collection administrators to enable auditing on an entire site collection.

Configuring Site Collection Auditing

Each organization will decide differently which items to audit. Bear in mind that the more you collect in the audit logs, the more space it will consume and the larger the log reports will be. Here are some general guidelines:

Standard Business Environment This would characterize a typical small to mid-sized business where a limited number of users have access to the network and little of the information is sensitive or subject to compliance regulations. This type of environment will most likely give many users read and edit rights to larger areas of content and there is little concern over who reads and edits documents they have rights to. The primary concern would be tracking misplaced or deleted data and monitoring security settings.

What to audit:

- Moving or copying items to another location in the site
- Deleting or restoring items
- Editing users and permissions

Enterprise Business Environment At times, large organizations face the problem of needing to recover the history of a document that has been moved and copied multiple times through its life cycle. If a file is moved from a library with versioning turned on to a library without versioning, then the history of changes to that document will be lost. The primary concern would be tracking the historical actions on a document and being able to report on activities that modify data.

What to audit:

- Editing items
- Checking out or checking in items

- Moving or copying items to another location in the site
- Deleting or restoring items
- Editing users and permissions

High-Security Environment Where the information in SharePoint is sensitive in nature—such as legal files, medical records, or intellectual property—it is advisable to audit all access to the content, including reading and viewing it. This may even apply to the search queries that users execute, since they may be part of a pattern of an employee seeking unauthorized information.

What to audit:

- Editing items
- Checking out or checking in items
- Moving or copying items to another location in the site
- Deleting or restoring items
- Searching site content
- Editing users and permissions

In some high-security environments, it may also be necessary to audit the following:

- Opening or downloading documents
- Viewing items in lists
- Viewing item properties

Auditing these activities will generate a high number of log entries and can use a large amount of database space. We recommend that you only enable this option after careful consideration and planning.

There are two additional settings not included in the environment categories just described:

- The ability to track editing content types and columns is used when an organization has implemented a highly structured metadata taxonomy that is used as part of a regulatory compliance requirement. Changes to the content types or columns may violate compliance, so these changes should be audited.
- Any changes made to the audit settings themselves are automatically logged and available through audit reports.

Manage Auditing and Audit Reports **453**

To configure auditing on an entire site collection:

1. Navigate to the home page at the root of a site collection for which you are the site collection administrator.
2. Select Site Actions, then Site Settings.
3. In the Site Collection Administration section, click Site Collection Audit Settings. The Configure Audit Settings page opens, shown partially in Figure 15.1.

Figure 15.1: Configure Audit Settings page

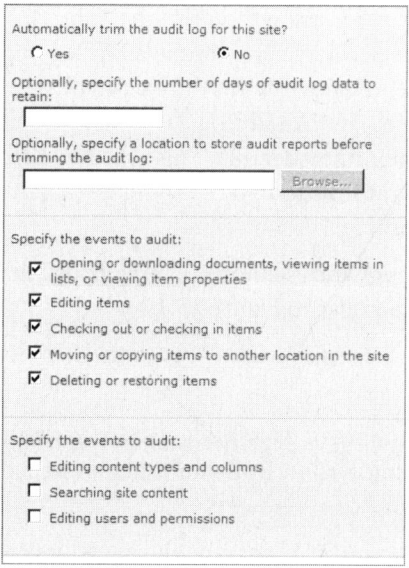

4. Optionally, set the log trimming settings. See the next section, "Managing Audit Log Growth and Size," for details.
5. Choose the events to audit
6. Click OK.

Managing Audit Log Growth and Size

SharePoint stores all audit entries in the content database table AuditData. By default, SharePoint does not delete entries in this table and the table can grow significantly over time. This was a notable problem with SharePoint

2007 farms where many administrators found that the AuditData table became larger than any of the other tables that stored site content.

To estimate the amount of data that you are likely to log, a good approach is to perform a baseline series of actions on the site to simulate a typical user during a period of the workday, then count the number of log entries that adds to the AuditData table. You can then multiply this baseline by the number of users who will be using SharePoint and the length of a typical workday to yield a rough estimation of the number of log entries per day. Log entries range from 1 KB to 4 KB in size, but 2 KB is used as a typical average size for estimation purposes.

Depending on your internal policies, it may not be necessary to keep all log entries. To minimize the growth in the content database, SharePoint 2010 allows you to periodically trim the audit log and, optionally, save copies of the entries before they are deleted. SharePoint is configured with a timer job named Audit Log Trimming, which is scheduled to run once per month by default. This schedule can be adjusted by the farm administrator if desired.

To configure audit log trimming:

1. Follow steps 1–3 in the previous section, "Configuring Site Collection Auditing" and refer to Figure 15.1.

2. Click the Yes option at the "Automatically trim the audit log for this site?" prompt.

3. Optionally, enter the number of days of log history to retain in the database when the timer job runs. By default, the site collection will be purged.

4. Optionally, specify a document library in which to store deleted log entries before trimming. To do so, click the Browse button and select the library you want to use.

5. Click OK.

> **NOTE** If you store audit reports, they continue to take space in the content database. To reclaim the space, you must download the reports from the library and delete them from SharePoint.

Viewing Audit Reports

Site collection administrators can run a number of reports to display audit details in Excel 2010 format.

To view and run reports:

1. Navigate to the home page at the root of a site collection for which you are the site collection administrator.
2. Select Site Actions, then Site Settings.
3. In the Site Collection Administration section, click Audit Log Reports.

NOTE The Audit Log Reports link is enabled via a site collection feature. If you do not see the link, then click the Site Collection Features link and activate the Reporting feature.

On the View Auditing Reports page, the following reports are available:

Content Modifications Any changes made to items such as checking out, checking in, and editing.

Content Type And List Modifications Any changes to content types in the site collection.

Content Viewing Opening documents or viewing items and properties.

Deletion Any items or lists deleted or restored from the recycle bin.

Run A Custom Report Filtered report displaying data for a specific location, date range, user, or action type.

Expiration And Disposition Any automated deletion or processing of items by an information management policy.

Policy Modifications Any changes to information management policies.

Auditing Settings Any changes to auditing settings.

Security Settings Any changes to users, groups, permission levels, and permission assignments.

4. Click one of the report links; then in the Save Location box, browse for the document library that you want the report placed into when it is generated.
5. Click OK.

The report is generated as an XLSX file and placed in the designated library. The results page contains a link to open the report directly.

An example of a section of a Content Modifications report is shown in Figure 15.2.

Figure 15.2: Audit report details

User Id	Document Location	Occurred (GMT)	Event
SYNERGY\afuller	it/Documents/Solar.docx	2011-01-14T16:07:59	Update
SYNERGY\afuller	it/Documents/Solar.docx	2011-01-14T16:08:00	Update
SYNERGY\afuller	it/Documents	2011-01-14T16:08:00	Update
SYNERGY\afuller	it/Documents/FW test.eml	2011-01-14T16:08:55	Delete
SYNERGY\afuller	it/Documents/Hydropower.docx	2011-01-14T16:08:56	Delete
SYNERGY\lcallahan	it/Documents/Solar.docx	2011-01-14T16:08:56	Delete
SYNERGY\mpeacock	it/Documents/Renewables.docx	2011-01-14T16:17:59	Update
SYNERGY\mpeacock	it/Documents	2011-01-14T16:17:59	Update
SYNERGY\mpeacock	it/Documents/Renewables.docx	2011-01-14T16:17:59	Update
SYNERGY\mpeacock	it/Documents/Renewables.docx	2011-01-14T16:18:13	Delete
SYNERGY\Administrator	it/Documents/test.eml	2011-01-14T16:18:13	Delete

Each audit report contains the following information about user activities:

Site ID   GUID of the site collection where the action occurred

Item ID   GUID of the item

Item Type   Values include Site Collection, Site, List, Document, and Item

User ID   Authentication account that performed the action

Document Location   Relative URL of the item or document within the site collection

Occurred (GMT)   Date and time of the action in Greenwich Mean Time

Event   Type of event, such as Edit or Delete

Custom Event Name   Additional information about the action

Event Source   Usually has a value of `SharePoint`

Event Data   Details about the action, such as the version number of the document checked in

Audit reports contain a concise listing of information that provides the essential details in a relatively raw format. Some information is not provided in a readily usable form. For example, the site collection and item are identified through their GUID rather than their URL; the date and time are reported in GMT rather than the local time zone where the report is run; and the user account is represented as the login rather than the full name of the user. It is best to consider the audit reports generated by SharePoint as data exports rather than as presentable reports found in other areas of the application. Third-party add-ins are available from SharePoint market vendors that generate fully formatted reports.

Configure Web Analytics Reporting

The purpose of web usage analysis tools is to provide statistical information on the usage paterns of a web application. A primary benefit of this reporting is to determine the total utilization of SharePoint among the user base for growth and scalability projections. You can also use this information to identify possible issues or areas for improvement in the system by noting sites and pages with low traffic or search queries that return no results.

An important point about all these benefits is that they require a proactive and recurring schedule of monitoring to be effective. It is a good idea for each organization to have at least one IT staff member who is responsible for periodically viewing the usage reports and looking for trends or patterns that should be considered.

Configuring Web Analytics

In SharePoint 2010, usage analysis data is enabled by the Web Analytics service application, which runs as a shared service. The configuration of the Web Analytics service is discussed in Chapter 4, "Creating Service Applications." Once the service application is created, ensure that the Web Analytics Web Service and Web Analytics Data Processing Service are started on each WFE server. These services can be viewed in Central Administration on the Services On Server page.

Once the services are running, you need to enable usage data collection and configure the data to be logged. Do the following:

1. From SharePoint 2010 Central Administration, click Monitoring.
2. In the Reporting section, click Configure Usage And Health Data Collection.

3. In the Usage Data Collection section, click the Enable Usage Data Collection check box.

4. In the Event Selection section, shown in Figure 15.3, check the boxes for types of events you want to log. Generally, all events are logged for usage analysis; however, this does add overhead to the server and takes up more log space on the disk, so you may choose to not log specific events.

Figure 15.3: Choosing events to log

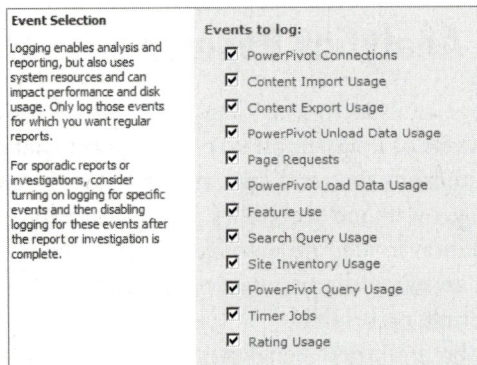

5. In the Usage Data Collection Settings section, shown in Figure 15.4, specify the physical directory where the usage log files will be stored. The log files contain the usage data collected in binary format. Ensure that you select a directory on a drive with sufficient free disk space. To ensure that disk usage does not grow uncontrollably, you can specify a maximum size for usage log files. When the limit is reached, SharePoint will delete older logs to make room.

Figure 15.4: Usage Data Collection Settings section

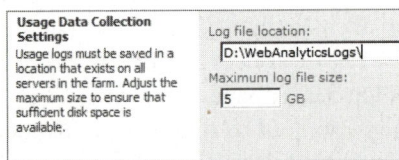

6. The processing of log files and generating of analyzed results is handled by two timer jobs. Both jobs run every 30 minutes by default. To change the schedule for the timer jobs, click the Log Collection Schedule link, and then click each job to edit the schedule.

The timer jobs are:

Microsoft SharePoint Foundation Usage Data Import Job   Collects the log files and stores the data in the web analytics database

Microsoft SharePoint Foundation Usage Data Processing Job   Compiles the raw data into summarized results

7. Click OK.

Viewing Analytics Reports

SharePoint 2010 offers three categories of web analytics reports: Traffic, Search, and Inventory. The reports are generated and viewable at different scopes within SharePoint, including the site level, the site collection level, the web application level, and specialized reports for the search service. Most reports show a default data view of 30 days and can be adjusted to show up to 25 months of data.

Viewing Site Collection Reports

To view site collection reports:

1. Navigate to the home page at the root of a site collection for which you are the site collection administrator.
2. Select Site Actions, then Site Settings.
3. In the Site Actions section, click Site Collection Web Analytics Reports. The Summary page is displayed as shown in Figure 15.5. This page displays overall statistics for the site collection both in total and averaged per day.

Figure 15.5: Site Collection Web Analytics – Summary page

Category	Metrics	Value (Current)	Value (Previous)
Traffic			
	Total Number of Page Views	260	260
	Average Number of Page Views per Day	55	55
	Total Number of Daily Unique Visitors	26	26
	Average Number of Unique Visitors per Day	24	24
	Total Number of Referrers	6	6
	Average Number of Referrers per Day	3	3
Search			
	Total Number of Search Queries	15	15
	Average Number of Search Queries per Day	2	2
Inventory			
	Total Number of Sites	26	26
	Total Storage Used (MB)	155.19	155.19

Viewing Site Reports

To view site reports:

1. Navigate to the home page at the site for which you are the site owner.
2. Select Site Actions, then Site Settings.
3. In the Site Actions section, click Site Web Analytics Reports. The Summary page is displayed. (The Summary page for site reports is very similar to the Summary page for site collection reports, shown in Figure 15.5.)

To view web application reports:

1. From SharePoint 2010 Central Administration, click Monitoring.
2. In the Reporting section, click View Web Analytics Reports. The Web Analytics Reports – Summary page is displayed showing Total Number Of Page Views, Total Number Of Daily Unique Visitors, and Total Number Of Search Queries.
3. Click the link for the web application that you want to see details on. The Summary page for the web application is displayed showing aggregate values very similar to those shown in Figure 15.5.

Understanding Reports

Reports are generally presented in one of two forms:

Trend Report A trend report displays how a specific measurement changes over time. It is typically shown as a line chart. (See the Number Of Page Views report in Figure 15.6.)

Figure 15.6: Number Of Page Views report

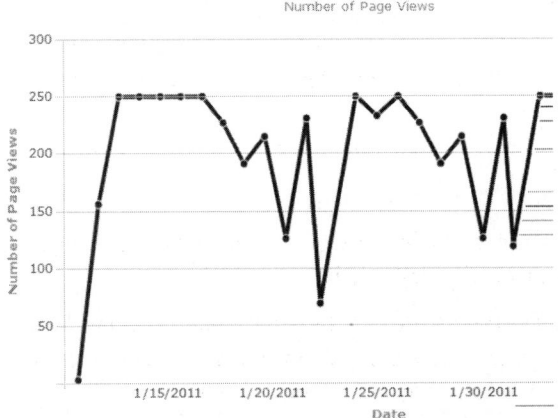

Rank Report A rank report shows a comparison of the top 2,000 results for a specific measure relative to each other. It is typically presented as a bar graph. (See the Top Pages report in Figure 15.7.)

Figure 15.7: Top Pages report

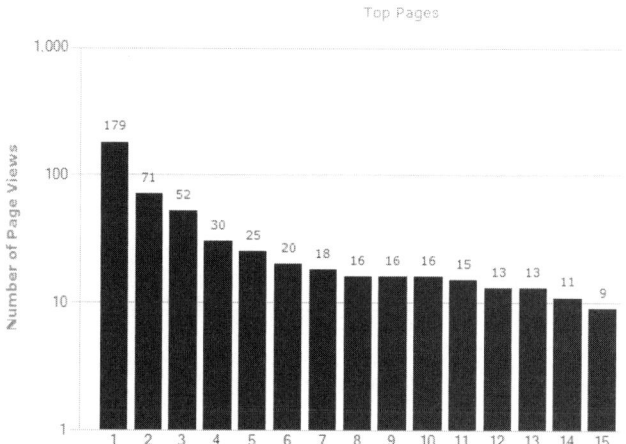

To change the date range for a report, click the Change Settings link at the top of the report and select a date range for the report.

There are three categories of reports available from the web analytics summary page: Search, Traffic, and Inventory.

Search reports are used to better understand the types of queries that users are making within the site collection in order to tune searches to provide better responses. Search reports are covered in detail in Chapter 9, "Configuring Search Scopes and Search Results."

The traffic reports show aggregated data on the number of visitors and page views in the site collection. Here is a brief description of each report:

First, trend reports:

Number Of Page Views Page visits per day.

Number Of Daily Unique Visitors Unique visitors per day. Anonymous visitors are identified by IP address.

Number Of Referrers Unique referrer websites per day. A referrer is a website that a user navigated from to get to this site.

Next, rank reports:

Top Pages   Most popular pages during the specified period of time

Top Visitors   Most frequent visitors during a period of time

Top Referrers   Sites that referred users to this site the most often

Top Destinations   Sites that users most often navigated to by clicking a link on this site

Top Browsers   Most popular web browsers used by visitors

Table 15.1 shows which traffic reports are available at each scope in SharePoint.

Table 15.1: SharePoint traffic reports by scope

Report	Site	Site Collection	Web Application
Number Of Page Views	X	X	X
Number Of Daily Unique Visitors	X	X	X
Number Of Referrers	X	X	X
Top Pages	X	X	X
Top Visitors	X	X	X
Top Referrers	X	X	X
Top Destinations	X	X	X
Top Browsers	X	X	X

Inventory reports show sum totals for usage, number of sites, and top site statistics. The following inventory reports are available.

For trend reports:

Storage Usage   Total space used in megabytes (MB) and the maximum limit set by quota for the site collection per day

Number Of Sites   Total number of sites existing in the site collection per day

Number Of Site Collections   Total number of site collections existing in the web application per day

For rank reports:

Top Site Product Versions For SharePoint farms that have been upgraded from a previous version, this report shows how many sites are using which version of the product.

Top Site Languages Languages most commonly assigned to sites in the site collection.

Table 15.2 shows which inventory reports are available at each scope in SharePoint.

Table 15.2: SharePoint inventory reports by scope

Report	Site	Site Collection	Web Application
Storage Usage		X	
Number Of Sites	X	X	
Top Site Product Versions	X	X	
Top Site Languages	X	X	
Number Of Site Collections			X

Use the Health Analyzer

SharePoint 2010 introduces a new tool to help administrators identify and correct problems in the farm. The SharePoint 2010 Health Analyzer is a built-in service that constantly monitors the state of SharePoint against a set of rules. When any issue is detected that violates one or more rules, SharePoint provides a visual indicator—a message at the top of the home page in Central Administration (see Figure 15.8). The notification is highlighted in yellow if only warning issues have been detected or in red if critical issues have been found.

Figure 15.8: Health Analyzer critical issue notice

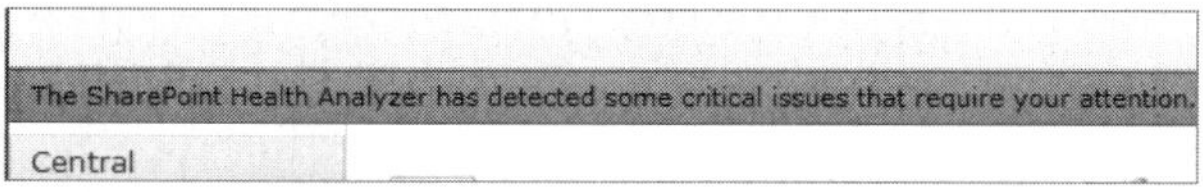

The Health Analyzer can be turned on or off in Central Administration. If you are concerned about the overhead of processing all the data, then you can disable data collection by doing the following:

1. From SharePoint 2010 Central Administration, click Monitoring.
2. In the Reporting section, click Configure Usage And Health Data Collection.
3. In the Health Data Collection section, click the Enable Health Data Collection check box.
4. Click OK.

Reviewing Problems and Solutions

To review problems that the Health Analyzer has detected, click the link View These Issues In The Health Analyzer message on the home page of Central Administration. Alternatively, click the Monitoring link in Central Administration; then in the Health Analyzer section, click the link Review Problems And Solutions. The health problems reporting page groups issues by category of problem, as shown in Figure 15.9.

Figure 15.9: Review problems and solutions page

	Title	Failing Servers	Failing Services	Modified
Category : Security (2)				
	The server farm account should not be used for other services.		SPTimerService (SPTimerV4)	3/13/2011 9:01 PM
	Accounts used by application pools or service identities are in the local machine Administrators group.	SPSERVER	SPTimerService (SPTimerV4)	3/17/2011 9:00 PM
Category : Configuration (3)				
	The PowerPivot service application identity should not be a member of the local Administrators group.	SPSERVER	MidTierService	3/17/2011 9:00 PM
	One or more categories are configured with Verbose trace logging.		SPTimerService (SPTimerV4)	3/17/2011 9:01 PM
	Built-in accounts are used as application pool or service identities.		SPTimerService (SPTimerV4)	3/13/2011 9:00 PM
Category : Availability (2)				
	Drives are running out of free space.	SPSERVER	SPTimerService (SPTimerV4)	3/18/2011 2:00 AM
	Database has large amounts of unused space.		SPTimerService (SPTimerV4)	3/13/2011 9:01 PM

To view the full details of a problem, click the link of the problem, which will open the Review Problem And Solutions dialog box shown in Figure 15.10.

Figure 15.10: Review the details of the problem in this dialog box

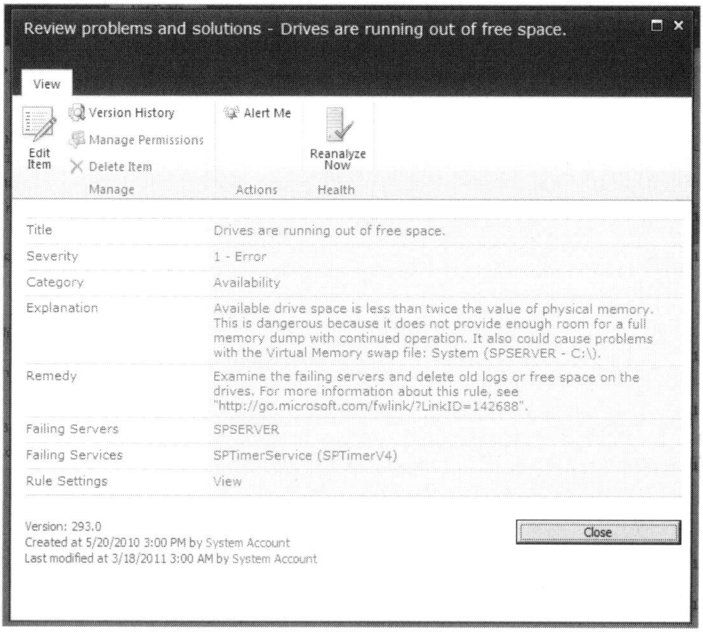

![Review problems and solutions dialog box showing details for "Drives are running out of free space" with fields: Title, Severity (1 - Error), Category (Availability), Explanation, Remedy, Failing Servers (SPSERVER), Failing Services (SPTimerService (SPTimerV4)), Rule Settings (View). Version: 293.0, Created at 5/20/2010 3:00 PM by System Account, Last modified at 3/18/2011 3:00 AM by System Account.]

The information displayed on the Review Problem And Solutions dialog box includes the following details:

Title The name of the health rule that identified the problem.

Severity One of five values: 1 - Error, 2 - Warning, 3 - Information, 4 - Success, or 0 - Rule Execution Failure.

Category One of these values: Configuration, Security, Performance, or Availability; or you can configure custom values for this field.

Explanation Details about the rule and conditions that caused the alert.

Remedy Recommendations on how to resolve the problem.

Failing Servers The server(s) that the issue is occurring on.

Failing Services The service(s) having the problem.

Rule Settings The View link takes you to the specific health rule that identified the problem.

Version Automatically incremented every time an alert is updated.

Reviewing Rule Definitions

To view a list of the problems that the health analyzer is monitoring, from the Monitoring page, click Review Rule Definitions. The Health Analyzer Rule Definitions page appears, as shown in Figure 15.11.

Figure 15.11: Health Analyzer Rule Definitions page

Title	Schedule	Enabled	Repair Automatically
Category : Security (4)			
Accounts used by application pools or service identities are in the local machine Administrators group.	Daily	Yes	No
Web Applications using Claims authentication require an update.	Daily	Yes	No
The server farm account should not be used for other services.	Weekly	Yes	No
The Unattended Service Account Application ID is not specified or has an invalid value.	Daily	Yes	No
Category : Performance (17)			
Application pools recycle when memory limits are exceeded.	Weekly	Yes	No
Databases used by SharePoint have fragmented indices.	Daily	Yes	Yes

SharePoint 2010 Enterprise Edition installs 73 separate rules. To view a specific rule, click on the link for its name. Individual rules can be edited. If you have determined that a rule is flagging an issue that you have accepted as part of the design of your farm and that is not an issue of concern, then you can disable the rule. To disable a rule definition, click the link for the rule to open it, click the Edit Item button, and on the Edit page, deselect the Enabled option.

Configure Diagnostic Logging

SharePoint 2010 includes two built-in mechanisms for capturing information about internal events and errors:

Event Logging   SharePoint writes messages to the Application event log made available through the Event Viewer utility in the Windows operating system. The event log is primarily intended for administrators and support staff to understand what configuration and maintenance problems SharePoint reports.

Trace Logging   SharePoint writes information into a set of log files stored in a specified directory. The trace log is primarily intended for developers and Microsoft support teams to identify internal errors and issues that often indicate more complex problems with the system.

Working with the Event Log

To access the SharePoint event log, log onto a SharePoint server and from the Start menu, select Administrative Tools; then click Event Viewer. SharePoint events are logged to the Application event log, as shown in Figure 15.12.

Figure 15.12: Application event log

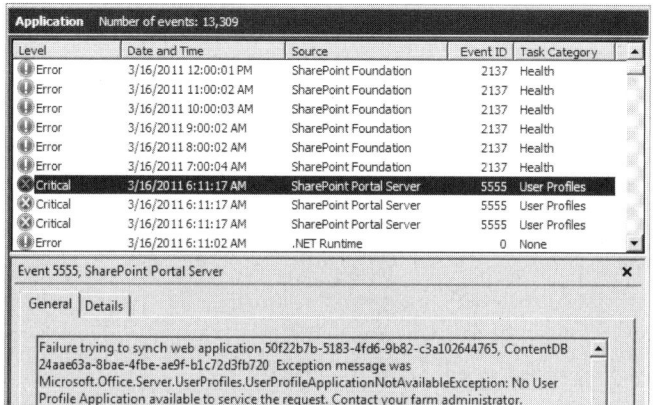

The messages that appear in the event log will correspond to one of five levels, as shown in Table 15.3. These message levels also correspond to the logging levels that SharePoint can be set to output so that you can configure the log for greater or fewer messages. In general, the lower in the table that the level is listed, the more messages are likely to appear in the event log.

Table 15.3: Event log message levels

Logging Level	Explanation
Critical	Indicates a serious problem resulting in the failure of a process.
Error	Indicates a significant problem that may be temporary or lead to permanent problems and should be tracked over time.
Warning	Indicates a potential problem that should be investigated for preventive maintenance.
Information	No issue has occurred but the information may be useful in diagnosing problems.
Verbose	Detailed informational messages that only appear when specifically enabled in SharePoint.

Working with the Trace Log

The trace log is also referred to as the ULS (Unified Logging Service) log. It generates files with more details than the event log. By default, these files are created in the `C:\Program Files\Common Files\Microsoft Shared\Web Server Extensions\14\LOGS` directory, but the administrator can change this location if necessary. Files are given a name based on the pattern *[SERVER NAME]*-*[DATE]*-*[TIME CREATED]*.LOG. For example, the file SPSERVER-20110217-4:17p.m.log was created on February 17, 2011 at 2:17 p.m. Events are logged using the time zone of the server that the event was recorded by. Columns of data include Area (what part of SharePoint is involved), Category, and Level, as shown in Figure 15.13.

Figure 15.13: Trace log

```
TID       Area                   Category      EventID  Level
0x0D5C    SharePoint Foundation  Monitoring    b4ly     Medium
0x0F44    SharePoint Foundation  Monitoring    nasq     Medium
0x0F44    SharePoint Foundation  Topology      8xqz     Medium
0x0F44    SharePoint Foundation  Monitoring    b4ly     Medium
0x0964    SharePoint Foundation  Topology      e5mc     Medium
0x149C    SharePoint Foundation  Monitoring    nasq     Medium
0x11BC    SharePoint Foundation  Monitoring    nasq     Medium
0x15E0    SharePoint Foundation  Monitoring    nasq     Medium
0x149C    SharePoint Foundation  Monitoring    b4ly     Medium
0x11BC    SharePoint Foundation  Monitoring    b4ly     Medium
0x15E0    SharePoint Foundation  Monitoring    b4ly     Medium
0x0BBC    SharePoint Foundation  Monitoring    nasq     Medium
0x0BBC    SharePoint Foundation  Monitoring    b4ly     Medium
0x0964    SharePoint Foundation  Topology      e5mc     Medium
0x1570    SharePoint Foundation  Monitoring    nasq     Medium
```

The messages that appear in the trace log correspond to one of five levels, as shown in Table 15.4.

Table 15.4: Trace log message levels

Logging Level	Explanation
Unexpected (Critical)	A condition has caused a component to throw an exception and fail. Some messages, such as those logged by the Health Analyzer, will use the term Critical, which is equivalent to Unexpected.
Monitorable	A condition prevented an operation from completing but did not throw an unrecoverable exception.
High	A high-priority or high-risk operation occurred in SharePoint but did not generate an error.
Medium	Informational messages.
Verbose	Informational messages intended to provide additional details for developers to determine the internal processing of a component.

One consideration is the size that these logs may grow to. While the trace logs in SharePoint 2010 have been optimized to be half the size as those in SharePoint 2007, they still grow based on the rate at which messages are entered into the logs. A new log file is created every 30 minutes and the default setting is to retain 14 days of logs (336 files). Files may be 5 to 10 MB in size. Under normal conditions, it is not unusual for the log files to consume 5 GB or more of disk space. However, log files could grow substantially if SharePoint encounters a recurring issue that logs large numbers of events. If SharePoint runs out of disk space on the drive storing the log files, it will stop the logging service and log a message in the event log.

Configuring Diagnostic Logging Settings

The settings for both the event log and the trace log are configured on the same screen. To configure these settings, do the following:

1. From SharePoint 2010 Central Administration, click Monitoring.
2. In the Reporting section, click Configure Diagnostic Logging.
3. Use the Event Throttling portion of the page to define how detailed the log events should be. By reducing the number of events logged, the log files will be smaller but less information will be logged. When an issue requires greater detail, the logging level can be increased to output more events. Begin by selecting the specific categories of events that you want to see more detail on by checking the box next to each, as shown in Figure 15.14.

Figure 15.14: Event categories

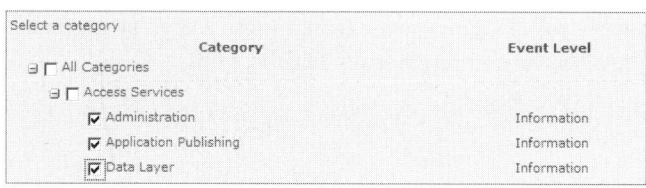

4. Underneath the categories of events, optionally make choices in the drop-downs labeled "Least critical event to report to the event log" and "Least critical event to report to the trace log," as shown in Figure 15.15. To reset the logging levels back to the installed defaults, open the drop-down for the log you want to reset and select the Reset To Default option at the top of the list.

Figure 15.15: Logging Level selection

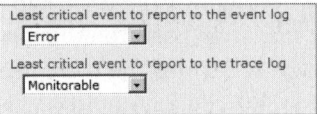

5. Choosing Enable Event Log Flood Protection allows SharePoint to automatically detect when the same event is being logged repeatedly and to suppress the duplicate events. Enabling this option is the recommended setting.

6. In the Trace Log settings, shown in Figure 15.16, enter the path to the local directory where you want SharePoint to place the trace log files. We recommend that you specify a physical drive other than C: to minimize contention.

Figure 15.16: Trace Log settings

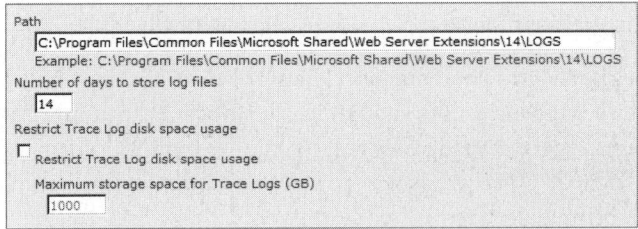

7. Specify the number of days to keep files for. SharePoint will automatically delete older files.

8. Optionally, you may choose to restrict the amount of disk space that SharePoint can use for trace logs to a specific number of gigabytes. Values can range from 1 GB to 1 TB.

9. Click OK.

Manage Timer Jobs

SharePoint 2010 uses the SharePoint 2010 Timer service (owstimer.exe) to execute all scheduled operations on all servers in the farm. Timer jobs are automatically created when SharePoint services are installed and configured. Developers can create custom timer jobs for specialized purposes.

Viewing Timer Jobs

To view existing timer jobs, perform the following steps:

1. From SharePoint 2010 Central Administration, click Monitoring.
2. In the Timer Jobs section, click Review Job Definitions.

   On the Job Definitions page, shown partially in Figure 15.17, you can view the alphabetical list of timer jobs and the web application they are associated with, along with the interval of scheduling.

   Figure 15.17: Job Definitions page

   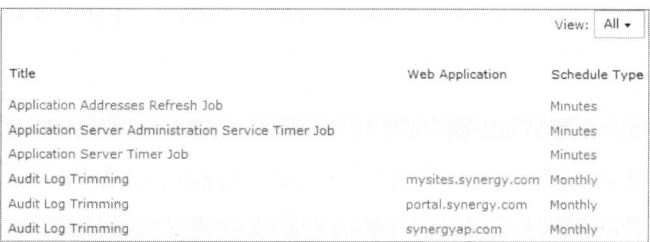

3. To view details about any job, click the link for the job name. The Edit Timer Job page will appear, shown partially in Figure 15.18.

   Figure 15.18: Edit Timer Job page

   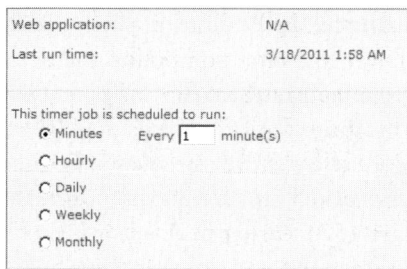

To view the current status of any timer job, from the Monitoring page, in the Timer Jobs Section, click Check Job Status. The Timer Job Status page, shown partially in Figure 15.19, displays the server that the timer job runs on, the web application it is associated with, and the next time the job will run.

Figure 15.19: Timer Job Status page

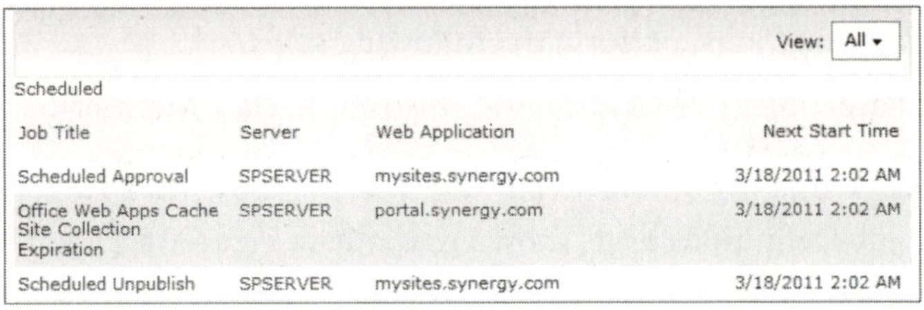

Scheduled			View: All ▼
Job Title	Server	Web Application	Next Start Time
Scheduled Approval	SPSERVER	mysites.synergy.com	3/18/2011 2:02 AM
Office Web Apps Cache Site Collection Expiration	SPSERVER	portal.synergy.com	3/18/2011 2:02 AM
Scheduled Unpublish	SPSERVER	mysites.synergy.com	3/18/2011 2:02 AM

Running a Timer Job

SharePoint 2010 provides users with the ability to trigger jobs to run on demand. To do so, go to the Edit Timer Job page, shown in Figure 15.18, and click the Run Now button at the bottom of the page. Bear in mind, the job may take a few seconds or minutes to start running. SharePoint queues the job for execution and may not be able to execute the job immediately if the server is very busy. It is always a good idea to reopen the Edit Timer Job page after a minute or so and check to ensure that the job ran as expected.

Managing Timer Job Schedules

When timer jobs are created, SharePoint configures them with a default schedule that is designed to meet the needs of the majority of cases. These schedules can be edited and, if your needs require it, adjusted to a different frequency. For example, the Expiration policy timer job reviews documents that are subject to a retention policy and determines if they have expired. The default interval for this policy is once per week. This is effective for most noncritical records management scenarios, but may not meet more stringent requirements. To modify the retention policy so that it is checked on a daily basis, open the Edit Timer Job page, shown in Figure 15.18 earlier in this chapter, change the schedule to Daily, and set a start and end time for the job. Bear in mind that setting schedules to run more frequently will add overhead to the server, so these changes should always be monitored afterward to gauge the impact on performance.

16

Managing Backup and Restore

IN THIS CHAPTER, YOU WILL LEARN TO:

▶ **BACK UP THE FARM** (Pages 474 – 484)
- Performing a Complete Farm Backup (Page 474)
- Understanding Farm Backup Sets (Page 480)
- Using PowerShell to Automate Farm Backups (Page 481)

▶ **RESTORE THE FARM** (Pages 484 – 488)
- Understanding Farm Restore (Page 485)
- Using Central Administration to Restore the Farm (Page 486)

▶ **BACK UP AND RESTORE A SITE COLLECTION** (Pages 488 – 491)
- Using Central Administration to Back Up a Site Collection (Page 489)
- Using PowerShell to Back Up a Site Collection (Page 489)
- Using PowerShell to Restore a Site Collection (Page 490)

▶ **EXPORT AND IMPORT A WEBSITE, LIST, OR LIBRARY** (Pages 491 – 495)
- Using Central Administration to Export (Page 492)
- Using PowerShell to Export (Page 493)
- Using PowerShell to Import (Page 494)

▶ **RECOVER DATA FROM AN UNATTACHED CONTENT DATABASE** (Page 495 – 498)
- Restoring a Content Database (Pages 496)
- Using Central Administration to Recover Data from an Unattached Content Database (Page 497)
- Restoring or Importing Content (Page 498)

SharePoint supports backups of the farm and more granular levels, including site collections, websites, lists, and libraries. This chapter will provide you with a solid overview of backup and restore, including step-by-step procedures on how to perform each type of backup or restore operation.

Back Up the Farm

A farm backup is the most holistic form of backup that SharePoint supports. When you run a farm backup, SharePoint coordinates the backup with farm servers to ensure you get a consistent and consolidated backup. There are four primary types of farm backups that can be taken, and each is described in subsequent sections:

- Complete farm backup
- Differential farm backup
- Configuration-only backup
- Component-level backup

While somewhat flexible, SharePoint's farm backup does have some limitations that are worth pointing out up front. One is that you cannot back up directly to tape since SharePoint only supports file system-based locations. If you need to archive to tape, you must employ an additional backup solution to archive the files generated by SharePoint's backup.

SharePoint's farm backup engine doesn't scale well to farms with a number of large content databases. In general, if the total amount of content in your farm exceeds 500 GB, you should consider using SharePoint-compatible, third-party products instead. Many good ones exist, including System Center Data Protection Manager 2010 by Microsoft and DocAve by AvePoint.

While a farm backup is running, the farm can still be used for normal operations. However, the backup places a sizable load on the servers, so expect the performance to be affected. For this reason, try to schedule your farm backups during off-peak hours.

Performing a Complete Farm Backup

Among all the backup types covered in this chapter, a complete farm backup is the most important of all. It is the most complete in terms of backup coverage and offers the most flexibility in the number of restore options you have. If fact, if you do not run any other type of backup, a complete farm backup will leave you reasonably well protected.

Here is a summary of what is included in a farm backup:

- Most farm configuration settings
- Web application settings and all content databases
- Service application settings and databases, including search indexes

A complete farm backup also backs up and truncates the transaction log for each database, preventing runaway log files.

Despite being the most complete type of backup, there are some notable components that are not included in a complete farm backup. Table 16.1 describes these components and how to back up and restore them.

Table 16.1: Components not included in a complete farm backup

Components	Backup Procedure
Farm configuration settings such as managed account passwords, which services are running on which servers, service application associations, and changes to timer job schedules.	Document and reapply manually if doing a restore.
IIS settings not configurable through SharePoint, including SSL certificates and IIS logging details.	Document and reapply manually if doing a restore.
Web application folders stored on each WFE server. By default, these are stored at `Inetpub\wwwroot\wss\VirtualDirectories`.	Back up manually or include in an OS backup of the server.
DLL files manually deployed into the global assembly cache (GAC). This is commonly done when manually deploying custom code.	Back up manually or include in an OS backup of the server.
Any changes made within the SharePoint Root (14 Hive). By default, located at `Program Files\Common Files\Microsoft Shared\Web Server Extensions\14`. This is often done when manually deploying custom code or altering files located here.	Back up manually or include in an OS backup of the server.

For more details on how to protect components not included in a complete backup, see "Plan for Backup and Recovery" on TechNet at `http://technet.microsoft.com/en-us/library/cc261687.aspx`.

Complete farm backups can be made with Central Administration or PowerShell. Regardless of which of these methods you use, the resulting backup set is the same. If you back up using one method, you can restore with another.

> **NOTE** Although STSADM is a viable method for most backup and restore operations, it will not be covered in this chapter since PowerShell is the preferred method.

Using Central Administration to Perform a Complete Farm Backup

Here are the steps to perform a complete farm backup using Central Administration:

1. Click Backup And Restore, and then select Perform A Backup.
2. In Select Component To Back Up, select the Farm component at the top, as shown in Figure 16.1. This tells SharePoint to automatically include all farm components, or the "complete farm."

Figure 16.1: Selecting all components for farm backup

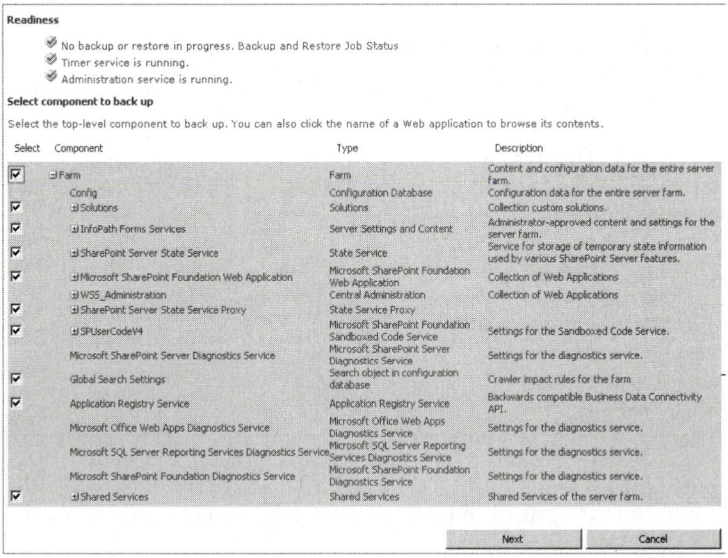

3. Click Next to go to the Select Backup Options page (shown in Figure 16.2).

Figure 16.2: Setting backup options for complete farm backup

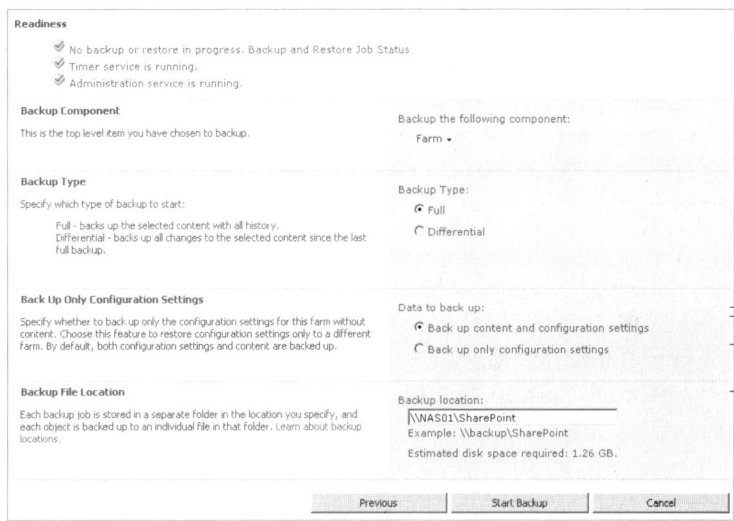

4. For Backup Component, Farm should be automatically chosen and doesn't need to be changed.
5. For Backup Type, ensure that Full is selected.
6. For Data To Back Up, ensure that Back Up Content And Configuration Settings is selected.
7. For Backup Location, be sure that a valid Universal Naming Convention (UNC) path is listed, for example, \\NAS01\SharePoint. When the backup is issued, farm servers are responsible for backing up SharePoint-centric details such as farm configuration. Database server(s) also back up each of their databases to this location. This means that each SQL server must be able to write to this location.
8. Click Start Backup to begin. SharePoint creates a new timer job for the backup and schedules it to run immediately.

> **NOTE** As shown at the bottom of Figure 16.2, SharePoint provides you with an estimate of the amount of disk space needed for the backup. This estimate is almost always on the high side as it includes the actual size of current database log files, which are not backed up in entirety. However, if you do not have the estimated amount of space available, an error is displayed, and you cannot run the backup using Central Administration. If you are unable to free up enough space, you can use the Backup-SPFarm cmdlet with the -force switch from PowerShell as described in "Using PowerShell to Automate Farm Backups," later in this chapter.

After starting the backup, you are redirected to a Backup And Restore Job Status page. This allows you to monitor the progress while the backup is running. Since a timer job is processing the backup, you can safely close this window and return to it later. To return to the status page, click Backup And Restore, and then select Check Backup And Restore Job Status.

The amount of time the complete farm backup takes can vary widely, from minutes to over 24 hours. The primary factors are the size and number of content databases, the speed of your database servers, and the speed of the network in between the SQL servers, query servers, and the file server location specified in the UNC path.

Using Central Administration to Perform a Configuration-Only Backup

A configuration-only backup instructs SharePoint to back up only essential farm configuration settings. You can conceptually think of this as backing up the configuration database, but SharePoint does not actually do this. Instead, it captures many of these details and stores them in a series of XML and binary files. These settings include:

- Web application settings, including managed paths
- Farm solutions
- Incoming/outgoing email settings
- Timer jobs
- Diagnostic logging settings
- InfoPath Forms Services settings

Running a configuration-only backup is almost exactly the same as running a complete farm backup. Follow the steps in the previous section, "Using Central Administration to Perform a Complete Farm Backup," but in step 6, select Back Up Only Configuration Settings. A configuration-only backup shouldn't take more than a few minutes in most cases.

Using Central Administration to Perform a Component-Level Backup

A component-level backup is the backup of a single component within the farm. A component can mean one of many different SharePoint objects, such as a web application. When you select a component, all its subcomponents are also included and cannot be excluded. For example, when you select a web application, all content databases for that web application are included. Or you can back up all service applications or just a single service application. Within a web application, the smallest component that can be selected is a content database.

> **NOTE** Some service applications such as the State Service application cannot be backed up as a single component.

Unfortunately, you are always limited to a single component. So, you cannot back up just two of the four content databases within a web application. Similarly, you cannot back up a single web application and a single service application together. This would be considered two components and requires two separate backup jobs. This limitation applies to PowerShell as well.

A component-level backup is run almost exactly the same as when you're running a complete farm backup. Here are the steps:

1. Click Backup And Restore, and then select Perform A Backup.
2. In Select Component To Back Up, select a single component. You can expand and collapse components to see their subcomponents.
3. Click Next to go to the Select Backup Options page, as shown in Figure 16.2, earlier in this chapter.
4. For Backup Component, the selected component is shown.
5. For Backup Type, ensure Full is selected.

6. For Backup Location, be sure that a valid UNC path is listed.
7. Click Start Backup to begin. SharePoint creates a new timer job for this backup and schedules it to run immediately.

> **NOTE** SharePoint also supports differential backups, in which only the changes since the last full backup are captured. Differential backups apply only to databases and not all components. When performing a restore from a differential backup, you must have both the differential and corresponding full backup available.

Understanding Farm Backup Sets

When any type of farm, configuration, or component backup is run, SharePoint keeps track of it in a separate folder within the UNC path provided for the backup location. The naming convention for each backup folder is SPBR*xxxx*, where *xxxx* is a number that begins with 0000, and increments to 0001, 0002, and so on.

In each backup folder, you'll find a lot of BAK files. Some of these are XML-formatted files. some (the largest) are database backups, and some are other unreadable binary files. In addition, you'll find two files useful for troubleshooting and performing restores:

spbackup.log This text file lists what was included in the backup and all logging details. A summary of the number of errors and warnings is listed at the end of this file.

spbackup.xml This XML file also lists what was included in the backup and describes what component is included in which BAK file. For example, you can identify which BAK file contains one of your content databases. This information can be used to restore the database directly from SQL Server, separate from SharePoint.

In the top-level folder (the parent of all the SPBR*xxxx* folders), you will find one more XML file named spbrtoc.xml. This file, called the table of contents, keeps track of each backup that was run and the corresponding SPBR*xxxx* folder. SharePoint uses this file when performing a farm restore.

Using PowerShell to Automate Farm Backups

All of the backup combinations available under Central Administration can also be run as PowerShell cmdlets. To run any type of farm backup, use the `Backup-SPFarm` cmdlet. Running a farm backup from PowerShell does not create a timer job, but the backup can still be tracked from the Backup And Restore Status page.

Here is the syntax with most of the commonly used options shown:

```
Backup-SPFarm -BackupMethod <Full | Differential>
-Directory <UNC Path> [-ConfigurationOnly] [-Force]
[-Item <Named component>]
```

Here are some examples on how it can be used.

- To run a complete farm backup:

    ```
    Backup-SPFarm -BackupMethod full -Directory
    \\NAS01\SharePoint\Backup
    ```

- To run a configuration-only backup:

    ```
    Backup-SPFarm -BackupMethod full -Directory
    \\NAS01\SharePoint\Backup -ConfigurationOnly
    ```

- To back up just the web application named "Intranet - 80":

    ```
    Backup-SPFarm -BackupMethod full -Directory
    \\NAS01\SharePoint\Backup -item "Intranet - 80"
    ```

Central Administration makes farm backups very easy, but it does not support automating regular backups on a schedule. While a programmer can write a custom timer job for this, it is more complex, so the more common solution is to create a PowerShell script and run it as a scheduled task under Windows. Listing 16.1 is a script that we use to automate farm backups. This script will also archive old backup sets. Save this script as a text file named **FarmBackup.ps1**.

Listing 16.1: FarmBackup.ps1

```
#FarmBackup.ps1
Add-PsSnapin Microsoft.SharePoint.PowerShell

# Parameter:Days of backup that should be retained
$days = 3

# Parameter:Backup Folder
$backupFolder = "\\NAS01\backup"

# Run complete backup
Backup-SPFarm -BackupMethod full -Directory ↵
$backupFolder

# Archive older backup sets. With credit to
# Marco (http://blog.wauwwie.nl)

# Location of TOC
$spbrtoc = $backupFolder + "\spbrtoc.xml"

# Import the Sharepoint backup report xml file
[xml]$sp = gc $spbrtoc

# Find backup sets in TOC
$old = $sp.SPBackupRestoreHistory.SPHistoryObject ↵
| ? { $_.SPStartTime -lt ((get-date).adddays(-$days))}
if ($old -eq $Null) { write-host "No backups older ↵
than $days days found" ; break}

# Delete the old backups from spbrtoc.xml file
$old | % {$sp.SPBackupRestoreHistory.RemoveChild($_)}

# Delete the physical folders no longer used
$old | % { Remove-Item $_.SPBackupDirectory -recurse}

# Save the revised backup TOC
```

```
$sp.Save($spbrtoc)

Write-host "Backup(s) entries older than $days days ↵
have been removed from spbrtoc.xml and $backupFolder"
```

There are two parameters you will need to adjust:

$days Any backups older than the number of days specified here are automatically removed.

$backupFolder Contains the UNC path where you want the backups to be stored.

To automate, you can schedule this script to run as a Windows scheduled task. This task can be created on any of your WFE servers. Here are the steps:

1. Run Task Scheduler (Start ➢ All Programs ➢ Administrative Tools ➢ Task Scheduler).
2. In the Actions pane, select Create Task. The Create Task dialog box appears.
3. For Name, enter a suitable name for the task.
4. Click the Change User Or Group button and provide the username of the farm account or other account that has PowerShell access to all SharePoint databases. (See Chapter 14, "Managing Security," for more information on granting PowerShell access.)
5. Click the Run Whether User Is Logged On Or Not radio button.
6. Click the Run With Highest Privileges check box.
7. Select the Triggers tab.
8. Click New and enter the schedule details—for example, whether you want to run the task daily or weekly.
9. Click OK to save the schedule.
10. Select the Actions tab.
11. Click New to create a new action.
12. For Program/Script: enter **Powershell.exe**.

13. For Add Arguments (Optional), enter the full path to where you have saved the previous script file—for example, `D:\scripts\FarmBackup.ps1`
14. Click OK to save the action.
15. Click OK to save the task.
16. When prompted, enter the password for the account you specified in step 4. Click OK to save.

> **NOTE** To get the previous script to run correctly, you may need to alter your WFE server's configuration policy for running PowerShell scripts. The recommended setting is RemoteSigned. For more information on changing this, see the article "Set-ExecutionPolicy" at http://technet.microsoft.com/en-us/library/dd347628.aspx.

Restore the Farm

While we hope you will never have to do a farm restore, you should know the steps to be able to perform one with confidence. There are many situations where you need to rely on a farm restore to bring your environment back online. These include:

- Loss or major corruption of one or more databases or database servers
- Accidental or malicious removal of data at the farm level (i.e., using Central Administration or PowerShell)—for example, deleting a web application

On the other hand, a farm restore is not always needed. Here are two situations where you do not need to do a farm restore:

- Loss of a WFE or application server. In many cases, you can remove the old server from the farm, install SharePoint on a new server, join it to the farm, and configure the services that should be running on it. Depending on your environment, however, there may be additional third-party software that needs installation, or other custom changes that you need to apply.

- You need to restore data from within a content database (e.g., restore a website or file). For this type of restore, see "Recover Data from an Unattached Content Database," later in this chapter.

A farm restore can be done with Central Administration or PowerShell, but since restores are usually done ad hoc when needed, we will detail these steps using Central Administration only. Furthermore, performing a restore from the command line is much more difficult, and there is a higher probability of making a typo, causing the restore to fail.

Understanding Farm Restore

Just like a backup, when doing a farm restore, you have the option of restoring the complete farm, just its configuration, or a single farm component. If you did a complete farm backup, you are not required to do a complete restore. You can do a component restore from a complete farm backup. For example, you can restore a single content database or service application from your complete farm backup.

When doing a farm restore, you have the following choices:

Restore to the Same Configuration SharePoint replaces the existing component when doing the restore.

Restore to a New Configuration You can rename the component during the restore. A common example of using a new configuration is when you are restoring a content database—you can restore the database to a different server or as a different database name.

SharePoint does not store managed account passwords in any backup. Consequently, when you restore a web application or service application, you will need to know the application's managed account password. If you don't know the password, you will need to reset it within Active Directory prior to starting the restore. When starting the restore, SharePoint will prompt you for all the passwords needed, as covered in the next section.

If you have a major farm failure and the configuration database is unavailable, you will first need to create a new farm before doing a restore. SharePoint's farm restore can only be run when the farm is online.

Using Central Administration to Restore the Farm

Using Central Administration to perform a farm restore is the recommended approach. It is the easiest approach since you have a graphical interface when reviewing and adjusting the configuration settings, including when you're entering the managed account passwords.

Here's how to restore the farm:

1. Click Backup And Restore, and then select Restore From A Backup.

2. For Backup Directory Location, the most recent backup path is shown with the backup sets found. If you have moved your backup files to an alternate path, change it here and click the Refresh button.

3. Select the backup set that you wish to restore. These are pulled from the `spbrtoc.xml` file that is processed from this directory location.

4. Click Next.

5. SharePoint displays a tree view of all components. Check boxes are listed next to those components that are available for restore from this backup set. Select the component that you wish to restore. Just with the backup, you can restore only one component at a time, and any subcomponents are automatically included.

6. Click Next.

7. This page's contents will vary depending on what you selected for restore on the previous page. If you are performing a farm restore, you must choose Restore Content And Configuration Settings or Restore Only Configuration Settings.

8. Under Restore Options, you are asked what type of restore you want to perform. Your choices are New Configuration or Same Configuration (see Figure 16.3).

9. If a web application or service application is included in the restore, the Login Names And Passwords section contains all the managed accounts that SharePoint will re-create when performing the restore. You must provide the current password for each account. If you do not know the password, you will need to reset it in AD.

Figure 16.3: Restoring a web application

Restore Component	
This is the top level item you have chosen to restore.	Restore the following component: Farm\Microsoft SharePoint Foundation Web Application\SharePoint - 80 ▼
Restore Options	
To restore to a farm with the same computer names, web application names and database servers as those in the backup farm, select 'Same configuration'. To restore to a farm with different computer names, web application names or database servers, select 'New configuration'.	Type of restore: ⊙ New configuration ○ Same configuration
Login Names and Passwords	
For each object or group of objects, specify the login name and password that the objects will use. For Web Applications and Service Applications, provide the login name and password to be used by the associated application pool. If using SQL Server authentication, provide a SQL Server login name and password for each database listed.	SharePoint - 80 Login name: HAWMETAL\sp.apppool Password:
New Names	
If you choose to restore with a 'New configuration', you must specify new web application URLs and names, new database and database server names, and the new directory names where database files are located.	SharePoint - 80 New web application name: SharePoint - 80 New web application URL: http://intranet Classic_Content New directory name: D:\Program Files\Microsoft SQL Server\ New database name: Intranet_Content New database server name: sql.hawmetal.com

10. If you are restoring to a new configuration and are restoring content databases, then in the New Names section you must provide the new directory name for the database files, the new database name for the database to restore, and the new database server name. You have these three options for each content and service application database. If you are restoring to the same configuration, the information in this section cannot be changed.

11. Depending on the components you selected for restore, other names such as web application URLs and service application names may be listed.

> **CAUTION** Before clicking Start Restore, double- and triple-check your settings! The restore may take hours, and it will be frustrating to have to do it again because you had one setting wrong.

12. Click the Start Restore button to begin the restore. A timer job is created and you are redirected to the backup and restore status page.

If you are doing a complete farm restore, you will find there is more work that needs to be done to finalize the environment. Tasks include:

- Reapplying manual IIS configuration changes, such as SSL certificate bindings
- Restarting services on the correct servers
- Reconfiguring service application associations
- Reapplying manual changes made to `web.config` files
- Redeploying any DLL files (assemblies) that were manually deployed into the GAC
- Reapplying any manual changes to the SharePoint Root (14 Hive)
- Reestablishing any cross-farm trust relationships
- Testing each essential SharePoint function to be sure it is working correctly

To perform a farm restore using PowerShell, use the `Restore-SPFarm` cmdlet. For more information, see the article "Restore a Farm (SharePoint Foundation 2010)" at `http://technet.microsoft.com/en-us/library/ee428311.aspx`.

Back Up and Restore a Site Collection

A site collection backup is a complete, full-fidelity backup of a single site collection. *Full-fidelity* means that all content and the state of the site collection are preserved in entirety. Site collection backups are useful when you need a full-fidelity backup but do not want to back up a whole content database. For example, you might have a training area stored in a site collection, and you periodically need to restore it to its original state.

When a site collection backup runs, SharePoint extracts from the content database only the table rows that are specific to the site collection. This makes a site collection backup more overhead intensive and slower than a content database backup. For this reason, try to avoid running regular site collection backups for site collections larger than 15 GB and only do so during off-peak hours.

When a site collection backup runs, SharePoint places a read-only lock on the site collection to preserve its integrity. During this time, the site collection can be used, but the UI is modified to prevent changes.

This behavior can be adjusted as covered in the "Using PowerShell to Back Up a Site Collection" section.

Unlike a farm backup, a site collection backup is stored as a single file. The backup command can be issued from Central Administration or PowerShell and whichever way you run it, the resulting backup file is the same. A site collection backup can only be restored using PowerShell.

Using Central Administration to Back Up a Site Collection

To perform a site collection backup using Central Administration, follow these steps:

1. Click Backup And Restore, and then select Perform A Site Collection Backup.

2. As shown in Figure 16.4, select the site collection.

   Figure 16.4: Site collection backup

   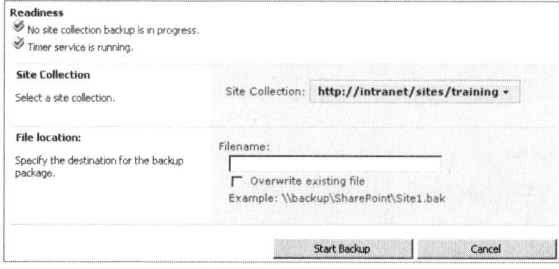

3. For Filename, specify the full path and filename where the backup should be stored. While this can be a local path, we recommend that you use a UNC path. Make sure that the farm account has read/write permissions to this share and the underlying NTFS folder.

4. Optionally, choose to overwrite the existing file at this path. If a file already exists and this option is not checked, the backup will fail.

5. Click Start Backup. SharePoint creates a new timer job for this backup and schedules it to run immediately.

Using PowerShell to Back Up a Site Collection

The PowerShell cmdlet you use to perform a site collection backup is Backup-SPSite. When you use it to back up a site collection, a timer job is not issued, and the backup is done on the fly within the PowerShell process.

Here is the syntax with the most common parameters:

```
Backup-SPSite <URL> -Path <BackupFile> [-Force]
[-NoSiteLock] [-UseSqlSnapshot]
```

The parameters are as follows:

- The -Force switch is used to overwrite the backup file.
- The -NoSiteLock switch tells SharePoint not to apply a read-only lock on the site collection during backup. We don't recommend that you use this switch in normal situations.
- The -UseSqlSnapShot switch tells SQL Server to create a database snapshot during the site collection backup. Using a snapshot allows the site collection to remain writable during backup. This feature is only available if you are running the Enterprise version of SQL Server. To learn more about database snapshots, see the article "Database Snapshots" at http://msdn.microsoft.com/en-us/library/ms175158.aspx.

Here is a basic example of backing up a single site collection:

```
Backup-SPSite http://intranet/sites/training
-Path \\NAS01\Backups\Training.bak
```

The following is a more advanced example. This sequence of cmdlets iterates through each site collection in a web application and issues a site collection backup for each one:

```
Get-SPWebApplication "SharePoint - intranet" |
Get-SPSite -limit all | ForEach-Object { $filename =
"\\NAS01\Backups\" + $_.Url.replace("http://","").
replace("_","__").replace("/","_") + ".bak" ;
Backup-SPSite $_.Url -path $filename -force}
```

Using PowerShell to Restore a Site Collection

A site collection backup is most commonly restored using PowerShell. The cmdlet that restores a site collection is Restore-SPSite, and the syntax is similar to Backup-SPSite:

```
Restore-SPSite <URL> -Path <BackupFile> ↵
[-Force] [-DatabaseName <DbName>]
```

The -Force switch is used if you will be restoring on top of an existing site collection. In this case, the existing site collection is first deleted.

The -DatabaseName switch allows you to specify which content database to use when restoring the site collection. This saves you from having to manually adjust each database's status as covered in Chapter 2, "Creating and Managing Web Applications." The content database must already exist and be associated with the web application.

This example restores a site collection into the designated content database:

```
Restore-SPSite http://intranet/sites/training ↵
-Path \\NAS01\Backups\Training.bak ↵
-ContentDatabase Training_Content
```

When you're restoring a site collection, the managed path does not need to match what was used when backing up. For example, you can also restore the training site collection to the following URL: http://intranet/sites/training_copy. You just need to make sure that a matching wildcard or explicit managed path already exists. To learn more about managed paths, see Chapter 3, "Creating and Managing Site Collections."

> **NOTE** You cannot restore a duplicate copy of a site collection within the same content database where the original is currently stored. This is because objects in a site collection are uniquely identified by a GUID, and these GUIDs must be unique across the database.

SharePoint also lets you restore site collections across web applications and farms. If you restore to a different farm, it must be the same SharePoint version and should be the same build (patch level).

Export and Import a Website, List, or Library

In addition to farm and site collection backups, SharePoint allows you to back up and restore a website hierarchy or even a single list or library. Unlike a site collection backup, these are not full fidelity since some details—including workflow settings, file checked-out status, alert subscriptions, and personal web part settings—are not captured in the backup.

If you export a website, that website and its subsites are included in the backup. If you export just a list or library, only the list or library is backed up. When performing an import, the content can be either merged with existing content or created.

Exporting content is a resource-intensive operation, much more so than a site collection backup. Thus, we don't advise you to export content if the total size of the backup exceeds 1 GB. Instead, back up the site collection or content database.

Exports can be run from Central Administration or PowerShell. The resulting backup file is the same, assuming the same options are used. Importing must be done using PowerShell.

Using Central Administration to Export

To use Central Administration to perform an export, follow these steps:

1. Click Backup And Restore, and then select Export A Site Or List.

2. In the Site Collection area, as shown in Figure 16.5, select the site collection where the content you want to export exists.

Figure 16.5: Site Or List Export

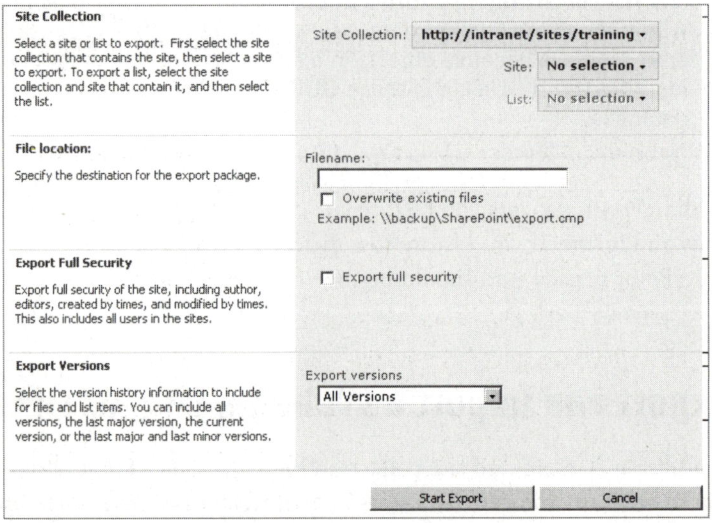

3. Optionally, select a website in the site collection. This can be the top-level website or a website at any other level. If nothing is selected, the website hierarchy from the top-level site and down is exported.

4. Optionally, choose a list or library from the selected website. If you do not choose a list or library, you will get a website export.

5. For Filename, specify the full path and filename where the backup package should be stored. If the amount of data exported is larger than about 25 MB, the backup will be split into multiple files. Each file in the package must be kept in order to import.

6. Optionally check Overwrite Existing Files to replace any previously exported packages.

7. Optionally, check Export Full Security. Enabling this switch preserves object permissions and inheritance settings. It also preserves item create and modified timestamps.

8. Choose how to handle export versions. You have four options: All Versions (the default setting), Last Major Version, Current Version, or Last Major And Last Minor.

9. Click Start Export to begin the export. A timer job is created and is scheduled to run immediately.

Using PowerShell to Export

The cmdlet you use to run an export using PowerShell is Export-SPWeb. Here is the syntax with the most common options:

```
Export-SPWeb <URL> -Path <ExportFile> [-CompressionSize
<number>] [-Force] [-IncludeUserSecurity]
[-IncludeVersions <LastMajor | CurrentVersion |
LastMajorAndMinor | All>] [-ItemUrl <path>]
```

Here is a brief explanation of each parameter:

URL The absolute URL to the website to export.

ExportFile The full path and filename to be exported.

Force Used to replace (overwrite) the current export file.

CompressionSize Sets the maximum size (in MB) for each export file in the package. The default size is 25 MB. If the export package is larger than this, the backup will be split into multiple files.

IncludeUserSecurity Includes information about users, groups, and permissions in the backup.

IncludeVersions Specifies which versions to include in the backup. You have the same four choices available as from Central Administration. This parameter must be used if you want files within libraries to be exported.

ItemUrl Specifies the path to the list or library, relative to the website defined in URL—for example, `"Shared Documents"`.

The following example exports just the tasks list for the IT website:

```
Export-SPWeb http://intranet/IT -Path
e:\Backups\IT-Tasks.cmp -ItemUrl "lists/tasks"
```

Using PowerShell to Import

An import is able to either merge or create the same content that was exported. When importing websites, the topmost website that was exported must already exist in the destination URL with the same site definition (e.g., team site, blog). Any subsites in the hierarchy that do not exist will be created. When importing a list or library, SharePoint creates the list or library if it doesn't exist. If it does exist, SharePoint can create just missing items in the list.

This merge concept is very powerful as it can be used to restore missing data. For example, if a few files are accidentally deleted from a library, you can recover these files by doing an import. Of course, always try to recover files from a Recycle Bin first.

The PowerShell cmdlet used for importing is `Import-SPWeb`. Here is the syntax with the most commonly used options:

```
Import-SPWeb <URL> -Path <ExportFile>
[-IncludeUserSecurity] [-UpdateVersions
<Append | Overwrite | Ignore>]
```

IncludeUserSecurity re-creates users and groups in the site collection and restores the security permissions included in the export package.

The **UpdateVersions** parameter defines how the merge works if an item already exists. **Append** restores the item as the most recent version, keeping original versions. **Overwrite** replaces the item with the version(s) from the export package. **Ignore** skips items that already exist.

To perform a basic import:

```
Import-SPWeb http://intranet/sites/training -Path ↵
e:\Backups\Training.cmp
```

To perform an import from an exported package and only create files that are missing:

```
Import-SPWeb http://intranet/IT -Path ↵
e:\Backups\IT-Docs.cmp -UpdateVersions Ignore
```

> **NOTE** If your export package contains multiple files, you only need to reference the first file in the package with the -Path parameter. SharePoint will automatically read each file in sequence when doing the import.

Recover Data from an Unattached Content Database

Being able to recover data from an unattached content database is quite a useful feature. The primary benefit is that you do not need a separate recovery farm when restoring site collections, websites, or lists and libraries. Here is a broad overview of the steps for using this feature:

1. Restore the content database from backup to any network-accessible SQL server.
2. Point SharePoint to this restored database (this is where the term *unattached content database* applies) and either back up the site collection or export the websites/list/library that need to be recovered.
3. Restore the site collection or import the websites/list/library.

The unique capability is in step 2, where SharePoint is able to access this database even though it is not actively attached to your farm.

With this feature, your recovery options open up significantly, provided you have made a complete farm backup. Recall in the "Using Central Administration to Perform a Component-Level Backup" section, earlier in this chapter, that the smallest component backed up is a content database.

What if you lose just one website or a site collection gets corrupted? If you restore the whole content database, all site collections in the database are restored to a previous state. You will lose the data in the site collections that changed since the last backup.

Using unattached content database recovery, it's a different story. You can point to the single site collection that is corrupted and just restore it. Or you can point to the website or library and just restore it. In other words, you have more granular restore options, even though you only have a farm backup.

Performing unattached content database recovery requires using a mixture of administration tools. Step 1 usually involves doing a restore from SQL Server. Step 2 can be done with Central Administration or PowerShell. Step 3 requires PowerShell and is the same type of restore or import as covered in previous sections.

Restoring a Content Database

When performing an unattached content database recovery, the first step is to restore the content database. It is best to restore directly from SQL Server Management Studio, the administrative program for SQL Server.

> **WARNING** If you intend on restoring the database to the same SQL server, be very careful that you do not restore to the same database name. Instead, use a temporary name.

You can also restore the database to any network-accessible SQL server, provided your SharePoint Farm account has dbcreator and securityadmin server role permissions and the version of the SQL server is the same or newer.

When restoring the database, you can restore it from any farm-level SharePoint backup that includes the content database as a component— for example, a complete farm backup. To identify which database backup file to restore, see the `spbackup.xml` file found in the corresponding `SPBRxxxx` folder. See "Understanding Farm Backup Sets," earlier in this chapter, for more information. If your DBA has been taking direct backups of your content databases from SQL Server, this backup can also be restored.

For specific steps on how to restore a database from SQL Server, see the article "How to: Restore a Database Backup (SQL Server Management Studio)" at http://msdn.microsoft.com/en-us/library/ms177429.aspx.

Using Central Administration to Recover Data from an Unattached Content Database

Once the database is restored, you can perform an unattached content database recovery. As a reminder, in this procedure you will back up or export the site collection or website/list. This must be done before you can issue the restore or import. Here are the steps:

1. Click Backup And Restore, then select Recover Data From An Unattached Content Database.

2. As shown in Figure 16.6, specify the database server where the database was just restored.

Figure 16.6: Unattached content database recovery

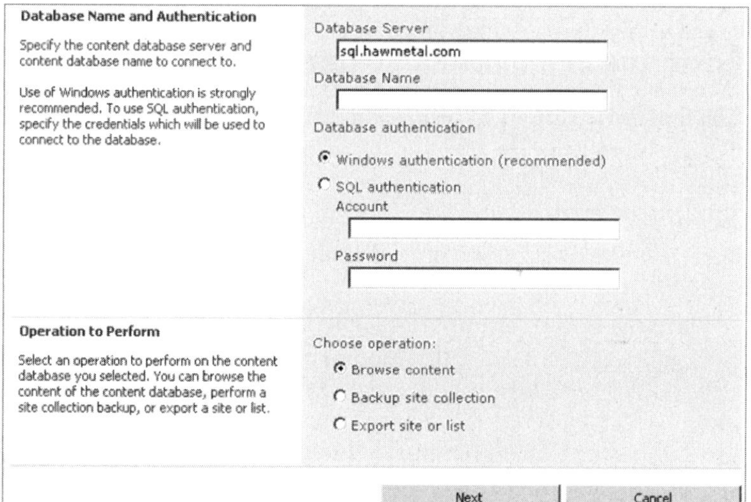

3. Enter the database name.

4. For Operation To Perform, the easiest choice is to select Browse Content (the default).

5. Click Next.

6. To browse content, first select the site collection in the content database.

7. Optionally, select the website in this site collection. If you do not select a website, you can only back up the site collection.
8. Optionally, select a list or library from the selected website.
9. For Operation To Perform, depending on what you did in steps 7 and 8, select either Backup The Site Collection or Export Site Or List.
10. Click Next.
11. The options presented on this final page depend on whether you selected Site Collection Backup or Export Site Or List. Either way, they are the exact same options you see when using Central Administration to back up a site collection or to export a website/list, so review the previous sections if you need more details.
12. Click Start Backup. A timer job is created and is scheduled to run immediately.

Restoring or Importing Content

The final procedure is to restore the site collection or import the website/list generated from the previous section. This is done using PowerShell, and you can use either `Restore-SPSite` or `Import-SPWeb`. There is nothing special about this type of restore, so consult the "Using PowerShell to Restore a Site Collection" or the "Using PowerShell to Import" section earlier in this chapter.

Once the restore or import completes, and you have confirmed all is working, you can delete the temporary database that was restored.

Index

Note to the Reader: Throughout this index, **boldfaced** page numbers indicate primary discussions of a topic. *Italicized* page numbers indicate illustrations.

A

AAMs (alternate access mappings)
   editing, **69–70**, *70*
   multiple servers, 167–168
   overview, **68**
   URLs, **69**, *69*
.accdt extension, 119
Accept Content Deployment Jobs settings, 414, *414*
Access Services application, **118–119**
accounts
   managed, **426–430**, *428*
   Search service, **257–258**
   User Profile service, **224–225**
Action Editor, 370, *371*
activating
   features, **216–218**, *217*
   in-place records management, 364
   SharePoint Server Publishing Feature, 394, *394*
   site collection publishing, 393–394, *394*
Active Directory (AD)
   authentication with, 45, 47–48
   requirements, 7
   synchronization with, 224–225
   trust relationships, 170
Add A New Path settings, 76
Add A Workflow dialog box, 320
Add Audience Rule page, 247–248, *247*
Add Best Bet dialog box, 301, *301*
Add Content Database window, 184
Add Crawl Component window, 177, *177*
Add Crawl Database window, 178, *178*
Add Crawl Rule page, 273–274, *274*
Add/Edit Port Rule dialog box, 162, *163*
Add Federated Location page, 303, *304*
Add Host To Cluster option, 164
Add Keyword page, 300, *300*
Add New Mapping settings, 237
Add New Synchronization Connection page, 239, *239*
Add Permission Policy Level dialog box, 434
Add Query Component window, 180, *180*
Add Rules option, 285
Add-SPShellAdmin cmdlet, 426
Add-SPSolution cmdlet, 207
Add To A Hold option, 390, *390*
Add To Default Proxy List option, 115
Add Trusted Data Connection Library page, 129
Add Trusted File Location option, 126
adding
   Best Bets, **300–301**, *301–302*
   content databases, **190–193**, *191*
   crawl rules, 273
   farm administrators, **425–426**
   farm solution packages, **207**
   nodes to clusters, **164–165**, *165*
   servers, **150–151**, *151*
   site collection administrators, **437–438**, *438*
   SQL servers, **183–184**
   users to SharePoint Groups, **441–442**

addresses
    clusters, 160, *161*
    Excel Services, 126
    IIS websites, 46
Admin settings in Search service, **266**
administrators
    farms, **424–426**
    service applications, **116**, *116–117*
    site collections, 79, *79*,
        437–438, *438*
Advanced Search feature, **291**
alerts
    search, 264
    SMS, 204, *204*
Alias option in search, 237
All Content scope rule, **287**
Allow Cross Domain Access
    option, 124
Allow External Data option, 127–128
Allow External Data Using REST
    option, 128
Allow Fill-In Choices option, 353
Allow manual submission from the
    Send To menu option, 379
Allow Multiple Values option, 351
Allow RSS Feeds In This Site
    Collection option, 102
Allow This Property To Be Used In
    Scopes option, 297
Allow users to choose the language of
    their personal site option, 252
Allow users to edit values for this
    property option, 237
Allow Writers To View Cached
    Content option, 407
alternate access mappings (AAMs)
    editing, **69–70**, *70*
    multiple servers, 167–168
    overview, **68**
    URLs, **69**, *69*
Always Follow Web Settings option,
    102
analytics reports, **457**
    configuring, **457–459**, *458*
    viewing, **459–463**, *460–461*
anonymous access
    site collections, 446

web application security, **434–435**
anonymous authentication, 307
Anonymous Cache Profile
    settings, 409
Anonymous Policy, 435
anonymous users, 46
antivirus settings, **435–436**
Application event log, 467
application pages, 97
Application Pool For Search Admin
    Web Service settings, 261, *261*
Application Pool For Search Query
    And Site Settings Web Service
    settings, 261, *261*
application pools, **43**
    configuring, **52–53**, *52*
    Search Service, 261, *261*
    service applications, 115
    User Profile service, 229, *230*
    web applications, 336
application servers
    overview, **5–7**, *5*
    scaling out, **168**
        cross-farm services,
            169–175, *171*
        search application, **175–182**,
            177–178, *180–181*
applications
    service. *See* service applications
    for User Profile service, **228–231**,
        230–231
    web. *See* web applications
applying
    master pages, **96–98**, *97*
    site collection policies, **388**, *388*
Article Page layout, 398
assigning search scopes, **289–291**,
    289–290
associating service applications to
    web applications, **140–141**
audiences, **246**
    compilation scheduling, **249**, *249*
    creating, **246–248**, *247*
    deleting, **248–249**
    editing, **248**
    user profiles, 224
    views, 323

auditing and audit reports
  log growth and size, **453–454**
  overview, **450–451**
  policies, **384–385**, *385*
  site collections, **451–453**, *453*
  viewing, **454–457**, *456*
Auditing Settings reports, 455
Authenticated Cache Profile
  settings, 409
authentication
  Claims-Based Authentication,
    47–51, *47–48*
  Classic, **51**, *51*
  crawl rules, 274–275
  crawler service databases, 178
  extended web applications,
    66–67
  Federated Search locations, 307
  groups, 440
  output caches, 409
  User Profile synchronization
    connections, 240
  web applications, **44–45**, *45*,
    66–67, 336
Authentication Information
  settings, 417
Authentication Providers dialog
  box, 435
authoritative pages, **297–299**, *298*
authors in Federated Search
  locations, 304
automatic operations
  farm backups, **481–484**
  installation, **33–37**, *35*
  site collection deletion, **87–88**, *87*
  updates, 402
Automatically Create And Manage
  Snapshots For Content
  Deployment option, 420
AutoSPInstaller, **34–36**, *35*
availability
  clustering for, 185
  scaling for, 149, 156, 168
Available For Tagging option, 348,
  350, 359
Available In All Locations By Default
  record control, 365

B

Background Activity setting, 264
Backup And Restore Job Status page,
  478, 481
Backup-SPFarm cmdlet, 478, 481
Backup-SPSite cmdlet, **489–490**
$backupFolder parameter, 483
backups
  component-level, **479–480**
  farms. *See* farms
  site collections, **488–490**, *489*
backward-compatible updates,
  32–33, *33*
barcodes policy, **385–386**, *386*
base permissions, **431**
Basic Authentication, 49
Basic Page layout, 398
BCS (Business Connectivity
  Services), 119
  permissions, **121–122**
  User Profile Service synchronization,
    243, *243*
BDC (Business Data Connectivity)
  configuring, **119–120**, *120*
  importing models, **120–121**
  permissions, **121–122**
  User Profile Service
    synchronization, 239
Best Bet Suggestions report, 310
Best Bet Suggestions Action History
  report, 310
Best Bet Usage report, 310
Best Bets in searches, **300–301**,
  301–302
"Best Practices for Using
  Fine-Grained Permissions", 443
BIN folder, 20
binary files
  installing, **12–15**, *13*
  in updates, 29, 32
Binary Large Objects (BLOB)
  caches, **411–413**
  remote, **42**
bindings, IIS, 60, *60*
Block Delete record
  control, 365

Block Edit And Delete record
  control, 365
Blocked File Types setting, 65
blocking keywords, 359
breaking permission inheritance, 443
Browser File Handling setting, 61–62
Business Connectivity Services
  (BCS), 119
  permissions, 121–122
  User Profile Service synchronization,
    243, *243*
Business Data Catalog service
  application, 115
Business Data Connectivity (BDC)
  configuring, 119–120, *120*
  importing models, 120–121
  permissions, 121–122
  User Profile Service
    synchronization, 239
business environments,
  auditing, 451–452

C

cache profiles, 403–407, *404–407*
Cache Profiles page, 404, *404*
Cache Profiles - New Item page,
  404–405, *405*
Cacheability settings, 406–407, *407*
caches
  application pools, 43
  BLOB, 411–413
  Excel Services, 125, 128
  object, 409–411, *410*
  output, 407–409, *408–409*
  Visio Graphics Service, 136–137
Caching Of Unused Files setting, 125
Calculation Behavior settings, 127
capacity settings for content
  databases, 195
cascading-style sheets (CSSs), 98
CBA (Claims-Based
  Authentication), 45
Central Administration, 23
  content databases, 191–192, *191*
  crawler services, 176–177
  for exporting, 492–493, *492*

farm backups, 476–480, *476–477*
farm restores, 486–488, *487*
installed services, 154
managed paths, 75–76, *76*
quota templates, 80–82, *81*
recovering data from unattached
  content database,
  497–498, *497*
site collections
  backups, 489, *489*
  creating, 77–79, *77–79*
  managing, 85–88, *85–86*, *88*
web applications, 44
  application pools, 52–53, *52*
  authentication, 44–45, *45*
  content databases, 53–54, *53*
  IIS website settings, 45–46, *46*
  multiple servers, 166–168, *167*
  public URLs, 52
  security, 46–51, *46–49*
.cer extension, 59
certificates
  configuring, 58–60, *59–60*
  content deployment, 415
  farm search administration, 265
  SMS, 204
  STS, 170–172
Change Site Collection
  Administrators option, 437
Check Backup And Restore Job Status
  option, 478
checkouts
  explicit, 315–317, *316*
  file ownership, 317–318, *318*
  implicit, 315–316
Claims-Based Authentication (CBA),
  45, 47–51, *47–48*
Classic authentication, 45, 51, *51*
Cluster Parameters page, 160, *161*
clusters
  creating, 159–164, *159–161*, *163*
  load-balancing, 156–158, *156*
  nodes, 164–165, *165*
  for scaling, 185
co-authoring feature, 316
collections. *See* site collections
color in site themes, 98–99

comments for PerformancePoint
    Services, 131
common authentication, **307**
compatibility mode, **30**, *30*
compatibility of updates, **32–33**, *33*
Complete Certificate Request
    option, **59**
complete farm backups, **474–478**,
    476–477
Compliance Details dialog box,
    367–368, *368*, **390**
component-level backups, **479–480**
Condition Editor, 370, *370*
conditions
    Content Organizer rules, 332
    Records Center rules, 376, *377*
    records declarations, 370, *370*
    views, 323
config.xml file, 34
configuration-only farm backups,
    478–479
Configuration Wizard
    farms
        creating, **15–21**, *16–19*
        joining, 151
        removing, 151–152
    language packs, 27
    multiple servers, 166
    service applications, 113
    service packs, **31**, *31*
    updates, 29, 32–33
Configure Alternate Access Mappings
    option, 70
Configure Audit Settings page,
    453, *453*
Configure Diagnostic Logging option,
    24
Configure Incoming Email Settings
    option, 197
Configure Metadata Navigation page,
    355, *355*
Configure Service Application
    Associations dialog box, 141, *141*
Confirm Site Use And Deletion
    option, 87
Connect An Existing Server Farm
    option, 22

Connection Lifetime setting, 125
Connection Security settings,
    415, *415*
connections
    content deployment, **415**, *415*
    Excel Services, **124–125**
    farm search time-out settings, 265
    portal site, **106–107**, *107*
    Send To, **377–380**, *378*, *380*
    User Profile synchronization,
        238–241, *239–240*,
        243–244, *244*
consuming farms, 169–171
consuming service applications,
    174–175
contacts
    farm search administration, 264
    keywords, 300
    Secure Store Service, 134
    term sets, 348
content approval
    configuring, **319–321**, *321*
    enabling, **319**, *319*
content databases, **190**
    adding, **190–193**, *191*
    configuring, **53–54**, *53*, **194–196**
    moving, **196**
    moving site collections to, **89–90**
    recovering data from, **495–498**, *497*
    removing, **193**
    restoring, 488
    site collections, **82–83**, *82*
    working with, **41–42**, *41*
content deployment
    configuring, **413–415**, *414–415*
    jobs, **418–420**, *419–420*
    paths, **415–418**, *416–417*
Content Deployment Settings page,
    414, *414–415*
content management, **103–104**, *103*
Content Modifications report, *455*
Content Organizer, **330**
    configuring, **330–331**
    rules, **331–332**
content source for Search service
    creating, **267–269**, *267–268*
    types, **269–270**, *270*

Content Source scope rule, **287**, *287*
Content Type And List Modifications report, 455
Content Type Hub property, **338–339**, *339*
Content Type Publishing Hubs page, 341, *341*
content type syndication
    hubs
        configuring, **338–342**, *339–340*
        creating, **335–338**
    overview, **334–335**
content types
    creating, **324–326**, *325*, **337–338**
    planning, **337–338**
    publishing, **340–342**, *341*
Content Viewing report, 455
copying
    Federated Search locations, 308
    permissions, 439
    Records Center documents, 379
Core Results web parts, **308**, *308*
CPU
    core requirements, 7
    quota point calculations, 214
Crawl Schedules settings, **269**, *269*
Crawl Status setting, 264
Crawled Property Selection dialog box, 297
crawls and crawlers, 258, **271**
    databases, 277
    logs, **275–276**
    properties, **295–297**
    rules
        host distribution, **277–278**
        impact, **262–263**, *262*
        managing, **273–275**, *273–274*
    scaling, **176–179**, *177–178*
    schedules, 269, *269*, **271–272**, *272*
    settings, 264, **266**, 269
Create A New Quota Template option, 81
Create A New Server Farm option, **16**, *16*
Create Certificate Request option, 58
Create Content Deployment Job page, 419, *419*
Create Content Deployment Path page, 416, *416*
Create List Workflow dialog box, 370
Create New Access Services Application dialog box, 114, *114*
Create New Web Application dialog box, **44–46**
Create Scope page, **285**, *285*
Create Task dialog box, 483
credentials for Secure Store Service, **134–135**
Critical logging level, 467
cross-farm services, **169**
    publishing farms, **172–173**
    service applications
        consuming, **174–175**
        publishing, **174**
    trust relationships, **170–172**, *171*
Cross List Query Cache Changes settings, 410
cryptography. *See* encryption
CSSs (cascading-style sheets), 98
Cumulative Updates (CUs), **28–29**
Current Navigation, **99–100**
Custom Event Name information, 456
custom repositories, 270
Custom zones, 68
Customize Your Term Set option, 352, *352*

D

Daily Time Window For Large Queries setting, 63, *63*
Data Source Query Time-Out setting, 131
Database Authentication settings, 53, 54, 178
Database Information settings, **194**
Database Server settings, 6
database servers
    content databases, 53, 54
    roles, **5–7**, *5*
    scaling, **182–183**
    Search service accounts, **259**, *259*
databases
    content. *See* content databases

Disabled cache profiles 505

crawls and crawlers, 176, **178–179**, *178*, 277
mirroring, **184–185**, *184*
naming conventions, 53
property, **179–182**
recovering data from, **495–498**, *497*
Search service, 266
SQL servers, 183, 185
User Profile service, **229–230**
dates for retention policies, 383–384
$days parameter for farm backups, 483
deactivating features, **216–218**, *217*
Debug Cache Information settings, 409
declaring records
  manual process, 367–368, *367–368*
  through retention policies, 371–372
  through workflow, 369–371, *369–371*
dedicated NICs for Windows-based NLB, 158
dedicated site collections, **336–337**
dedicated web applications, **335–336**
Default Content Access Account setting, 264
Default Proxy Group settings, **231**
Default Quota Template setting, **61**
default SharePoint groups, **440**
Default Time Zone setting, **61**
Default User Profile Subtype setting, 236
Default Value for Managed Metadata columns, 353
Default zones, 68
Define Managed Paths dialog box, 76
Delegation Of Control wizard, 225
Delete Data Associated With The Service Applications option, 116
Delete Items permission, 439
Delete Selected Paths option, 76
Delete Selected Users option, 432
Deleted From End-User Recycle Bin option, 105
Deletes information in crawl logs, 276
deleting
  audiences, **248–249**

Federated Search locations, 308
  keywords, **358–359**
  profiles, **245–247**, *246*
Search service indexes, 280
service applications, **115–116**
site collections, **86–88**, *87*, **90**
web applications, **71–72**, *72*
websites, 104
Deletion report, 455
denying permissions, 431
Deploy User Names option, 418
deployment
  content
    configuring, **413–415**, *414–415*
    jobs, **418–420**, *419–420*
    paths, **415–418**, *416–417*
  farm solution packages, **207–210**, *208–209*
descriptions
  content types, 326
  Excel Services, 126
  Federated Search locations, 304
  information management policies, 382
  site collections, 78
  term sets, 348
  terms, 350
Destination Central Administration Web Application settings, *416*, *417*
destination site collections
  creating, 413–414
  selecting, 417–418, *417*
Destination Web Application list, *417*, 417
diagnostic logging, **466**
  adjusting, **24–25**, *24*
  event logs, **466–467**, *467*
  settings, **469–470**, *469–470*
  trace logs, **468–469**, *468*
differential backups, 480
Disable Embedded Fonts? option, **138**, 140
Disable-SPFeature cmdlet, 219
Disable Word 97-2003 Document Scanning? option, **138**, 140
Disabled cache profiles, 403

disabling
    SharePoint Designer, **64–65**, *64*
    User Profile properties, 236–237
Disconnect From This Server Farm option, 152
disk space
    backups, 478
    query services, 181
    requirements, 7
Dismount-SPContentDatabase cmdlet, 193
Display Granular External Data Errors setting, 128
Display Information settings, 306, *306*
Display Name setting, 134
Display settings for User Profile properties, 237
DNS (Domain Name System), 46
Do Not Disconnect From This Server Farm option, 21
Do Not Require Encryption option, 415
Document Conversions Load Balancer Service, 155
Document ID Service, 328, 337
document IDs, 328–330
Document Location information in audit reports, 456
document management, **312**
    content approval, 319–321, *319*, *321*
    Content Organizer, 330–332
    content types, 324–326, *325*
    document IDs, 328–330
    document sets, 327–328, *328*
    draft item security, 318, *318*
    explicit checkouts, 315–317, *316*
    ownership of checked-out files, 317–318, *318*
    restoring document versions, 314–315, *315*
    versioning, 312–314, *313*
    views, 321–324
document sets, 327–328, *328*
Domain Name System (DNS), 46
draft item security, 318, *318*
Drop Off Library, 374, 379–380
Duplicate Submissions option, 331
.dwp extension, 93

E

ECS (Excel Calculation Services), **123**
eDiscovery, **388–390**, *389–390*
Edit Authentication dialog box, 435
Edit Managed Metadata Service Connection page, 340, *340*
Edit permission for BCS, 122
Edit Policy page, 383, *383*, 385–386, *385*
Edit Rule dialog, 376, *376*
Edit Scope Display Group page, 290, *290*
Edit Setting section for User Profile properties, 237
Edit Timer Job page, 471–472, *471*
Edit Users dialog box, 433
editing
    alternate access mappings, 69–70, *70*
    audiences, **248**
    Federated Search locations, 308
    file types, **279**
    keywords, **358**
    managed accounts, **428**
    permissions, **445**
    profiles, **244–245**
    User Profile synchronization connection filters, **243–244**, *244*
electronic document and records management systems (EDRMSs), 362
email
    incoming, **197**
        enabling, **197–199**, *198*
        forwarding messages, **200–201**, *201*
        library configuration for, 201–202, *202*
        SMTP service, **199–200**
    outgoing, **203–204**, *204*
Enable Automatic Password Change option, 428

Enable Event Log Flood Protection option, 470
Enable Output Cache option, 408, *408*
Enable-SPFeature cmdlet, 218–219
Enable-SPSessionStateService cmdlet, 135
Enable Usage Data Collection option, 458
enabling
    content approval, **319**, *319*
    incoming email, **197–199**, *198*
    keyword tagging, **357–358**, *357*
    Self-Service Site Creation, **228**
    site collection required features, **337**
    versioning, **312–314**, *313*
encryption
    certificates, **59**
    content deployment, **415**
    Excel Services, **124**
    Secure Store Service, **133**, *133*
    SSL, 47
enterprise business environments, auditing, **451–452**
Enterprise Edition, **111**
Enterprise keywords, **356–357**
    blocking, **359**
    deleting, **358–359**
    editing, **358**
    moving, **359**
    tagging, **357–358**, *357*
    viewing, **358**
Enterprise Search Center site template, **291–294**, *292*
Enterprise Wiki template, 393
enumerating site collections, **88–89**
Error logging level, 467
error logs, 342
errors in crawl logs, 275
Establish Trust Relationship dialog box, **171**, *171*
event information in audit reports, 456
event logs, **466–467**, *467*
Event Selection settings, **458**, *458*
Event Throttling setting, 469
Excel Calculation Services (ECS), **123**
Excel Services application, **122–123**

global settings, **123–125**, *123*
trusted data connection libraries, **128–129**
trusted file locations, **126–128**
user-defined function assemblies, **129–130**
Exchange public folders, 270
Exclude All Items In This Path option, 274
Exclusion Filters For Groups settings, 244
Exclusion Filters For Users settings, 244, *244*
Execute permission for BCS, 122
Expiration And Disposition report, 455
explicit checkouts, **315–317**, *316*
explicit managed paths, 75, 226
Export-SPWeb cmdlet, 493
exporting
    Federated Search locations, 308
    site collection policies, **388**
    term sets, **349**
    User Profile properties for, **235**, *235*
    website, lists, and libraries, **491–494**, *492*
extending web applications, **65–68**, *66–67*
external data
    Excel Services, **125**, **127–128**
    FAST, 282
Extranet (Published Site) cache profile, 404
Extranet zones, 68

F

Failed Queries report, 310
failover servers
    content databases, **54**, 195
    query components, 181
    in scaling, **184–185**
Farm Configuration Wizard, **112–113**
farms
    administrators, **424–426**
    backups
        automating, **481–484**
        complete, **474–478**, *476–477*

farms (*continued*)
    configuration-only, **478–479**
    overview, **474**
    sets, **480**
  content deployment, 413–414
  creating
    Configuration Wizard, **15–19**, *16–19*
    PSCONFIG.EXE, **19–21**, *20*
  features, **218**
  joining, **21–23**, *22–23*
  for My Site, **225–228**
  Office Web Apps installation on, **26**
  overview, **4–5**
  restores, **484–488**, *487*
  search administration, **263–265**, *263*, *265*
  security, **424–426**
  selecting, **12–13**, *13*
  servers
    adding, **150–151**, *151*
    removing, **151–153**, *152*
  solution packages, **206–207**
    adding, **207**
    deploying, **207–210**, *208–209*
    removing, **211**
    retracting, **210**
  topologies, **144**
    large farms, **148–150**
    medium-server farms, **147–148**, *148*
    single-server farms, **145**, *145*
    three-server farms, **146–147**, *146–147*
    two-server farms, **145**, *146*
  trust relationships between, **170–172**, *171*
  updates on, **30–33**, *31*
  with User Profile service, **224**
FAST Index option, **305**, **307**
FAST search component, 261
  Federated Search locations, 305, 307
  overview, **281–282**
FBA (Forms-Based Authentication), **45**, **49–51**, *49*

features
  activating and deactivating, **216–218**, *217*
  managing, **215–216**
  PowerShell for, **218–219**
Federated Search feature, **302–303**, *303*
  locations
    creating, **303–307**, *304*, *306–307*
    importing, **307–308**
    web parts, **308–309**, *308*
File Access Method in Excel Services, **123–124**
file icons in Search service, **280**
File Location tab, 14
file shares in Search Service content sources, 270
file types in Search service, **278–279**
filters
  Metadata Navigation, **354–356**, *355–356*
  Search service, **278–279**
  User Profile synchronization connections, **243–244**, *244*
  views, 323
FIM (Forefront Identity Manager) services, 224, 233
folders
  Content Organizer, 331
  views, 324
fonts in site themes, 98–99
Forefront Identity Manager (FIM) services, 224, 233
Forefront Identity Manager Synchronization Service, 233
form pages, 97
formats for Managed Metadata columns, 351
Forms-Based Authentication (FBA), **45**, **49–51**, *49*
forwarding messages, **200–201**, *201*
FQDNs (fully qualified domain names), 46, 200
frequency of content deployment jobs, **420**, *420*

Frequency With Which To Start Conversions (Minutes) setting, 138
Full Control option for administrators, 116, *117*
full crawls, **271**
Full deployment type, 418
full-fidelity backups, 488
Full Read permission, 434–432
fully qualified domain names (FQDNs), 46, 200

G

galleries, **91**
    Master Pages And Page Layouts, **91–93**, *92–93*
    Solutions, **95–96**, *95–96*
    Web Parts, **93–95**, *94*
GALs (global address lists), 198
General Settings for web applications, **61–62**, *61*
Get-Help cmdlet, 56, 195
Get-SPCertificateAuthority cmdlet, 170–171
Get-SPClaimProvider cmdlet, 172
Get-SPContentDatabase cmdlet, 195
Get-SPFarm cmdlet, 172
Get-SPFeature cmdlet, 218
Get-SPMetadataServiceApplication cmdlet, 173
Get-SPSecurityTokenServiceConfig cmdlet, 171
Get-SPServiceApplicationSecurity cmdlet, 172
Get-SPSite cmdlet, 88
Get-SPSiteAdministration cmdlet, 88–90
Get-SPTopologyServiceApplication cmdlet, 172–173
Get-SPWeb cmdlet, 426
Get-SPWebApplication cmdlet, 490
global address lists (GALs), 198
global audiences, 246
global navigation, **99–101**, *99*
global settings
    Excel Services, **123–125**, *123*
    Visio Graphics Service, **136–137**
Gradual Site Delete job, 86
Grant Permissions dialog box, 425, 441, 445
Group By setting, 323
Group Managers setting, 346
groups
    content types, 326
    Secure Store Service, 135
    site collection, **440–442**
    term set, **345–347**, *346*
    views, 323
growth issues with logs, 453–454, 469
guest users, 46
GUIDs
    in audit reports, 456–457
    publishing farms, 172–173
    uniqueness, 491

H

hardware-based load balancers, 165–166
Health Analyzer Rule Definitions page, 466, *466*
Health Analyzer tool, **463–464**, *463*
    problems and solutions reviews, **464–465**, *464–465*
    rule definitions, **466**, *466*
Health Insurance Portability and Accountability Act (HIPAA), 342
hierarchical term sets, 343, *343*
high availability
    clustering for, 185
    scaling for, 149, 156, 168
High logging level, 468
high security environments, auditing, 452
HIPAA (Health Insurance Portability and Accountability Act), 342
histories, version. *See* document management
holds, **388–390**, *389–390*
host distribution rules, 179, **277–278**
Host Headers in IIS websites, 46

host interfaces in Windows-based
    NLB, 158
host parameters for clusters, 160, *160*
"How to: Restore a Database Backup
    (SQL Server Management
    Studio)", 496
HTML, reusable, 401–403
HTTP 401.1 Unauthorized Error
    handling, **25**
hubs, syndication
    configuring, **338–342**, *339–340*
    creating, **335–338**
    designating, **334–335**

I

icons, file, **280**
IDC (International Data Corporation)
    study, 257
IDs, document, **328–330**
IFilters, **278–279**
IGMP (Internet Group Management
    Protocol) Multicast, **162**
Ignore SSL Certificate Name
    Warnings option, 265
IIS. *See* Internet Information
    Services (IIS)
IISRESET command, 233, 241
impact rules for crawlers,
    262–263, *262*
Impersonation method, 124
Implicit checkouts, **315–316**
Import-SPWeb cmdlet, 494–495, 498
importing
    BDC models, **120–121**
    Federated Search locations,
        307–308
    lists and libraries, **494–495**
    site collection policies, 388
    term sets, 349
    User Profile properties for,
        233–234, *234*
    websites, 494–495, 498
in-place records management
    activating, **364**
    declaring records
        manual process, **367–368**,
            367–368

through retention policies,
    371–372
through workflow, **369–371**,
    369–371
lists and libraries, **365–367**, *366*
overview, **363**
record declaration settings,
    364–365, *364*
Include All Items In This Path
    option, 274
Include User Who setting, 247
incoming email, **197**
    enabling, **197–199**, *198*
    forwarding messages, **200–201**, *201*
    library configuration for,
        201–202, *202*
    SMTP service, **199–200**
incremental crawls, **271–272**
Incremental deployment type, 418
incremental synchronization, **242**
index partitions
    multiple, **179–181**
    Search service, **266–267**
Index Reset command, 280
Indexed properties, 237
indexes
    content sources. *See* crawls and
        crawlers
    Metadata Navigation, **354–355**
    resetting, **280–281**
Indexing Schedule settings, 260
Individual Quota template option, 86
Information logging level, 467
information management policies
    auditing, **384–385**, *385*
    barcodes, **385–386**, *386*
    creating, **382–383**
    labels, **386–387**, *387*
    overview, **381–382**
    retention, **383–384**, *383–384*
    site collection, **387–388**, *388*
inheritance of permissions,
    442–444, *442*
Initial Retrieval Limit setting, 131
Inline Editing setting for views, 323
Install-SPFeature cmdlet, 218
Install-SPSolution cmdlet, 210–211
installation

IFilters, **279**
SharePoint
  automating, **33–37**, *35*
  binaries, **12–15**, *13*
  farms, **15–23**, *16–20*, *22–23*
  postinstall operations, **23–28**, *24*
  preparing for, **4–9**, *5*
  prerequisites, **10–12**, *11*
  steps overview, **9–10**
  updates, **28–33**, *30–31*, *33*
SMTP service, **199–200**
Windows-based NLB, **158**
installed services, viewing, **154–155**, *154*
instances, service, **112**
internal URLs, **69**, *69*
International Data Corporation (IDC) study, *257*
Internet Group Management Protocol (IGMP) Multicast, **162**
Internet Information Services (IIS), **56**
  logging path, **57–58**, *57*
  relationship with, **42–43**
  SSL certificates, **58–60**, *59–60*
  User Profile services, 233
  website settings, **45–46**, *45*, **336**
Internet zones, 68
Intranet (Collaboration Site) cache profile, 404
Intranet zones, 68
inventory reports, 462
IP addresses
  clusters, 160, *161*
  IIS websites, 46
IPsec encryption, 124
Item Count setting for views, 324
Item ID information in audit reports, 456
Item Type information in audit reports, 456

J

Job Definitions page, 471, *471*
jobs
  content deployment, **418–420**, *419–420*
  timer. *See* timer jobs
joining farms, **21–23**, *22–23*

K

Keep drafts for the following number of major versions setting, 314
Keep the following number of major versions setting, 313
Kerberos authentication, 19
  Excel Services, 124
  overview, **48–49**
keywords, **356–357**
  blocking, 359
  deleting, **358–359**
  editing, 358
  moving, 359
  search scopes, **299–300**, *300*
  tagging, **357–358**, *357*
  viewing, 358
KPI Icon Cache setting, 131

L

labels policy, **386–387**, *387*
LanguagePacks folder, 35
languages
  language pack installation, 27
  My Site, 252
  term sets, 345
large farms, **148–150**
layouts, page, **92**, **397–399**, *398–399*
LDAP (Lightweight Directory Access Protocol) authentication, 45
Least critical event to report to the event log setting, 469
Least critical event to report to the trace log setting, 469
Length Of Time Before Conversion Status Is Monitored (Minutes) setting, 139
levels
  event log messages, **467**
  permissions, **431–434**, **438–439**

libraries
    data connection, **128–129**
    document versioning for, 313
    email configuration, **201–202**, *202*
    exporting, **491–494**, *492*
    importing, **494–495**
    in-place records management, **365–367**, *366*
    Records Center, **374–375**
    views, **321–324**
license keys, 14
Lightweight Directory Access Protocol (LDAP) authentication, 45
line-of-business data content, 270
links
    navigation, 100, *100*
    to Office client applications, **254**
list administrators, 365
List Workflow menu, 369, *369*
lists
    Access Services, 118
    exporting, **491–494**, *492*
    importing, **494–495**
    in-place records management, **365–367**, *366*
    views, 321
load balancing, **156–157**, *156*
    Excel Services, **124**
    hardware-based, **165–166**
    IIS websites, 46
    with updates, 32–33
    for user solutions, **212–213**, *213*
Local option for Excel Services load balancing, 124
Location Type settings
    Excel Services, 126
    Federated Search, **305**
locations in Federated Search
    creating, **303–307**, *304*, *306–307*
    importing, **307–308**
locked files, 316, *316*
locked term sets, 343
locks for site collections, **85–86**, *85*
logical operators for shared search scope rules, 286
logs
    content type publishing, 342
    crawls, **275–276**

diagnostic, **466**
    adjusting, **24–25**, *24*
    event, **466–467**, *467*
    settings, **469–470**, *469–470*
    trace, **468–469**, *468*
farm search, 264
growth and size, **453–454**, 469
IIS paths, **57–58**, *57*
Network Load Balancing Manager, 163, *163*
SQL servers, 183
web analytics reports, **457**
look and feel of web pages, **96**
    master pages, **96–98**, *97*
    site collection navigation, **99–101**, *99–100*
    site themes, **98–99**

M

major versions, 313–314
    pending approval, **319–320**
    publishing files as, **93**, *93*
Manage Content And Structure option, 104
Manage Excel Services Application page, 123, *123*
Manage Federated Locations page, 303, *303*
Manage Schedules page, 272, *272*
Manage Servers In This Farm option, 151
Manage Service Applications page, **123–124**
Manage the Graphics Service Applications page, 136, *136*
Manage Web Applications screen, 71
managed accounts
    configuring, **426–427**
    creating, **427–429**, *428*
    editing, **429**
    removing, **429–430**
Managed Metadata columns
    creating, **351–353**, *352*
    working with, **353**, *354*
Managed Metadata Service application, 334

content type. *See* content type syndication
databases, 115
Enterprise keywords, **356–359**, *357*
permissions, 173
purpose, 111
term sets. *See* term sets
troubleshooting, **350–351**
managed paths
defining, **74–77**, *74*, *76*
for My Site, **226**
managed properties, **295–297**, *296*
Managing Crawl Rules page, 273, *273*
manual processes
Records Center uploads, **379–380**
records declarations, **367–368**, *367–368*
service application creation, **113–115**, *114*
User Profile synchronization, **241**
mappings
alternate access, **68–70**, *69–70*, 167–168
metadata properties, **294–297**, *295–296*
server names, **276**
User Profile properties, **236–238**
master pages, **91**, *96–98*, *97*
Master Pages And Page Layouts gallery, **91–93**, *92–93*
Maximum Application Log Size setting, 119
Maximum Cache Age setting, 137
Maximum Chart or Image Size setting, 127
Maximum Chart Render Duration setting, 127
Maximum Concurrent Queries Per Session setting, 128
Maximum Conversion Attempts setting, 139
Maximum Measures To Load In Select Measure Control setting, 131
Maximum Members To Load In Filter Tree setting, 131
Maximum Number Of Items setting, 132
Maximum Private Bytes setting, 125
Maximum Recalc Duration setting, 137
Maximum Request Duration setting, 127
Maximum Retrieval Limit setting, 132
Maximum Sessions Allowed Per User setting, 124
Maximum SharePoint Database Schema version setting, 195
Maximum Size Of Workbook Cache setting, 125
Maximum Template Size setting, 119
Maximum Unused Object Age setting, 125
Maximum Upload Size setting, **62**
Maximum Web Drawing Size setting, 136
Maximum Workbook Size setting, 127
Medium logging level, 468
medium-server farms, **147–148**, *148*
Members group, 440
memory
Access Services, 119
application pools, 43, 52
Excel Services, **125**
requirements, 7
Memory Cache Threshold setting, 125
messages
email. *See* email
SMS, **204–205**, *205*
metadata, 334
Managed Metadata Service. *See* Managed Metadata Service application
property mappings, **294–297**, *295–296*
Metadata Navigation feature, **354–356**, *355–356*
Metadata Navigation and Filtering feature, 354–355
Metadata Property Mappings page, **295**, *295*
Microsoft Cluster Service, 158
Microsoft SharePoint Foundation Incoming Email service, 154

Microsoft SharePoint Foundation
    Usage Data Import Job, 459
Microsoft SharePoint Foundation
    Usage Data Processing Job, 459
Microsoft SharePoint Foundation
    Web Application service, 154
Microsoft SharePoint Foundation
    Workflow Timer Service, 154
Minimum Cache Age setting, 136
minor versions, 313–314
mirroring database, **184–185**, *184*
mirrors, query component, 179,
    181–182
Mobile setting for views, 324
Monitorable logging level, 468
monitoring content type
    publishing, **342**
Most Authoritative Pages setting, 298
Mount-SPContentDatabase
    cmdlet, 193
mounting databases, 193
Move-SPSite cmdlet, 89–90
moving
    content databases, **196**
    keywords, 359
    Records Center documents, 379
    site collections, **89–90**
.msi extension, 206
Multi-Tenancy, 378
Multicast cluster mode, **162**
multiple farms, 169
multiple index partitions, **179–181**
multiple languages
    language packs, **27**
    My Site, 252
    term sets, **345**
multiple query components, **179**
multiple servers, **166–168**, *167*
My Site Host Location settings,
    251, *251*
My Site Host sites, **227**
My Site Host URL setting, 231, *231*
My Site Managed Path setting,
    231, *231*
My Sites
    farm preparation for, **225–228**
    Office client application links, **254**
    overview, **249–250**

personalization site links,
    253–254, *253*
setting up, **250–252**, *251–252*
trusted host locations, **252–253**
user profiles, 223

N

names
    Content Organizer rules, 332
    content types, 326
    databases, **53**, 192
    Federated Search locations, 304
    information management
        policies, 382
    managed properties, 296
    My Site, 252
    network interfaces, 158
    publishing farms, 172
    rules, 376
    Search service, 260, *260*
    server mappings, **276**
navigation
    Metadata Navigation, **354–356**,
        355–356
    site collections, **99–101**, *99–100*
network interface cards (NICs),
    157–158, 162
Network Load Balancing (NLB), 156
    IIS websites, 46
    Windows-based. *See* Windows-
        based NLB
Network Load Balancing Manager,
    159
Network Load Balancing Manager
    log, 163, *163*
Never Allow The Manual Declaration
    Of Record option, 366
New Audience option, 247
New Content Source page, 268, *268*
New Content Type page, 325, *325*
New Managed Property page,
    296, *296*
New Page dialog box, 396
New Send Connector dialog box,
    200–201, *201*
New-SPClaimsPrincipal cmdlet, 172
New-SPContentDatabase cmdlet, 192

New-SPManagedAccount cmdlet, 429
New-SPManagedPath cmdlet, 77
New-SPSite cmdlet, 79–80
New-SPWebApplication cmdlet, **55–56**
New Web Application page, **336**
New Workbook Session Timeout setting, 127
NICs (network interface cards), 157–158, 162
NLB (Network Load Balancing), 156
   IIS websites, 46
   Windows-based. *See* Windows-based NLB
No Restriction option, 306
No Restrictions record control, 365
No Result Queries report, 310
NoCache option, 407
nodes, clusters, **164–165**, *165*
Not Available In All Locations record control, 365
notifications for managed accounts, 428
NTLM (Windows NT LAN Manager), 19, 48
Number Of Conversions To Start (Per Conversion Process) setting, 139
Number Of Daily Unique Visitors report, 461
Number Of Page Views report, 461
Number Of Queries report, 310
Number Of Referrers report, 461
Number Of Site Collections report, 462
Number Of Sites report, 462

O

Object Cache Flush option, 410
Object Cache page, 410, *410*
Object Cache Reset settings, 410, *410*
object caches, **409–411**, *410*
object permissions in BCS, **121–122**
Occurred (GMT) information in audit reports, 456
Office client applications, links to, **254**
Office Data Connection (ODC) files, 128

Office Mobile Service (OMS), 204
Office Web Applications
   installing, **25–26**
   purpose, **111**
officialfile.asmx service, 380
Offline content database status, 194
OMS (Office Mobile Service), 204
OpenSearch option, 305, **307**
operating system requirements, 7
optimizing SQL server databases, 183
Organizer rules for Records Center, **375–377**, *376–377*
outgoing email, **203–204**, *204*
output caches, **407–409**, *408–409*
Overwrite Existing Files option, 493
Owner setting for term sets, 348
Owners group, 440
ownership of checked-out files, **317–318**, *318*
owstimer.exe service, 470

P

page layouts, **92**, **397–399**, *398–399*
Page Output Cache Policy settings, 409
page properties, **399–400**, *400*
pages, publishing, **394–397**, *394–396*
Parent Content Type setting, 326
passwords and passphrases
   farm restores, 486
   farms, 17–18, *18*, 22–23, *23*
   FBA, 50
   managed accounts, 427–428
   Search service accounts, 258
   Secure Store Service, 135
PATH environment variable, 20
paths
   content deployment, **415–418**, *416–417*
   content deployment jobs, 419, *419*
   crawl rules, 274
   IIS logging, **57–58**, *57*
   managed, **74–77**, *74*, *76*, **226**
   Managed Metadata columns, 352
patterns for Federated Search locations, **305**
PDF IFilters, 279

People Picker, 47–48, *48*
Percentage Of Memory setting, 138
Perform ACL Check option, 405
performance, scaling for, 168
PerformancePoint Services, **130–132**
permissions, **8–9**
   base, 431
   BCS, **121–122**
   cache profile, 405
   errors, 20
   farm administrators, 425
   inheritance, **442–444**, *442*
   levels, **431**
   My Site, 252
   publishing farms, 173
   service application administrators, 116, *117*, 427
   SharePoint groups, 441
   site collection, **438–439**, **444–447**, *447*
   User Profile service, **224–225**
   web application, **431–434**
   web parts, **94–95**
personal settings for site collections, 102
Personal Site Location settings, 251, *251*
personal views, 322
personalization site links, **253–254**, *253*
policies
   information management. *See* information management policies
   web application, **431–433**, *432*
Policy Modifications report, 455
pools. *See* application pools
Populate Containers list, 240, *240*
portal site connections, **106–107**, *107*
ports
   IIS websites, 46
   TCP, 18, *18*, 21
postinstall operations, **23–24**
   diagnostic logging, **24–25**, *24*
   HTTP 401.1 Unauthorized Error handling, **25**
   language packs, 27
   Office Web Apps, **25–26**

WCF Data Services fix, **28**
web applications and site collections, **25**
PowerPoint 97-2003 Presentation Scanning setting, 139
PowerPoint Service application, **139**
PowerShell
   content databases, **192–193**
   for exporting, **493–494**
   farm administrators, **425–426**
   farm backups, **481–484**
   for features, **218–219**
   for importing, **494–495**
   managed paths, 77
   site collections, 88
      backups, **489–490**
      creating, **79–80**
      deleting, 90
      enumerating, **88–89**
      moving, **89–90**
      restores, **490–491**
   web applications, **55–56**
Preferred Search Center settings, 250, *251*
prefixes for Federated Search locations, **305**
PrerequisiteInstallerFiles folder, 36
prerequisites, **10–12**, *11*, **36–37**
Prerequisites Installer, **10–11**
Preserving Context option, 331
previews, FAST, 281
primary site collection administrators, 79, 438
primary SQL server databases, 185
principal SQL server databases, 185
principals, 444
Principles and Functional Requirements for Records in Electronic Office Environments, 363
priorities
   clusters, 160
   Content Organizer rules, 332, 376
   nodes, 164
   Search service content, 269
privacy settings
   cache profiles, 407
   User Profile properties, 237

Profile Database settings, **229–230**, *230*
Profile Synchronization Instance list, 231
profiles
   cache, **403–407**, *404–407*
   user. *See* User Profile Service application
Project Page layout, 398
Propagation Status setting, 264
properties
   crawled, **295–297**
   metadata, **294–297**, *296*
   page, **399–400**, *400*
   User Profile service, **233–238**, *234–235*
property databases, **179–182**, 266
property extractors, 282
Property Mapping For Synchronization settings, 237
Property Query scope rules, **287**, *287*
proxy servers, 264–265
PSCONFIG.EXE
   creating farms, **19–21**, *20*
   removing servers, 151–153
Public cache profiles, 407
Public Internet (Purely Anonymous) cache profiles, 404
public URLs
   configuring, **52**
   extended web applications, 67, *67*
   overview, **69**, *69*
public views, 322
Publish as a major version option, 320
publishing
   caches
      BLOB, **411–413**
      object, **409–411**, *410*
      output, **407–409**, *408–409*
      profiles, **403–407**, *404–407*
   configuring, **392–393**
   content types, **340–342**, *341*
   links to Office client applications, 254
   page creation, **394–397**, *394–396*
   page layout, **397–399**, *398–399*
   page properties, **399–400**, *400*
   reusable content, **401–403**, *401–402*
   service applications, **174**
   SharePoint Server Publishing Feature, **394**, *394*
   site collection, **393–394**, *394*
publishing farms, 169, 171, *171*
   configuring, **172–173**
   as major version, **93**, *93*
Publishing Portal, 393, 398
Push-down Content Type Publishing updates option, 340

Q

queries
   Access Services, 118
   logging, 264
   rates, 264
   scaling, **179–182**, *180–181*
query component mirrors, 179, 181–182
Quick Deploy deployment type, **418–419**
quotas
   quota point calculations, **213–215**, *214*
   recycle bins, 106
   resources, **95**, *95*
   site collections, **85–86**, *85*
   templates, **61**, **79–82**, *79*, *81*, **85–86**, *85*

R

RAM
   Access Services, 119
   application pools, 43, 52
   Excel Services, **125**
   requirements, 7
rank reports, **461–463**
ratings information
   FAST, 282
   Wiki pages, **396**
RBS (Remote BLOB Storage), **42**
re-extending web applications, 70–71
Ready content database status, 194

Really Simple Syndication (RSS) settings, **102**
Recent Crawl Rate setting, 264
Recent Query Rate setting, 264
Record Library, 374
Recording Declaration Settings page, 364–366, *364*, *366*
Records Center, 363
   Content Organizer rules, 375–377, *376–377*
   libraries, 374–375
   overview, 372–373
   record submissions, 379–381, *380–381*
   Send To connections, 377–380, *378*, *380*
   sites, 373–374
records management
   eDiscovery and holds, 388–390, *389–390*
   in-place. *See* in-place records management
   overview, 362–363
   policies. *See* information management policies
   Records Center. *See* Records Center
recovering data from unattached content databases, 495–498, *497*
recycle bins, **104–106**, *105*
Recycle Threshold setting, 138, 140
Redirect Page layout, 398
Redirect Users To The Drop Off Library option, 331
Refresh all published context types on next update option, 342
regional settings for site collections, **101–102**
release-to-manufacturing (RTM) version, 196
releasing hold items, 390
relevance ranking in FAST, 282
Remember User Filter Selections For setting, 131
Remote BLOB Storage (RBS), **42**
Remove SharePoint From IIS Web Site option, 71, *71*
Remove-SPContentDatabase cmdlet, 193
Remove-SPManagedAccount cmdlet, 430
Remove-SPShellAdmin cmdlet, 426
Remove-SPSite cmdlet, 90
Remove-SPSolution cmdlet, 211
Remove-SPWebApplication cmdlet, 72
removing
   content databases, **193**
   defined policies, 432
   farm administrators, 425–426
   farm solution packages, **211**
   hold items, 390, *390*
   managed accounts, 429–430
   permissions, **445**
   search result items, **302**
   servers, **151–153**, *152*
   site collection administrators, 437–438, *438*
reports
   search results, 309–310
   web analytics, 457–463, *458–461*
Representational State Transfer (REST), 28
republishing content types, 341
Request Certificate form, 58, *59*
Require Encryption (Recommended) option, 415
requirements, 6–8
Reset To Default option, 469
resetting Search service indexes, **280–281**
Resource Throttling settings, **63–64**, *63*
resources
   quota point calculations, 213–215, *214*
   user solutions, 95, *95*
REST (Representational State Transfer), 28
Restore From A Backup option, 486
Restore-SPFarm cmdlet, 488
Restore-SPSite cmdlet, 490–491, 498
restores
   data from unattached content databases, **495–498**, *497*
   document versions, **314–315**, *315*
   farms, **484–488**, *487*
   recycle bin items, 105

site collections, **490–491**, 498
Restrict Usage settings, 306, *307*
retention policies
  creating, **383–384**, *383–384*
  record declarations through, **371–372**
  record submission through, **381**
retracting farm solution packages, **210**
Retrieve Results Asynchronously option, 309
reusable content, **401–403**, *401–402*
reverse proxies, 69
Review Problem And Solutions dialog box, **464–465**, *464*
Role Definitions Only option, 418
roles
  permission levels, 431
  servers, **5–7**, *5*
Root Authority Certificates, 172
Round Robin With Health Check option, 124
RSS (Really Simple Syndication) settings, **102**
RTM (release-to-manufacturing) version, 196
Rule Managers setting, 331
rules
  Content Organizer, **331–332**
  crawls
    host distribution, **277–278**
    impact, **262–263**, *262*
    managing, **273–275**, *273–274*
  Health Analyzer tool reviews, **466**
  Records Center, **375–377**, *376–377*
  shared search scopes, **285–287**, *286–287*
Run A Custom Report, 455
running timer jobs, **472**

S

Safe E-mail Servers settings, 199
Safe For Authenticated Use option, 407
SAML (Security Assertion Markup Language)-based tokens, 45
sandboxed solutions, **95–96**, *95–96*, **211–212**
load balancing for, **212–213**, *213*
quota point calculations, **213–215**, *214*
Sandboxed Solutions With Code Limits option, 82
SANs (storage area networks), 184
Sarbanes-Oxley act, 342
scaling out
  application servers, **168**
  cross-farm services, **169–175**, *171*
  search application, **175–182**, *177–178*, *180–181*
  database servers, **182–185**, *184*
  farms, 149
  FAST, 281
  web servers, **156–157**, *156*
    hardware-based load balancers, **165–166**
    multiple servers, **166–168**, *167*
    Windows-based NLB. *See* Windows-based NLB
schedules
  audience compilation, **249**, *249*
  crawls, 269, *269*, **271–272**, *272*
  farm backups, 483
  farm search administration, 264
  page properties, **400**, *400*
  timer job, **472**
  User Profile synchronization, **241–242**
scopes
  content deployment jobs, **419–420**, *419*
  features, 215
  search. *See* search scopes
Scopes Needing Update setting, 264
Scopes Update Schedule setting, 264
Scopes Update Status setting, 264
Search Admin Web Service Application Pool account, 258
Search Administration screen, **263–264**, *263*
Search Alerts Status setting, 264
Search And Add To Hold page, **389**, *389*

search application scaling, **175**
   crawlers, **176–179**, *177–178*
   overviews, **175–176**
   query services, **179–182**, *180–181*
search center tabs, **291–294**, *292*
Search Index On This Server
   option, **305**
Search Query and Site Settings
   Web Service Application Pool
   account, **258**
search results
   removing items, **302**
   reports, **309–310**
search scopes
   assigning, **289–291**, *289–290*
   authoritative pages, **297–299**, *298*
   Best Bets, **300–301**, *301–302*
   Federated Search. *See* Federated
      Search feature
   keywords, **299–300**, *300*
   managing, **284–285**
   metadata property mappings,
      294–297, *295–296*
   overview, **284**
   search center tabs, **291–294**, *292*
   shared, **285–288**, *285–287*
   site collections, **288**
   updating, **288**
Search Server setting, **195**
Search service, **257**
   accounts, **257–258**
   configuration steps, **257**
   content sources
      creating, **267–269**, *267–268*
      types, **269–270**, *270*
   crawls. *See* crawls and crawlers
   creating, **260–262**, *260–261*
   farm search administration,
      263–265, *263*, *265*
   FAST, **281–282**
   file icons, **280**
   IFilters and file types, **278–279**
   index resetting, **280–281**
   server name mappings, **276**
   SharePoint Foundation
      configuration, **258–260**, *259*
   topology, **265–267**, *266*

Search Service Application Web
   Analytics reports - Summary
   page, **310**
Search settings
   site collections, **289**, *289*
   User Profile properties, **237**
Searchable Items setting, **264**
searching for hold items,
   389–390, *389*
Second-Level Authoritative Pages
   setting, **299**
secondary site collection
   administrators, **79**, **438**
Secure Sockets Layer (SSL), **46–47**
   certificates, **58–60**, *59–60*
   content deployment, **415**
   Excel Services, **124**
   SMS, **204**
Secure Store Service (SSS) application
   configuring, **132–135**, *133*
   databases, **115**
   PerformancePoint Services, **132**
Secure Store Service Application
   setting, **131**
security, **424**
   farm-level, **424–426**
   managed accounts, **426–430**, *428*
   service accounts, **430**
   site collection. *See* site collection
      security
   web applications, **46–51**, *47–49*,
      51, **430–431**
      anonymous access, **434–435**
      antivirus settings, **435–436**
      permission policy levels,
         433–434
      policies, **431–433**, *432*
Security Assertion Markup Language
   (SAML)-based tokens, **45**
Security Settings report, **455**
Security Token Service (STS)
   certificates, **170–172**
Select Backup Options page,
   477, *477*, *479*
Select Component To Back Up page,
   476, *476*
Select Template Later option, **78**

Selectable In Clients permission, 122
self-service site creation, 84, 227–228
Send To connections, 377–380, *378*, *380*
Sending To Another Site option, 331
Server cache profiles, 407
Server Type tab, 13–14, *13*
ServerAndPrivate option, 407
servers
    adding, 150–151, *151*
    farms. *See* farms
    name mappings, 276
    removing, 151–153, *152*
    roles, 5–7, *5*
    SQL
        adding, 183–184
        aliases, 17
        clustered, 185
        database mirroring, 184–185, *184*
        requirements, 7
service accounts
    creating, 8–9
    security, 430
    settings, *259*, *259*
service applications
    Access Services, 118–119
    administrators, 116, *116–117*
    associating to web applications, 140–141
    Business Connectivity Services, 119–122, *120–121*
    connection settings, 54–55, *54*
    consuming, 174–175
    creating, 112–115, *114*
    deleting, 115–116
    Excel Services, 122–130, *123*
    framework, 110–112
    instances, 112
    overview, 110
    PerformancePoint Services, 130–132
    PowerPoint Service, 139
    publishing, 174
    restoring, 486
    Secure Store Service, 132–135, *133*
    State Service, 135
    Visio Graphics Service, 135–137, *136*
    Web Analytics Service, 137
    Word Automation Service, 137–139, *138*
service packs (SPs), 28, 31, *31*
service principal names (SPNs), 49
Services On Server screen, 119
Session Timeout setting, 126
sessions
    Access Services, 119
    Excel Services, 124–127
Set Object Permissions dialog box, 121, *121*
Set Permissions permission, 122
Set-SPContentDatabase cmdlet, 195–196
Set-SPManagedAccount cmdlet, 429
Set-SPPassPhrase cmdlet, 23
Set-SPServiceApplicationSecurity cmdlet, 173
SetInputs.xml file, 34
sets
    document, 327–328, *328*
    farm backup, 480
    term. *See* term sets
setup.exe program, 12
shared search scopes, 285–288, *285–287*
Shared Service Provider, 110
shared services. *See* service applications
SharePoint Designer
    disabling, 64–65, *64*
    managing, 107–108
    workflows, 369, *369*
SharePoint Foundation (SPF), 11
    installing, 12–14, *13*
    purpose, 110–111
    site collections, 91
SharePoint Preparation Tool wizard, 11, *11*
SharePoint Server (SPS), 14–15, 91
SharePoint Server Publishing Feature, 393–394, *394*
SharePoint Server Publishing Infrastructure Feature, 393

SharePoint services
  configuring, **155**
  managing, **153–154**
  starting and stopping, **155**
  viewing, **154–155**, *154*
Short Message Service (SMS), **204–205**, *205*
Short Session Timeout setting, **126–127**
similarity searches, 282
Simple Mail Transport Protocol (SMTP) service, 197, **199–200**
single-server farms, 145, *145*
Site Bindings dialog box, 60, *60*
site collection security, **436–437**
  administrators, **437–438**, *438*
  permissions, **444–447**, *447*
    inheritance, **442–444**, *442*
    levels, **438–439**
  SharePoint groups, **440–442**
Site Collection Web Analytics Reports - Summary page, 310, **459**, *459*
site collections, 74
  analytics reports, **459**, *459*
  auditing, **451–453**, *453*
  backups, **488–490**, *489*
  Central Administration for, **77–79**, *77–79*, **85–88**, *85–86*, *88*
  content and structure management, **103–104**, *103*
  content databases, **82–83**, *82*
  creating, 25, 74
  dedicated, **336–337**
  deleting, **86–88**, *87*, 90
  destination, **413–414**
  enumerating, **88–89**
  features, **217**
  galleries, **91–96**, *92–96*
  look and feel of web pages, **96–101**, *97*, *99–100*
  managed paths, **74–77**, *74*, *76*
  moving, **89–90**
  navigation, **99–101**, *99–100*
  overview, **40–41**, *41*
  policies, **387–388**, *388*
  portal site connections, **106–107**, *107*
  PowerShell for, **79–80**, **88–90**

  publishing, **393–394**, *394*
  quota templates for, **80–82**, *81*
  recycle bins, **104–106**, *105*
  regional settings, **101–102**
  required features, **337**
  restores, **490–491**, **498**
  RSS settings, **102**
  search results reports, 310
  search scopes, **288**
  security. *See* site collection security
  self-service site creation, **84**
  SharePoint Designer, **107–108**
Site Content and Structure utility, **103–104**, *103*
Site ID information in audit reports, 456
Site Master Page setting, **97**
Site Naming Format settings, **231**, **251–252**, *252*
Site Quota Information settings, 86
site reports, **460**
Site Settings page, 437
SitePages library, 394
sites. *See* websites
Sites To Demote setting, 299
size
  content databases, **82–83**
  logs, **453–454**, 469
  recycle bins, 106
slipstreaming, 12
SMS (Short Message Service), **204–205**, *205*
SMTP (Simple Mail Transport Protocol) service, 197, **199–200**
Social Tagging Database section, 230, *230*
software requirements, 7
Solution Resource Usage Log Processing job, 215
Solution Resource Usage Update job, 215
solutions, 206
  farm, **206–211**, *208–209*
  user, **211–212**
    load balancing for, **212–213**, *213*
    managing, **95–96**, *95–96*
    quota point calculations, **213–215**, *214*

Solutions gallery, **95–96**, *95–96*
sorting
 links, 100, *100*
 views, 323
SP.Install folder, 34
spbackup.log file, 480
spbackup.xml file, 480, 496
spbrtoc.xml file, 480, 486
Specific Sites Within The Site Collection option, 420
Specify A Different Content Access Account option, 274–275
Specify Authoritative Pages page, 298, *298*
Specify Client Certificate option, 275
Specify Compilation Schedule page, 249, *249*
Specify Configuration Database Settings screen, 17, *17*
Specify Form Credentials option, 275
Specify Quota Templates option, 81
SPF (SharePoint Foundation), 11
 installing, **12–14**, *13*
 purpose, **110–111**
 site collections, 91
SPNs (service principal names), 49
SPs (service packs), 28
SPS (SharePoint Server), **14–15**, 91
SQL servers
 adding, **183–184**
 aliases, 17
 clustered, **185**
 database mirroring, **184–185**, *184*
 requirements, 7
SSL (Secure Sockets Layer), 46–47
 certificates, **58–60**, *59–60*
 content deployment, 415
 Excel Services, 124
 SMS, 204
SSS (Secure Store Service) application
 configuring, **132–135**, *133*
 databases, 115
 PerformancePoint Services, 132
Stage Properties page, 383, *384*
Stakeholders setting for term sets, 348
stand-alone servers, 12–13, *13*
Standard Edition, **111**
Start Full Crawl option, 269
Start Options window, 371, *371*
Start-Sleep cmdlet, 211
Start this workflow to approve publishing a major version of an item option, 320
Started content database status, 194
starting
 SharePoint services, **155**
 User Profile services, **232–233**, *232*
State Service application, **135**
Stop Inheriting Permissions option, 95
Stop When Refresh On Open Fails option, 128
Stopped content database status, 194
stopping SharePoint services, **155**
storage area networks (SANs), 184
Storage Limit Values settings, 81
Storage Usage report, 462
store permissions in BCS, **122**
Strict setting for browser, 62
structure management for site collections, **103–104**, *103*
STS (Security Token Service) certificates, 170–172
STSADM method, 476
Style setting for views, 323
Submission Policy setting, 348
submissions to Records Center, **379–381**, *380–381*
subscriber sites, publishing in, **341–342**, *341*
Successes entry in crawl logs, 275
Supported File Formats setting
 PowerPoint Service, 139–140
 Word Automation Service, 138
Synchronization Connections page, 239, *239*
Synchronization Database settings, 230, *230*
synchronization in User Profile service, **238**
 accounts, **224–225**
 connection filters, **243–244**, *244*
 connections, **238–241**, *239–240*
 manual process, **241**
 schedules, **241–242**
 settings, **242–243**, *243*
 status, 232

syndication hubs
  configuring, **338–342**, *339–340*
  creating, **335–338**
  designating, **334–335**
synonyms for keywords, 300
System Master Page setting, 97
system settings, **190**
  content databases, **190–196**, *191*
  email
    incoming. *See* incoming email
    outgoing, **203–204**, *204*
  feature management, **215–219**, *217*
  SMS messaging, **204–205**, *205*
  solutions, **206**
    farm, **206–211**, *208–209*
    user, **211–215**, *213–214*

T

tabs for search scopes, **291–294**, *292*
tag clouds, 357–359
tagging
  content, 356
  keywords, **357–358**, *357*
Target Application ID setting, 134
Target Application Type setting, 134
tasks lists for views, 322
Taxonomy feature, **350–351**
TCP ports, 18, *18*, 21, 46
TEMP environment variable, 12, 14–15
templates
  Access Services, 119
  Enterprise Search Center site, **291–294**, *292*
  quota, **61**, **79–82**, *79*, *81*, **85–86**, *85*
  Records Center, 363, 374–375
  site collections, 78, *78*
Temporary Location Of Index setting, 177
term sets, 236
  creating, **347–348**
  groups, **345–347**, *346*
  importing and exporting, 349
  overview, **342–343**, *343*
  term store tool, **343–345**, *344*
  terms, **349–350**, *349*

Wiki pages, **397**
  working with, **350–356**, *351*, *354–356*
Term Store Management Tool page, **344–349**, *344*
term store tool, **343–345**, *344*
testing crawl rules, 273
text, reusable, 401–403
themes, **98–99**
Third-Level Authoritative Pages setting, 299
.thmx extension, 98
three-server farms, **146–147**, *146–147*
thumbnails in FAST, 281
time zone setting, **61**
timeouts
  Excel Services, 126–127
  farm search administration, 265
Timer Job Status page, **471**, *472*
timer jobs, **470**
  content databases, 195
  page properties, 400
  quota point calculations, 214–215
  running, **472**
  schedules, **472**
  viewing, **471**, *471–472*
  web analytics reports, **457–458**
Timer service, 470
titles for site collections, 78
Token Issuer Certificate setting, 172
Token Issuer Description setting, 172
Top Browsers report, 462
Top Destinations report, 462
Top Federated Results web parts, 309
Top Level Errors in crawl logs, 276
top-link navigation, **99–101**, *99*
Top Pages report, 461–462, *461*
Top Queries report, 310
Top Referrers report, 462
Top Site Languages report, 463
Top Site Product Versions report, 463
Top Visitors report, 462
topologies, **144**
  large farms, **148–150**
  medium-server farms, **147–148**, *148*
  single-server farms, **145**, *145*

three-server farms, **146–147**, *146–147*
two-server farms, **145**, *146*
Total Worker Processes setting, 140
Totals setting for views, 323
trace logs, 466
  settings, 24, *24*, **469–470**, *469–470*
  working with, **468–469**, *468*
trend reports, **460–462**, *460*
Trigger settings, **304–305**, *304*
Trust Children setting, 126
trust relationships between farms, **170–172**, *171*
trusted content locations, 132
trusted data connection libraries, **128–129**
Trusted Data Connection Libraries Only setting, **127–128**
trusted file locations, **126–128**
trusted host locations, **252–253**
Trusted Identity provider authentication, 47
trusted identity providers, **51**
tunable relevance ranking, 282
two-node load-balancing clusters, 156, *156*
two-server farms, **145**, *146*

U

UAG (Unified Access Gateway), 165
UDC (Universal Data Connection) files, 128
ULS (Unified Logging System) logs, 24, 468
unattached content databases, recovering data from, **495–498**, *497*
Unattended Service Account setting
  Excel Services, 125
  PerformancePoint Services, 131
Unattended Service Account - Application ID setting, 137
undeclaring records, **368**
Unexpected logging level, 468
unextending web applications, **70–71**, *71*

Unicast mode for clusters, **162**
Unified Access Gateway (UAG), 165
Unified Logging System (ULS) logs, 24, 468
Uninstall-SPFeature cmdlet, 219
Uninstall-SPSolution cmdlet, **210–211**
Universal Data Connection (UDC) files, 128
unpublishing content types, **341**
updates, **28**
  farm search administration, 264
  on farms, **30–33**, *31*
  process, **29–30**
  search scopes, **288**
  types, **28–29**
Updates folder, 35
upgrading content databases, **194–195**
URLs
  content deployment, 413
  Content Type Hub, 339
  document IDs, 328
  Excel Services, 124
  Federated Search locations, 305
  internal, **69**, *69*
  managed paths, 74, *74*
  multiple servers, 167, *167*
  My Site Hosts, 231, *231*
  My Sites, **253–254**
  public, **52**, 67, *67*, **69**, *69*
  Records Center, 374, 378
  service applications, 174
  SMS, 204
  Wiki pages, 396
Usage Data Collection settings, 458, *458*
Use a Managed Term Set option, 352, *352*
Use A Site Collection Policy option, 388
Use Cookie For Crawling option, 275
Use Restriction option, 306
Use The Site Collection Default Setting option, 366
User Can Override option, 237
user contexts in FAST, 282
user-defined function assemblies, **129–130**

User ID information in audit reports, 456
User Profile Service application, 115, **223**
 accounts and permissions, 224–225
 applications for, **228–231**, *230–231*
 configuring, 223–224
 farm preparation, 225–228
 profiles
  creating, 245
  deleting, **245–247**, *246*
  viewing and editing, 244–245
 properties, **233–238**, *234–235*
 starting, **232–233**, *232*
 synchronization. *See* synchronization in User Profile service
User Profile Service - Social Data Maintenance Job, 396
User Profile Service - Social Rating Synchronization Job, 396
User Profile Synchronization Service startup screen, *232*, *232*
user solutions, 211–212
 load balancing for, **212–213**, *213*
 managing, **95–96**, *95–96*
 quota point calculations, **213–215**, *214*
usernames
 FBA, 50
 managed accounts, 427
 Secure Store Service, 135
users
 adding to SharePoint groups, 441–442
 permissions, **446–447**

V

Vary By Custom Parameter setting, **406**, *406*
Vary By Query String Parameters setting, **406**, *406*
Vary By User Rights setting, **406**, *406*
VDW files, 135
Verbose logging level, 467–468
versions and versioning
 content databases, **194–195**

enabling, **312–314**, *313*
Federated Search locations, 304
restoring, **314–315**, *315*
View Auditing Reports page, 455
View External Content Types page, **120**, *120*
View pages, 97
View Web Analytics Reports option, 310
viewing
 analytics reports, **459–463**, *460–461*
 audit reports, **454–457**, *456*
 crawl logs, 275–276
 crawl rules, 273
 crawled properties, **295**
 installed services, **154–155**, *154*
 keywords, 358
 profiles, 244–245
 search results reports, 309–310
 timer jobs, **471**, *471–472*
views, creating, 321–324
Virus Scanning application programming interface (VS API), 436
viruses, **435–436**
Visio Graphics Service application, **135–137**, *136*
Visitors group, 440
Visual Best Bets feature, 281
Volatile Function Cache Lifetime setting, 127
VS API (Virus Scanning application programming interface), 436

W

W3SVC (World Wide Web Publishing Service), 31
w3wp.exe process, 43
WANs (wide area networks) and farms, 5
Warn On Refresh setting, 128
Warning logging level, 467
Warnings in crawl logs, 275
WCF (Windows Communications Foundation)-based web services, 174

wide area networks (WANs) and farms **527**

WCF Data Services fix, **28**
Web Address scope rules, **286**, *286*
web analytics reports, **457**
 configuring, **457–459**, *458*
 viewing, **459–463**, *460–461*
Web Analytics Service application, **137**
web applications, **40**
 alternate access mappings, **68–70**, *69–70*
 application pool configuration, **52–53**, *52*
 associating service applications to, **140–141**
 authentication, **44–45**, *45*, **66–67**, **336**
 Blocked File Types setting, **65**
 components, **40–42**, *41*
 content database configuration, **53–54**, *53*
 creating, **25**, **44**
 dedicated, **335–336**
 deleting, **71–72**, *72*
 extending, **65–68**, *66–67*
 features, **218**
 General Settings, **61–62**, *61*
 IIS settings, **45–46**, *45*, **56–60**, *57*, *59–60*
 for My Site, **226**
 operation, **42–43**
 PowerShell for, **55–56**
 public URLs, **52**
 Records Center, **373–374**
 Resource Throttling settings, **63–64**, *63*
 restoring, **486**, *487*
 security, **46–51**, *47–49*, *51*, **430**
  anonymous access, **434–435**
  antivirus settings, **435–436**
  permission policy levels, **433–434**
  policies, **431–433**, *432*
 Service Application Connections settings, **54–55**, *54*
 SharePoint Designer disabling, **64–65**, *64*
 unextending and re-extending, **70–71**, *71*
web.config files
 BLOB caches, **412**
 extended web applications, **68**
 modifying, **50–51**
web content publishing. *See* publishing
web front end (WFE) servers, **5**, *5*
 description, **6**
 IIS websites on, **42**
 requirements, **7**
 Windows-based NLB, **157–158**
web pages look and feel, **96**
 master pages, **96–98**, *97*
 site collection navigation, **99–101**, *99–100*
 site themes, **98–99**
Web Part Picker, **93**, *94*
Web Parts gallery, **93–95**, *94*
web parts in Federated Search, **308–309**, *308*
web servers, scaling out, **156–157**, *156*
 hardware-based load balancers, **165–166**
 multiple servers, **166–168**, *167*
 Windows-based NLB. *See* Windows-based NLB
.webpart extension, **93**
websites
 exporting, **491–494**, *492*
 features, **216**, *217*
 importing, **494–495**, **498**
 Records Center, **373–374**
 Search Service content sources, **270**, *270*
 themes, **98–99**
Welcome Page layout, **399**
WFE (web front end) servers, **5**, *5*
 description, **6**
 IIS websites on, **42**
 requirements, **7**
 Windows-based NLB, **157–158**
wide area networks (WANs) and farms, **5**

Wiki pages
   creating, **394–396**, *395–396*
   ratings information, **396**
   term sets, **397**
wildcard characters in crawl rules, 274
wildcard managed paths, **75**, 226
Windows authentication, **48–49**, 440
Windows-based NLB, **157**
   clusters
      creating, **159–164**, *159–161, 163*
      nodes, **164–165**, *165*
   installing, **158**
   WFE servers, **157–158**
Windows Communications Foundation (WCF)-based web services, 174
Windows Live, 45
Windows NT LAN Manager (NTLM), 19, 48
Wise Technology Management study, 363
Word Automation Service application, **137–140**, *138*
Word Automation Services page, **138–139**, *138*

Workbook Cache Location
   setting, 125
Workbook Calculation Mode
   setting, 127
Workbook Properties settings, **127**
workbook URLs, 124
workflow
   approvals, **320–321**, *321*
   for record declarations, **369–371**, *369–371*
   for record submission, **380–381**, *381*
Workflow Settings page, 370–371
World Wide Web Publishing Service (W3SVC), 31
.wsp extension, 95, 206
WSS Solution Packages, 206
WSS_UsageApplication application, 262

Z

zones
   AAM, 68–69
   extended web applications, 67–68, *67*